O BRAVE NEW PEOPLE

O BRAVE

NEW PEOPLE

THE EUROPEAN INVENTION

OF THE AMERICAN INDIAN

JOHN F. MOFFITT

SANTIAGO SEBASTIÁN

University of New Mexico Press, Albuquerque

First paperbound printing, 1998.
Library of Congress Cataloging-in-Publication Data

Moffitt, John F. (John Francis), 1940–
    O brave new people : the European invention of
the American Indian / John F. Moffitt, Santiago
Sebastián. — 1st ed.

            p.   cm.

    Includes bibliographical references and index.
    ISBN 0-8263-1639-5, cloth
    ISBN 0-8263-1989-0, paper
    1. Indians—Public opinion—History. 2. Public
opinion—Europe—History. 3. Indians—Pictorial
works—History. 4. America—Description and
travel—Early work to 1800.   I. Sebastián, Santiago.
II. Title.
E59.P89M63   1996
973.1—dc20   94-48680
                                                CIP

Grateful acknowledgment is given to the Program for
Cultural Cooperation Between Spain's Ministry of
Culture and United States' Universities for support of
this volume.

Frontispiece:

*Jan van der Straet (Stradanus), Allegory of the European
Discovery of America: Vespucci Meets the Amazon, 1590.*

In Memoriam
Erwin Walter Palm (1910–88)
Colleague and Mutual Friend
and
Santiago Sebastián
López (1931–95)
Co-author, Colleague, and Beloved
Friend

O, Wonder!
How many goodly creatures are there here!
How beauteous mankind is! O brave new world,
That has such people in't.
                    —Shakespeare, *The Tempest,* v, 1, 182–5

. . . thou Angel bringst with thee
A heaven like Mahomets Paradice . . .
Licence my roaving hands, and let them go,
Before, behind, above, below.
O my America! my new-found-land,
My kingdome, safeliest when with one man
          man'd,
My Myne of precious stones: My Emperie,
How blest am I in this discovering thee!
                    —John Donne, *Elegie* xix:
                        "To his Mistress Going to Bed"

CONTENTS

3

4

5

LIST OF ILLUSTRATIONS

O BRAVE NEW PEOPLE

Introduction

THE EUROPEAN INVENTION
OF THE AMERICAN INDIAN

Both the authors of this book are art historians, one American and the other Spanish. Our mutual purpose here has been to gather together the fruits of some of our earlier research and, through these, to provide some new—and we hope useful and objective—perspectives on the problem of the initial European, mostly Spanish, perceptions and vision of Columbian and post-Columbian America, especially as focused upon the Native Americans. Preferring to let the historical evidence speak for itself, we have additionally (as much as possible) tried to avoid the imposition of the kind of theoretical constructs that so bedevil current, postmodernist academic writing. In retrospect however, we do see that this does now seem a textbook example of deconstruction, in this case a somewhat systematic demolition of various myths of European colonialism. Given our (mostly) Spanish focus, the Indians—*los indios*—discussed here turn out to have been, for the most part, natives inhabiting the Caribbean areas; however we also include, a bit later in time, increasing references to South American natives. To balance the historical composition, we shall moreover make occasional reference to related events belonging to regions settled for the most part by Anglo-Saxon European colonists, and also to some peoples (both "red" and "white") dwelling in those more northerly latitudes.

Taking a more traditional approach, it has been our desire to let the source documents carry the weight of the historical argument. When not classical or medieval in origin, our sources, texts and illustrations, belong to the Renaissance era, known in Spain as either *el Renacimiento* or, more commonly, *el Siglo de Oro,* the Golden Age. Sometimes this extended post-medieval timespan is referred to by (general) historians as the Early Modern era (as probably derived from German historiographic terminology, *die Neu-zeit*). That temporal notion can however be further broken down, with reference to currently recognized thematic and stylistic changes occur-ring in both literature and in the visual arts. Thus the art historian might begin by speaking of an initial Renaissance period proper, which includes the close of the fifteenth century and extends well into the mid sixteenth century, with this phase being succeeded around 1550 by (according to current art historical terminology) a stylistically self-conscious Mannerist phase and the full cycle finally concluding after around 1620 with the so-called Baroque movement. This is an extended time period—from 1492 until around 1680—that also embraces the emergence (around 1520) of a Protestant Reformation movement which, in its turn, provokes a nearly immediate reaction, the Catholic Counter-Reformation. These religious controversies also, as we shall point out, fundamentally affected Europeans' perceptions of America and its diverse peoples.

As becomes readily apparent when one consults the primary docu-ments (either textual or pictorial) resulting from the European discovery of America, the landscape and, particularly, the inhabitants of the New World were viewed with a certain emotional reaction—naturally enough, largely surprised amazement—by the first *conquistadores* coming from the Old World. Their immediate reaction was to evaluate America and the Americans—actually to "invent" them—according to certain culturally en-shrined patterns that seemed most natural or logical to them. Their ini-tial perceptions directly, almost inevitably, arose from what the Europeans already brought with them in their heads: a fixed context, a psychologi-cal baggage of hoary myths and legends, many of them dealing with India and the Asiatic Indians. If one doubted in particular the enduring power of those pre-established Gangetic images, one need now only recall how Native Americans are still, most tenaciously, called "Indians."

This book treats topics that have either been presented in extremely scattered studies—as cited in our chapter endnotes and comprehensive bibliography—or which have never really been synthesized into a single narrative presentation. To complement previous, mostly disparate, efforts, a great deal of new material is now sequentially presented and, where possible, illustrated. We trust this work will prove to be of interest to, besides art historians and Native Americans, literary historians, those interested in the history of ideas, historians of the Americas (either Hispanic or Anglo-Saxon), social historians, mythologists and other collectors of legendary detritus, anthropologists or ethnologists, and naturally, anyone concerned with how the initial momentous encounters between European and Native American civilizations might affect us today.

We intend to show how, as conceived in the collective Renaissance mind, the "savagery" routinely attributed to New World peoples could embody either positive or negative values. Either way for the civilized European the tangible, even blatantly visible manifestations of (non-European) savagery were hunting and gathering, not systematic agriculture and (eventually) urbanization; emotion, and not reason and philosophical detachment; pagan superstition and demonic subjugation, not Christian doctrine (and dogma); exclusively spoken language, not literacy and the fixed (and dogmatic) word, evermore firmly established as it was now being mechanically manufactured by the printing press. Like all the rest, these figurations of "the primitive" and of "barbarism" represent cultural stereotypes; as such, they are essentially figures of speech imposed upon a living but passive "savage" being disdainfully perceived by his uninvited "civilized" spectators as representing the Other.

For the early Spanish *conquistadores,* the fundamental division lay between *los paganos* (heathens) and *los cristianos* (Catholics). The Christian tradition broadly defined generic "Man" in terms of his receptivity to divine grace. In short, if he accepted the articles of The Faith, then the pagan could officially become a Man. Following early receipt of positive notices from missionaries in the Indies suggesting a capacity for conversion on the part of Native Americans, in 1537 Pope Paul III issued a bull, *Sublimis Deus,* which generously declared that "the Indians are true men." Unfortunately, this bucolic picture is complicated by the fact that the Renaissance was notoriously "classical" in content. Unfortunately for all those *indios,* the classical tradition had defined *homo sapiens* primarily as a rational being. The question now arose, what was the strictly *legal* (or secular) status of the Indians? In these areas, jurisprudence, the major authority was a long dead Greek, Aristotle, and his status was especially formidable among Spanish jurists.

Like all his peers, Aristotle drew a careful distinction between Greeks —real men—and the *barbaroi,* near beasts. A Hellene was rational; the semi-human barbarian was only emotional, irrational for being only "ruled by his passions." In his *Politics,* to which Spanish authorities customarily made obligatory reference, Aristotle advanced a dangerous thesis about those who *need* to be ruled by their more rational betters. As "masters," these superior humans may even properly make slaves of their cultural inferiors, those hopelessly "ruled by passions." As Aristotle declared (*Politics,* I.2), "barbarian and slave are, by nature, identical." In this world, there are but two kinds of men, "that kind which naturally rules, and that which naturally is ruled." Moreover, "he who is able to supply physical labor is, by nature, ruled; he is a slave to the superior being." Further on (*Politics,* I.5), he defines the "difference between slave and free" men. This natural condition is seen "even as to their bodies—making the former [the slave] strong, with a view to their doing the menial work, and it makes the free people upright, useless for servile work but suitable for political life, which is divided into the tasks of war and peace." The condition of slavery is, he suggests, good for the slave, and proceeds to make his point by means of a simile: "Domesticated animals are, by nature, superior to untamed animals; it is better for all the former to be ruled by man, since in this way they obtain security." Aristotle is the same venerable authority who dogmatically declared (likewise in *Politics,* I.5) that, "as regards male and female, the former is superior, that latter inferior: the male is ruler, the female is subject." In short, Aristotle tacitly, often explicitly in America, provided a license for Spanish *encomenderos* to enslave the *indios americanos,* for that condition was only "natural," since "barbarian and slave are, by nature, identical."

Although modern researchers in the principal European and American nations have busily occupied themselves with the historical image of the New World and its central protagonist, the American Indian, their interest contrasts with a paucity of investigations in Spain along similar lines. This must seem ironic: Spain discovered America, was the first nation to attempt its systematic colonization, and for many centuries, Spaniards accordingly knew it better than any other European peoples. Even though there are a considerable number of chronicles written by Spanish authors during the Renaissance period that deal in plentiful detail with the native fixtures and peoples of the Americas (some of which we will quote here), nevertheless there seems to have been maintained in these publications, at least those issued in Spain, something like a tacit silence in the strictly visual sense. As a result, the actual work of the "illustration" of the Americas in publications issued during the Renaissance was largely left to non-Spanish artists. But why did this happen?

Even though we do not have all the answers, by a close reading of some contemporary images of New World Indians, as "explained" to aghast Europeans in various kinds of Renaissance publications (and for various purposes), we can at least provide our readers with some valuable insights into the first attempts at visualizations—and timely "inventions"—of Native Americans during the Renaissance. The results of our equally iconographic and iconological investigation are of more than mere antiquarian interest. Some of these graphic materials actually exerted an enormous historical impact. Indirectly, most of this imagery is still with us. Reinforcing some already preformed European images of Native Americans, as generally derived from previous notions of "barbarism," the illustrative material devised during the Renaissance was either of a positive, "noble," trend, or it could—increasingly—partake of a negative nature, so making for an "ignoble Indian." As we shall also show, during the course of the sixteenth century European depictions of Native Americans increasingly began to be deployed for the spread of a so-called Black Legend, *la leyenda negra*. Although the martyred Native American was the ostensible focal point of the Black Legend, the real impetus behind the image was as much religious as political. The real context is the Protestant Reformation and its temporal rebuttal, a Catholic Counter-Reformation mainly funded by Imperial Spain. With that development, once again American Indians reverted to the status of Noble Savages—and the Spaniards, by comparison, were turned into wholly Ignoble Savages by mostly Protestant publishers, writers, and graphic artists.

In effect, our book deals with equally anthropological and culturally symbolic analyses of targeted pictorial materials, mostly book illustrations.

We use these to reveal the actual workings of a literally "illustrative" process by which post-Columbian America was being opportunely "invented" by usually scarcely disinterested Europeans. As we demonstrate, the complex process of an evolving iconographical invention of America, particularly as applied to its native inhabitants, was made possible largely due to two factors: the new technology of the printing press and old mythic contexts established in late medieval Europe. Although the chronological framework of the Columbian discovery is clearly Renaissance, the actual results of an extremely original European illustration of America were mainly due to a variety of significant, unfortunately still largely ignored, pre-Renaissance influences, sometimes pseudo-classical and sometimes Christian. As we discuss them here, the presently obscure legacy of the Renaissance illustrations of the New World embraced such suggestive and largely "primitivist" topics as the Noble Savage, the (Ignoble) Cannibal, the Asiatic quasi-Christians, the Amazons, pygmies and giants, the Age of Gold, the Age of Iron, potential Utopias, lost Edens, a Paradise on Earth regained, then another lost again, and so forth. During these baleful moments following an abortive and largely acrimonious Columbian quincentennial, it seems appropriate that these illustrative issues be critically reexamined, if only because many of their propositions can be shown still to be operational in current, but mostly subconscious, evaluations of Native Americans.

The major objective pursued in this book is the manner of the entrance of the Native Americans into written, really meaning "printed," history. Since the American Indian lacked a "history," meaning that he had none that was immediately apparent to the Renaissance European, the kind of history that Native Americans immediately acquired was one imposed upon them by Europeans, and particularly Spaniards. Given the complexity of investigating its sources, it is scarcely surprising that the still-novel topic of the means of entry of the American Indian into European history has yet to acquire an interdisciplinary, even international, character. It is axiomatic that one picture is worth a thousand words; therefore, for an accessible methodology by which to unravel the historical problem of initial European definitions of Native Americans during the Renaissance, we have conveniently turned to detailed iconographical analyses. We were particularly interested in situating our designated visual imagery within a matrix of historical contexts, which, as it turned out, now seem largely pseudo-anthropological or legendary. As we show, these mythical impositions could also be exploited for polemical purposes essentially having nothing to do with Native Americans. Most logically, as it also turned out, implicit meanings belonging to the strictly pictorial materials are tacitly clarified by reference to plentiful documentary notices contained in the American chronicles composed by mostly Spanish authors, some of whom actually *were* explorers of a strange New World that first began to unfold its nearly inexhaustible marvels before astounded European eyes and minds late in 1492.

There is, we think, both a timely and a useful aspect to this book. A kind of collective hangover left by the five-hundredth anniversary of Columbus's initial voyage to the Americas makes the chronological context of our contribution literally timely, but the documentation provided is also useful in the context of a new (and largely unexpected) polemic since stirred up by that largely symbolic occasion. The original plan for the quincentennial was to make it a *celebration* of European appropriations of previously unknown lands across the Atlantic; at least, that was the scheme that had been envisioned a few years ago by numerous promoters, either altruistic or (mostly) mercenary. Alas, for their ambitious plans, times have since changed; now the new buzzword is political correctness. Columbus's once immaculate image finds itself repainted in despicable colors. Now, what happened way back in 1492 is no longer called a "discovery," rather just an "encounter" (lower-case). Various partisan groups, particularly in the United States and ranging from the National Council of Churches to the American Indian Movement, chose to denounce the proposed "Celebration" of yet another "Dead White European Male." According to the politically correct, or revisionist, view in America, Columbus is a figure representative, like nearly all of his European Renaissance entourage, of greed, duplicity, material exploitation, cultural imperialism, paranoia, and bestial cruelty.

The real context of the new acrimony is probably just another crisis in American intellectual life. The recent Columbian controversy pitted those anxious to prove the presumed evils of Eurocentric thinking against those who treat all attacks on the Western tradition as constituting a threat to Eurocentric Civilization itself. In short, the burning question now becomes: Was 1492, after which peoples of European stock unquestionably took over the Americas in both the physical and the spiritual sense, a "Good Thing" or "Bad Thing"? This book certainly will not resolve the partisan questions recently raised by this quincentennial polemic. What it *will* do, however, is document, in a specific instance—wholly visualized, but always textually supported—the manner in which the Western (which again in this case just happens to be Eurocentric) tradition typically tends to divide the world's populations into Civilized and Other. For this typically Eurocentric peculiarity we provide, and comment in some detail upon, the strictly visual documentation dealing with what resulted from a single momentous event, the European invention of America after 1492.

By means of graphic particulars attending this historic occurrence, what we shall show are the specific ways that psychological boundaries were tacitly established between *Us* (Europeans) and *Them* (American Indians). As is revealed here, long before the discovery of America and its Native Americans, Europeans customarily employed certain kinds of wholly conventionalized verbal imagery to convey subcultural essences belonging to an ubiquitous non-European Primitive Other. This inevitably misunderstood Other (*alius,* whence "alienated") was generally taken to represent the primal childhood of human evolution. The imagery that went along with standard definitions of the Other relied heavily on standard metaphors of fear and darkness, meaning motifs pointing to superstitious pagan ignorance and spiritual darkness, unchecked eroticism and bloody beastliness. The persistent European pattern of, equally, attraction and repulsion toward the Other was fixed in medieval texts, especially in those indebted to a somewhat precocious revival (*renaissance*) of classical themes. Accordingly, from 1492 onward, the Native Americans were quickly discovered, subjugated, reinvented, and so commoditized, thus stripped of their contextual social and cultural ties. That, alas, is a still-living legacy of the Renaissance in America.

Our major art historical conclusions about various artistic (more or less) representations initially dealing with those newly invented Native Americans can be quickly summarized, also observing that basic themes first introduced during the Renaissance have since continued as iconographic staples, and well into the twentieth century. In sum, imagery by which *los indios americanos* were originally presented to Europeans—at first only in crude prints, later via paintings and sculptures—was created in order to embody certain attitudes belonging wholly to European whites. In this case the inventors were typically patrons and publishers, and also included in a lesser role artists actually charged with visually fixing various notions passed on to them, and tacit accomplices were their designated audiences, the European public. This understood psychological collusion should be perfectly obvious.

The principal themes developed by such commissioned imagery, whether textual or graphic in nature, were basically three. The essential polemics embodied in imagery dealing with European domination of the Americas dealt with nature, conquest, and civilization. Nature, as focused upon the lands and peoples of the Americas, could be discussed in terms either geographical-topographical or ethnographic-anthropological in focus. During the Renaissance any discussion of nature necessarily addressed issues belonging to the traditional scholastic disciplines of philosophy, science, and religion. The topic of conquest, as again focused upon the lands and peoples of the Americas, properly included reference to imperial politics, international law, and religion. The arguments for civilization, as a "gift" to the lands and peoples of the Americas, included obligatory discussions of history, the liberal arts (poetry to architecture), and religion. Obviously, the unifying theme of all the emerging American topics and issues was, at bottom, religion. Moreover, as an iconographic analysis of our sixteenth- and seventeenth-century print portfolios will particularly reveal, there were basically only three generic ways to treat the *indios americanos.* They must be pictured *either* as existing in a state considered to be "primitive"—that is, enviably innocent of civilization, *or* they are to be presented in a state taken to be inherently "savage"—that is, one belonging to implacable enmity, *or* they are to be shown to be "doomed"—in which case they represent the products of their own technological obsolescence in the face of European superiority, whether spiritual or merely material in nature.

Thus redefined by others (Europeans) in new ways, those representing essentially *Old* World mythic settings, the stunned inhabitants of the *Orbe Novo* eventually became thoroughly reconceptualized, and so made to fit conveniently within preexistent European medieval-Renaissance imagery. So viewed, Native Americans came to serve conveniently certain cultural, economic, political, mythic, and ideological needs, even polemics, belonging to wholly alien peoples, arriving—completely uninvited after 1492— from wholly alien, or other, societies previously established on the far-eastern shores of the Atlantic, Europe in short.

Unfortunately, in many instances, our real subject becomes an investigation of a graphic process performing something like the progressive *de*humanization of Native Americans. Therefore, the anthropological picture that really emerges deals not so much with Native Americans, but rather much more with the Europeans, specifically those who redrew them in the Renaissance according to their own culturally engrafted prejudices. It is only recently, particularly after the abortive *fiesta colombiana* of 1992, that American peoples frequently reverse the poles of prejudice, now seeing Europeans—and particularly their Euro-American progeny—as the misfit Other. Either or, we or them: In either case, prejudice demands pictures. It should be axiomatic that the seeing eye (whosoever's) is an organ of cultural traditions and, in our particular example—the European graphic invention of the Native Americans during the sixteenth century—the final result does not always present a pretty picture. Worse, its effects have been only slightly dissipated, but not yet wholly expunged from the historical record.

A final word may explain the respective contributions of the two authors. Professor Moffitt is wholly responsible for the first two chapters of this book, which deal in some detail with diverse images, mostly textually transmitted, associated in medieval European thought and art with both Asian India and the peoples inhabiting those Gangetic regions. As is here revealed in an extended and thoroughly documented manner, medieval European legends about India and the Indians—particularly the ones associating these places, *las Indias,* with the Earthly Paradise—had a considerable impact upon post-Colombian myths increasingly attached to the natives of the New World by the first Europeans who had to deal with them. Two chapters that follow this lengthy Edenic exposition include a portfolio of rarely seen book illustrations drawn from mostly inaccessible Renaissance publications, mainly by Spanish authors, dealing with the then-recent history—*conquista* and *colonialización*—of what was becoming Spanish America. These two segments are mostly the product of painstaking research conducted by Professor Sebastián in various European libraries, but mainly in Valencia. The final, or fifth, chapter is a collaborative effort, summarizing the results of our mutual investigations into other aspects of this fascinating but complex topic.

And what is the utopian goal of this study, now that it has reached the hands of a presumably sympathetic reader? Hopefully, following a painstaking dissection of the intricate anatomy, symptomology, and etiology of an initial process of stereotypification, a centuries-long syndrome of generally malignant dehumanization applied to Native Americans, first wrought in Europe during the Renaissance, can be finally restrained, if not wholly arrested. In short, our investigative prophylaxis, a tardy prescription written long after a first contagion and onset of some dramatically alarming symptoms, suggests that a final cure can be proposed by revealing the initial causes and exact evolution of the original malady, in this case one establishing its insidious workings half a millennium ago. So doing, we are only following a historiographic precedent set some two millennia ago by a considerably artful Roman historian, Titus Livy, about whom we shall have much more to say. As he put it in the preface to his *Ab urbe condita* (a "History of Rome," arranged in "Decades," which was read by many early Spanish *cronistas* of the Americas), "the study of history is the best medicine for a sick mind; for in History you have a record of the infinite variety of human experience . . . and in that record you can find for yourself—and for your country—both examples and warnings." As he also observed (Book XXXIV, 4.8), "Diseases must be known before their cures are found; by the same token, appetites come into being before there are laws to limit their exercise."

So be it . . .

Laus Deo, atque Indios Americae:
July 4, 1994.

John F. Moffitt
New Mexico State University

Santiago Sebastián López
Universitat de Valencia

1

"INDIA" AND THE
"EARTHLY PARADISE"

The Contribution of the

European Middle Ages

to the American Legend

India and Eden in Columbus's Quest

As everybody knows, the most common name applied to Native Americans is "Indians." But why is that, and exactly *how* did this clearly impossible appellation come about? In order to arrive at an answer to a question that has never really been adequately framed, it becomes necessary to probe the various meanings held by the first European "inventors" of America, those currently applied in their minds to India itself. Such an investigation reveals in turn the real significance for Europeans around 1492 of the native inhabitants, "Indians," of a then largely fabled Asiatic land.

With the acrimonies stirred up by the quincentennial anniversary of the discovery of America by Christopher Columbus in 1492 still fresh in our minds, a new look at an endlessly overlooked observation by Columbus is definitely in order. First, we must remind our readers that Columbus was never looking for "America." That name, attached to what was only much later recognized to be a separate continent, arrived some years after Columbus's death. What Columbus was really seeking, and what he always thought he *had* found in those places we now dub "America," was instead "India." This was a name then, in 1492, commonly signifying an even broader idea than now, namely, the Far East, or all of tropical southeastern Asia and the Spice Islands. Not wishing to belabor a point already resolved by competent scholars, that is, Columbus's continuous quest for India,[1] we need only quickly remind our audience of a clear declaration of original intent contained in the first notice of the New World to reach the Old World. This was a letter to Europeans composed by Columbus himself and published early in 1493.

Its Latin title, summarizing all of its forthcoming contents, is *De Insulis Indiae supra Gangem nupter inventis,* and means, that this was a timely report "Concerning the Indian Islands, Located Beyond the Ganges River, Which Have Just Been Newly Rediscovered." In fact, the Gangetic idea proved so persistent that, for many years, even centuries afterward, Spaniards continued to call their Caribbean possessions *las Indias.* Moreover, and again to belabor a point, Native Americans are still erroneously labeled *Indians.*

Now, granted that Columbus was *only* looking for India, or *las Indias* (essentially the same generic idea), and of course never for America, then exactly what was it, and in his own terms, that he thought he *had* found over here? It was—as nearly every historian of the epoch-making Columbian adventure conveniently chooses to ignore—nothing less than "Paradise-on-Earth." As employed by Columbus, the term precisely meant a specific place described in the Book of Genesis as having been initially inhabited by Adam and Eve. In fact, the exact terminology used by Columbus was "*el Paraíso terrestre* [or *terrenal*]." This is the exact Spanish equivalent for a standard medieval Latin term employed for the scriptural setting of primeval man, namely *Paradisus terrestris,* or "the Earthly Paradise."

We may now proceed to quote (in an English translation) the exact words employed by Columbus to describe his paradisiacal encounters in America. One will first, however, observe that all these statements were extracted from his private journals, the *Diario,* as it is now called in Spanish. Although evidently Columbus composed his ship's log for eventual presentation (presumably following much editing) to the Spanish monarchs, the Journals represent a document that its author *never* intended to be published. In fact, the *Diario* remained completely forgotten for centuries. The statements by Columbus recorded in his Journals are, moreover, completely intimate revelations; as such, their sincerity cannot for a moment be doubted. Unfortunately, the original holograph manuscript is now lost; fortunately, however, we do have an accurate, although somewhat truncated or paraphrased, transcription that was preserved by Columbus's friend and sympathetic biographer, Padre Bartolomé de Las Casas. Happily, this gentleman, later appointed bishop of Chiapas in Mexico, chose to include the *Diario* in his pioneering *Historia de las Indias,* composed between 1527 and 1560—but, likewise, only published centuries later.[2]

The first Edenic entry in Columbus's *Diario* was dated February 21, 1493. These remarks were written once Columbus had reached the shelter of the Azores, just after leaving America behind him for the first time. As recorded by Las Casas, as soon as Columbus sailed out of European waters on his initial bold venture,

> He always found a great mildness to characterize both the winds and the seas. The Admiral's conclusion was that the Holy Theologians and the wise Philosophers were absolutely correct in stating that the Earthly Paradise is to be found in the Far East, [if only] because that is the most temperate place on Earth. The result is that those lands which he had just discovered [in America] are, he says, the Far East.[3]

We learn from this statement that America—a place paradoxically found by Columbus in "the Far East" by sailing due west—in fact represented to Columbus *el Paraíso terrenal.* America appears, moreover, to have been so conceived nearly from the very first moment Columbus came to lay his amazed eyes on this brave New World, "just found/invented" or *nupter inventis.*

The composition of a really long statement by Columbus that deals in some detail with the situation of an Earthly Paradise in America was delayed for more than five years, until August 1498. At that time he found himself anchored in the Gulf of Paria, between Venezuela and Trinidad. Whatever we may happen to call it today, for Columbus this spot was situated, of course, *supra Gangem,* that is, just "beyond the mouth of the Ganges River." Since this statement is much too long to quote here in its entirety (it is, moreover, published in full elsewhere),[4] we will cite only the most significant passages.

Approaching South America for the first time during his third voyage to the New World, Columbus again notices the distinctive ambience belonging to what he perceives as the Earthly Paradise. This means that once again he observes that "the climate was becoming gradually more temperate." Coasting toward Venezuela, he finds these effects due to "the fact of this land being the most elevated in the world." This supposition leads him to a further bizarre conclusion: "I affirm that the globe is not [wholly] spherical, but that there is instead a difference in its form." The ultimate authority for this argument is God Himself; according to the admiral, "When Our Lord made the Sun, it was first seen in the extreme point of the Far East and that was where light was first seen, that is, right here, in the Far East. This is [therefore] the place where that most elevated point of this world must be found." Since Columbus now believes himself (as he always did) to be sailing in the Far East, namely tropical Asia, he identifies "this place," the Gulf of Paria—our "America"—with the legendary *Paraíso terrenal* as follows:

> The Holy Scriptures record that Our Lord made the Earthly Paradise, and that He planted in it the Tree of Life, and that from that spot there issues a fountain. From this place the four principal rivers of the world take their courses, namely, [*nota bene*] the Ganges, in India, and [also] the Tigris and Euphrates. . . . I do not now find, nor have I ever encountered any account by either the Romans or the Greeks which fixes, in a documented manner, the actual site of the Earthly Paradise. Nor have I ever found it to have been placed upon any world maps—except that I do know that it is to be found here [in Paria, belonging to "America"], and that conclusion is firmly based upon certain authoritative arguments. Some authorities have placed Eden in Ethiopia at the sources of the Nile . . . [nevertheless] St. Isidore, Bede, Strabo, Petrus Comestor, St. Ambrose, and Duns Scotus, along with all the other orthodox theologians, are all in agreement that the Earthly Paradise is situated in the Far East, and so forth. I have already laid out my ideas concerning this [American] hemisphere and its [unique] shape, and I have no doubt that, if I could only pass below the Equator, I would then reach that highest point. . . . It is not that I really suppose that such an elevated point would be attainable by navigation, nor even that there is sufficient water there [for navigation]. Instead, I simply believe that it is impossible to ascend [by ship] to that place. Because I remain, nevertheless, quite convinced

that this place [the Gulf of Paria] really represents the location of the Earthly Paradise, then this is a place where no man can go, except with God's permission. . . .

I do not suppose that the Earthly Paradise is in the form of a rugged mountain, such as the writings about it would have us believe. Instead, I imagine that it is placed upon the heights of that site I have described as being in the form of the breast-shaped, upper part of a pear. The approach to Paradise has to be made from a great distance and it must be made by means of a constant and gradual ascent. . . . I also believe that the waters [of the Orinoco] which I have been describing must issue from that place [Paradise] even though their sources are far away. . . . There are many factors pointing to this place as being the Earthly Paradise. In fact, all its details wholly conform to the opinions of all the holy and learned theologians whom I have already cited. The other evidence agrees with this conclusion. I have never either read, nor even heard of fresh water arriving in such huge streams and then mixing with seawater. The [Edenic] hypothesis is further corroborated by the mildness of the temperature. Therefore, if this fresh water which I am describing does not actually issue from the Earthly Paradise, then it must be all the more marvellous for that fact.

Even though Columbus's Journals were not read until centuries later, his fortuitous discovery of the Earthly Paradise in what he thought were the East Indies did, however, soon become widely known to literate Europeans. The vehicle was the first comprehensive published history of the New World, the *Decades de Orbe Novo* by an Italian humanist, Peter Martyr of Anglería (1456–1526). Begun in 1493, the *First Decade* of Martyr's exhaustive, ten-part chronicle, which was based on extensive interviews with the actual explorers, including Columbus himself, was published as early as 1511 (in a pirated edition—the complete, authorized version of the *Ten Decades* only appeared in 1530). In the *First Decade* Martyr observed how, in the eyes of informed Europeans,

even the parrots and many other things [brought back by Columbus] indicate that these [American] islands, either due to proximity or by nature, do really seem the products of Indian soil. The argument rests mainly on Aristotle, as put toward the end of his book *De coelo et mundo,* but also Seneca and other wise cosmographers, who all testify that, toward the west, the beaches of India are not separated by any great stretch of the Ocean from Spain itself.[5]

Martyr also observes how Columbus himself had told him that, when he first came across Cuba,

> he judged that it represented the end of our East, where the Sun sets, and of the West, where it rises. For this reason, he states that the beginnings of extreme Gangetic India lie just a bit further to the west [of Cuba], whereas its furthest ends stretch almost to the [Mediterranean] Levant. This conclusion is, however, not at all peculiar [to Columbus] because the cosmographers have left indeterminate the actual limits of Gangetic India. As a result, there are not wanting those who do believe that the coasts of India are not much distant from Spanish beaches. . . . Leaving behind Jamaica, he sailed westwards . . . and it seemed to him that then he had arrived not far from the Golden Cheronese [Indonesia], which represents the beginnings of our East.[6]

Speaking later of Columbus's third voyage, including his passage through the Gulf of Paria, which contained his Earthly Paradise, Martyr remarks how subsequent explorers still "hold it to be the continent of the India of the Ganges. This conclusion arises because such a great mass cannot be taken for a mere island, unless we so consider the earthly orb, calling it too an island in the literal sense."[7] Columbus was not the only European to have found India in America. Martyr additionally reports that the Pinzón brothers "sailed more than 600 leagues around the coast of Paria and, as they imagined, they had gone further than the city of Cathy and the coast of India, even further [than Columbus] and beyond the Ganges."[8] In sum, as late as 1510, Martyr continues to report that "several navigators have skirted the coasts of Paria—which they all believe to be the continent of India—and have come across many new oriental regions, but others with new western lands, all full of gold and spices."[9]

The preceding materials document the initial premise impelling this investigation: The unmistakable geographical goal of Columbus and his immediate followers was India. Given this, the next conclusion reached by Columbus may now seem foregone. Having found, as he believed, India, Columbus then directly finds the Earthly Paradise, apparently a perfectly logical geographical extension of sub-Gangetic India. As he could not have suspected, but as we do know, Columbus had really found his Eden on Earth in (South) America—and not in India as he believed. Given those unquestionably authentic statements composed by Columbus himself—which paraphrased are: "I am really looking for India," and, furthermore, "In India I have found (just as I knew I would) the Earthly Paradise"—a strictly historiographic question is now called for.

This query is: By which bizarre chain of events did Eden come to land in India? In answering this question, we must first say that, as far as we can tell, the question has never before been posed in such a forthright manner, let alone analyzed in any kind of a methodical fashion. In order to resolve what none have really seen as a significant historical problem— let alone a latent factor in the obviously momentous European discovery of America—we intend to illustrate the evolution of the now largely forgotten myth of Eden in India by means of some old maps and, especially, through a whole series of often obscure medieval texts.

How a Quattrocento Painter Placed Eden

An anonymous, Middle English poem (ca. 1325) that was dedicated to the fabulous exploits of "Kyng Alisaunder," describes Eden in the following manner: "Beyonde the dragouns, gripes, and beste, / Paradys terrene is righth in the Est, / Where God Almightty, thorough his grace, / Fourmed Adam our fader that was. / The kyng thennes went forth, / Ayein into Ynde in the north."[10] In order to illustrate in a concrete, specifically visual manner the way that Alexander the Great's "Paradys terrene"—derived of course from the Latin, *Paradisus terrestris,* and meaning Eden on Earth—took up an extended, but now nearly wholly forgotten, residence in India (or Ynde), we may examine in some detail the case of a painting from the Early Renaissance in Italy.

Laurinda Dixon published (in 1985) an incisive iconographical analysis of Giovanni di Paolo's panel painting, *Expulsion from Paradise* (see Fig. 1).[11] In her fascinating article, Dixon explored the sources and meanings of several unusual aspects of Giovanni's enigmatic depiction of the Expulsion (or "Paradise Lost"), showing a chagrinned God pointing to the image of a concentrically circular universe surrounded by the Zodiac. Dixon specifically traces those cosmological motifs to the *De Sphera mundi* (ca. 1225)

1.

Giovanni di Paolo, Expulsion from Paradise, ca. 1445. New York, Metropolitan Museum of Art
(Lehman Collection).

of Johannes Sacrobosco (John Holywood), still a standard school text in
the early quattrocento. As the credibility of her larger conclusions seems
unquestionable, the point of the investigation immediately following is
to enhance Dixon's identification of the odd disklike device placed in the
exact center of Giovanni's cosmological diagram.

The centric emblem in Giovanni di Paolo's *Expulsion* represents the
Orbis terrarum, or world disk, containing the canonical continental triad of
Europe-Africa-Asia (Fig. 2). The disk with the three contiguous divisions
of the Earth is depicted just as it would have been viewed from On High
by the omnivoyant *Deus Pater.* As Dixon correctly pointed out, on one level
Giovanni's planisphere is indeed the representation of a staple of high medi-

eval cartography, namely a *mappamundi* (world map). As, however, she failed to recognize, Giovanni's map of the world is considerably more "medieval" and, therefore, much more "conventional" in its content and composition than has been supposed by the few scholars who have bothered to mention it. As such, Giovanni's peculiar (to us) conception of the cosmos will serve to demonstrate on a popular level the persistence of certain characteristically medieval worldviews long after the reception of Renaissance ideas in art. Nevertheless, in the particular matter of its geographical misconceptions, Giovanni's weltanschauung is scarcely unique for its time and place. Its aberrant features are, in fact, closely paralleled in other, equally old-fashioned *mappaemundi,* including some Italian examples that are nearly contemporaneous with the accepted date (ca. 1445) for the execution of the Lehman panel.

This contemporaneous cartographic identification serves a useful purpose and carries significant implications ranging far beyond the confines

2.

Detail of Figure 1: Giovanni's mappamundi.

of the visual arts. The larger purpose is both grandly mythical and mystical and, additionally, narrowly cartographic. We mean to locate a more or less tangibly geographical representation of Eden in the collective mind of Giovanni's contemporaries. As we shall see, tracing both the invention and the survival of Eden on Earth (let alone in India) is a rather complicated matter. Most prominently, there is the fact of an enormously popular conflation of the Judeo-Christian *Paradisus voluptatis* (as delineated in Genesis) with a preexisting, but generally vague background composed of certain classical motifs descriptive of the Golden Age. These ancient topoi survived and were vigorously revived in the secular and neopagan literary traditions of the Renaissance.

There were two predominant, different but complementary, forms of poetic landscapes in the classical literary legacy: the arcadian pastoral, celebrating the delights of rural ease (indolence nearly to the point of sloth); and the georgic, represented by largely ethical poetry championing the earnest moral virtues of sweaty agricultural labors. In either case, the bucolic poets implicitly locate vice and degeneracy in the noisy and overcrowded city (the *urbs*), and virtue and beauty reside in a topographical opposite, the *locus amoenus,* or rustic and pleasurable garden spot.[12]

Complementing the classical imagery of "the amenable [garden] spot" that was so vigorously revived during the Renaissance, there is since at least the second century of the Christian era the thriving patristic tradition of a postlapsarian Eden on Earth that was believed to still survive in a very tangible form, albeit in a supposedly inaccessible geographical situation. According to the church authorities, the Earthly Paradise is always far, far away, and very often perched high atop a mountain. A highly popular, late medieval account of this legendary place is found toward the end of the wholly fictional *Travels of Sir John Mandeville* (ca. 1357):

> Paradys es closed all aboute with a wall; bot whare of the wall es made, can na man tell. It is all mosses begrowen and covered so with mosse and with bruschez that men may see na stane, ne nowt elles wharof a wall schuld be made. And ye schall wele understand that na man liffand may ga to Paradys: For by land may na man ga thider by cause of wilde bestez that er in the wilderness and for hillez and roches, whilk na man may passe, and also for mirk placez, of whilk ther er many thare. By water also may na man passe thider, for thas rivers commez with so

grete a course and grete a birre and wawes that na schipe may ga ne saile agayne tham. Thare es also so grete noyse of waters that a man may nowt here another, crie he never so hie. Many grete lordes has assayd diverse tymes to passe by thase rivers to Paradys—bot thai myght nowt spede of theaire journee; for sum of tham died for weryness of rowyng and ower travaillyng, sum wex blind and sum deef for the noise of the waters, and sum ware drouned by violence of the wawes of the waters. And so ther may na man, as I said before, winne thider, bot thurgh speciall grace of Godd.[13]

Our immediate purpose, a generic one, is physically to place Giovanni di Paolo's Garden of Paradise upon a modern map, that is, very specifically in India. As we shall see, the idea of Eden in India was in any event scarcely unique to Giovanni and it was, in fact, supported in Italy (as elsewhere) by a extended and, at times, extremely prestigious literary tradition. As Dixon explains, the *mappamundi* in "the Lehman panel presents the world in the shape of the medieval *oikoumene* (inhabited world), situated in the center of the universe." As portrayed by Giovanni di Paolo, the element of earth is colored brown and the water around it is green in hue.

Dixon however proposes to situate this particular "Garden of Eden" in the same locale as did a Spanish theologian, Jacobo Pérez de Valencia, whose *Commentaria in Psalmos* was first published in Valencia in 1484. Pérez had postulated that Eden was located on top of what he called the "Mountains of the Moon," a largely fanciful mountain range that rose steeply from the eastern fringes of the southern African seacoast. However that may be, given the date of its *editio princeps*, Pérez's *Commentary on the Psalms* was not, therefore, a work known to Giovanni, even though, states Dixon, "it is acknowledged to be a commentary on an earlier treatise," which is, she adds, "unknown to us."[14] Dixon additionally points to what she feels are two likely cartographic sources for the painter's microcosm: the *Este Map*, dated about 1450, and the *Mappamundi of Fra Mauro*, now known only in a copy completed in 1459.[15] Even though these two other cartographic sources postdate the execution of Giovanni's panel, the best reason to doubt their direct applicability as iconographic sources for Giovanni's cosmographic conception was provided by Dixon herself: "One of the most significant breaks with cartographic tradition evident in the Mauro and Este maps was the transfer of 'East' to a less prestigious position at the right edge of the page, a move that banished the Holy City of Jerusalem (visually, at least) from its former place of honor at the center of the world."[16] Before this moment in cartographic history, Jerusalem's prestigious axial location had been largely due to the authority of Ezekiel 5:5, announcing that God had set the Holy City "in the midst of the nations and countries that are around her."

To the contrary, Giovanni's essentially symbolic (versus strictly cartographic) "east" is clearly situated at the top of his *mappamundi,* not to the right. It is only in later humanistic world maps of the sixteenth century that "north" is invariably placed at the top of charts, and only then does "east" move to the center of the right-hand edge, where we now always expect to find it. This was an innovation of orientation specifically due to renewed study of the models of global projection verbally presented in the *Geographika* by Claudius Ptolemy, who died around the year A.D. 165. The particular case of Jerusalem's fall from cartographic grace in the exact center of the European *mappaemundi* was the result of previous changes in the practice of composing maps. According to modern historians of geography, the Italian world maps cited by Dixon belong to the "transitional" (to modern) period of cartography, beginning around 1300 and lasting to around 1460, that resulted from recent explorations in western Africa and, particularly, Central Asia.[17] On the other hand, a search for any particular cartographic source seems a futile enterprise; as will be directly explained, the most likely origins of Giovanni's cartographic curiosities were mainly textual in nature rather than exclusively pictorial. Nonetheless, when we carefully scrutinize Giovanni's simulated *mappamundi* it appears that it is, in fact, in complete conformity to the schemata of older medieval cartographic traditions. This mainly means that it is still, according to the conventions of much earlier practice, "oriented," meaning that a largely metaphorical "east" — *Oriens* — is still conventionally located at the symbolic "top" (*principium*) of Giovanni's world disk.

In the way that Giovanni's world map was really meant to be read, the darker parts of the world, Europe, lie on the enshadowed bottom — representing the West, or place of the setting sun — and this northern continent is characterized by rugged, snow-clad mountain ranges in the polar regions. If we were to read Giovanni's schematicized map like a clock, the Mediterranean would be seen at "five o'clock"; like a finger, it points diagonally upward toward the center of the world, Jerusalem. Persia and Arabia cover the regions distributed from two to three o'clock. Africa occupies the clock face from three to four o'clock. The rest of the disk comprises the biggest continent of all, Asia, stretching from around nine to two o'clock. At the very top, twelve noon, representing the broadly symbolic, or non-cartographic, idea of the East, is the tip of the farthest extending eastern regions. This symbolic point is represented by the triangular peninsula of the vast Indian subcontinent. This pointed area, tangent to the top of Giovanni's world map and corresponding to the situation of modern Madras and Ceylon (for us, lying in "the south"), has a great mountain at its tip. From this elevated place there flow downward (or north and west) the Four Rivers of Paradise, mentioned by name in the Book of Genesis (2:10–15).

According to the authorized, or King James version, "the name of the first [river] is Pison," and this was, as we shall soon see, most often identified with the Ganges, and:

> the name of the second river is Gihon: the same is it that compasseth the whole land of Ethiopia. And the name of the third river is Hiddekel: that is it which goeth toward the east of Assyria. And the fourth river is Euphrates [flowing through the middle of the lands of Mesopotamia]. And the Lord God took the man [Adam], and put him into the garden of Eden to dress it and to keep it.

Paradise upon Earth and on the Medieval Mappaemundi

This same situation was graphically illustrated in Venice a bit earlier, in 1436, by a professional chartmaker, Andrea Bianco (see Fig. 3). Even though his map was most likely not Giovanni's direct iconographic source, at the very least we may take this particular example to represent, in contemporary and decidedly graphic terms, the closest equivalent to certain, still-current medieval ideas that were common to both these designers of quattrocento *mappaemundi*. The key issue is what we may call Moralized Christian Geography, and our two cartographic examples demonstrate the vigorous *Nachleben* of some once commonplace, and decidedly unscientific notions that were to be found displayed in innumerable earlier world maps of the European Middle Ages. Just as in Giovanni di Paolo's *mappamundi,* at the very top (*Oriens*) of the Bianco map we see the southernmost tip of the vast Indian subcontinent. At this spot—clearly labeled *Paradixo terrestro*—are depicted

3.

Andrea Bianco Mappamundi, 1436 (as redrawn by L. A. Brown, 1979).

Adam and Eve and the Tree of the Knowledge of Good and Evil, all shown perched upon a tall, steep-sided mound. From this same, steeply elevated spot—the Earthly Paradise—the Four Rivers of Eden flow downward into Greater Asia and thence toward a spiritually darkened Europe.

The major continental divisions of the Bianco *mappamundi* also closely correspond to the general layout of Giovanni's *mappamundi*. If one compares the lay of the land in both these examples, even the outlines of the major land masses depicted by the two Italians generally indent at about the same points, and thus the clock face scheme works equally well. Africa, parallel to Persia and Arabia in Bianco's chart, covers the entire right side of the disk, from one o'clock to five o'clock; the Mediterranean is found at six o'clock and points upward towards "Ieruxalem." Europe (excluding "Ispania") runs from seven o'clock to nine o'clock and includes the Polar Alps along the left side, and Asia (excluding "Rosie") stretches from nine to twelve o'clock. As in Giovanni's painting, India—symbolically representing both the East and Eden—is located at twelve o'clock on Bianco's *mappamundi*.

In short, Giovanni di Paolo's painted *mappamundi* belongs wholly to the cartographic conventions of the time and place of its execution. For our purposes, it additionally documents in an unquestionable, and wonderfully graphic, manner the vigorous currency in Italy of the anomalous idea of Eden in India during the Early Renaissance. This is, therefore, the real, albeit pseudo-geographical, context of Columbus's discovery of Eden in India-America after 1492. In a broader sense, it also explains why Native Americans have always been called Indians. In part, this enduring misappellation arose because the life-style originally attributed to them—that is, by the first European interpreters of the newly uncovered New World— was inevitably likened to traditionally Noble Savage customs commonly attributed by medieval writers to the supposedly Edenlike customs of India.

The major differences between these two quattrocento *mappaemundi* is that Bianco's map is, to our eyes, somewhat less vague for the configurations of the major land masses than is Giovanni's and, additionally, Bianco's is a bit more probable in the light of our current geographical knowledge. Being a real world-map (that is, as real as was possible around 1435), Bianco's representation is of course lavishly labeled with terse but appropriate Latin inscriptions. Additionally hewing to contemporary fashion, Bianco's map is densely populated with miniature pictures of the diversely exotic inhabitants of the world, and all of these features were laid out according to the conventionalized "schemata" familiar to the popular (versus erudite) fancies of the early fifteenth century.[18] Giovanni's *mappamundi* is not so labeled; his scene, the expulsion from the Earthly Paradise, unfolds at a time when the other parts of the *Orbis terrarum* were not yet named. It was, of course, only after the Fall and the Expulsion that mankind began to explore the world beyond Eden. Only then could these other parts of the Earth be so named (or inscribed).

Like Giovanni di Paolo, Andrea Bianco certainly did not invent the microcosmic cartographic scheme that nearly inevitably situated Paradise in the most distant regions of the Far East. In both of these mid-fifteenth-century examples, the Edenic site is not only generally situated in Asia, but also quite specifically in India, in fact, at the southernmost tip of the great Asian subcontinent. In fact, all of the relevant details of Giovanni's and Bianco's heterodox geographical program—Eden in India—had been first laid out in textual form long beforehand, and both these quattrocento Italian artists were merely "illustrating" quaint ideas about world geography that had been in existence, indeed flourishing in verbal form, for well over seven hundred years. The contrasting idea of Jacobo Pérez, placing Eden in Africa, definitely was not very current, neither previously, nor then, nor presently. And that is why Columbus explicitly rejected that idea.

One today reads in the King James version of the Bible, "And the Lord God planted a garden eastward in Eden; and there he put the man whom he had formed" (Genesis 2:8). Nevertheless, no such compass direction was given in the Vulgate, the only version of the Scriptures that would have been available to Giovanni di Paolo and, additionally, to all the other late medieval cartographers; as we instead read there: "Plantaverat autem Dominus Deus paradisum voluptatis a principio, in quo posuit hominem quem formaverat." Merely stating that Paradise had been "planted in the beginning," St. Jerome had omitted the crucial *in oriente* setting. Nevertheless, Jerome's "a principio" was customarily read as suggesting "a principio temporibus"—that is, "at the beginning of time." In that case, the first day was born, or dawned with the sun brightly arising at a certain extremely elevated point in the easternmost, or beginning, edge of the Earth. It set (or died), of course, in the far west, representing a *finis Terrarum.* This omissive error of geographical location in the Vulgate of St. Jerome was only rectified by later exegetes who had more carefully read the original Hebrew texts in the Pentateuch referring to the site of "a garden eastward in *Eden,"* a Hebrew word signifying *delight,* also notably absent in the Vulgate (Latin) account.[19]

The principal authority for more particularized and strictly medieval (which is to say Christian vs. Jewish) ideas about world geography, specifically Paradise, was St. Isidore of Seville, whom Columbus explicitly cited (and which was also a textual source already imputed to Giovanni di Paolo).[20] A contextual study of the minutely detailed explanations contained in Isidore's encyclopedic masterwork, the *Etymologiae* (completed in the year 630), reveals that the widely read Visigothic scholar had derived most of his (often erratic) geographical lore from standard classical authorities, including Strabo, Ptolemy, Mela, and Pliny. Nevertheless, whereas those pagan scholars obviously had nothing to say about the Paradise of the Christians, Isidore certainly did, and he puts *Paradisus* in the Far East, namely in Asia (*Etym.*, XIV), which, he states,

> is so called because of the name of a woman who ruled over the East in ancient times. It is the third part of the Orb, and it contains, to the East, the place where the Sun rises. The Ocean is found to the South, and to the West is Our Sea [*Mare Nostrum*, the Mediterranean]. To the North [of the center of the world, i.e., Jerusalem] are the Meotic Marshes [on the Black Sea] and the Tanis [Don] River. Asia has many provinces and regions, of which we shall briefly give the names and places, beginning with Paradise.

According to Isidore's further observations about its paradisiacal ambience (*Etym.*, XIV, 2–4),

> Paradisus is a place situated in the regions of the East [*Oriens*]. Its name in Greek, as translated into Latin, is *Hortus*. In Hebrew, one says *Edem*, which in our tongue signifies *deliciae*, and, uniting both terms together, we form *Hortus deliciarum* [the Garden of Delights]. It is so called for being abundant in all kinds of fruit-bearing trees, including as well the Tree of Life. In this place there is neither cold nor heat, but instead a constant tempering of the air. In the middle of this place is a fountain which waters the entire garden, whence there arise four rivers. The gates of this place were closed after the Fall. It is surrounded on all sides by swords of fire, that is, by a wall of fire, the flames of which almost unite with the heavens. A cherubim, that is to say, an angelic fortress, is so placed as to separate evil spirits; that means, the flames keep them away from mankind, and the good angels will be separated from the evil ones, and in this way the Gates of Paradise shall be left open to neither the flesh nor to the spirit of transgression.

Immediately following this equally moral and topographical analysis of *Paradisus,* there follows another geographical excursus by Isidore (*Etym.*, XIV, 5—7), dealing with

> India, which is so called because of the Indus River, delimiting its western parts. It extends from the Southern Sea [*Mare Meridianus*] up to the place of exit of the Sun, and, from the north, up to the Caucasus Moun-

tains. It includes many races and peoples [and various lands]: the island of Taprobana [Ceylon], inhabited with elephants; the islands of Crise and Argyre, most fertile in gold and silver, and the island of Tylon, full of trees with evergreen leaves. India has rivers, including the Ganges, the Indus and the Hypasis. Due to its westerly winds, India provides two harvests every year. Instead of winter, it has yearly winds [*etesii*, the monsoons]. There live colored peoples; it is filled with enormous elephants, unicorns, parrots, ebony woods, cinnamon and pepper trees, and aromatic [sugar] canes. India also provides ivory, precious stones — like beryl, topaz, diamond, carbuncle, lignite and pearls, and the union pearl, making noble ladies burn with desire. There are mountains of gold, which [unfortunately] are impossible to reach, due to the presence of dragons, griffons and enormous human monsters.[21]

Mainly as a matter of textual sequence, Isidore certainly did put *Paradisus* and India in very close proximity to one another within the sprawling confines of Asia. Isidore's statement seems to have been a primary source for the conclusions of the Venerable Bede (672–735). It was Bede who apparently first championed the idea of Eden being immensely far away from the civilized (or specifically European) lands. According to his *Hexameron,*

> some would have it that the site of Paradise is in the eastern part of the world's circumference. It is, however, separated [from us] by a great distance, both of land and sea, from all those regions which the human race now inhabits. The result is that not even the waters of the Flood, which covered deeply the whole surface of our Earth, could reach to it. But indeed, whether it is there, or elsewhere, God only knows. We only know that there was such a place, and we may not doubt but that it was terrestrial, that is, a place indeed most pleasant, shaded with fruitful groves and made fertile by a great spring.[22]

Paradise on Earth in the Exegetical Tradition

Before Isidore and Bede, the most prominent, and rather circumstantial statement about Paradise issued from the pen of St. Augustine (354–430). In his *De Genesi contra Manichaeos* (II, 9), one reads a dual, historical-symbolical interpretation of the luxuriant *locus amoenus* that is central to all exegetical geography. "Let us now look at that happiness of man," Augustine announces,

> which is meant by the word *Paradisus* . . . with which word the spiritual delights, which are the possessions of a happy life, are to be figuratively explained, together with the fact that Paradise is planted *in Oriente*. . . . "In the East" means the light of wisdom in Eden, that is, in immortal and intelligible delight. For *Eden* may mean either delights or pleasure or feasts, if it is translated from Hebrew into Latin. It is put thus, however, without translation, to appear to mean some place, or, rather, to serve as a metaphor. We take all the trees which were produced from the Earth to signify every spiritual joy. . . . The Tree of Life, however, is planted in the center of Paradise, which means that Wisdom by which the soul ought to know that it is placed in the center of things.[23]

Augustine embroidered his vision of the spiritually central Earthly Paradise further in his *De civitate Dei* (XIV, 26), here stressing the mildness of its subtropical climate and the moderated life-style enjoyed there. "And, as in Eden itself," he states, "there was never a day too hot or too cold, so too in Adam, who lived there, no fear or desire was ever so passionate as to worry his will. Of sorrows, there was none at all, and of joys, none that was vain. . . . Finally, neither leisure nor labor had ever to suffer [in Paradise] from boredom or sloth."[24]

Such a tempting picture of prelapsarian pastoral ease naturally invited further embellishments, and one such was written in the twelfth century by Ernaldus of Bonneval, who included precise topographical, and certain literally olfactory, details that far exceeded the visual and aromatic limits previously imposed by SS. Augustine and Isidore. "That place was called Eden," Ernaldus affirms,

> that is, Pleasure, and a Garden of Delight, because of the fertility of its soil and its fruitful orchards. From its center there flowed a crystal spring, thoroughly watering and refreshing every herb, yet not too copiously flowing, but by underground infiltration moistening the garden's extent. Spreading leaves upon the tall trees shaded the grass beneath, and both the moisture below, and the equitable atmosphere above maintained an everlasting verdure in the turf. There was a gentle breeze arising at midday, which blew away and drove off the heat, if, by chance, there were

any. The place was entirely free of snow and hail, and was jocund with an unbroken and perpetual spring. There arose from the fruits and the very twigs a spicy emanation, and from the trunks there exuded perfumed gums . . . and, since the aromatic gum oozed forth without force of the press, the whole region was bathed in countless sweet odors . . . and that was like a kind of ecstasy, symbolizing the bodily senses, yet not lulling man to sleep, nor calling him away from his duties, but sharpening the mind's subtlety and cleansing it for zealous work.[25]

Long before the topography of the Garden of Eden came to be so tangibly equipped, such amenable details had already been associated with Heaven. A kind of precedent was set by Saint John the Divine in his Book of Revelations, saying, "to him that overcometh will I give to eat of the tree of life, which is in the midst of the paradise of God" (Rev. 2:7). This particular Paradise was, however, not situated upon the Earth. It is, rather than Eden, instead yet *another* Paradise, an alternative Paradise which is located directly upward, in the sky itself: "I looked, and, behold, a door was opened in heaven" (Rev. 4:1). This place is not only above the earth but, being only a prophesy, it also only lies in the afterward, that is, in the future to come: "Come up hither, and I will shew thee things which must be hereafter" (Rev. 4:1). "Up there," and "later," one sees how "a throne was set in heaven"; this is a place for the dead, those who "liveth for ever and ever" (Rev. 4:10).

The *other* Paradise, the one "up there" in Heaven, was a place, at least at the time John saw it, that was densely populated with, namely, "an hundred and forty and four thousands of all the tribes of the children of Israel," not counting, additionally, "a great multitude, which no man could number, of all nations, and kindreds, and peoples, and tongues" (Rev. 7:4, 9). Some of these thronging folk were, however, eventually consigned to "the bottomless pit," or Hell (described at length in the ninth chapter of the Book of Revelations). Finally, and quite to the contrary of the pristine garden of Eden, John's prophetic vision of the alternative Paradise in Heaven is thoroughly architecturalized, even urbanized: "I, John, saw the holy city, new Jerusalem, coming down from God out of heaven" (Rev. 21: 2ff., with the complete architectural particulars).

The wholly urbanized Paradise in Heaven did not, however, prove quite as popular as did the primordial garden vision, the one belonging exclusively to Eden—which had, of course, never quite left the earth-bound world of mortal men. The earliest known, fully developed, and post-Johannine Christian vision of Heaven is the so-called *Apocalypsis Sancti Petri* that dates from the mid second century. In this work the links with pagan Other World descriptions are nothing less than overt. For our purposes, the most important feature is a reversion to a wholly dearchitecturalized version of Eden that additionally betrays clear-cut, even explicit analogies with the gardenlike features of the Hellenic Elysian Fields. Like the *Elysium* of the ancient Greeks, this newly Christianized, fruitful, and blissfully Edenic Land of the Dead is oddly placed in the Far West. In this narrative, God speaks, saying,

> We are paid according to our deeds. Then I will give my elect and righteous the baptism and the salvation that they sought from me in the field of Acherousia that is called *Elysium*. . . . I have told this to you, Peter, and declared it to you. Go, therefore, to the Land of the West, and enter the vineyard that I will tell you of. . . . And my Lord, Jesus Christ, our king, said to me, "Let us go to the holy mountain." . . . And he showed me a great garden [in the Land of the West], open and full of fair trees and blessed fruits, and of the odor of perfumes.[26]

This pagan-derived vision, a religious-poetic conflation of *Elysium* and all the other, more generalized *loci amoeni,* was further elaborated slightly later in the *Visio Sancti Pauli,* a text of the late fourth century. This must be the particular Urtext that precociously introduced into the Christian canon the geographical motif of an ocean-girdle that entirely surrounds Paradise, thus explicitly making it *insula,* an island, just like the first *Indias americanas* discovered by Columbus in 1492. In this case, the author's guide to the Other World is an angel, and, he states,

> from the Firmament, he led me to the Gates of Heaven. The beginning of its foundation was on the river that waters all the Earth. I asked the angel and said, "Lord, what river of water is this?" And he said to me, "This is the Ocean." . . . And I said, "Lord, what place is this?" He said to me, "This is the Land of Promise." . . . I looked around that land and saw a river, flowing with milk and honey. There were planted at the brink of the river trees full of fruit. Now every tree bore twelve harvests each year, and they had various and diverse fruits. . . . The trees were full of fruit, from the roots to the upper branches. . . . I said to the angel,

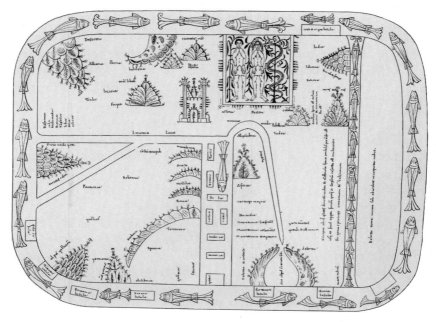

4.

Mappamundi Beati, after the original of 787 (as copied by L. A. Brown, 1979).

"What are these rivers that encircle this city?" He said to me, "These are the four rivers that flow abundantly for those who are in this Land of Promise. These are their names: the river of honey is called 'Physon,' and the river of milk 'Euphrates,' and the river of oil 'Geon,' and the river of wine is the 'Tigris.'"[27]

Eden's Eastward Translations

A very early medieval world map, attached to one of the many copies of the Spanish Beatus Manuscripts (initially composed between 776 and 786), is faithful to the textual particulars of Isidore's *Etymologiae* (Fig. 4).[28] As was already customary, this *mappamundi* is *oriented* to the East, and so that spot is placed at the very top of the chart. This is the place where, like the resurrected Christ, the reborn sun daily reappears to announce the golden "beginning" (*principium*) of each new earthly Day following the metaphorical "spiritual darkness" of Night. It is also in the East, at the very top of the world, where Adam and Eve are shown standing in the Paradise Garden, next to the Tree of Knowledge with a devious serpent tightly wrapped around it. In this very early cartographic example, Eden lies somewhere past the eastern shores of the Mediterranean, a rectangular trough filled with a great fish swimming west (or downward) toward the Atlantic. In modern geographical terms, Eden is seen to be situated exactly between the Caucasus Mountains, to the left-north, and India, to the right-south. Jerusalem (Ihalm) is however placed rather nearer to Eden, in fact just a bit further away to the northwest. This is a schematic and didacticizing picture that we may take to represent the canonic, highly moralized, and specifically *early*, medieval view of the World Entire.

As one may now ask, what had happened in the meantime to impel two much later cartographers—Andrea Bianco and Giovanni di Paolo—to move (or translate) the Paradise Garden so far to the top of the oriented map, at that time meaning completely toward what we would now call the south, and then into India? Their's was, however, a cartographic quirk that had became obviously canonized somewhat earlier. This is a fact documented by the famous *Hereford Mappamundi*, executed sometime between 1276 and 1283, that shows Adam and Eve standing upon a circular island located vaguely in what we may call the Farthest East (Fig. 5).[29] The kind of historicized cartographic conventions hewed to by Andrea Bianco and Giovanni di Paolo much later are even better illustrated by the topographical situation outlined in the *Ebstorfer Weltkarte* of about 1235–50 (which was destroyed in World War II).[30] A detail taken from the very top of this evidently stereotypical *mappamundi* shows a box-enframed head of Christ placed at the very top, or *Oriens* of a cartographic *composition moralisée* (Fig. 6). Immediately adjacent to His right side is a rectangular picture depicting Adam and Eve in Eden, and directly below the frame of their picture one easily reads the name of their putative geographical location: India.

The textual basis, supplying the tangible and historical context of Giovanni's and Bianco's assimilations of the idea of Eden in India two hundred years later, may be briefly explained as follows (and unquestionably, this is also a context pertinent to Columbus's ruminations about his felicitous discovery of the Earthly Paradise in *las Indias* toward the close of the fifteenth century). Beginning in 1096, the Crusades had of course made innumerable Europeans intimately familiar with the physical topography of the regions

5.

The Hereford World Map, ca. 1280. Hereford Cathedral.

immediately adjacent to Jerusalem. The direct result was that it quickly became obvious that this arid area, the Holy Land (*Terra Sancta*), was quite
incapable of supporting the luxuriant vegetation that was nearly inevitably
attributed to the Edenic site by patristic traditions. This place was schematically described in the Bible as being "a garden eastward in Eden . . . and
out of the ground the Lord God made to grow every tree that is pleasant
to the sight, and good for food. . . . A river went out of Eden to water
the garden; and from thence it was parted, and became into four heads"
(Genesis 2:8–10, according to the King James Bible).

Besides being considerably embroidered in the strictly topographical
sense by the likes of Ernaldus of Bonneval (as quoted above), Eden became

more tangibly geographical. The twelfth-century *Relation of Enoch and Elias* had, for instance, unequivocally stated that Paradise was specifically to be found in India, where it might be seen situated on the top of four mountains.[31] In so doing, the anonymous author of this *Relation* was probably echoing points previously raised by Hugh of Saint Victor (1096–1141), who described Paradise as though it were any other recognized country. "Asia has many provinces and regions," states Hugh,

> whose names and location I shall set forth briefly, beginning with *Paradisus*. Paradise is a place in the East, planted with every kind of timber and fruit trees. It contains the Tree of Life. No cold is there nor excessive

6.

"Eden in India": detail from the Die Ebstorfer Weltkarte, ca. 1235 (destroyed in World War II).

heat, but a constantly mild climate. It contains a fountain which runs
off in four rivers. It is called *Paradeisos* [a park, or garden] in Greek, *Edem*
[delight] in Hebrew, both of which words in our [Latin] language mean
a *Hortus deliciarum*.[32]

Later statements situating the Asiatic Eden specifically in India seem to
have arisen, more or less logically, from two previously distinct literary
traditions. The first of these deals with a mythical people called the Camerini, first encountered in the *Liber Junioris Philosophi,* the Latin translation
of a Greek work (from Alexandria or Antioch) of the mid fourth century.
The Camerini, "extremely pious and good," constantly reappeared in Christian stories of the Earthly Paradise composed during the medieval period.
According to the original version of this story,

> it is said that the people of the Camerini live in the East. Moses called
> their country Eden. From it a very great stream is said to flow and to
> be divided into four rivers, whose names are Geon, Phison, Tigris, and
> Euphrates. The men who live in the said country are extremely pious
> and good and, among them, there is found no evil, either of body or
> soul. . . . Living, therefore, in such great happiness, they know not how
> to labor, nor are they wearied by any weakness of disease, except this
> alone—that they leave the body [and] when the day of death begins
> to approach, each makes for himself a sarcophagus of various aromatic
> woods, for there are many aromatic trees in their country [etc.].[33]

In the later Middle Ages, the place of the Camerini was taken over by the
Brahmins, a wholly unimaginary people who still populate the vast Indian
subcontinent.

Alexander the Great in Paradise

Although the Brahmins had been written about since the time of Alexan-
der the Great, for our purposes the most important text was the *Res Gestae
Alexandri* ("The Exploits of Alexander the Great"), a Latin version by Julius
Valerius of an earlier Greek work, probably composed in the second or third
century of the Christian era, by an author known as Pseudo-Callisthenes.
It was especially the various, specifically postclassical Alexander epics that

supplied the complementary literary components placing Eden in India. Here we also find the basis for the rather later legends of non-Christian peoples living in southern Asia whose way of life was essentially Christian. Certainly the life-style associated with the kingdom of Prester John, later repeatedly located in the same Gangetic regions, was unquestionably Christian. The Valerius text also appears to represent the first narrative link leading up to the fanciful *Roman d'Alexandre* of the Gothic period. The immediate predecessor of the well-known French texts was, however, the *Alexandri Magni Iter ad Paradisum* ("The Journey of Alexander the Great into Paradise"), a short Latin prose narrative of unknown authorship that began to circulate early in the twelfth century. Since the story in the *Iter* is basic to what follows, as much in art as in literature, a close synopsis is called for.

In the farthest, or southernmost parts of India, King Alexander came among a hitherto unknown people who lived by the seashore. Surprised by the Greek king's graciousness toward them, they entertained him and generously provided supplies for his entire army. In this far-flung territory, the Hellenistic foreigners had come upon a great river which, as the natives told them, was either called the Ganges, or (at the same time) the Physon. This river was the one that was so named (or recorded) in the Book of Genesis; as this text would have it, Alexander "venit ad fluvium Gangem quod Physo[n] Sacra Scriptura memorat." As was additionally stated, the Ganges-Physon arose in Paradise. Alexander observed strange leaves floating down the stream; when dried in the sun, they were seen to yield exceedingly fine spices. Frustrated in his efforts to find their source, he sighed, "In all this world I have won nothing unless I win a part in this delight." Alexander fortuitously found a ship tied to the banks of the Ganges. With five hundred of his best men, he outfitted the craft for a summer's sail upstream, and so he and his hardy soldiers-turned-sailors ventured forth to find Paradise on Earth. For a month there was very hard going, and their strength was beginning to fail, equally due to the force of the current and to the deafening roar of its cataracts. Eventually, they perceived, far off, what they assumed was a great city. For three days they passed from south to north alongside its high, sheer walls, but they could not land due to the slipperiness of the muddy and mossy banks. The walls of the seeming city presented an unbroken, smooth face, without either buttresses or turrets.

Finally, on the third day, they espied a small aperture, and Alexander sent in a small party to present his demands to the inhabitants. His emissaries said that "we are the envoys, not merely of a king, but of the King of Kings, Alexander, to whom all the world is subject." To this, they added a threat: "If you have any care for your safety or peace, follow the way of all other peoples and render him tribute." By way of reply, the citizens of the hidden place girdled by steep walls gave Alexander's men a magical stone, and, they said, when the King came to understand the significance of the occult properties of the stone, all ambition would then leave him. Taking the wondrous *lapis* with him, he and his men immediately reembarked and sailed downstream. Back at their starting-place, an old Jew explains to them the meaning of both the stone and the place from whence it was derived, namely *Paradisus*. The latter is not a city, he says, but "rather a solid garden-wall, impenetrable to all flesh." This is the place where the Universal Judgment Day will appear, when all the flesh shall be resurrected: "quam in terminum ulterius progrediendi statuit universorum conditor justorum spiritibus carne solutis et ibidem corporis resurrectionem prestolantibus."[34]

It appears that the *Res Gestae Alexandri* and the *Iter ad Paradisum* are also major sources for the credibility later accorded to the legendary priest-king Prester John, the ruler of the mythical Christian empire of Kara Khitai. A widely circulated letter (in Latin, ca. 1165) was supposedly sent from him to the Byzantine emperor Manuel Comnenus. In his much-quoted epistle, Prester John also appears to situate his Edenic kingdom alongside the banks of the Indus River, which has its source in Paradise: "In the country," writes Prester John, "through one of our provinces, there flows a river which is called Ydonus [Indus]. This river, flowing out of Paradise, winds through the whole province." In this country, located far to the East, there was also a shady grove, situated near the foot of Mount Olympus, and "whence a transparent spring arises, possessing every kind of taste [and located] not far from Paradise, from which Adam was expelled." It was also said that "if anyone . . . tastes of that spring, he will. . . . always be as a man thirty-two years old, however long he may live." Besides the Fountain of Youth, this letter also mentions the fact that "there are no paupers among our people, . . . no division among us," and concludes by claiming that "we have no ruling vice."[35]

The virtues belonging to Prester John's subjects were commonplace in this Edenic state; according to the much earlier *Gestae Alexandri* of Pseudo-Callisthenes, in India

the Brahmins are not a people withdrawn from the world by choice, like
monks, but have received this way of living from on high and from the
judgment of God. They dwell by a river [the Ganges] in a state of nature,
living in nakedness [and] have a climate which is brisk and invigorating
and, in all respects, very fair. . . . Being wanderers in the woods, they
sleep on beds of leaves . . . and the land produces still other fruits upon
which they live. The men inhabit the ocean-side of the river Ganges;
this river flows into the Ocean. And their wives are on the other side of
the Ganges, towards India. . . . We [Brahmins] rest in view of the trees
and of heaven, and we listen to the melodious voices of the birds and to
the eagle's call, and we are roofed over with leaves, and we live in the
open air, and we eat fruits and drink water. We sing hymns to God, and
we gladly accept the future, and we listen to none who are not of profit
to us.[36]

And in this manner there was described an enviably bucolic and carefree
life-style that is still sought by myriads of ecologically self-conscious youths
in lands that Columbus came to call *las Indias.*

A Nearly Christian India

The idea of the essentially Christian India had been around for quite a
while. In fact, according to these traditions, also including a somewhat
apocryphal mission of the Apostle Thomas to India, tropical Ceylon, always
known to be an island located far south of India, was noted as being
an especially Christian place. Besides that, it was obviously one of those
often legendary islands belonging to *las Indias.* For example, we learn from
the *Topographia christiana,* written around 530 by Cosmas Indicopleustes (or
"India-journeyer"), that

> even in Taprobane [Ceylon]—an island in Further India, where the
> Indian Sea is—there is a Church of Christians, with clergy and a body of
> believers, but I know not whether there be any Christians in the parts
> beyond it [to the East]. In the country called Malé [Malabar], where
> the pepper grows, there is also a church, and at another place, called
> Calliana [Kalyana, near Bombay], there is, moreover, a bishop, who is

appointed from Persia. In the island, which is called the island of Dios-
corides [Socotra], which is situated within the same Indian Sea, and
where the inhabitants speak Greek, having been originally colonists sent
thither [from Egypt] by the Ptolemies, who succeeded Alexander the
Macedonian, there are [Christian] clergy. They receive their ordination
in Persia, and are sent on to the island, and there is also a multitude of
Christians. I sailed along the coast of this island, but did not land upon
it. I met, however, with some of its Greek-speaking people, who had
come over into Ethiopia. And so likewise among the Bactrians and the
Huns and the Persians, and the rest of the Indians, the Perarmenians,
and the Medes and the Elamites, and throughout the whole land of Persia. There is no limit to the number of churches here [on the shores of
the Indian Ocean], with bishops and with very large communities of
Christian people, as well as many martyrs, and monks also, who live as
hermits.[37]

Besides the largely fanciful texts dealing with the topic of Eden in India—
a standard topos by the mid-fifteenth century and standing for a tropical Paradise always subscribing to Christian virtues (either literally or only
figuratively)—there were also contributions resulting from some very real
physical contacts with the fabled Eastern World.[38] Largely impelled by the
promise of great commercial gain, European explorers, missionaries, and
traders soon pressed ever further toward the fabled Far East, meaning well
past the traditional boundaries of the Holy Land. In the middle of the fourteenth century, after the Black Death had halted further Asian contacts, a
very widely read spokesman for these new opinions was "Sir John Mandeville" (evidently a French monk who never went anywhere near the Far
East). In the *Travels,* the fraudulently peripatetic explorer claimed that the
"paradyse terrestre where Adam and Eve were sette" is adjacent to "the
first flode [which] is called Physon or Ganges, and that runneth through
Inde." This is, of course, the same place that comprises the most attractive
part of Prester John's kingdom, and in Mandeville's *Travels,* its description
immediately follows a detailed account of Taprobane, the old name for
Ceylon.[39]

As a result of the early explorers' reports (whether authentic or wholly
fictional), Eden gradually moved east with the missionaries and commercial travelers, and then south, that is toward the really lush, tropical zones
of the newly known Old World. These incursions into what had recently

been terra incognita created—besides Eden in India—a popular new literary genre, the Marvels of the East.[40] Besides Sir John Mandeville, the best-known figure in a new school of fabulous travel diaries is, of course, the doughty Venetian merchant and raconteur, Marco Polo, who dictated *Le livre du Marco Polo, citoyen de Venise, dit Million, ou l'ont conté les merveilles du monde* (i.e., *The Travels of Marco Polo*) to Rustichello da Pisa some time before 1299.[41] As we now know, and quite to the contrary of Mandeville's highly popular inventions, Polo's reports were usually solidly grounded in fact.

In fact, it is Marco Polo's widely read travel book, *Il Milione* (that many, a "million lies" were ascribed to it by detractors), that most vividly re-creates for us today the sources of the geographical anomalies that are equally shared by Giovanni's panel and Bianco's map, which means that they were also notions largely shared by most literate Italians interested in the widening problems of world geography around 1440. In the first place, there was the communality of a Paradise that had now become definitely situated well beyond the traditional confines of the Holy Land, that is, far, far away in the Far East. As we have seen in various ways, and for reasons as much cartographical as textual and legendary, Eden had clearly been moved into Asia. But, by Marco Polo's time, the geographical displacement was much further east and then south than Isidore or anyone else had originally put it. As a second and complementary factor, it was now even accepted by many that Adam had dwelled—and was even buried—in Ceylon, which is to say far into the equatorial southern extensions of Asia.

Marco Polo probably did not know that what he called *Paradiso* represented a word borrowed from the Old Persian language, wherein *pairi-daèza* originally meant a garden enclosure, a walled park, and as was further implied in the original context, this paradise garden was also the setting for a palace. After Polo leaves Persia, passing beyond the immense and largely sterile plains of the Dry Tree, he arrives, as he says, at the "Land of Mulehet, which means 'heretics' according to the law of the Saracens," and this place seems generally to conform to modern Uzbekistan (in what used to be the USSR). In former days, these regions were ruled over by Sheikh Alaodin (Alladin, or Al ud-Din, d. 1255), who, states Polo,

> had made in a valley, between two mountains, the biggest and most beautiful garden that was ever seen, planted with all the finest fruits in the world and containing the most splendid mansions and palaces that

were ever seen . . . [and] there were fair ladies there and damsels, the loveliest in the world, unrivaled at playing every sort of instrument and at singing and dancing. And he gave his men to understand that this garden was Paradise. That is why he had made it after this pattern; because Mahomet assured the Saracens that those who go to Paradise will have beautiful women to their hearts' content, to do their bidding, and they will find there rivers of wine and milk and honey and water. So he had had this garden made, like the Paradise that Mahomet promised to the Saracens, and the Saracens of this country believed that it really was Paradise.[42]

Viewed textually, this Edenic land of Mulehet incorporates all the significant features of the strictly Islamic version of Paradise. As, for example, one reads in the Koran (suras 37:41–49; 38:50–54),

For them [the blessed], there is a known provision, Fruits. And they will be honored in the Gardens of Delight, on couches facing one another . . . and with them are those [maidens] of modest gaze, with lovely eyes, pure as if they were of hidden eggs. . . . For those who ward off evil, there is a happy journey's end, the Gardens of Eden, whereof the gates are opened for them, wherein, reclining, they call for plenteous fruit and cool drink therein. And with them are those of modest gaze, [female] companions. This is that which you are promised for the Day of Reckoning.[43]

Curiously, the strictly Islamic vision of a Paradise pleasure garden, which is usually said to be deliciously equipped with beautiful and compliant damsels, seems to have become current with some Christians during the Renaissance. According to the decidedly unmystical evaluation of Lorenzo de'Medici,

Paradise means nothing more than a most pleasant garden, abundant with all pleasing and delightful things, of trees, apples, flowers, vivid running waters, song of birds and, in effect, all the amenities dreamed of by the heart of man; and, by this, one can affirm that Paradise was where there was a beautiful woman, for here was a copy of every amenity and sweetness that a kind heart might desire.[44]

Eden Even into Ceylon

Even though he had never actually seen a place now called Sri Lanka with his own eyes, Marco Polo asked his readers to allow him to digress a bit, to hear what must have been an often repeated travelers' tale (in fact, it was by then nearly a thousand years old). "Let us turn to a delightful story that I forgot to tell you when we were dealing with Ceylon . . . I am sure it will impress you." The attention of his audience caught, Polo then says, "Ceylon, as I told you earlier in this book, is a large island. Now it is a fact that in this island there is a very high mountain, so ringed by sheer cliffs that no one can climb it except by one way. . . . It is said that on top of this mountain is the monument of Adam, our first parent. The Saracens say that it is Adam's grave, but the [Buddhist] idolaters call it the monument of Sakyamuni Burkhan,"[45] and that term, signifying *divinity* in Mongol, corresponds to "Enlightened One," or *Buddha,* in Sanskrit. After giving us a more or less accurate account of the life of the Holy Man, from Bodhisattva to Buddha, also describing "how idols first originated," Marco explains that "idolaters from very distant parts come here on pilgrimage, just as we Christians go to the shrine of Messer St. James," meaning Santiago de Compostela, in Spanish Galicia. As the Venetian traveler further explained,

> the Saracens, who also come here in great numbers on pilgrimage, say that it is the monument of Adam, our first parent, and that the teeth and hair and bowl [venerated there] were his also. So now you have heard how the idolaters say that he is that king's son who was their first idol and their first god, while the Saracens say that he is Adam, our first parent. But God alone knows who he is or what he was. For we do not believe that Adam is in this place, since our Scripture of the Holy Church declares that he is in another part of the world.[46]

Even though the church (and St. Isidore) might have believed otherwise, many others eagerly accepted the "fact" that lushly tropical southern India, attached to which is Ceylon, was the original dwelling place of Adam and Eve, and therefore, it was none other than Eden, or Paradise on Earth. For example, according to Marco Polo, the Great Khan had heard that the hair, teeth, and bowl of Adam could be found upon the great Ceylonese mountain. The Mongol ruler made up his mind that he must have these relics. As Marco concludes,

So he sent here a great embassy, in the year of our Lord 1284. What more shall I say? You may take it for a fact that the Great Khan's envoys set out with a great retinue on their way and journeyed so far by sea and land that they came to the island of Ceylon. They went to the king and so far succeeded in their mission that they acquired the maxillary teeth [of Adam], which were very large and thick, and some of the hair and the bowl, which was made of a very lovely green porphyry. . . . Then the Great Khan ordered that all the people, both monks and others, should go out to meet these relics, which they were given to understand belonged to Adam. Why make a long story of it? [47]

Although rather large in size, Ceylon is, of course, an island. Well over a century ago, an English scholar had cited a twelfth-century *mappamundi* that described Eden as being an "Island of Paradise in the Ocean in the Far East," which the anonymous mapmaker had carefully situated it off the southern coast of India at a spot corresponding to Ceylon.[48] Curiously, this Indian Ocean placement of the Earthly Paradise was also evidently current with Scandinavian navigators. According to an Icelandic narrative of the fourteenth century, *Eiriks Saga Vídförla,* Prince Eirik posed a geographical question to the emperor in Constantinople, "And what's to the south of the Earth?" The imperial riposte is that "Oh! there is the end of the world, and that is India." Unsatisfied, Eirik again queries, "and, pray, where am I to find the Deathless Land?" "Paradise, I suppose you mean," answers the emperor, "that lies slightly east of India." Having obtained these geographical insights, Eirik goes to southern India where, of course, he finds the Earthly Paradise. As described in *Eiriks Saga,*

> the island [of Paradise] was most beautiful, and the grass as gorgeous as purple; it was studded with flowers, and was traversed by honey rills. The land was extensive and level, so that there was not to be seen mountain or hill, and the sun shone cloudless, without night and darkness; the calm of the air was great, and there was but a feeble murmur of wind, and that which there was, breathed redolent with the odor of blossoms.[49]

Another standard source (actually a late medieval "best-seller") composed about the same time—the aforementioned *Travels of Sir John Mandeville*— omitted the *locus amoenus* topography but stated very much the same thing: "In that isle of Silha [Ceylon] there is a high mountain, and on the very top of it is a great loch full of water. Men of that land say that Adam and Eve wept for a hundred years on that hill after they were expelled from Paradise, and that the water [in the lake] was collected from their tears."[50] As it turns out, in this instance the ultimate source of Mandeville's vastly popular tale was the (authentic) *Viaggio del Beato Odorico da Pordenone* (1318–30). In 1321, the Franciscan noted that

> I passed by another island, called Ceylon. . . . In this country there is a huge mountain, where, the inhabitants of that region report, Adam mourned for his son Abel the space of five hundred years. In the midst of this mountain there is a most beautiful plain, wherein is a little lake containing a great amount of water, which the inhabitants report to have come from the tears of Adam and Eve. However, I proved that to be false, because I myself saw the water flow into the lake.[51]

Siting Eden in Dante and Milton

Doubtlessly drawing from the same common fund of geographical mis-information, a few years earlier (ca. 1320), Dante Alighieri similarly placed the Garden of Eden on an island, specifically upon the top of a very steep mountain, and this paradisiacal place he definitely situated well toward the Equator. As he stated (*Purgatorio,* I, 22–30), the *Paradiso terrestre* was perched high atop a great mountain that lay at the center of the Southern Hemi-sphere, near the mouths of the Ganges and exactly opposite Jerusalem in the northern half of the world: "a man destra . . . all'altro polo . . . opposita a lui cerchia, uscia di Gange fuor colle bilance." As Dante adds (*Purg.,* IV, 79ff.),

> There is where my intellect seemed wanting: the middle circle of the highest movement, that which is called the Equator by some fashion, and which is always located between the Sun and the Winter, and, for the reason given, it [the Earthly Paradise] lies far to the opposite end of the North, and the Hebrews were also accustomed to see it, down toward the warmer parts [of the world].

As it turns out, this same Indian Ocean placement of Eden, figuring so vividly in Dante's epic poem, was to be reiterated, centuries later, by John

Milton. In his own, equally monumental verse saga, *Paradise Lost* (published in 1667), Milton similarly places the Earthly Paradise immediately before "them who sail / Beyond the Cape of [Good] Hope, and now are [well] past / Mozambic" (PL, IV, 159–61). Elsewhere (PL, XI, 929–34), Milton states that, after the Fall, and after the Universal Flood, the postlapsarian Eden-now described as being an extremely elevated island-had been washed out into the Indian Ocean, far away from its original site in Mesopotamia:

> this Mount / Of Paradise [was] by might of waves . . . moved / Out of this place, pushed by the horned flood, / With all his verdure spoiled, and trees adrift, / Down the great [Tigris] river to the opening / [of the Persian] Gulf, / And there [to] take root, an island salt and bare, / The haunt of seals, and orcs, and sea-mews clang

Even though this of course largely represents an epic simile, nevertheless the distinctive residue of traditional medieval pseudo-geography remains clear.

Given the immense cultural significance of these two poetic epics, a question is definitely in order. Where did Dante (and thus Milton after him as well) tangibly acquire knowledge of this peculiarly insular Earthly Paradise that is situated in the middle of an ocean which lies, in this case, in the near-equatorial Far East? Briefly put,[52] it turns out that the textual tradition of Paradise as an island is perhaps even older than the Bible itself because, as one may read in the *Odyssey* (IV, 561–68), "the Elysian Fields [lie] at the world's end, where all existence is a dream of ease." This place must be an island because it is cooled by "mild and lulling airs from Ocean . . . the West Wind is always blowing." The insular setting of the pagan Paradise of the Dead is even more apparent in Hesiod, who said (*Works and Days,* 60–65) that beatified souls "lived untouched by sorrow in the Islands of the Blessed along the shores of deep swirling Ocean." An insular setting was also often implied for the mythical Golden Age that typically unfolded at the end of the world.

The first recorded descriptions by Columbus—and various other Europeans (to be cited in chapters following)—of the American Indians, living on some islands that were found in 1492 to be lying at the end of the world, were initially couched in the then-familiar terms of the Age of Gold. Although the term *Tempus Aureum* was only later invented by the Romans, for Homer its equivalent was the Elysian Fields—a place for the

Golden Race—and, for Hesiod, their reward was the Islands of the Blest. The ultimate conflation—Islands of the Blest and Golden Age—appears in Horace's *Epode* XVI: where "the Happy Fields of the Blessed" (41–42: "arva, beata . . . et insulas") are observed to be "shores for a righteous folk . . . [living in] the Age of Gold" (63–64). Centuries later, John Milton also picked up on the idea, then defining America as the New Eden, an unspoiled place where native peoples still live in the innocent bliss of the Golden Age. Toward the close of *Paradise Lost* (IX, 1, 113–18), Adam and Eve, now shamed and so newly clad in fig leaves in their postlapsarian Earthly Paradise, are invidiously compared to the newest, meaning strictly contemporaneous, Renaissance models of Edenic existence. Now Eden acquires a dual historical significance, namely with reference

> To that first naked glory. Such of late
> Columbus found the American [Indian] so girt
> With feathered cincture, naked else and wild
> Among the trees on isles and woody shores.

Marco Polo and all the other authors quoted here who discussed the apocryphal placement of Eden in India do not really explain the odd topographical details that were repeatedly cited in Dante's famous description of the *Paradiso terrestre*. The best guess has it that Dante's topography—the picturesque appearance of a steeply walled Edenic *insula* completely surrounded by seawater in the middle of a tropical Ocean—arose in a more chronologically immediate sense from the famous legendary voyage of St. Brendan, an Irish monk of the sixth century. The Latin text of the immensely popular *Navigatio Sancti Brandanni* was first written down in the late ninth or tenth century and was often recopied thereafter. As Dante might have perhaps read here, with his picked sailing companions Brendan eventually found that

> all gloom departed, and gladly they started to the eastern regions. For forty days they were blown by helpful winds, so that nothing except sea and air fell upon their sight. Then, however, by the grace of our Lord Jesus Christ, they approached that belt of darkness which surrounds Paradise. . . . About it a wall appeared to them, which, reaching to the clouds, was exceedingly high. Its material was unknown to the travelers, its whiteness, brighter than that of snow. . . . That wall surrounding Paradise was built upon a high mountain, whose summit was of gold and

whose base, which came down to the sea, was of marble. . . . A huge gate
was the entrance [and] they joyfully entered the gates of Paradise [and]
they looked upon a land fertile in watered groves, with orchards and
meadows unceasingly in bloom. Flowers of a wonderful kind and sweet
perfumed the air, as is proper in the habitation of the just. Beautiful trees
and delightful flowers, precious fruits and pleasing odors, gave forth the
greatest pleasure. The trees and flowers in that part of the Zodiac (where
the Sun may be) do not fade, but always produce their fruits. An ever-
present, gentle summer provides a ready supply of fruits. The groves are
full of animals and the streams full of fish. The rivers there flowed with
milk and dew. . . . The clouds never gathered there to shade the bright-
ness of the sun. The inhabitants of this place will never suffer from heat,
cold, sadness, hunger, thirst, poverty, nor other adversity. They will have
a supply of all good things; but what is more, their will shall be done in
all things.[53]

Later, Brendan and his mates land on an island called Jasconius, where they
celebrate mass—until it sinks beneath their feet. They had disembarked
upon a whale! John Milton certainly also knew the fabulous story, a whale
of a tale, because of his bizarre mention (PL I, 201ff.) of another such island
cetacean. Although this was a story originally unique to the *Navigatio,* it
later became widely spread through important intermediaries, including
(besides Dante) the *Historia de gentibus septentrionalis* (1567) by Olaus Magnus
(but see also Fig. 48, an engraving of 1621 showing Brendan's Whale Island,
which might also have been known to Milton).

To conclude we find that both Andrea Bianco and Giovanni di Paolo
(among many other late medieval cartographers) had evidently heard of the
same tall story about Eden in India, probably learning some of it directly
from Marco Polo's vastly popular travel book and, most likely, much (if not
all) of the rest from Mandeville's even more popular *opusculum.* That explains why both the chartmaker and the quattrocento painter had chosen to
put Eden in India, especially way down south in the Indian Ocean, alongside Ceylon, so treated as part of *las Indias.* Viewed in a larger perspective,
our two cartographic anomalies from Italy become significant documents
of contemporary culture inasmuch as they reveal something intrinsic to the
eclectic state of the emerging science of geography in the early quattrocento. This was a time when traditional travelers' accounts (remade, in the
case of Sir John Mandeville, into pure fairy tales) were increasingly scruti-

nized and put into competition with the newly reemphasized classical, or humanist, sources of geographical knowledge. One contemporary reader now known to have avidly consumed Mandeville's geographical fantasies was Christopher Columbus.

The conflict was, however, only to be resolved well after 1492, when another Italian interested in maps, Christopher Columbus, fortuitously dis-covered (and thus invented) a whole New World in the endlessly replayed Edenic mode. Being a creature of his times, Columbus first took the island of Cuba in the Caribbean and, later, the Gulf of Paria to represent the site of the Earthly Paradise. As he always believed, he was sailing in regions that he had rediscovered in a place, Eden, that one then knew to be located south-east of the southernmost ends of India, as embraced by the blanket term *las Indias*. The Native Americans first found by him, therefore, inevitably were assumed to partake of those same Indian-Edenic characteristics that had been discussed throughout the Middle Ages in Europe as belonging to peoples inhabiting the sub-Gangetic regions. There is, therefore, really no mystery about why—and *how*—he came to call Native Americans *indios*.

Columbus's contemporaries also called these newly invented places in the Far West the setting of the Age of Gold, but that idea (to be further explored in later chapters) was just a secularized and humanistic transposi-tion of everything that Eden stood for. As we just saw, like the Indies, the topographical setting of the innocent, peaceful, and endlessly bountiful *Tempus Aureum* was often insular. Even without that literary reference to a topos that proved so appealing to many of his learned contemporaries, when Christopher Columbus first saw the New World he believed that he had, singlehandedly, recovered Eden in India. Previously, without any solid knowledge of this long-standing pseudo-geographical tradition, Eden in India, modern students of Columbus's explorations and written statements have (should they even deign to mention them) merely dismissed his rumi-nations upon the *Paraíso terrenal* in various parts of tropical America as just an idle delusion. Now, finally, the single most plausible explanation for his geographical and exegetical suppositions has been provided.

In spite of such persistent delusions, all of which are directly attrib-utable to the results of the strictly moralized, geographic and cartographic conventions of the later Middle Ages, in 1492 a *Mundus Novus* had indeed miraculously appeared in the Far West. As a direct result, all the old *mappae-mundi* subsequently had to be completely recast in the light of authentic eyewitness accounts and scientifically verifiable information. As one minor result, after 1498, Eden was finally removed in a definitive fashion off of (nearly) all the maps of India. That other cartographic omission mainly resulted from the momentous voyage of Vasco da Gama, which had opened up a whole new sea route to the Indian Ocean by turning the Cape of Good Hope.

Curiously, that momentous voyage was initially motivated by a similarly medieval delusion. It was the desire of the Portuguese monarch, King João II, to lay down a transoceanic path of communication with Prester John. As we just heard, that fabulous fellow was known to be the wise and wealthy ruler of the Rivers of Paradise and the Fountain of Youth (which Juan Ponce de León fruitlessly sought in Florida). As one now also begins to understand, King João II must have known probably as much as did Columbus about the miraculous situation and benefits of Eden in India. Accordingly, even as late as the last decade of the fifteenth century, the physical attainment of Paradise on Earth still seemed well worth the effort, and one, then wholly unforeseen, result of a wholly medieval quest was a huge continent we now call America.

In order to summarize all these diverse arguments in a memorable manner, a final piece of evidence may be introduced. It sticks in the mind as it is both visual in nature and conveniently labeled (Fig. 7). A typically medieval *mappamundi* of the sort we have been reviewing was included in a tome published in Paris as late as 1522, and most oddly called *La Salade nouvellement imprimée* ("The Newly Printed Salad").[54] This early sixteenth-century world map is modern inasmuch as it does place north at the top of the planisphere. In spite of its late date, some thirty years after Columbus's Great Discovery, it still gives no indication of the existence of the New World. Nevertheless, and probably reflecting news of the recent Portuguese voyages toward India, it does show sub-Equatorial Africa to be circumnavigable, that is, by way of what is called here the *Mare Antipodes et Incognitum*. The way toward the exotic Far East through the Unknown Antipodean Sea then leads one to an outsized Ceylon (labeled Tapbano), north of which sprawls the great Indian subcontinent (labeled Inde). The tip of India is here called Asian India. Far to the north of this tropical place is found Asia-Aise, and yet further north is Cathay. Directly to the east of the Gangetic coasts — and exactly opposite to, or facing the European Atlantic coasts, stretching

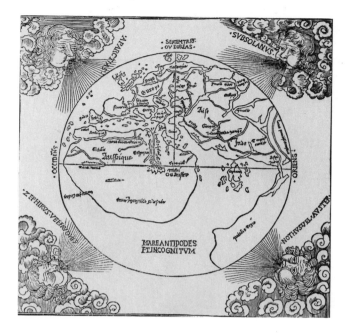

7.

"The World Map," from La Salade nouvellement imprimée *(Paris, 1522).*

from the Canary Islands north to the English Channel—there is found yet another Asian coastal region. Representing the furthest *Oriens,* this huge tract of seacoast is clearly labeled, announcing itself to be none other than the *locus paradisi terrestrie.* Quite literally, this means, of course, "the Site of the Earthly Paradise."

This contemporaneous cartographical placement of Eden on Earth exactly corresponds to Columbus's geographical expectations, meaning exactly as those carefully written down by the admiral in various passages of his *Diario.* As the example of this anachronistic *mappamundi* confirms, one, now forgotten, result of the great Columbian invention of America in 1492 (and immediately afterward) was the renewal of Eden on Earth. Just as in the Middle Ages, that Edenic epiphany had to occur in India, later to be known as *las Indias.* Accordingly, all of its potentially Edenic inhabitants ought to be called *indios.*

Due to Columbus's delusions however, the long-awaited renewal of Eden on Earth happened, however briefly, in the as-yet-unnamed Americas. Those of us who are intimately familiar with the subsequent history of the Americas, south and north, might now pause to think of several cogent reasons accounting for a quick dismantling of the idea of Eden in contemporary America.

2

MEDIEVAL LITERARY
CONVENTIONS IN
THE FIRST EUROPEAN
ENCOUNTERS WITH
THE AMERICAN INDIANS

Art in the Invention of an Edenic America

It seems a particular distinction of the psychology of Homo sapiens that nothing really exists *for* it until a thing is described *by* it. Therefore verbalization must attend, in order to define, even the most rudimentary facts of cognition.

At the successful conclusion of his first voyage of discovery to the New World in February 1493, with a certain amount of self-satisfaction Christopher Columbus wrote that he had indeed found *el Paraíso terrenal,* Eden on Earth. As he put it, "both the theologians of the Sacred Scriptures and the learned philosophers had rightly said that the Earthly Paradise is [to be found] in the Far East"; given this presupposition, "therefore, those lands, which I have recently discovered, are in the Far East."[1] Here too, obviously, was the location of the Earthly Paradise. Now we know in some detail the nature of that body of largely textually transmitted (and considerably fictitious) traditions that had led Columbus, nearly inevitably, to arrive at this (to us) fabulous geographical conclusion. The result was the great Columbian invention of 1492—not "America" (as yet unnamed), but the renewal of Eden on Earth.

As we have seen, the idea of the Earthly Paradise was certainly nothing new. Regardless of the varieties of its possible geographical appearances, whoever believed in Paradise had to see it in a certain way, according to a mode dictated by long-standing rhetorical traditions and a well-established Edenic format. Because the idea of Paradise does not seem very real to us today, at least not in any tangibly geographical sense (notwithstanding the lucrative encomia of travel-agents), we must assume that it has always been a dream, a product of the human mind and wishful thinking. So viewed, *Paradisus,* whether on Earth or situated in Heaven, may be called art.[2] Derived from the Latin—*ars, artis*—the classical term now signifies many of the same things in modern English: "Human contrivance or ingenuity, as in adapting natural things to man's use" (as in the commonplace definition afforded by *Webster's Collegiate Dictionary*). Besides representing an artful distortion of the facts of nature through the will of the human imagination, art also suggests to the modern lexicographer a "systematic application of knowledge or skill in effecting a desired result."

The earliest applications of the standard terminology of Eden by Columbus to the quite accidentally arrived at American experience also suggest that Paradise had once again become artifice. According to the same lexical source, this other term—*artifice*—also signifies the intervention of a human agency in the perception of "workmanship; a skillfully contrived work. . . . crafty device; an artful, ingenious, or elaborated trick . . . expedient . . . machination . . . imposition, imposture." Returning to our original postulate, it was all simply an invention, even *inventio* in the accepted, literal Latin sense of "discovery." In this light it is interesting to discover that Columbus's ecstatic descriptions of the lands he had recently *re*discovered (as he thought) in the tropical regions of southeastern India include all the standard Edenic literary topoi—*topoi* literally meaning *places*—that had been commonly employed by pagan literary artists since the classical period.

The first lands that Columbus encountered were only some fly-blown and low-lying sandy islets dangling at the southern edges of the Bahamas. These were evidently not the sort of places that would stir the hardy sailor's dormant poetic instincts. A fortnight later, however, Columbus drew near the immense island of Cuba, which he assumed was terra firma, the eastern and southernmost parts of Greater Asia itself. According to the *Diario* of the first voyage, on October 24, 1492, the admiral took this to be "the island of Cipango, of which marvellous things are told. It was with these hopes that I [first] saw it and, according to the manner that Cipango is represented in the *mappaemundi,* this must be its location."³ Four days later he described the Edenic appearance of Cipango-Cuba as follows and, according to Bartolomé de Las Casas's scrupulously paraphrased transcription of Columbus's *Diario,*

> The Admiral says that he never saw a more beautiful place. It was so full of trees that they even grew over the river. These are lovely and green and different from ours. They have flowers, and each kind bears fruits according to its fashion. There are many birds, and some of the little ones were singing most sweetly. There was a great quantity of palm-trees, but these are different from those in Guinea [in Equatorial Africa] or the ones we have [in southern Spain]. They are of middling height, and they have no covering at their bases. Their large leaves are used as roofing materials. The land [here] is rather flat. . . . It was a great pleasure to see all this lush vegetation and the forests. There were so many birds all around us that you could never leave them behind you. He says that this island is the most lovely place ever seen by his eyes. It is filled with many good ports and deep rivers. It seems as though the tides never rise very much here because the shrubbery grows on the beaches, nearly reaching to the edges of the sea. This cannot happen where the seas are typically tempestuous. Up to this point, he had yet to find any place in those islands where the seas were rough. He says that all over the island [of Cuba] there are some very beautiful mountains. Even though they are not very great in extension they are rather high. The rest of the land is elevated in the manner of Sicily.⁴

Another dazzling piece of descriptive landscape painting appeared in the *Diario* in an entry for December 13, a week after Columbus had sighted the adjacent island that he dubbed Española (now combining the modern nations of Haiti and the Dominican Republic). Padre de Las Casas recorded these equally Edenic and arcadian expressions as follows:

> They also spoke of the great beauty of the lands which they had seen, saying that they bore no comparison whatsoever with Castille, even its

most beautiful and fruitful parts. The Admiral's perception of these lands was always in comparison to those other places which he had seen, and which he kept before him [in his mind's eye]. It was said that what they saw could not be compared with any other valleys and fields, like those [for example] around Córdoba; there was as much dissimilarity as between day and night. It was also stated that those lands were all under cultivation, and that through the middle of this valley an immensely wide river flowed, and this watered all the fields. There were green trees that were full of fruits, and all the bushes were in bloom and grew very tall. There were very good, wide roads. The air was like that of Castille in April. The nightingales and other smaller birds were singing, just as they do in Spain during that same month. So they said that this place must represent the greatest pleasure in the whole world. At night, various small birds were softly singing; many crickets and frogs could also be heard. The fish are [as good] as they are in Spain.[5]

Given the scriptural turn of the admiral's mind, naturally he decided to call this place Paradise: "Puso nombre al valle del Paraíso.' " A week later another highly idealized landscape picture was drawn into the *Diario:*

Throughout this region there are found extremely high mountains. They seem to reach up to the sky. The one that is on Tenerife [a reference to El Pico de Teide] seems like nothing at all when compared with these in either altitude or in beauty. They are all so green and covered with groves that it is like a miracle. In the middle of them are luscious meadows. In the south, at the base of this port [Port Paix, in Haiti], there is another huge meadow, so big that your eyes cannot even reach far enough to see the end of it—even though there are no mountains to block your view. It seems to be about fifteen or twenty leagues in extension, and a river runs through the entire length. It is completely populated and heavily cultivated. Now, it is so green that you would think you were in Castille in either May or June.[6]

The Classical Pedigree of American Landscapes

Somewhat curiously, eighty years later these same topographical features were, to cite only one literary example, to reappear in a pastoral poem written by a notable English author, Sir Philip Sidney (they also surface later in

John Milton's *Paradise Lost*). Since Columbus's unpublished *Diario* certainly cannot be the source for either Sidney or Milton, then we have further evidence for an independently flourishing literary tradition about Edenic geography. The only significant change by the 1570s is botanical—given the nationality and tastes of the considerably more artistic Elizabethan poet, it is only natural that Sidney should now place some blood-red rosebushes into Columbus's prototypical Haitian landscape, now dubbed in Britain (as elsewhere) "Arcadia." According to Sidney's temperate transposition of the Edenic *Hortus deliciarum,*

> It [Arcadia] was indeed a place of delight [i.e., a *locus amoenus*]; for thorow the middest of it, there ran a sweete brooke, which did both hold the eye open with her azure streams, and yet seeke to close the eie with the purling noise it made upon the pibble stones it ran over: the field itself being set in some places with roses, and in al the rest constantly preserving a flourishing greene; the Roses added such a ruddy shew unto it, as though the field were bashfull at his owne beautie: about it (as if it had bene to inclose a Theatre) grew such a sort of trees, as eyther excellency of fruit, stateliness of growth, continuall greennes, or poeticall fancies have made at any time famous.[7]

The same bucolic literary pattern also appeared eighty years earlier in the more formal, and rather brief, *Carta de Colón* (Columbus's Letter). Composed by Columbus himself, and dated February 15, 1493, it was shortly afterward published—usually with an illustration—throughout Europe in various languages (see Figs. 16–19). In this printed form, the *Carta* constitutes the official version of the Earthly Paradise that Columbus had rediscovered to the Far West. As amazed Europeans learned from it (in this example, the Castilian version),

> This island [of Española] and all the others [in what Columbus thinks is the southeastern Indian Ocean] are very fertile to a limitless degree, and this island is extremely so. In it there are many harbors lying on the coast of the Sea [of India], and these are not to be compared with the others I might know of in Christian lands. There are many good and large rivers. It is like a miracle [*es una maravilla*]. The lands here are elevated and there are many mountain ranges and high peaks, all beyond comparison with [the Pico de Tenerife on] the [Canary] island of Tenerife [12,200 feet

high]. All of these are exceedingly beautiful and in a thousand different shapes, but all are accessible and full of trees of a thousand different kinds. Some are so high that it seems that they reach to the heavens. I have it on authority that they never lose their leaves. I can understand this, for I saw them to be as green and lovely as their like in Spain in the month of May. They all flower, and many bear fruits while others prepare to do so, each according to its manner. Nightingales were singing and so were other smaller birds in a thousand different ways, all this in the month of November, and wherever I chose to walk. There are six to eight different kinds of palm trees. They are an admirable sight for their beautiful deformities, and the same applies to the other trees, fruits and plants. There are marvelous stands of pines and there are many immense, cultivatable fields. There is honey and many kinds of birds and diverse types of fruits and vegetables. Inland, there are many mines and a great number of people. . . . On this island there are many sources of spices and large mines, producing gold and other [valuable] metals.[8]

Perhaps both eastern Cuba and northern Haiti actually *did* once have this pristine and Edenic appearance. Perhaps not; it really does not matter. These are written descriptions, and as we have shown in many other ways, Columbus's perceptions were often conventional and essentially medieval. Certainly those anomalous nightingales represent an obvious European ornithological interpolation, being a motif common to medieval romances albeit never ones native to the American landscape. As any student of medieval literature additionally knows, descriptions of nature written during the Middle Ages were not meant to represent the raw facts of uncooked reality.[9] The minds of Columbus and his men were unquestionably filled with predigested literary formulas. As applied to the tropical wonders of the Indies these set textual patterns were, of course, largely derived from Marco Polo and, especially, the fraudulent, pseudonymous traveler, Sir John Mandeville. That was the new, or postclassical and medieval, literary formula of topography: Exoticism. But an even older *schematum* seems to be at work here as well.

Medieval science has often been aptly characterized as representing natural philosophy without nature. The older medieval conventions for poetic landscape descriptions were derived from the rhetorical school exercises of late antiquity. Even if all of those amenable and delicious features—

trees, rivers, mountains, and animals (and even European nightingales)—
had also been in Cuba and Haiti at the time of Columbus's landing, they
were present long before, in spirit if not in corporeal fact, in antique poetry
and rhetoric. *Any* learned reader of Columbus's *Carta* in the Renaissance
would have admitted the analogy. Two of the most ancient examples of
extended landscape description will suffice to illustrate this essentially rhetorical point. These venerable texts illuminate in a concrete fashion the
way art and artifice were actually imposed by one representative, somewhat literate European mind—Columbus's—upon the actual landscape of
the central Caribbean in late 1492. Thus was a raw America immediately
invented in the conventional European poetic mold.

The initial long *Diario* entry (October 8, 1492) drew the picture of an
idyllic and uninhabited island landscape. Being without people, it is additionally like Eden, that is, well before the fall, *ante homines,* before men,
white or red, ever trampled its virgin verdure. Although Columbus probably never read it, it turns out that a similarly ravishing bit of heroic, but
unpopulated island scenery had appeared millennia before to astounded
sailors in the *Odyssey* (IX, 132ff.):

> Now a rough island stretches along outside the harbor, not close to the
> Cyclops' coast nor yet far out, covered with trees. On it innumerable
> wild goats breed; no tread of man disturbs them; none comes here to
> follow hounds, to toil through woods and climb the crests of hills. The
> land is not held for flocks or tillage, but all unsown, untilled, it ever-
> more is bare of men and feeds [only] the bleating goats. . . . For here are
> meadows on the banks of the gray sea, moist, with soft soil; here vines
> could never die; here is smooth plowing-land; a very heavy crop, and
> always well in season, might be reaped, for the undersoil is rich. Here is
> a quiet harbor, never needing moorings, throwing out anchor-stones, or
> fastening cables; but merely to run in and wait awhile, till sailor hearts
> are ready and the winds are blowing. Just at the harbor's head a spring
> of sparkling water flows from beneath a cave; around it poplars grow.
> Here we sailed in, some god our guide.[10]

The actual geographical setting of Homer's pre-Christian, verdant Edenic
landscape surrounded by the sea is, at best, vague. A Roman poet, Horace,
was however to give this typological insular Paradise a much more concrete

situation, namely the *Insulae Fortunatae,* and those Islands of the Blessed were always taken to lie in the Far West of the Ocean Sea. As one may read in Horace's *Epodi* (XVI, 40ff.),

> The encircling stream of Ocean awaits us; let us seek those fields, those blessed Elysian Fields, and the Fortunate Islands. Here the unplowed earth distributes the gifts of Ceres year by year, here the vine blooms untouched by the pruning knife; here the olive buds always ripen, and the dark fig adorns its trees, here honey drips from the hollow oak, and, from the high mountains, the smooth stream trips down with splashing foot. . . . Many other wonders we shall happily behold [in the Fortunate Islands]: watery Eurus never tears up the fields with his downpours, nor are the rich seeds burned in the dry glebe; both rain and sun are tempered by the King of the Gods. . . . Jupiter hid those island shores for virtuous folk, when he alloyed the Age of Gold with bronze; after the Bronze Age, and then he hardened the [last of the Four] Ages with iron. Nevertheless, as I prophesy, escape from them both [the Ages of Bronze and Iron] is open [only] to the Virtuous[11]

Columbus's later landscaped entries, particularly the ones written in December 1492, described (as quoted above) yet another kind of Edenic scene in Haiti. That one was, however, not only populated but, additionally, heavily cultivated. This situation, a *Hortus deliciarum post homines,* also has its (doubtlessly inadvertent) *locus classicus* in Homer. In this case, the prototypical *locus amoenus* is represented by a poetical landscape trope called the Gardens of Alcinous (*Odyssey,* VII, 112):

> In the King's house are fifty serving maids, some grinding at the mill the yellow corn, some plying looms or twisting yarn. . . . Without the court, and close beside its gate, is a large garden, covering four acres; around it runs a hedge on either side. Here grow tall, thrifty trees— pears, pomegranates, apples with shining fruit, sweet figs and frugal olives. On them fruit never fails; it is not gone in winter or in summer, but lasts throughout the year, for constantly the west wind's breath brings some to bud and mellows others. Pear ripens upon pear, apple on apple, cluster on cluster, fig on fig. Here too the teeming vineyard has been planted. . . . And here trim garden-beds, along the outer line, spring up in every kind and all the year are gay. Nearby, two fountains

rise, one scattering its streams throughout the garden, one bounding by another course beneath the court-yard gate toward the high house; from this the townsfolk draw their water. Such at the palace of Alcinous were the gods' splendid gifts.[12]

The quintessential Latin equivalent of Homer's Doric meter would be (about a thousand years later) the elegant *Eclogues* of Virgil. All medieval studies of the *artes poeticae* began with the *First Eclogue,* from which only the first couplet need be cited: "Oh Tityrus, you recline beneath the shadowing beech-tree to woo a muse of the woods with your slim pipe." The vivid result, once it became repeatedly pictorialized in the painterly mode of the High Renaissance, would be one of the sensuously painted Venetian *poesie,* either by Gentile Bellini, Giorgione, or the younger Titian, collectively celebrating pastoral utopias set in an archetypal Arcadia that metaphorically signified bliss and beauty. As was commonly understood during the Renaissance, those bucolic virtues were fugitive and distant from contemporary man, both in time and place.[13] In this way, Arcadia is functionally the same thing as Eden. In either case, Hellenic or Roman—or even medieval—these standard poetic figures of the classical landscape originally represented what Ernst Robert Curtius calls

> the place of heart's desire, beautiful with perpetual spring, as the scene of a blessed life after death; the lovely miniature landscape which combines tree, spring, and grass; the wood with various species of trees; the carpet of flowers. . . . The minimal ingredients [of the *locus amoenus*] comprise a tree (or several trees), a meadow, and a spring or brook. Birdsong and flowers may be added. The most elaborate examples also include a breeze.[14]

The Christian Pedigree of the American Landscape

In all cases, in either literature (art) or in Cuba and Haiti (reality), well-watered and largely unassisted fertility is made an essential feature of the ideal landscape, either the one belonging to Eden or its complement Arcadia, drawn by classical and pagan poets. The devout Christian European, Christopher Columbus, must give this poetic configuration a name and an understood, moralized, and medieval valence: the Earthly Paradise. In short, in Columbus's case, life imitates art, or, as Shakespeare put it, "the art itself is Nature" (*Winter's Tale*, IV, iii, 96). Those scenes of lush Caribbean bounty so carefully painted in words by Columbus are like folios torn from the perennial textbook of the *Paradisus voluptatis terrestris*, soon to be repainted by the Renaissance poets and renamed Arcadia in a newly secularized format. As the literary art of the sixteenth century reveals, besides the immediate *locus classicus* in the Book of Genesis, Eden, the amenable landscape figures so lovingly limned in the admiral's album could have been drawn as easily from classical antiquity as from the modern classicizing currents. All these motifs blend together seamlessly late in 1492. In retrospect, it appears somewhat paradoxical that the Renaissance proves to be the cultural entity that chronologically enframes Columbus's essentially medievalizing reconnaissances of the Far East-Far West.

In his Journal, Columbus initially drew the pastoral picture of an Eden before the fall. Columbus, of course, had intensely studied the Bible. According to the sequence laid down in the Book of Genesis, before God the Father had created the *Paradisus voluptatis*, he had brought into being an androgynous mankind that would take over and tame a raw nature. As is stated in Genesis 1: 26–28 (King James version),

> And God said, Let us make man in our image, after our likeness; and let them have dominion over the fish of the sea, and over the fowl of the air, and over the cattle, and over all the earth, and over every creeping thing that creepeth upon the earth. So created man in his own image, in the image of God created he him; male and female created he them. And God blessed them, and God said unto them, Be fruitful, and multiply, and replenish the earth, and subdue it; and have dominion over the fish of the sea, and over the fowl of the air, and over every living thing that moveth upon the earth.

Columbus was, therefore, not at all surprised when he found that what he called the prelapsarian *Paraíso terrenal* was populated. As he also knew, he and his rapacious men were scripturally intended to "have dominion over every living thing that moveth over the earth." In the *Carta*, Columbus described the inhabitants of the Earthly Paradise in such a way as to suggest that this place was Eden before the fall. Before the fall and the well-deserved expulsion from Paradise, humanity went stark naked; it was only afterward that (Genesis 3: 21–24)

> Unto Adam also and to his wife did the Lord God make coats of skins and clothed them. And the Lord God said, Behold, the man is become as one of us, to know good and evil. . . . Therefore the Lord God sent him forth from the garden of Eden. . . . So he drove out the man; and he placed at the east of the garden of Eden Cherubims, and a flaming sword which turned every way, to keep the way of the tree of life.

To the contrary, the first Indians seen by Columbus and his men in their Edenic landscape setting were, he observed, "as naked as the day they were born." For them, there was (as yet) no Paradise Lost. All this was made perfectly clear in Columbus's published *Carta:*

> The people of this island, and all the other islands which I have found and of which I have information, all go about naked, men and women, just as their mothers bore them, although some women cover a single place with the leaf of a plant or with a net of cotton which they have made for the purpose.[15]

These points were first raised in the private *Diario* early in November 1492. Since this longer statement was in effect private, intended only to be read by the Catholic Monarchs, Columbus additionally felt free to discuss the potential usefulness of his Indians as a kind of *materia prima* (raw materials) for "dominion" and "subduing" into the fabric of the Catholic church. Dominion and subjection were a given for anyone who read Genesis 3. The acquisition of *los indios* by the church would also, Columbus shrewdly adds, ensure a strong measure of divine approval for the Spanish monarchs and promises of greater glory yet for them in the hereafter. In his own words, from the outset Columbus believed that he was dealing with prelapsarian souls:

> They are a people most innocent of wickedness and warfare. They are all naked, men and women, just as their mothers bore them. It is true that the women wear only a piece of cotton, large enough to cover their genitals and no more. They are of good appearance, and are not black, certainly much less so than even the Canary Islanders. I hold, Most

Serene Princes, that, as they are predisposed towards devoutly religious instincts, once they became further disposed by language [i.e., learned Spanish], they should all become good Christians. I trust by Our Lord that Your Majesties will be determined to effect this with great diligence, and thus you will return to the fold of the Church such great populations. They will converted [by you], just as you have liquidated all those [Muslims and Jews] who did not accept the Father, the Son, and the Holy Ghost. Following your days, for we are all mortal, you shall have left their kingdoms in a state of peace that is free from heresy and evil. Thereby, you will be well received before the Eternal Creator, Whom it may please to grant you long life and an even greater increase of yet greater kingdoms and territories, and to grant you the will and inclination to spread yet further the Holy Christian religion, just as you have done, up to the present time. Amen.[16]

The coverings placed over the loins of the Carib maidens are naturally taken by Columbus to represent a sign of quasi-Christian modesty, due to sexual awakening. Most of the medieval theologians had, of course, connected the eating of fruits from the Tree of Knowledge of Good and Evil in the Garden of Eden with the attainment of sexual maturity. One of those authorities was Tertullian (*De anima*, 38):

> For as Adam and Eve, upon acquiring knowledge of good and evil, felt that they must cover their pudenda, so we, from the time we experience the same feeling, recognize that we have attained knowledge of good and evil. From this age [of puberty] on, sexuality is more bashful, and it covers itself, and concupiscence employs the eye as its minister and communicates its desire and understands what these [sexual organs] are, and girds itself against the lascivious touch as by the apron of fig-leaves, and it leads man out of the Paradise of Innocence.[17]

As described by Columbus, besides potentially providing an unmistakable biblical context—Eden—these Indian inhabitants of *el Paraíso terrenal* were also living representatives of a currently revived classical idea, namely that of the Golden Age, a long-gone time before the advent of civilization—the Iron Age—and its discontents. At such a time—the Paradise of Innocence— and in such an Edenic setting, there is no war and there is no selfishness. According to Columbus's first published impressions of these prelapsarian peoples in his *Carta,*

They have neither iron nor steel. Neither do they have weapons, nor are they suited to their use. This is not because they are not built for it [warfare], for they are of handsome stature; rather, they are instead amazingly fearful. They have no other kinds of weapons, but they do have some canes and, when it is time to plant seeds, they put a sharp point at the end of the thin pole. But they do not dare to make [offensive] use of these. Many times, it has happened to me that when I sent ashore a couple of men to some hamlet to talk with them, in great numbers they would flee from them.[18]

Columbus's conclusion was that the Tainos "son así temerosos sin remedio"—due to their natures, are hopelessly fearful. Peace-loving and wholly ignorant of the arts of warfare, they were also precocious subscribers to a kind of open-handed communism *avant la lettre (columbienne)*. According to Columbus's recollections in the published *Carta*,

After they have been reassured, and have thus lost their fear, they are so guileless and so generous with all they possess, that no one [that is, no European] would believe it who has not seen it. Anything they may possess, once it is requested of them, they can never refuse its donation. Instead, they invite anyone to share it, and display so much love as if they would give [to the recipients even] their hearts. Whatever the thing given them may be, whether of great value or even of small price, whatever trifle it may be, for all that they are quite content with it.[19]

America, the New Cradle of Golden Age Primitivism

This idea, a kind of primitive communism, evidently appealed to the European intelligentsia during the Renaissance. There had never been the like in Europe, at least not on the universal scale imputed to the benign practices of the New World. In 1516, Sir Thomas More wrote his famous treatise *Utopia* ("Noplacia"). It purports to be the report of a certain Portuguese explorer who "saw much to condemn in the New World, but he also discovered several regulations which suggested possible methods of reforming European society. . . . I lived there for more than five years, you know, and the only reason why I ever left was that I wanted to tell people about the New World."[20] When More's New World explorer gets around to telling his listeners about the social organization of Utopia in America, we find ourselves reading what appears to be a paraphrase of Columbus's widely read *Carta:*

> The products of every household are collected. . . . When the head of a household needs anything for himself or his family, he just goes to one of these shops and asks for it. And whatever he asks for, he's allowed to take away, without any sort of payment, either in money or in kind. After all, why shouldn't he? There's more than enough of everything to go around. . . . Under such a system, there's bound to be plenty of everything and, as everything is divided equally among the entire population, there obviously can't be any poor people or beggars.[21]

If More had not read Columbus's Carta, then he must have been familiar with (among his other possible American sources) the contents, to the same effect, of the well-known *Decades de Orbe Novo* by Pietro Martire d'Anghiera (ca. 1457–1526) also known to English readers as Peter Martyr. Although the official date of appearance for the *Decades* is 1515, significant parts had already been published in pirated versions since as early as 1505. Besides making the term *New World* (*Orbe Novo*) current, this Italian scholar, who never left Europe, must additionally be given much of the credit for initially giving the definitive Renaissance format to Columbus's newly invented American Eden. The immediate result was that a universal mythic mold for America became the *Tempus Aureum.* Peter Martyr's vision, however, went beyond mere poetic artifice, and penetrated into the deeper matter of a social structure properly befitting a genuine Earthly Paradise reshaped to conform to current Renaissance concerns. According to this enthusiastic advocate of primitivist economic values and political near lawlessness (*anarcia,* or *anarchia*),

> It is certain that among them [the Indians], the land is as common as the sun and water, and that "Mine" and "Thine" (the seeds of all mischief) have no place with them. They are content with so little that, in so large a country, they have rather superfluity than scarceness. So that (as we have said before) they seem to live in the Golden World, without toil, living in open gardens, not entrenched with dikes, divided with hedges, nor defended with walls. They deal truly one with another, without laws, without books, and without judges. They take him for an evil and mischievous man who takes pleasure in doing hurt to others.[22]

"Mine and thine"—"meum et tuum"—is an interesting phrase, one that was to become a kind of equally poetic and ethical topos in its own right during the later Renaissance. The trope seems to have had its immediate *locus classicus* in Peter Martyr; in any event, when it was afterward employed by European literary artists—including by the likes of Montaigne, Ronsard, Cervantes, Lescarbot, etc.[23]—it was then always set in the context of Martyr's original coinage, namely the Age of Gold. But did Martyr himself invent the term? We rather doubt it; although we cannot cite a classical source (which is what one would have expected to have found for it), we do find that the phrase was clearly used by a much earlier travel writer— and within the same psychological, and even the same geographical context of equally Edenic and primitivist Indian felicity that Martyr was to describe nearly two hundred years later within a wholly New World setting. As one reads in the *Viaggio del Beato Odorico da Pordenone* (1330), the peripatetic Franciscan friar had reached the island of Lamory (Sumatra), where, he states,

> in regard of extreme heat, the people, both men and women, go stark naked, from top to toe. Seeing me apparelled, they scoffed at me, saying that God had [in the Garden of Eden] made Adam and Eve naked. In this [East Indian] country, all women are [sexually] held in common, so that no man can say, this is my wife. Also, when any of the said women bears a son or a daughter, she bestows it upon any one that hath [sexually] consorted with her. Likewise, all the land of this region is possessed in common, so that there is not mine and thine, *nec meum aut tuum,* nor any other propriety of possession in the division of lands.[24]

Whereas Odorico is completely of the medieval cut, both Thomas More and Peter Martyr were typical Renaissance men, meaning that, as humanists, they were applied students of classical literature. That is, of course, the source of their knowledge and enthusiasm for the idea of the fugitive Golden Age.[25] If they knew, for instance, Porphyry's essay *On Abstinence,* then they would have read there the following comments (*De abstinentia,* IV, i, 2):

> Dicaearchus the Peripatetic says of the men of the earliest [Golden] age that they were akin to the gods and were by nature the best men and

lived the best life, so that they are regarded as a Golden Race in comparison with the men of the present time, who are made of a base and inferior matter [iron]. . . . All things then presumably grew spontaneously, since the men of that [primitive] time themselves produced nothing, having invented neither agriculture nor any other art. It was for this reason that they lived a life of leisure, without care or toil, and also—if the doctrine of the most eminent medical men is to be accepted—without disease. . . . For they [primitive men] did not eat any food too strong for their constitutions, but rather such food as their constitutions could absorb, nor did they exceed the limits of moderation, in consequence of having so much food available. . . . And there were no wars or feuds between them [during the Golden Age]; for there existed among them no objects of competition, none of such value as to give anyone a motive to seek to obtain them by those [bellicose] means. Thus it was that their whole life was one of leisure, and one of freedom from care about the satisfaction of their needs, one of health and peace and friendship. Consequently, this manner of life of theirs naturally came to be longed for by men of later times [especially in the Renaissance!] who, because of the immensity of their desires, had become subject to many evils.[26]

As is particularly evident from the remarks of Sir Thomas More and Peter Martyr, the newly rediscovered inhabitants of a Golden World in the Far East-Far West were the square pegs that were made to fit into the round hole of the ancient literary trope of the *aurea aetas*. Like the doctrines of the four elements, the basis of medieval physics, and the scheme of the four humors, representing medieval physiology, the theory of the four ages of man was the given proposition of medieval allegorized historiography. Since all grand concepts came in fours during the Middle Ages, three continents were not enough, and a fourth, America, needed invention. So said Saint Isidore of Seville around 630:

Besides the three continents originally known, there must also be a fourth one; this one must lie on the other [western] side of the [Atlantic] Ocean. It must be in the South, but it has been made unknown to us due to the heat of the Sun. It lies in the Antipodes, in which parts there will additionally have been produced fabulous inhabitants.[27]

America and the Reborn Christian Golden Age of the Renaissance

America, lying west and south of Europe, filled a long felt need by supplying, through timely invention, the missing fourth part of the *Orbis terrarum*. Once opportunely invented, America needed conventionalized descriptions to make it comprehensible. As we are beginning to recognize, the assimilation of America by Europeans was rapid and relatively easy because there was little — besides the name — that was completely new, meaning little or nothing lacking some kind of tradition, in this case specifically a textual precedent. Europeans were already completely primed by a long medieval tradition of dramatic travel narratives that told of very similar primitive cultures, exotic flora and fauna, and tropical lands full of immense wealth and carefree peoples enjoying desirably unclothed, libertine, and Edenic lifestyles. Nearly all of those traits were, as we saw, long since associated with India.

The role of Peter Martyr in this business of the European invention of America was an important one, but he mainly served to give the old idea of the primordial Age of Gold a tangible new geographical *locus*. The spread and acceptance of this venerable topos, and long after the non-Asian-Indian identification of the Americas had been established by geographers, is demonstrated in a famous soliloquy in *Don Quijote* (I, xi) that employs the same kind of terminology as did Peter Martyr's encomium on the pristine New World. This nostalgic rhapsody played out upon a lost Edenic Age of Gold that was vigorously perpetrated by classical poetry reappears on a grand scale in the eleventh chapter of Miguel de Cervantes Saavedra's famous novel (1605) having the same name as its famous but befuddled hero. In the original Castilian, the passage begins: "Dichosa edad y siglos dichosos aquellos a quién los antiguos pusieron nombre de dorados . . ." Put otherwise, and adding the traditional Edenic-Arcadian landscape components, besides including Peter Martyr's *meum et tuum* trope emblematic of his *Orbe Novo*, Don Quijote exclaims,

> Happy the age and happy the times on which the ancients bestowed the name of "golden," not because gold, which in this iron age of ours is rated so highly, was attainable without labor in those fortunate times, but rather because the people of those days did not [then] know those two words "thine" and "mine" [*éstas dos palabras de "tuyo" y "mío"*]. In

that blessed age, all things were held in common. No man, to gain his common sustenance, needed to make any greater effort than to reach up his hand and pluck it from the strong oaks, which literally invited him to taste their sweet and savory fruit. Clear springs and running rivers offered him their sweet and limpid water in glorious abundance. In clefts of the rock and hollow trees, the careful and provident bees formed their commonwealth, offering to every hand, without interest, the fertile produce of their fragrant toil. Spontaneously, out of sheer courtesy, the sturdy cork-trees shed their light and broad bark, with which men first covered their houses, supported on rough poles only as a defence against the inclemencies of the heavens. All was peace then, all amity, all concord.

The broader, underlying cultural leitmotiv of the entire Renaissance period was the hope for a return to that lost Golden Age, ignorant of "mine" and "thine." At the time Columbus sailed west to find the Edenic East, the quest in Europe was for a lost, specifically Christian, Golden Age, and in the same Christian terms, its actual and unfortunately elusive geographical location was, of course, the Earthly Paradise. This is what Columbus sought, and this is what he found in the Indies. According to the theologians, some of whom Columbus must have read, this new Age of Gold had long before been prophesied by Virgil in his famous *Fourth Eclogue*. In the manner that Virgil's messianic *Fourth Eclogue* was read (or misread) by the Christian exegetes, "the boy" described by the Roman poet was none other than Christ Himself—and thus Dante took Virgil to be his not-quite-so-pagan guide through the *Inferno*. As Virgil put it,

Now is come the last age of the Cumaean prophecy: the great cycle of periods is born anew. Now returns the Maid [Astraea, or "Justice"], now returns the reign of Saturn [tutelary god of the Golden Age]: now from high heaven a new generation comes down. Yet do thou, at that boy's birth—in whom the iron race shall begin to cease, and the golden to arise over all the world—be thou, holy Lucina, gracious. . . . He shall grow in the life of gods, and shall see gods and heroes mingled, and himself shall be seen by them, and shall rule the world that his fathers' virtues have set at peace. . . . When once thou shalt be able now to read the glories of heroes and thy fathers' deeds, and to know Virtue as she is, slowly the plain shall grow golden with the soft corn-spike, and the

reddening grape will trail from the wild briar, and hard oaks shall drip
dew of honey. . . . Behold how all things rejoice in the golden age to
come! Ah, may the latter end of a long life yet be mine, and such breath
as shall suffice to tell thy deeds![28]

Before Columbus sailed, in the strictly geographical sense the world of
Latin Christendom had been considerably narrowed by the loss, in the
eastern Mediterranean, of Constantinople in 1453. Columbus restored the
balance of the Christian world by adding a whole New World, *ad Ocas-
sum,* into the path of the setting sun and well on the other side of the
traditional Christian ecumene. The theme of the recovered Golden Age —
inevitably postulated upon the utopian vision of a better society than that
one currently known in Europe — was repeated throughout the Renaissance
by innumerable poets, scholars, and church reformers. The universalist goal
was a renewed Christendom, and the communal ideal was, therefore, unity
and order; as such, it was, of course, a strictly utopian pursuit for earthly
perfection of a kind for which the standard model was, and has always been,
Paradise. In the matter of church reform, whether Catholic or Protestant,
after 1517 the historical goal was usually the "primitive values" of the early
church, usually situated in time just before the Peace of Constantine in 317.
An early and eloquent spokesman for the Catholic Reformation was Jacques
Lefevre d'Étaples. In his *Commentarii initiatorii in* IV *evangeliis praefatio* (1522),
he typically claimed that

> the model of faith may be sought in the primitive church, which offered
> to Christ so many martyrs, which knew of no other rule than the Gospel,
> and no other end than Christ. . . . If we rule our life by this [primitivist]
> example, the eternal Gospel of Christ will flourish now, as it flourished
> then. . . . Why may we not aspire to see our age restored to the likeness
> of the primitive Church, when Christ received a purer veneration, and
> the splendor of His Name shone forth more widely? . . . [More recently,]
> the new lands were discovered, and thereupon the name of Christ was
> propagated, by the Portuguese in the east [in India] and, in the south-
> west [in America], by the Spaniards, under the leadership of a Genoese
> [Columbus].[29]

It was a foregone conclusion that "the name of Christ was [to be] propagated" in all the lands found by Columbus. The admiral wrote the following

appraisal about the primitivist religious customs of the Caribs to his royal patrons in the secret *Diario* (November 12, 1492):

> I saw, just as I expected, that these people [of India] have no creed, nor are they idolaters. They are instead very gentle and do not know what it means to be wicked or to kill others or even how to steal. They are unarmed and are so fearful that a hundred of them run away from just one of our people, even when they are joking with them. They believe—know—that there is a God in Heaven. They are also sure that we have ourselves descended from heaven. They are also quick to repeat any prayer that we might repeat to them and they also [now know how to] make the sign of the Cross. Your Highnesses must therefore resolve to turn them all into Christians. I believe that, once you begin, in just a little while you will have achieved the conversion of huge numbers of peoples to our Holy Faith. You will, thereby, take for Spain immense territories and riches and all their inhabitants.[30]

Columbus's final, and most revealing, comment was that "doubtlessly, there are in these lands immense amounts of gold." It was all rather fitting; in an exotic landscape that was preshaped according to the lineaments of the ancient *Tempus Aureum* there must similarly be real gold littering the arcadian background. The mostly malevolent effects deriving from real gold eventually appearing in the Americas, and equally opposed in thought and deed to an essentially metaphorical situation belonging to that Age of Gold initially imposed in these parts, will be further pursued in Chapter 5.

The Onset of an Age of Iron

According to the Renaissance formula of the Golden Age that represented what was generally taken to be a probably unrecoverable past, the present age was a harsh and selfish, bellicose and mechanized Age of Iron. The contrast between the two periods—broadly representing artless simplicity versus duplicitous artifice—was inevitably invidious; as Don Quijote (I, xi) put it,

> In those days [of the Golden Age], the soul's amorous fancies were clothed simply and plainly, exactly as they were conceived, without any

search for artificial elaborations to enhance them. Nor had fraud, deceit, or malice yet mingled with truth and sincerity. Justice pursued her own proper purposes, as yet undisturbed and unassailed by favor and interest, which so impair, restrain, and pervert her today. . . . But now, in this detestable Iron Age of ours, no maiden is safe. . . . Therefore, as times rolled on, and wickedness increased, the order of knights errant was founded for their protection, to defend maidens, to relieve widows, and to succor the orphans and the need. Of this chivalric order am I.

The primitivist, or anti-modernist ideas expressed by Cervantes and all of his other nostalgic Renaissance contemporaries are truly ancient; indeed, they can in fact be traced (at least) back to the eighth century B.C. As may be initially read in Hesiod's *Works and Days* (ll. 109–20),

First of all, the deathless gods, who dwell on Olympus, made a golden race of mortal men who lived in the time of Cronos [Saturn] when he was reigning in heaven. And they lived like gods, without sorrow of heart, remote and free from toil and grief; miserable age rested not on them; but, with legs and arms never failing, they made merry with feasting, beyond the reach of all evils. When they died, it was [only] as though they were overcome with sleep, and they had all good things; for the fruitful earth, unforced, bore them fruits abundantly, and without stint. They dwelt in ease and peace upon their lands with many good things, rich in flocks and loved by the blessed gods.[31]

Hesiod also appears to have invented the Age of Iron, succeeding—in the present/our period—the Age of Gold.[32] It was the former age that so bedeviled Cervantes and his nostalgic contemporaries in the Renaissance, a period they would have probably called the New Age of Iron. According to the ancient Greek poet (*Works and Days*, 176–205),

Now truly there is a race of iron, and men shall never rest from labor and sorrow by day, and from perishing by night; and the gods shall lay sore trouble upon them . . . and Zeus shall destroy this race of mortal men; [making them so degenerate that] they will come to have grey hair on their temples at their birth. The father will not agree with his children, nor the children with their father, nor a guest with his host, nor comrade with comrade; nor will both be dear to brother as previously.

Men will dishonor their parents as they grow quickly old, and will carp at them, chiding them with bitter words, hard-hearted they, [now] not knowing the fear of the gods. They will not repay their aged parents the cost of their nurture, for might shall be their [only] right: and one man will sack another's city. There will be no favor for the man who keeps his oath, nor any for the just, or any for the good; but instead men will [only] praise the evil-doer and his violent dealings. Strength will [solely] be right, and reverence will cease to be. . . . Envy, foul-mouthed, delighting in evil, with scowling face, will go along with wretched men, one and all, . . . and [only] bitter sorrows will be left for mortal men, and there will be no help against evil.[33]

Whereas Hesiod was scarcely known to Europeans at the time of the European invention of America, Ovid certainly was, and it was his detailed and often grimly frightening picture of the Age of Iron that was taken by many (including Cervantes) to provide a classical counterpart to the Age of Iron that was felt to dominate the material culture of the Renaissance. Ovid explained his precocious blueprint for the Renaissance in the first book of his widely read *Metamorphoses:*

Last of all arose the age of hard iron: immediately, in this period, which took its name from a baser ore [than gold], all manner of crime broke out; modesty, truth, and loyalty fled. Treachery and trickery, deceit and violence, and criminal greed took their place. Now sailors spread their canvas to the winds, though they had as yet but little knowledge of these. . . . The land, which had previously been common to all, like the sunlight and the breezes, was now divided up far and wide by boundaries, set by cautious surveyors. Nor was it only corn and their due nourishment that men demanded of the rich earth: they explored its very bowels, and dug out the wealth which it had hidden away, close to the Stygian shades; and this wealth was a further incitement to wickedness. By this time, iron had been discovered, to the hurt of mankind, and gold, more hurtful still than iron. War made its appearance [in the Age of Iron], using both those metals in its conflict, and shaking clashing weapons in bloodstained hands. Men lived on what they could plunder: friend was not safe from friend. . . . All proper affection lay vanquished and, last of the immortals, the maiden Justice [Astraea] left the blood-soaked earth.[34]

The medieval exegetes quickly invented a concrete geographical location for the arcadian activities of the inhabitants of the Age of Gold invented by the Greek poets. That place was, of course, Eden. Since the works of St. Isidore of Seville were more influential than the other early medieval authorities in passing on these ideas to posterity, he alone need be cited in order to establish the connection between Arcadia and Eden. In the tenth chapter of his treatise *De ordine creaturarum,* he affirmed that "paradise was the home of the first men." The way Isidore tells it, the blissful life in Christian Eden was just like the one enjoyed by the primordial and happily slothful inhabitants of the Age of Gold who had been described by the pagan poets:

> Life in that land [Eden] was entirely happy, and it was carried on without any labor, but, presently, when they had sinned and degenerated, the very world was changed by their vice. . . . Accordingly, it lost its beauty and fruitful power, if not entirely, at least to a very large degree, so that the things which had increased the blessed happiness of those living well [in Eden] augmented the punishment of those living ill [outside of Paradise].

The baleful results of this fall from Divine Grace—Paradise Lost—were exactly those that were to be re-recorded one thousand years later in England by John Milton in his *Paradise Lost.* According to Genesis 3:23, "God sent him [Adam] forth from the Garden of Eden, to till the ground from whence he was taken." In short, after the expulsion, indolent mankind had, immediately and forever more, to wrest a living from a now demanding, even hostile nature, a "cursed land" that also came to be known as the wilderness. Any modern wage-earner can appreciate the ultimate significance of Isidore's grim picture of the economic consequences of Paradise Lost:

> When the dweller in Paradise sinned in the place of his earthly bliss, he was thrust out to dwell into a land accursed, and, straightaway, all those things which he had previously possessed [without effort], he lost in part, and, in part, he preserved [some of] these by labor. And when he was shut out from the abode of bliss, the possibility of returning there was precluded, and it was so done in the case of the fallen angel, who, cast out of the high serenity of Paradise with his troop, was apportioned

this [present] realm of darkness [roughly corresponding to Ovid's Age of Iron]. So, too, man was excluded from the earthly blessedness of his Paradise into the habitation of this cursed land.[35]

During both the Middle Ages and the Renaissance, besides Virgil, the best-loved classical poet was Ovid. He, too, spoke in moving figures of the now lost, and probably irretrievable, *aurea saeculi*. As one reads in the *Metamorphoses* (I, 89ff.),

> In the beginning was the Golden Age, when men of their own accord, without threat of punishment, without laws, maintained good faith and did what was [inherently] right. There were no penalties to be afraid of; no bronze tablets were erected; no carrying threats of legal actions; no crowd of wrong-doers, anxious for mercy, trembled before the face of their judge: indeed, there were no judges, men lived securely without them. . . . The peoples of the [primordial] world, untroubled by any fears, enjoyed a leisurely and peaceful existence, and had no use for soldiers.

At the outset, Ovid's initial enframing idea was one of untutored political harmony, the immediate fruits of which are security and peace. As he also makes clear, this came about because of the absence of restrictive laws (and opportunistic lawyers, still a problem in the modern age). In that sense, the ideal arrangement of the utopian Golden Age is pure *an-archia,* ungoverned "lawlessness" in the literal sense of the Greek word *anarcia.* Ovid concludes however by putting his anarchic Age of Gold into a specifically described, semitropical, landscape setting.

The Edenic Landscape of the Primitivist Age of Gold

In this case, the widely read Ovidian mise-en-scène, a semitropical, landscape setting, is none other than the topography of that *Paradisus voluptatis terrestris.* This was the same kind of *paysage moralisé* that was to so fascinate a multitude of Christian writers during the Middle Ages, particularly in the lineaments of some equally fabulous *Insulae Fortunatae* often identified with real Atlantic archipelagoes, particularly the Canaries. The pagan but canonic equivalent of the Eden of the Golden World appears as follows in Ovid's *Metamorphoses* (I, 100–12):

> The earth itself, without compulsion, untouched by the hoe, unfurrowed by any plowshare, produced all things spontaneously, and men were content with foods that grew without cultivation. They gathered arbute berries and mountain strawberries, wild cherries and the blackberries that cling to thorny bramble bushes, or acorns, fallen from Jupiter's spreading oak. It was a season of everlasting spring, when peaceful zephyrs, with their warm breath, caressed the flowers that sprang up without having been planted. In time, the earth, though untilled, produced corn too, and fields, that never lay fallow, whitened with heavy ears of grain. Then there flowed rivers of milk and rivers of nectar, and golden honey dripped from the green holm-oak.[36]

In a decisive fashion, some time around A.D. 387, St. Ambrose, the bishop of Milan, succeeded in fusing the previous disparate, but communally paradisiacal themes of Genesis and the classical poetic evocations of the lost Golden Age. According to his *Hexaemeron* (III, 10), in a parallel kind of Age of Gold, now placed securely in Eden,

> spontaneously, the earth bore all fruits; although it could not be plowed, in the absence of a plowman—for no farmer yet existed—nevertheless, it abounded in the richest harvests, and, I do not doubt, with an even larger yield [than now], since the slothfulness of the husbandman could not yet rob the soil of its richness. For now the fertility of a piece of land is in proportion to the labor expended upon it, and neglect . . . is punished by the barrenness of the soil. In those days, however, the earth of itself everywhere brought forth its fruits, since He so commanded, He Who is the fullness of all things. For the word of God fructified upon the earth, nor had the soil as yet been laid under any curse. For the time of the birth of the world [in Eden] is more ancient than our sins, and the guilt [due to the Fall], because of which we have been condemned to eat our bread in the sweat of our brow, to know no food without sweat, is much more recent.[37]

About a century and a half later, locked away in a dreary prison near Rome, Anicius Manlius Torquatus Severinus Boethius was to compose (ca. 525) his influential *Consolation of Philosophy.* In such a hellish place, the thoughts of Boethius naturally went back in time to the lost but idyllic Golden Age. Alongside Ovid, Boethius must be accounted the major source in the Middle Ages for the standard landscape picture of this Edenic period of man's earliest existence, ideal and idle, before the Fall of Mankind and before the Age of Iron. As he stated in the *Consolatio philosophiae* (II, 5),

> Oh, happy was that [golden] early age of men, contented with their trusted and unfailing fields, not yet ruined by the wealth that enervates. Easily was the acorn gotten that used to satisfy their longwhile fast. They knew not Bacchus' gifts [wine], nor honey mixed therewith. They knew not how to tinge with Tyre's purple dyes the sheen of China's silks. Their sleep kept health on rushes and grasses; the stream gave them to drink as it flowed by: the lofty pine to them gave shade. Not one of them [in pre-historical times] yet clave the ocean's depths, nor, carrying stores of merchandise, had visited new shores. Then was not heard the battle's trump, nor had blood made red with bitter hate the bristling words of war. For why should any madness urge them to take up first their arms upon an enemy, such ones as knew no sight of cruel wounds nor knew rewards that could be reaped in blood? Oh, would that our [iron] times could but return to those old ways! But love of gain and greed of holding burn more fiercely far than Etna's fires. Ah! Who was the wretch who first unearthed the mass of hidden gold, the gems that only longed to lie unfound? For, full of danger, was the prize he found.[38]

In the classical descriptions of the Age of Gold, the Edenic landscape setting (according to Ovid, "the land of milk and honey") was largely optional. For the Renaissance commentators on the bounteous New World, full of "the mass of hidden gold," it seems, conversely, to have been the essential component. However, for the other Renaissance commentators on the Golden Age, those who stayed home in Europe, a fundamental issue was the essentially political benefits that supposedly arise from social primitivism. Although primitivist socialism is a very popular idea today among idealists and naive youth, this point of view was actually a very old one and probably was best expressed originally in a text of Tacitus that had only been fully recovered in the Early Renaissance. As one could then read in the *Annales* (III, 26), dealing with the topic of the origins of law,

Primitive man had no evil desires. Being blameless and innocent, his life was free of compulsions or penalties. He also needed no rewards; for he was naturally good. Likewise, where no wrong desires existed, fear imposed no prohibitions. But when men ceased to be equal, egotism replaced fellow-feeling, and decency succumbed to violence. The result was despotism—in many countries, permanently. Some communities, however, either immediately or when autocratic government palled, preferred the rule of law. Laws were, at first, the unpolished inventions of simple-hearted men.[39]

Eden-Arcadia Fitted to Asian Indians and/or American Indians

As most students of postmedieval European culture now recognize, the Renaissance was propelled in large part by a nostalgic and antiquarian quest for the ethical values identified with the lost Golden Age. However, fewer recognize that this largely futile search often additionally took on the concrete shape of a specific topographical entity. The geographical model for the renewed *Siglo de Oro* was acquired through certain ancient texts describing a conventionalized vision of the Earthly Paradise; accordingly, this often-sought place took on new life and new trappings after 1493, meaning directly after the publication of Columbus's *Carta*. The living model of a tangibly Golden World was expanded in widely read accounts by Peter Martyr and Thomas More of a newly invented world situated in the Far East-Far West. This Golden World was initially presented as an Edenic Paradise whose inhabitants were not yet corrupted by contemporary European vices. The various conventional meanings arbitrarily applied by European social philosophers to the largely unparalleled American experience contribute to an understanding of the inner workings of the Renaissance intellect. They also illuminate the origins of certain overly inflated expectations entertained by much of the current population of the Americas.

These geographically transposed visions of Eden—or Arcadia, if you were an agnostic classicist during the Renaissance—mostly represent undiluted antiquarian nostalgia. But this Eden never actually occurred, any time or anywhere. In the context of venerable rhetorical tropes, America—painted as either Eden, from the late medieval viewpoint, or as an elegiac Arcadia, according to the newer humanistic format—represented a new haven, not only from a faulty present but also from a questionable future. In short, America—the ultimate Utopia-No-Place—served contemporary psychological needs: It could represent whatever pleased you.[40] Half a millennium later, it still does.

Previously we examined widely read medieval texts that told of the multitudes of Christian (or near-Christian) peoples that were believed to inhabit the Indian subcontinent. Columbus surely must have known of these tales because he ascribes exactly the same virtues to the simple Arawaks (or Tainos) of the Caribbean—whom he, of course, knew to be Gangetic *indios*. In his *Diario* (December 24, 1492), he sketched a preliminary draft of a private letter to Ferdinand and Isabella extolling the Christian potential of the inhabitants of the Indies:

> Your Majesties must believe that there are no more meek peoples in the whole world. Your Majesties must take great pleasure in this fact because, shortly, they will all be made into proper Christians. They will be given instruction in the good customs belonging to your realms. In this way, there will be no better peoples nor any better world.[41]

With an air of patronizing paternalism and Christian opportunism, Columbus also affirmed that "I graciously gave them a thousand good things which I brought with me. I did this so that they would acquire love [for us] and so that, by these means, they might become Christians—" meaning, of course, good Roman Catholics. He concluded that,

> In this way, they would [also] incline towards allegiance to the service of Their Majesties [Ferdinand and Isabella] and obedience to the whole Castilian nation. In this way, they would endeavor to help us and to give us those things which they have in abundance and which are essential to us. They do not subscribe to any idolatrous sects. Instead, they all believe that all power and all good resides in Heaven.[42]

The essentially Christian nature of the *indios*—seen as representatives of a natural, or inherent and innate, kind of strictly "primitive" Christianity, based upon communal industry and a concomitant disavowal of material possessions—was further remarked upon by Columbus:

> In all these islands, it seems to me that all men are quite content with one woman. To their chief or king, however, they give as many as twenty. It

appears to me that the women work more than the men do. I have not been able to ascertain if they do hold private property. Instead, it appears to me that all take an equal share in what an individual possessed, especially in the case of food.[43]

Columbus and his men, somewhat to their amazement, were taken by these simple but honest, quasi-Christian Indians to be rather like gods, that is, beings descended from Heaven, where "all power and all good resides." As Columbus tells it in his published *Carta*,

> They are very firmly convinced that these ships and men of ours all came down from the heavens. Once they had overcome their fears, in this belief they everywhere received me. This is not because they might be ignorant. To the contrary, they are men of subtle intelligence who navigate all of these seas, and of all these parts they have given us a marvellous accounting. It is rather that they have never seen clothed peoples, nor any like vessels. . . . They are always assured that I come from Heaven. . . . Wherever I went, they went running from house to house and to the neighboring hamlets with loud cries of, "Come, come and see the people from Heaven!" Therefore, all of them, men and women, once their minds were set at rest about us, came to us; no one, adult or child, remained behind. They all brought something to eat and drink, and this they gave us with astonishing affection.[44]

As we have observed, Columbus was unquestionably familiar with the medieval literature dealing with the "Marvels of the East"; these legends, told and retold by many authors, had determined the European concept of India for almost two thousand years. Concerning the monsters that supposedly inhabited India and the Indies, all we need to know about the current speculations in Europe may be conveniently summed up in one illustration (Fig. 8). This composite, picture-and-text image appeared in Hartmann Schedel's *Liber Chronicarum* (1493) at a date that is exactly contemporaneous to the composition of Columbus's widely read *Carta*. The caption explaining Schedel's bizarre illustrations states that

> Pliny, Augustine and Isidore write the following things concerning the various shapes of men. In the land of India there are men with dog's heads who talk by barking. They feed by catching birds and they wear the skins of animals. Others again have only one eye in the forehead, over

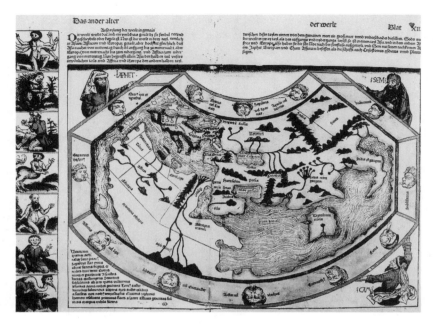

8.

"Monsters in the Far East," from H. Schedel, Liber Chronicarum (Nuremberg, 1493).

the nose, and they eat only the flesh of animals. . . . Close to Paradise, next to the River Ganges, likewise there live men who eat nothing. For they have such small mouths that they only absorb liquid nourishment through a straw; they live on the juice of flowers and apples, and they almost die from a bad smell. Likewise, there are people [in India] without noses and with otherwise flat faces. Many have such large underlips that they can cover their whole faces with them. Many have no tongues; they converse with each other by signs, like people in monasteries. . . . Likewise in the *Histories of Alexander the Great* we read that in India there are men with six hands. Many there dwell naked and rough in the rivers; there are many who have six fingers on their hands and feet, [and also] many, who dwell in the waters, who have half the form of men, half that of horses [meaning they that are centaurs]. Item, also [there are] women [in India] with beards down to the breast, but who have no hair on their heads.

Having provided us with the conventional, pseudo-scientific and proto-anthropological-zoological wisdom of his age concerning the exotic Indies,

Schedel now launches into some similarly conventional wisdom of his (and Columbus's) age that deals with matters strictly geographical:

> But men cannot believe, as St. Augustine writes, that the people who live [below the Equator] in the place opposite to us (where the Sun rises), and those who live where it sets [in the Far West], all must have their feet pointed towards ours [in the opposite end of the globe]. But there is great argumentation in the literature against the madness of the common man in wondering why either we, or those whose feet are turned towards ours [that is, the unknown peoples who must live in the Antipodes, or "Opposite Feet"], do not fall off the earth. For right around the Earth [that is, on the other side, on "the bottom"], people live there with their feet turned towards each other and their heads towards the sky. It would [however] be contrary to nature for them to fall off. For, just as the seat of fire is nowhere else than in fire, and that of water nowhere else than in the waters, and that of the spirit nowhere else than in the spirit, so too is the seat of the earth to be found nowhere else but in itself. This, presumably, means that the things of the Earth cannot fall away from, but only [inwardly] towards the Earth, to which they belong.[45]

This kind of pseudo-scientific conventional wisdom, however bizarre and misinformed it may appear to our eyes, was very much current at the time of Columbus's first voyage to the Indies. Our awareness of the exotic expectations instilled in him by his historical-cultural context finally explains the latent significance of the following statement from his *Carta:*

> In these islands I have, so far, found no human monstrosities, such as many would have expected. To the contrary, the whole population is [surprisingly] well formed. They are not Negroes, as in Guinea. Instead, they have flowing hair; they are not raised in a place where there is too much intensity in the rays from the Sun. It is true, however, that the Sun has great power here, even though it is twenty-six degrees distance to the north from the Equator.[46]

The *Carta* was, of course, composed as the official and public version of his first voyage to the Indies. In his *Diario,* however, we get the unofficial, and more authentic, version of Columbus's initial perceptions, and these show that he was reading the same materials about the marvels of the

Indian East as Hartmann Schedel. According to the entry in his *Journals* for November 4, 1492,

> I was given to understand that, not far from here [Cuba], there were men with one eye and also other kinds with the snouts of dogs. The latter eat men. When they grabbed one, they would rip out his throat, and then they customarily drank his blood and sawed off his genitals.[47]

The American Indies as East Asian Indies

And what is the specific geographical location (at least in Columbus's mind) for this monstrous anthropophagous apparition? Only a week and a half earlier (October 21), Columbus wrote that he was on the point of "departing for that much bigger island, which I believe to be Cipango. According to the information brought to me by the Indians, it is called Colba by them." As he concluded,

> I am even more determined than ever to go to the mainland, and from there to the city of Quinsay. There I can present my letters from Your Majesties [Ferdinand and Isabella] to the Great Khan; then I can ask for a reply from him and come back [to you in Spain] with it.[48]

The place where Columbus thought himself to be at this time, somewhere northward along the "Equinoctial Line," can be reconstructed on the basis of an exactly contemporaneous map (Fig. 9). As derived from his geographical researches in Lisbon, in 1492 Martin Behaim presented to his native city, Nuremberg, a world globe. The pioneering German cartographer had earlier accompanied Diogo Cão on his African voyages in 1484–85, and he no doubt met Columbus while they were both residing in Lisbon. In this case, there is no reason to think that Behaim's globe does not faithfully represent the same idealized picture that was shared by Columbus of the lands lying far out to the west in the Atlantic. In the upper right hand corner of the map designed by Behaim are the Azores and, immediately below them, the Canaries appear (cropped) at the far edge; southwest are the Cape Verde Islands. From right to left, below all these island groups, runs the checkered line of the Equinoccialis. All the rest, to the Far West, is wholly fanciful. A diminutively scaled *Insula Antilia* appears above a larger

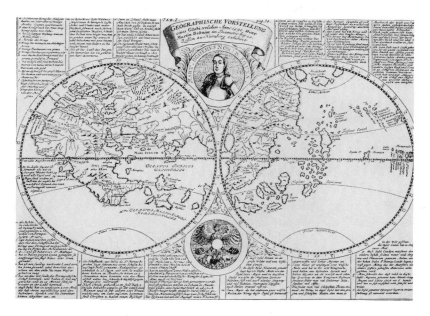

9.

"Martin's Behaim's World Globe of 1492," from J. G. Doppelmayer, Historische Nachricht (Nuremberg, 1730).

version of itself; according to the inscription, the bigger island is where "St. Brendan landed in the Fifth Century A.D." Further west is the huge island of Zipangut, described as being "the richest and most noble island," and also full of gold. Far to the northwest is the Asian mainland, containing (according to Behaim's labels) *Cambalu Cathai* and, below it, the Kingdom of *Mango.* Due west of *Cipango* is *Ciamba porto,* which may be taken to represent the general location of a Cantonese port Columbus called *Quinsay.* According to Marco Polo, Quinsay (Hangchow?) was the capital of the Great Khan. As Columbus's log reveals, he thought he was directly south of Cipango, and was, therefore, "determined to go to the mainland," meaning the terra firma lying to the north and west.

Far away to the southwest, and far off the western part of the Atlantic on Behaim's globe, now appearing in the other side of Behaim's (now-flattened) world sphere, was situated India proper and, below it, *Taprobana Ins[ula].* Even on a much later world map by Petrus Bertius, published in 1628 and showing "The Lands of the World According to Pomponius

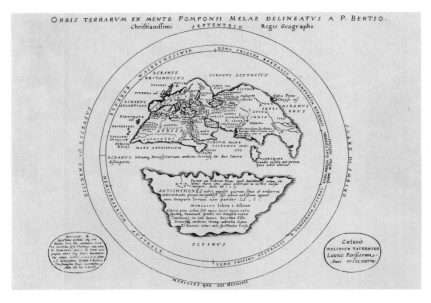

10.

"The Northern Hemisphere According to Mela," from P. Bertius, Variae orbis universi
(Rome, 1628).

Mela," Ceylon was still called *Taprobane* (Fig. 10). However, in this example
the inscription belonging to that tropical place, so often identified with
the Earthly Paradise during Columbus's era, is much longer, designating
Taprobane-Ceylon as being a "huge island" lying directly below, or due
south of India. Ceylon is, moreover, specifically stated here to be found
situated, like a gateway, exactly "in front of the first parts of the Other
World," and that term, *orbis alterius,* often conventionally referred to either
"Paradise" or "Heaven." Directly to the north of Taprobane on the Bertius-
Mela *mappamundi* one also sees the distant Himalayan sources of the mighty
Ganges fl[uvius] and, directly eastward, its six mouths are shown to be hugely
pouring out its streams of fresh water (like the Orinoco, as described by
Columbus) directly into the *Oceanus Eous.*

The evidence assembled here indicates that Columbus's real but un-
spoken goal was, besides meeting a somewhat legendary Khan, probably
the Earthly Paradise, and that all the authorities quoted by Columbus had
already situated this fecund and salubrious place, supposedly inhabited by

"soft primitive" Christian types, in the general region of India and, more specifically, in Taprobana-Ceylon. Given this situation, obviously, Columbus had to sail first *south,* and then much further *west* in order to obtain his real (but consistently disguised) goal, and in that case, this quest now turns out to have been as much spiritual as lucrative and geographical. Since this is a critical point, more evidence to the same effect may be presented. In the *Diario* entry of November 14, 1492, Columbus stated that, as he believes, he is sailing among certain "islands which, in the mappaemundi, are placed in the Far East." Therefore, and as he *always* continued to believe, "in them there are very great riches, precious gems and spices; they extend extremely far to the south and spread out in all directions."[49] To find the Golden Chersonese he obviously felt he must go further south. This was also his unshaken belief at the time of his second voyage to the Indies; according to his shipmate-secretary, Andrés Bernáldez, Columbus knew that "he had reached a point very near to the Golden Chersonese," meaning the Spice Islands of Indonesia.[50]

By reference to another contemporary map, we can literally see the global picture that had always been in Columbus's mind (Fig. 11). The first printed map of the New World was designed by Johannes Ruysch and published in his *Nova et universalitor Orbis cogniti tabula* (Rome, 1508). Ruysch's *mappamundi* was also the first printed chart to show Africa as a peninsula completely surrounded by ocean, thus also revealing the easy accessibility of India from this extreme southern direction. The western part of Ruysch's map of the Atlantic also shows what we now know to be the Caribbean islands in very close proximity to Greater Asia. Due north of the Caribbean is Greenland (*Gruenlanteus*) and the "Codfish-Land" (*Baccalaurus*), or Newfoundland, recently discovered by John Cabot, and both of these northern American sites are also shown in 1508 to be physically connected to Asia. Due south of these is *Antilia Insula,* and a long inscription in Latin explains that, although they have been long sought in vain, they were long ago discovered by Visigothic Spaniards seeking refuge from the Mohammedan barbarians. In the far south, along the same axis, is South America, called here the "Land of the Holy Cross, or the New World." Southwest of Antilia is Española (*Spagnola*), an island that had been discovered by Columbus only sixteen years earlier. Immediately west of this island is another, the western limits of which remain undefined. A bit further west and north, across the China Sea (*Plisacus Sinus*), is the port of *Quinsai* (curiously placed next to

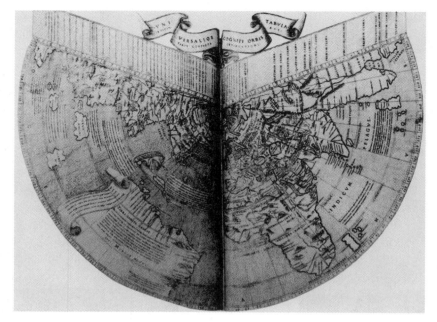

11.

"The Atlantic Ocean, the 'New World,' and the Far East" (right), and "The Indian Ocean with 'Taprobane, alias Zeilon' " (left), from J. Ruysch, Nova et universalitor Orbis cogniti tabula (Rome, 1508).

Tebet). To the south and west is *Java Maior,* and below that *Java Minor,* and even further south and west are the cropped edges of *Seylan.*

Although we now know that the central island with a Latin motto on its western edges is really part of Cuba, Ruysch's inscription identifies it as *Sipangus,* and he adds that it is abundant in gold and precious gems. Here we see manifested the confusion still existing between the medieval *mappaemundi* and the results of recent explorations in the Renaissance; as Ruysch explains with a certain amount of understandable puzzlement,

> As the islands discovered by the Spanish navigators exactly occupy this place [assigned to Japan-Cipango], I have not ventured to lay down this island, presuming that the land called Española by the Spaniards must be Cipango, especially as everything written about the former is equally applicable to the latter—excepting the idolatry.

Columbus, as we know, was searching for both the Spice Islands—what we now call Java and Sumatra—and as well the Earthly Paradise—which probably was most specifically identified by him with the Indies, also specifically including what we call Ceylon or Sri Lanka. Certainly, as we know from having read the private correspondence of Peter Martyr, Columbus believed that Paria and the lands around it "must represent the very continent of Gangetic India"; moreover, "he always sustains that this region is the continent of India of the Ganges River." [51] The other (eastern) half of Ruysch's map also helps to explain how Sumatra and Ceylon were seen at that time to represent the same place. As shown on the German cartographer's world map, an island called *Taprobane alias Zeilon* roughly corresponds, in the modern geographical sense, to the immense Indonesian island of Sumatra. Ruysch's inscription helpfully explains that Portuguese mariners had actually arrived there in 1507, three years after Columbus's last voyage to a "New World" containing his Parian *Paradíso terrestre*. The same inscription additionally states that elephants abound here and that the island was actually known to Alexander the Great.

Since Ruysch's world map so closely conforms to the world globe made by Behaim a dozen years before, geographical historians might assume that both conform to an earlier, now-lost prototype. Whatever the details of this putative shared cartographic archetype may have been, Columbus also knew it. If one were to sketch a composite drawing, representing a close synthesis between Behaim's and Ruysch's *mappaemundi,* then we would have in hand a close approximation of the world chart that was once to be found displayed in the private quarters of Christopher Columbus on his various flagships.

The Entrance of East Asian Man-Eaters into America

But, even on the first voyage, there were already certain premonitions of trouble brewing in the newly dubbed Earthly Paradise. Although initially enframed within a conventional literary context, as much medieval as classical, these ominous portents far exceeded the dreadfulness of the exotic, but essentially harmless curiosities cataloged by Hartmann Schedel in 1493 (see Fig. 8). In the unofficial *Diario,* Columbus wrote the following entry on November 26, 1492:

All the people whom I have encountered up to the present day say that they their greatest fear is of the Caniba or Canima. They also say that they live in this island of Bohío [Haiti], which must be quite a big one, or so it seems. They say that these Canibas are going to take their lands and homes away from them [which is likely] because they are quite cowardly and know nothing whatsoever about weapons. It appears that the Indians whom we have dealt with [so far] are not accustomed to settle upon the sea-coast because it is much too near to the Canibas' territories. The Indians say that, once they see the Canibas returning to their lands, they are quite unable to talk; this is because they are fearful that the Canibas will inevitably eat them. Their fear of the Canibas can not be taken from them. They said that the Canibas have but one eye and the faces of dogs. The Admiral took them to be lying, because he believed that the Canibas must really have escaped from the territories of the Great Khan, who must have [earlier] taken them prisoners.[52]

At first, Columbus took the name of the Canibas as a good omen. As late as December 11, 1492, he could still affirm: "Therefore, as I say again, as I have stated many times before, that 'Caniba' means nothing but 'the people of the Great Khan.' Therefore, I must be quite near to this place [Cathay]."[53] Soon afterward, however, Columbus was to discard the phonetically appealing idea that "Caniba" was derived from "Great Khan." Eventually, he also had to admit that the Arawaks were not lying about the dreadful Caniba, or, as we call them today, the "cannibals." As a result, they appear, albeit only briefly, in the official *Carta* that he prepared for publication a few months later:

As I have found no [Schedel-style] monsters, so I have no report of any. I did, however, receive notice [of something monstrous] on the island called Quaris [probably Dominica], which is the second upon entering into the Indies. This island is inhabited by a people who are regarded in all the islands as being very fierce. These ones feast on human flesh. They have many canoes, and with these they cruise throughout all the islands lying around India. They steal and take whatever they can. They are, however, no more deformed [physically] than are the other Indians. They do, however, have the custom of wearing their hair long, like women. They use bows and arrows and they have the same kinds of weapons, which are made from canes and have a small piece of [fire-hardened] wood at the tip. They do so for the lack of iron, of which they have none whatsoever. Among these other peoples, who are exceedingly cowardly, they make an indeed ferocious appearance. I will not, however, treat of them any more than I have of the others.[54]

Just as Columbus's descriptions of the Edenic topography of the Caribbean have been shown to concur with ancient poetic conventions, so too do his descriptions of the Edenic inhabitants fit the same kind of traditional literary patterns. One of those literary prototypes, the most obvious, was wholly late medieval, *The Travels of Sir John Mandeville*. Columbus expected to find in the Indies, just as we read, "men with one eye and others with the snouts of dogs." The most likely reason for this outlandish supposition was Mandeville, who had himself affirmed that in the islands surrounding the Indies:

> There are many different kinds of people in these [Indian] isles. In one, there is a race of great stature, like giants, foul and horrible to look at; they have one eye only, in the middle of their foreheads. They eat raw flesh and raw fish. In another part, there are ugly folk, without heads, who have eyes in each shoulder; their mouths are round, like a horse-shoe, in the middle of their chest. . . . Men and women of that isle have heads like dogs, and they are called Cynocephales [dog-headed]. . . . They go quite naked except for a little cloth round their privy parts.[55]

The cannibals were also a given for anyone who read—and believed—the stories filling the *Travels of Sir John Mandeville*. After all, did not this doughty world traveler tell the world how, on the "isle of Lamory" (Sumatra), the natives

> have an evil custom among them, for they will eat human flesh more gladly than any other. Nevertheless, the land is abundant enough in meat and fish and corn—and also gold and silver and other goods. Merchants bring children there to sell, and the people of the country buy them. Those that are plump they eat; those that are not plump they feed up and fatten, and then kill and eat them. And they say that it [human flesh] is the best and sweetest flesh in the whole world.[56]

In short, according to such popular medieval conceptions, those fearsome human-eating peoples who were eventually to be given an American name —"cannibals"—were all originally believed to be inhabitants of *las Indias*.

Already by 1493, at the end of Columbus's first voyage, we have been presented in written form the ethnographic materials for a complete re-creation by Europeans in America of the two complementary kinds of primitivism—respectively, "soft" and "hard"—that were equally current in European classical and medieval literature. In brief, soft primitivism conceives of primitive, or prehistoric life as a Golden Age, a period which is materially defined by effortless plenty, peace, and political innocence, and easeful (and nearly slothful) felicity. As all the ancient and modern writers tell us, this idyllic period represents civilized (from *civitas,* or city) life purged of urbanism and all its vices and materialist discontents. As is also apparent, that purge can only take place in the wholly literary (and wholly fictional) context of Utopia. Soft primitivism is also the literary context of nearly all of Columbus's initial written descriptions of the Indies and the Indians. It was also the format of a famous essay, *Des cannibales,* that was published in 1580 by Michel Eyquem, seigneur de Montaigne, who, like Sir John Mandeville, never went anywhere near the newly invented Americas.

Montaigne began his widely read treatise by reminding his European readers of the hoary legend of "a great Island called Atlantis, situated at the mouth of the strait of Gibraltar, [and] swallowed up by the Deluge." Wisely, he concludes that "there is no great apparency the said Island should be the New World we have lately discovered." The reason is that "our modern Navigations have now almost discovered that it [America] is not an Island but rather firm land and a continent." Montaigne was quite the library recluse; all of his information about the New World was, at best, secondhand. What he has mainly heard about this distant place (and he does not name his printed sources) is that "there is nothing in that nation that is either barbarous or savage, unless men call that barbarism which is not common to them." The main point is that here, at last, one now finds the reborn Age of Gold:

> What in those [Native American] nations we see by experience doth not only exceed all the pictures wherewith licentious Poesy had proudly embellished the Golden Age, and all her quaint inventions [in order] to feign a happy condition of Man, but also the conception and desire of Philosophy.

Even though the title of Montaigne's essay, *Des cannibales,* promises lurid details of cannibal feasts, we read nothing of these. Instead, the European essayist broadly extolls the Native Americans as living exponents of the Age of Gold and, once again, the literary context for this sort of commentary is pure soft primitivism. Because, in this case, the social context is largely lawless, then those depoliticized contexts discussed by Tacitus, in his *Annals,* and by Ovid, in the *Metamorphoses,* appear to be (alongside Peter Martyr and Amerigo Vespucci, and also probably López de Gómara and Jean de Léry) the most fitting published role models for Montaigne's bucolic ruminations. Although these run along the same lines as did classical speculations on the topic, a new twist is added; the setting for soft primitivism is now transposed to another time, the Renaissance, and another place, America. According to the French essayist, anarchic America

> is a nation, would I answer Plato, that has no kind of traffic, no knowledge of letters, no intelligence of numbers, no name of magistrate nor of politic superiority; no use of service, of riches or of poverty; no contracts, no successions, no partitions, no occupation but idleness; no respect of kindred but common, no apparel but natural, no manuring of lands, no use of wine, corn or metal. The very words that import lying, falsehood, treason, dissimulations, covetousness, envy, detraction, and pardon, were never heard of amongst them. . . . They contend not for the gaining of new lands, for to this day they yet enjoy that natural uberty and fruitfulness which, without laboring toil, doth in such plenteous abundance furnish them with all necessary things that they need not enlarge their limits. They are yet in that happy estate as they desire no more than what their natural necessities direct them. Whatsoever is beyond it, is to them superfluous.[57]

The Entrance of Hard Primitivism into America

But there is yet another point of view surfacing during the Renaissance: hard primitivism (to which we refer again at much greater length in Chapter 5). This anti-utopian perspective conceives of primitive life as an almost subhuman existence. Cannibalism, incidentally, necessarily belongs to this other kind of primitivist picture. According to those who hold this pessimistic viewpoint, the onerous and primitive, life-before-civilization is full of terrible hardships and devoid of all creature comforts and most spiritual benefits. In sum, it is strictly biological marginality. It also represents civilized life stripped of all its hard-won virtues. The most complete (and probably most widely read) recipe for hard primitivism as a historical model for the evolution of mankind was presented around 55 B.C. In Lucretius's treatise *On the Nature of the Universe,* recently recovered for Renaissance readers, the general development of humanity appears to have been a very bumpy ride.

According to this Roman author, initially one finds general bestiality; then comes the slow rise of a human civilization, characterized by speech and communications, social life, and technical innovations. At the third stage, one encounters a decline of social and moral standards; this leads to general anarchy—but not of the good, or thoughtless and spontaneous, sort. Finally, in the present, there is a new rise toward an era of lawfulness and the good things (material benefits) that follow from it. Because we are only interested in the precivilized stage of human existence, either hard or soft, we need only read the passages that pertain to this prehistoric (and so obviously pre-Columbian) epoch devoid of clothing and Christian shame. As we read in *De rerum natura* (v, 925ff.),

> The human beings that peopled these fields [at the beginning of time] were far tougher than the men of today, as became the offspring of tough earth. . . . Through many decades of the Sun's cyclic course, they lived out their lives in the fashion of wild beasts, roaming at large. No one spent his strength in building the curved plough. No one knew how to cleave the earth with iron, or to plant young saplings in the soil or to lop the old branches from tall trees with pruning hooks. Their hearts were well content to accept as a free gift what the Sun and showers had given and what the earth had produced unsolicited. . . . The lusty childhood of the Earth yielded a great variety of tough foods, ample for afflicted mortals. Rivers and springs called to them to slake their thirst. . . . They did not know, as yet, how to enlist the aid of fire, or to make use of skins, or to clothe their bodies with trophies of the chase. They lived in thickets and hillside caves and forests, and stowed their rugged limbs among bushes when driven to seek shelter from the lash of wind and rain.

As bleakly painted by Lucretius, this was certainly an age of anarchy, but scarcely an anarchy of the kind that leads to results mutually beneficial to the commonwealth. In this kind of anti-utopia, the absence of laws only denotes abysmal ignorance. Although rampant, sexuality at this time is similarly mindless, or grasping and devoid of apparent affection. According to Lucretius, the first or primordial human beings:

> could have no thought of the common good, no notion of the mutual restraint of morals and laws. The individual, taught only to live and to fend for himself, carried off on his own account such prey as fortune brought him. Venus coupled the bodies of lovers in the greenwood. Mutual [sexual] desire brought them together, or the male's mastering might and overriding lust, or a payment of acorns [to the female]. . . . When night overtook them, they flung their jungle-bred limbs naked on the earth, like bristly boars, and wrapped themselves round with a coverlet of leaves and branches.

At this time, human life was taken to be much as Thomas Hobbes saw it in his 1651 widely read book, *Leviathan:* unrelentingly "solitary, poore, nasty, brutish, and short." As Lucretius had himself put it long before,

> Then it more often happened that an individual [human] victim would furnish living food to a beast of prey; engulfed in its jaws, he would fill thicket and mountainside with his shrieks, at the sight of his living flesh entombed in a living sepulchre. Those who saved their mangled bodies by flight would press trembling palms over ghastly sores, calling upon death in heart-rending voices, till life was wrenched from them by racking spasms. In their ignorance of the treatment that wounds demand, they could not help themselves. . . . Then, when the mariner's presumptuous art lay still unguessed, it was lack of food that brought failing limbs at last to death. Now [in the present] it is superfluity that proves too much for them. The men of old, in their ignorance, often served poison to themselves. Now, with greater skill, they administer it to others.[58]

According to the Roman philosopher, in the very beginning of human history, life was at its absolute nadir. It did, however, measurably improve and, eventually, says Lucretius (*De rerum natura,* v, 1,015ff.),

> As time went by, men began to build huts and to use skins and fire. Male and female learnt to live together in a stable union and to watch over their joint progeny. Then it was that humanity first began to mellow. Thanks to fire, their chilly bodies could no longer so easily endure the

cold under the canopy of heaven. Venus subdued brute strength. . . . Then neighbors began to form mutual alliances. . . . It was still not possible to achieve perfect unity of purpose, yet a substantial majority kept the faith honestly. Otherwise, the entire human race would have been wiped out there and then instead of being propagated, generation after generation.[59]

In a nutshell, what happened in America—that is, according to the recent manner of its invention in Europeans' minds—was that this New World quickly went from soft indolence to hard and vicious primitivism.[60] Needless to say, the aboriginal natives of America had very little to say about their metaphorical, soft-to-hard metamorphoses. Most likely in fact, they remained more or less happily ignorant of the lofty debates raging between European intellectuals of opposing camps. In any event, as far as Columbus knew, in 1492–93 he *had* clearly found Eden on Earth. The immediate result of that amazing conclusion was that the newly invented Native American inhabitants must be then somehow fitted into the preexistent paradise-picture of a soft primitivism typically adhering to the ancient idea of the Golden Age. The same brand of soft primitivism was additionally essential to the distinctively late medieval *Imago mundi* of a specifically Gangetic-Indian *Paradisus terrestris*.

However, immediately after Columbus's brave westward venture, the general European viewpoint was commonly to become a strictly disillusioned one. The new mood became most apparent in America. As we shall explain in our final chapter, the initially soft idealism of the Golden Age was quickly turned into fire-hardened iron. In many cases, especially for those European settlers actually confronting the alien wildernesses of the New World, it was simply a matter of familiarity breeding contempt. In other cases (Montaigne in his comfortable European library), there was no familiarity, only a general disillusionment with humanity at large. In either case, a maxim later expressed by Jean-Jacques Rousseau may serve to stand as a representative of the harder attitude that was eventually to overturn the soft-primitive utopianism attached to the initial American reconnaissance—and to nearly all *other* European colonial experiences, belonging to all the *other* parts of the expanding European hegemony:

Quite unperceived by the stupid men of the earliest ages, and now but barely glimpsed by enlightened men in a much later age, that happy life, supposedly pertaining to "the Age of Gold," has always proved itself to be a stranger to the human race.[61]

Having presented the essential textual materials and contexts which set up a convenient rhetorical foundation, we may now proceed to analyze the actual results. In this case we refer to the various ways that artists, mostly commercial illustrators, employed (probably mostly unconsciously) these concepts in order to picture as vividly as possible the initial European contacts with Native Americans. As will be repeatedly emphasized in what follows, these various European illustrators of the *gestae americanarum* during the sixteenth century rarely—if ever—ever saw these exotic *indios*. Rather than ocular, their information, or inspiration, was essentially textual in its basis—and bias.

3

EARLY PICTURES
OF THE INDIAN IN
RENAISSANCE ART

The Mental Discovery of America

We have just pointed to the existence of a host of fanciful notions that were
initially attached to the New World "Indian" by his Old World "discoverers."
Such *capricci* prove to be mythic foundations for a chain of fundamental mis-
understandings of American realities entertained by Europeans throughout
the sixteenth and seventeenth centuries. Expanding further upon our initial
thesis of a preshaped mental invention in Renaissance Europe of America
and Native Americans, we may begin to look at evidence complementing
the strictly verbal testimonies. Analysis of a trail of pictorial documentation expressive of this enduring confusion will allow us to get to the heart
of the matter. Our mostly art historical observations complement in new
ways an ingenious thesis advanced some years ago by a notable Mexican
americanista, Edmundo O'Gorman, regarding the European discovery of the
Americas, namely that these lands and their native population were not so
much *discovered* as gradually *invented.* The result, inevitable from this inter-

pretive perspective, was that the Old World came to impose its own values, perceptions, and prejudices upon things—and the peoples—belonging to the New World.

A completely accurate or wholly objective *mental* discovery of complex physical realities wholly native to the American continents was long delayed. A tardy, but still incomplete, revelation only came about once the initial challenge presented by an ensemble of traditional prejudices, beliefs, and apocryphal attitudes was eventually overcome by a minority elite of increasingly alert and self-interested Europeans. The stubborn resistance generally offered by European cosmographers, philosophers, and artists to an ever-greater accumulating corpus of data flowing from the American discoveries is, as we shall see, unquestionable. Initially finding themselves incapable of assimilating this glut of confusing new knowledge, European intellectuals and humanists chose instead to bury themselves in perceptual routines belonging to their traditional, and thus limited, worldview. Only after some considerable delay was a mental readjustment eventually achieved that finally allowed America to be correctly fitted into the traditional framework of European perspectives.

J. H. Elliott has observed how sixteenth-century European reactions to the New World really represented nothing new; the results were in fact very much like medieval European reactions toward Islam, another alien and heretical culture. Like that older doctrinal challenge to comfortable mental habits, similarly the new American experiences could easily prove threatening. Elliott recalls the judgment of the Spanish humanist Hernán Pérez de Oliva in 1528, when he was rector of the University of Salamanca. In discussing Columbus, Pérez claims that the Genoese mariner had organized his second voyage in order to join together "the world, so to impose upon those strange lands the forms of our very own customs."[1] For Pérez, Columbus's reaction was the natural expression of bewilderment belonging to any other Renaissance European; it was additionally a spur to preshape the things of an unprecedented New World according to one's own preshaped or stereotypical thinking.

All this happened in Europe during the Renaissance, a period that should in no way be accounted a "Dark Age" but rather a time ripe for the opening of mental horizons through voyages of discovery. Still, this was also an age notorious for its veneration of classical models. Thus, just as occurred in the Middle Ages, this is a period in which inherited authority was still commonly to take precedence over immediate experience. On a more commonplace level, and with specific regard to the case of America, the egregious new data seeping in from those alien shores seemed incredible, often literally unbelievable, simply for being so very different from thousands of years of European experience.

The sorts of difficulties that Europeans were bound to encounter in coping with American realities were obvious, or at least so they should seem to us today. Equally explorers and colonizers found themselves incapable of describing accurately the physical characteristics of the New World, and even less able to relate the facts of a given historical formation leading to those social structures belonging uniquely to the Americas, for none of these solutions were easily accommodated to European standards. Such was the diversity of and the divergence from familiar norms that the first visitors to the New World seemed to lack even the vocabulary needed to articulate their impressions and so, for the most part, they limited themselves to monotonous statements of routinized wonderment. "Wonder," a concept solidly rooted in medieval traditions of the *mirabilia,* seems the central and consistent, equally emotional and intellectual, leitmotiv in the general European response to the momentous American encounter of the Renaissance.

An analogous perception is that of "the marvelous," a commonplace reaction familiar to students of medieval culture as a term encompassing a variety of shared metaphors, root perceptions, mimetic assumptions, and reactive operational procedures. For centuries, the all-encompassing concept of *lo maravilloso* had provided a pseudo-philosophical way for Spaniards (and Europeans in general) to tag, and so tame, the unfamiliar as the terrible-desirable and the alien-hateful. Even though litanies of tongue-tied awe were again to become current as literary fixtures among the earliest Spanish writers describing the New World *colonia,* what is amazing is how this stunned incoherence was to endure largely unabated centuries afterward. For instance, early in the nineteenth century, even the great, and otherwise relentlessly rational, German scientist Alexander von Humboldt was to fall into the muting trap of perceptual enthusiasm. As he exclaimed in a letter sent to his brother Wilhelm written shortly after his arrival in Venezuela,

> How pleased we were yesterday to have discovered a magnificent plant whose stamen is more than an inch long! Even more numerous however

are the most tiny plants—none of which have been previously observed! And what colors do these birds, fish, and even the crabs, have: from sky-blue to yellow! Up to this very moment we have been running around like mad-men. In these first days following our landing, we haven't even been able to fix our minds upon anything: we are always dropping one new thing in order to snatch at another novelty. My companion Bonpland assures me that he is going to lose his mind if these wonders don't quickly come to an end.[2]

Naturally, not every European visitor was like Humboldt, a trained *Naturwissenschafter* (natural scientist), but nearly all did fall prey to his kind of enthusiasm, a sense of stunned awe and wonder in the face of an apparently endless array of American exoticisms. If, for instance, the unprepared European observer of American phenomena happened to be an artist, then he would probably fall captive to all the perceptual limitations that were imposed upon him due to his professional Old World training. In this case, his natural powers of vision would inevitably become deformed by another kind of corrective lens, European culture, formulated with its own schemata, meaning long-established aesthetic biases and conceptual impositions. Traditional compositional formats, standard drafting tools and formularized rendering techniques, anatomical conventions, and standardized color schemes all contributed to preshape the early European pictorial vision of America. For the mere handful of trained artists who actually did make the dangerous voyage across the Atlantic, and for those even fewer draftsmen who did honestly seek to produce unbiased illustrations of their newly encountered, and for them largely unprecedented, American experience, there was an additional and very serious counter-argument to raw reality. These hardy journeymen-artists were working during a period of the great religious schisms in Europe. As a result, most of their on-the-spot illustrations of America—as it were visual journalism, *avant la lettre*—eventually became subject to political editing and religious manipulation back in Europe at the hands of engravers and publishers, partisans of one or another side, either Catholic or Protestant (see, for example, Figs. 53ff.).

The Mythic Context of the Period

A mythological element already notoriously latent in the Early Renaissance period, which was itself characterized by a wide variety of forms and expressions, came to be used in unexpected ways to define a peculiar historical situation, the European invention of America. Much earlier, beginning in the thirteenth century, great continental voyages of discovery—of a kind never before seen—were undertaken. Whereas Columbus was later to sail west, into the setting sun, the medieval evangelical precursors of the *conquistadores* marched eastward, into Asia and toward the rising sun. The first generation of Asiatic adventurers included figures like Giovanni da Piano Carpino (1245), Simon de St. Quentin (1247), and William of Rubruck (1253). Whether impelled by religious motives, mainly evangelization or spiritual colonization, or just for the sake of simple attractions offered to eager imaginations by novel prospects of mysterious lands, their journals recounting exhausting travels provided Europeans with some initial knowledge of the Far East. The sprawling Orient represented to Occidentals a mosaic of exotic lands that were generally treated by them as a storehouse of legendary anecdotes.

Besides providing a new awareness in the West of wholly different religious and artistic ideas flourishing in the mysterious East, writings produced by these doughty travelers set in place a new kind of literary vogue, the main feature of which was dramatic expositions of eastern *mirabilia*. Its culmination was achieved in the *Book of the Marvels of the World,* craftily composed by an ersatz Briton, "Sir John Mandeville," who appears never to have undertaken any journey beyond his library. Whoever may have been its real author and regardless of its essentially fictional character, the success of his *Book of Marvels* was unquestionably enormous; today more than three hundred handwritten manuscripts of Mandeville's spurious travelogue, translated into ten different European languages, are still extant. Moreover, by 1600, there were already some ninety printed versions of the same, late medieval "best-seller" and, as has already been remarked, this was certainly a book whose fabulous contents were very well known to Christopher Columbus, among (evidently) many other literate *conquistadores.*

While these travel tales generally focused on mostly sensationalistic *mirabilia* taken to typify the Orient, similarly marvelous materials had long since existed in the Occidental literary canon. We have already shown how their consistently bizarre formatting had been assimilated into a highly developed cartography of the imagination, namely the medieval *mappaemundi* (see Figs. 3, 4, 5, 6). This solidly entrenched, equally mythical and pseudo-geographical matrix gained new life with the discovery of America, an event that was itself produced during an age of psychological crisis resulting from the figurative transition from medievalism to modernity. This was a moment additionally propitious for the resuscitation of latent messianic and millenarian impulses. Among various objects of poignant nostalgia, most prominent was Jerusalem, the *Civitas Dei,* a holy city already generally recognized by reasonable Europeans, following the repetitious and disheartening failures of the Crusades, to be quite unrecoverable. As must become obvious to any one who has studied the new (1992) scholarly edition of Columbus's long-suppressed holograph *Libro de las profecías* ("Book of Prophecies"), among many of his contemporaries the admiral was himself yet another who wholeheartedly participated in various stubbornly medieval, but nonetheless fashionable, messianic and millenarian impulses still lingering in the early Renaissance period.[3]

Prominent among these anachronistic impulses was a portentous pseudo-geographical fancy, already discussed at some length, claiming that the Indies sheltered the Earthly Paradise within its sweltering tropical bosom, a notion still maintained in peripheral Renaissance cartography (as already shown in Figs. 6, 7). To cite another typical example of those rampant neo-medievalisms still flourishing during the era of the great discoveries, and for us especially significant for being one reviving the elusive Edenic motif, one might again mention the *Navigatio Sancti Brandanni Abbatis,* a famous Latin text composed by an anonymous monk from the Rhineland which had been, since at least the tenth century, often recopied. We shall later have occasion to refer to this early medieval text in the way that it was much later commented on in great detail, very much *à la baroque,* and also this time actually illustrated, by a mysterious Benedictine author, Honorius Philoponus (see Figs. 47–50).

Neo-medieval elements lurking beneath Renaissance humanism even physically shaped early phases of European invention of America. Modern scholarly research reveals, for instance, that Franciscan colonizers of New Spain—and especially Friar Jerónimo de Mendieta (1525–1604), the author of a massive *Historia eclesiástica indiana*—were determined to set up in America the seat of a future millenarian kingdom.[4] Ultimately, this blatantly utopian idea was derived from the writings of an Italian abbot of the Cistercian order, Joachim del Fiore (1145 — 1202). Besides establishing functional parallels between St. Francis and Christ, it now seems only natural that the "spiritual," or Joachimite branch of the Franciscans would additionally have concretely sought a realization of Joachim's mystical prophecy of the coming of the Third Kingdom, representing for him the millennium belonging to the implantation of a Universal Church. Inspired by this utopian vision, Franciscans saw themselves as setting up a truly renewed church in America, a spiritually virgin land that itself would make possible the installation of the desired millenarian kingdom. A French scholar, Alain Milhou, remarks that, even if America did not itself prove to be a true substitute for a Jerusalem irrevocably lost to the Muslims, at the very least, "it did turn into a fundamental component of the Spanish messianic scheme."

Such retrograde evangelical fervor, including all those complementary searches appearing during the Renaissance for primitive ecclesiastic precedents that we have already mentioned, really belongs to a broader historical pattern, the endless pursuit of an elusive and primitivizing Age of Gold. If we were to forget that the Age of Discovery in America was simultaneously the Age of the Inquisition as well as the Age of the Reformation and Counter-Reformation in Europe, we would misconstrue a fundamental psychological context determining the period immediately following the initial Columbian ventures. This was an age that eventually imposed a moral history onto the Spanish conquest of America, such as is clearly shown by arguments contained in a famous Jesuit chronicle, Father José de Acosta's *Historia natural y moral de las Indias* (1590).

Further evidence for these anachronistic impulses is found in an American art historical monument that has not previously been aligned with these spiritual-evangelical utopian phenomena. We refer here to an iconographic program in Mexico ordering the designs for a facade belonging to the Franciscan church of Huejotzingo (Estado de México). In fact, its decorative scheme appears to have been inspired by the same Jerónimo de Mendieta, a friar who resided in this very convent during the time in which he was actually composing his *Indian Ecclesiastical History*. Flanking the main entranceway leading into this church are two strangely carved column-and-capital ensembles. Each pseudo-architectural unit (neither serves any real load-bearing function) has a shaft covered in a kind of simulated basket-work and each is capped with a bizarrely carved capital that looks, in fact, quite like a pomegranate. Given that the bulbous forms of both pillars are wholly inexplicable as responding to any strictly stylistic inclination, nor certainly to any apparent structural purposes, the best explanation is that the significance of the paired columns must be wholly symbolic.

As such, they must have been deliberately conceived to evoke a pair of famous pillars that once adorned the nearly legendary Temple of Jerusalem. As we are informed (I Kings 7:15ff), besides having designs attributed to King Solomon—an archetypal "architect" whose masterwork was in turn directly inspired by God Himself—such anomalous architectural elements figuratively belonging to the legendary Templum Solomonis were even given specific names, "Joachim" and "Boaz," by the same spiritual source. Surely such manifestly Solomonic columns would not have been placed on the facade of this obscure Mexican church due to mere antiquarian fancy. We must instead interpret them in the broader sense, as responding to a contemporary spiritual problematic in a timely fashion. Accordingly, they must symbolize a recent installation of the messianic seat of the New Jerusalem re-created in the American New World. This was just what Mendieta had predicted would soon transpire in Nueva España.

Since any neo-medieval vision of the cosmos, including Mendieta's, would naturally be one given to millenarian eschatology, the quest of an ever-elusive Earthly Paradise was also to prove a constant factor in the thinking of his monkish contemporaries in the New World. This is only logical, and the evidence for such Edenic nostalgia has been demonstrated by our previous recital of any number of voyages dispatched out of Europe—mostly towards the east, but with the more imaginative efforts supposedly directed westward—occurring many centuries before Columbus's epic journey. Many of these expeditions were evidently planned, or at least were emotionally equipped with such anachronistic ends in mind. In retrospect, these now mostly forgotten legends may presently appear to us to have been a significant factor in the opening up of the Atlantic to the European imagination. That westward-lying and darkening body of water was, of course, "The Ocean" (Homer's wine-dark *ōkeanos, Oceanus*), a largely legendary, for being essentially wholly unknown region, a potentially infinite space where there had been vaguely situated since remotest antiquity famed properties of the mind; besides the likes of Atlantis and the Garden of the Hesperides, the Fortunate Isles were also located here by venerable tradition. Since the actual siting of these desirable places differed widely among various medieval authorities, none proved satisfactory and a dossier remained opened for each possible location. In the end, what lingered in the Christian European mind was a generalized psychological perception, a collective mood that has since been dubbed the "nostalgia for Paradise." That yearning had also long since become tangibly transoceanic in character and, as such, that hunger eventually fed upon something like geographical reality.

As we also saw, certain ideas became fixed in the head of Christopher Columbus as the cumulative result of his heterodox readings, and these caused him to conclude, already at the end of his first voyage, and even more so in the middle of his third, that he was in the proximity of the most privileged site of all these, the Earthly Paradise. Under the influence of Pierre d'Ailly's *Imago mundi,* and (as we are convinced) even more so Mandeville's *Marvels,* Columbus remained assured that the Garden of Eden was situated in the Far East, and even more specifically around Taprobane (with evidence for this assumption already shown in Figs. 6, 7, 11). This precociously quixotic *idée fixe* would have been supported by his systematic readings of any of the standard medieval *auctoritates,* called by him "todos los sacros theólogos," and whom we have already cited in detail. Hewing to the commonplace notion that Eden would reveal itself to be perched upon a great mountain, and that it must have a central spring, and that its waters would then divide into four mighty streams, and that all of these must eventually enter into the ocean with a great roar, he came, in fact, to fix the Earthly Paradise upon his mental map even more assuredly than had any of his predecessors, precisely in the Gulf of Paria, a place that he fittingly called "la Tierra de Gracia."[5] The South American chimera of Paradise on Earth lingered in the minds of Spaniards, and in the seventeenth century it was to receive its most elaborate exposition at the hands of Antonio León Pinelo in his magnum opus, *El Paraíso en el Nuevo Mundo* (1656). Like Columbus a century and a half earlier, Pinelo shared the same belief. With superior hindsight, however, he additionally knew that Eden, according to inscrutable divine plan, was hidden in the still-untrodden jungle fastness of what eventually became Brazil, and that its canonic fluvial quartet emerged in the many different streams comprising the principal rivers of South America: the Orinoco, Amazonas, Magdalena, and Plata.[6]

The Noble Savage

Since the topos of the Native American as a "Noble Savage" is a recurring theme in this book, we first need to trace its origins in remote antiquity and will then proceed to show evidence for some nearly endless extensions and myriad recombinations extending well into modern times. For our particular purposes, the way that the idea was specifically reinvented to serve the needs of a New World, and then further evolved, namely for the same geographical application, from the sixteenth into the seventeenth century, is especially significant. During the Renaissance, and apparently operating under mostly American local pressures, the ancient pseudo-ethnographical concept of noble savagery was vigorously revived. Then it was used to complement, even give new values, to yet another ancient myth, that of a paradisiacal life-style imagined by innumerable pagan authors as uniquely belonging to remote times (and peoples) preceding all recorded history. Pagan paradisiacal traditions had long since been integrated into the ubiquitous Christian tradition, itself long since complemented by a uniquely Hebrew contribution, the delicious topographical myth of Eden.

One eventual result of this eclectic conflation, surfacing early in the sixteenth century, was the timely imposition of noble savagery upon Native Americans. This reaction was, therefore, certainly not solely a product of Renaissance humanism. We have already shown how notions of noble savagery and its complementary Edenic lifestyle were medieval commonplaces, long before any thoughts were entertained concerning an auspicious European invention of America. Accordingly, it was only natural they were to become important components in any imaginative devising of a New World largely fashioned—or invented—in the manner of a very much older one, the primitivist Gold Age taken to precede all written history. Already in the Middle Ages, Franciscans (besides some other, more truly heretical sects) showed appreciation for a simple and impoverished, and largely idealized, life-style that was attributed by them to any manner of generically primordial peoples, including those much-discussed folk beatifically residing in the Indies. Their essentially primitivist life-style was assumed, in fact, to represent the goals of their own anti-materialistic and monastic ways. These monkish millenarians, eventually to be transplanted themselves to a spiritually virgin *Mundus Novus,* even proposed that the nudity of "savage" peoples would provide a concrete sign of their innocence and purity, in short, of their putative *nobilitasque honestas.* According to this line of idealizing primitivist thought, a quasi-Christian Utopia, wherever it might fortuitously be uncovered, might look something like a primeval nudist camp.

Treated more broadly, such is, as it were, the dress code of primitivism, for that is the perennial theme in European letters that broadly embraces nearly all of these notions, one aspect of which may be further explored here in various ways. In a broadly contextual view, the discovery of the Americas in the Far West tangibly served to merge evolving primitivist themes of Renaissance humanism into analogous but much older legends and lore, much of which had been recently illustrated in any number of older travel books, now issuing from printing presses, describing *mirabilia* attributed to the mysterious Far East (see Fig. 8). Those same textual-graphic sources also provided a ready-made iconography potentially applicable to some initially Edenic, so mostly noble, savagery. In tropical lands belonging to a New World unexpectedly emerging after 1492, it seemed as though a truly felicitous humanity was opportunely revealing its idyllic existence; as was repeatedly claimed, these carefree and unclothed folk must be the inhabitants of a legendary Age of Gold that had somehow managed to remain ignorant of a myriad of vices belonging to contemporary civilized societies in the Old World.

The initially noble American Savage, the designated (or invented) inhabitant of this newly rediscovered Golden Age, conveniently fit into an ancient mold; this was a model being whose praises had been sung millennia ago in antiquity, from Hesiod to Horace. It was particularly the latter, especially in his *Odes* (II, xxiv, 12–29), who referred to peoples experiencing this *Aetas aurea.* Nonetheless, at bottom, this Golden Age fashioned first by Greeks and Romans was nothing more than a myth, even if it was one that took on new life as a Christian adaptation of the Judaic figure representing the "delightfully" beatific innocence of man before the fall and the expulsion from the Garden.[7] Such were the essential components of the literary legacy of the Golden Age when a New World opportunely surfaced in the Far West to actively illustrate, *au vif,* the persistent myth in nearly all its hoary particulars. Then the Native American was opportunely employed to illustrate concepts of "natural religion" that earlier had been developed in Spain by the likes of Ramón Llull and Juan Manuel, who carefully distinguished between bad *idolatros* and some potentially good *paganos sin ley.*[8]

Since the first verbal pictures drawn of Native Americans generally conformed to this cliché—if indeed they were not actually preshaped by the same literary traditions—obviously this predetermined pattern was also bound to influence pictorial compositions of the American Golden Age myth that illustrated books published during the Renaissance. Columbus, of course, instigated the whole process. Just as soon as he found his Indies, he approvingly noted in his *Diario* (as we may again read) that these peoples

> all go about naked just as their mothers gave birth to them, even the women. . . . They are very well put together, with most handsome bodies and good faces. . . . Each and every one of them is of goodly stature, large they are, and with graceful movements; all are well made.[9]

This is the verbal picture of unclothed innocence that was to be repeated nearly verbatim by Pedro Mártir de Anglería and, above all, by Bartolomé de Las Casas. The latter actually used the term *Golden Age* (*la edad dorada*), the very one "sung by ancient authors, mostly poets." With reference to his wholly idealized picture of a life to be shared equally by "españoles e indios" in the realm of the "Vega Real de la Hispaniola," at a time and in a place when and where everyone would equally share worldly goods in a pre-Marxist communist state, the Dominican asks:

> What better argument can there be about the innocence and wonderful simplicity of these Indians? Could any more application of innocence and simplicity, any more evidence for so many marvels and delights, actually be encountered even in that Golden Age, of which the ancient authors, mostly poets, were accustomed to sing?[10]

Moved by an otherworldly, propertyless love of God, the monkish missionaries operating in America, above all the Franciscans, persisted in their idealized vision of universal fraternal harmony. Mendieta, for example, even supposed that these aboriginal American soul mates of the European friars might have been unclothed relatives to the angels, or their own brand of the *genus angelicum*. Neither was Columbus scandalized by the nudity of the natives; from his prolific readings, especially those prepared for him long before by Sir John Mandeville, he was already expecting to see this primordial state, "todo desnudo." Columbus actually discussed with the chronicler

Andrés Bernáldez a certain passage in Mandeville (*Libro de las maravillas del mundo,* book II, ch. 44) that referred to the same kind of "gentes de la mar océana que van desnudos."[11] Concerning these "naturally" naked folk belonging to the [East] Indies, described as nakedly cavorting "just as God made them," Mandeville further stated that no man "ought to feel shame if he sees himself just as God made him, for it is not abhorrent to exhibit natural things." Indeed, all the unclothed peoples discovered by Columbus in *his* West Indies did appear to confirm the truth of what he had previously read about the East Indies in popular writers like Mandeville, and this was a point underscored by him in a famous letter directed to his patron, Luis Santángel (1493), and soon to be widely published:

> The people on this island, and all the other islands which I have found and of which I have any information, all go about naked, men and women alike, just as their mothers bore them.

The American Cannibal and Other Marginal "Savage Barbarian" Races

A race of repugnant cannibals, previously known as the *anthropophagi,* was yet another wholly conventionalized literary type that had long since been included in discussions by medieval writers of collective masses of "the Savages," from the Latin *sylvestres homines,* literally meaning "wilderness folk" (this largely negative category will again be discussed, and in much greater detail, in Chapter 5). Before they were commonly called "savages," all non-European ethnic types, following a pernicious practice inaugurated by classical Greeks, were simply dismissed as "barbarians" (*barbaroi, barbari*).[12] All barbarian peoples, *les sauvages avant la lettre,* were usually viewed by their xenophobic, antique or modern, European discoverers with varying degrees of condescension, suspicion, scorn, and dread. Owing to his developed agrarian technology, urban establishments, economic and early industrial institutions, and conspicuous literary and artistic heritage, civilized man, meaning the *European* white male, conceived of himself as superior to lesser folk discovered (or "invented") by him elsewhere. Those typically designated as his spiritual inferiors usually happened to be, as it turns out, the peoples with whom Europeans competed for domination of the materially richer parts of the world. Consequently, the appellation "barbarian savage" becomes an essential psychological component of the colonial and/or missionary process, usually justified as "bringing [European] civilization to the uncivilized," and it has been so since the time of Homer.

It is all essentially pure rhetoric: The perennial concept of savage barbarism is, like its antonym, civilization, the invention of a self-styled civilized man. The function of this term for ancient and modern Europeans (including more recently White North Americans) has been, besides allowing an opportune excuse for material exploitation, a means of self-congratulation; it points to *his* superior level of material, intellectual, and moral evolution. Even when, as occasionally happens, real (or supposed) virtues are attributed to the savage barbarian, these positive traits are only discussed, but still essentially pejoratively, by the "civilized" commentator in order to applaud nostalgically what he takes figuratively to represent *his* own lost innocence. In this case, the collective loss of primal virtues, or fall from grace, represents archetypal moral virtues of pristine simplicity and material purity abandoned during a putative "progress" toward the delicious urbane vices belonging to fully developed, urbanized civilization. Among early European historians dealing with such cultural disparities, as much ancient Greeks as Renaissance Spaniards, the most that was generally conceded was that climate and geography might account for certain differences (usually *in malo*) between peoples, and that—maybe—a degree of objectivity was necessary to evaluate—really to judge, meaning morally, and usually *in malo*—foreign customs and ways of life.

Christianity, considered as a kind of spiritualized tribalism bent on conserving the positive aspects of Latin civilization, was no less forgiving of "heathen, Godless," savage barbarism. Once "saved" by his (often forced) conversion to Christianity, the savage barbarian lost his former identity, so figuratively advancing to the level of an "almost European." Although rarely stated as such, since religion only worked upon the soul, and never upon skin color, the converted heretic savage necessarily remains only an inferior representative of the barbarous, retarded, disoriented, irrational "infancy of mankind," a prehistoric time when, as Cicero noted, there were only those "sylvestres homines," peoples of the rain forest sharing the ravenous appetites of wild beasts.

In the specific instance of the cannibals and other marginal races, what they had in common with any other variety of savages is that they all lived like animals. That was however a designation neither intrinsically *in bono* nor *in malo,* but rather generally meaning that they pursued a state of nature, which here just means that they lacked (at least to civilized eyes) any apparent social organization and not even a trace of structured religion or government (see Fig. 22). An important, alternate, or people-eating, figure of the barbarian savage—soon after 1493 to be rediscovered in America, and so universally dubbed cannibal—was however a type wholly *malo.* Diet makes all the difference, but the underlying premise was neither really gastronomical, nor for that matter was the underlying issue anything really new. For instance, Aristotle had long ago made mention of the anthropophagi, announcing that they were beings who lived on the shaky borderline between two natures, animal and human.

During his first voyage into the Caribbean, Columbus had heard of the existence of certain *canibas* who were hugely feared by the gentle Taino peoples. The latter had indicated to him, or so he chose to think, that the *canibas* were subjects of the *Gran Kan,* who must similarly be found close at hand, and certainly the words *Kan* and *can-iba* did at least sound as if they ought somehow to be related one to another, as master to subject. Columbus distinguished between "peaceful Indians," in effect the Tainos of Cuba and Haiti, and that immensely more *belicosa* race, the *canibas* or *caribes,* who were those dreadful "comedores de carne humana." It was additionally stated by Columbus (or so he chose to hear) that the fearsome *canibas* took masses of good *indios* captive; since the latter never again returned to their homeland, the inevitable conclusion was that they had all been devoured in the line of duty. In any event, from that moment a coined term, "Caribbean," acquired, at least for Europeans, a double meaning: an American dweller of the Antilles (*Islas de los Caribes*) and a man-eater (*antropófago*).

Nonetheless, all such proto-anthropological Caribbean distinctions strictly hewed to medieval precedents. Columbus, for instance, carefully distinguished between the "buenos salvajes," who were "pacíficos y sin religión," and the "malos," for those were the recently designated "idólatras y antropófagos." As for the latter, these were already well known to Europeans, but as the "idolatrous man-eaters" who had, according to tradition, inhabited much colder climates. When previously encountered by Christians in such intemperate regions, they were actually Tartars and Mongols. Since the thirteenth century, these bellicose Asiatic nomad-warriors had provoked a kind of apocalyptic terror; of them it was commonly said that

they drank human blood and fed off the bodies of their vanquished enemies. Accordingly, it was obvious that one was only dealing with inhuman,
even bestial beings. In the absence of the Mongol's emblematic pony, and
with all their furs stripped off due to tropical heat, these two-legged Asiatic
beasts fortuitously happen to reappear as a malevolent subspecies known as
los indios.

The early, but firmly implanted characterization of the American (versus Asiatic) Indian as a partisan of *la antropofagía* was mainly due to a widely
known publication which originated (or so it was then claimed) as a printed
letter sent to Pier Francesco de'Medici by Amerigo Vespucci. Its authenticity is much discussed, and the date of its first publication in Latin is
uncertain—perhaps initially in Paris in 1503, but certainly by the next year
in Augsburg. But Vespucci's provocative epistle to the Europeans did seem
quite newsworthy at the time, and so other versions, now in the vernacular,
were subsequently published, with German and Dutch translations appearing in 1505. Most of these were provocatively illustrated (see Figs. 12, 20–23,
25–29). The author, whoever he may have been, painted his cannibalistic
anecdotes more vividly, or atrociously, than Columbus ever chose to do.
He states, for instance, with deadpan demeanor that he once had seen—
with his very own eyes—a father feeding upon his own wife and children,
and adds that yet another well fed *indio* claimed to have personally devoured more than three hundred men (but evidently not at one sitting).
Perhaps the European readers devouring this anthropological purple prose
savored even further the claim that the intrepid Italian once visited a certain town, "where I saw in their houses salted human meat hanging from
the roof-beams; it was just like we do, stringing up bacons and pig-meat."[13]
According to one's particular culinary preferences, the idea of feasting upon
those notorious human rashers and salamis could become literally tasty or,
more likely, wholly tasteless: *de gustibus non disputandum.*

Whereas we may today rashly claim that so-and-so "is a real pig," we
do not really ever actually intend to prepare him to be *eaten* as one. Nonetheless, if the *indios* really did so, as we were told on such good authority
throughout the sixteenth century, then we immediately must recognize
that they are themselves nought but *bestias.* Vespucci was certainly not the
only European to make Native Americans into promiscuous people-eaters.
Half a century later, in 1557, the German Hans Staden published a sensationally written book about his incredible adventures in a savage land we now

12.

"American-Cannibal-Cynocephalloi," from A. Vespucci, Carta Marítima (Strassburg, 1530).

call Brazil. Among other lip-smacking anecdotes enthusiastically recounted by the Teutonic traveler was one concerning the fate of a Portuguese sailor, Jorge Ferreira, whose flesh was first hung to age next to a chimney erected inside a native hut, and later those well smoked Lusitanian leftovers were kept in a wicker basket.[14]

There was, however, an eventual reaction to the specifically anthropological, or broadly bestial, smears. After all, in the early sixteenth century, when doctrinal schisms were already dividing neighbors, most Europeans would still choose to support the beatific picture of the Noble Savage inhabiting a notoriously bucolic Golden Age. They did so probably because, if there was any hope left for the human race, then it was most likely to be found in America, a New World where there lived a variety of peoples so often described as being handsome, naked, mindless of physical possessions and, therefore, all too "innocent" for their own good. Perhaps with luck, some of that undraped natural goodness might eventually wear off onto the Old World, now tightly wrapped in the joyless sackcloth of sectarian discord. One of the first European travelers who reacted against the image of the Indian as a subhuman being, in both psychology and physiology, was a Frenchman, André Thévet. In his book, *Singularités de la France antarctyque* (1558), Thévet generously proclaimed that Native Americans "come out of the wombs of their mothers as handsome as do the children born in our very own Europe."[15] Nonetheless, it was perhaps just as natural that most Europeans would wish to believe otherwise, that Americans did not function as did clothed folk, "in our very own Europe."

Since these unprecedented regions found across the seas were literally called a *Mundus Novus,* this anomalous New World, the *mundus alterius,* was often thought of as the place where various marginal (other) races would have long ago drifted in order to take up a permanent abode. Viewed *in malo,* as so often happened, these alien-other types were mostly monstrous in nature, one way or the other. Whether those aliens inhabiting the American Indies were viewed positively or negatively, unquestionably all the types encountered there, already represented "stock figures," descriptively enumerated in a proliferating torrent of writings composed in Europe, from, already, the Classical world up to the near present, the Renaissance. The pertinent source materials might be either "scientific" in spirit or just unabashedly mythological; some others constituted outright apocrypha. The modern *scientia* of the Renaissance, as represented by Columbus and his fellow explorers, quickly attempted to identify and transpose, or otherwise mentally situate, the familiar European literary types in America. Soon, the New World became populated with all manner of exoticisms formerly associated with any number of distant Old World lands discussed at length in the *encyclopediae* of Antiquity and the travel accounts of the Middle Ages.

Sir John Mandeville, Columbus's predecessor in more than one way, summed up the most fabulous aspects of various traditional beliefs embodied in a received pseudo-science passing for objective ethnography. Mandeville's standard work was, in fact, mostly based on the unquestioned authority of writings belonging to the most trustworthy sources of his late medieval era. His strictly anthropological observations were, for instance, derived from the likes of Pliny (*Historia naturalis,* book VII, chapter 11), St. Augustine (*De Civitate Dei,* XVI, 8), and Isidore of Seville (*Etymologiae,* XI, 3). It is thus scarcely surprising that, beginning with its initial circulation in the last third of the fourteenth century, Mandeville's *Book of the World's Marvels* would soon become one of the most commonly read texts of the late

Middle Ages. In fact, its readership was much greater than that belonging to a work much better known to us, the *Travels* of Marco Polo.

Although long known in manuscript form, it was only early in the sixteenth century that Mandeville's *Marvels* finally appeared in print, thus obtaining an even greater readership than before, and now his best-seller was even provocatively illustrated with simple woodcuts. Close scrutiny reveals that some of the prints depicting Mandeville's marginal East Indian races had actually been copied directly from Schedel's *Chronica mundi* (see Fig. 8).[16] The illustrations belonging to the famous Nuremberg chronicle were published early in 1493, meaning before any European could have had the opportunity to see really authentic pictures of Native Americans (which, in the event, probably only commonly date from after the mid seventeenth century; see Fig. 52) — or even pictures of the *East* Indians, who were being discovered at about this moment by Portuguese trader-sailors. No matter: Schedel's or Mandeville's Indians must be the same as Columbus's *indios* (see Fig. 8). As Columbus read in the introduction to his copy of Mandeville's *Maravillas*, in India, "hay hombres monstruosos de tales formas como en el presente libro hallaréis." And, after 1492, those "monstrous men" now must belong to tribes of strange peoples, *los indios*, whom Columbus actually did find in his fabulous Indies.

Much impressed by the literary pictures emphatically presented to him by his diverse readings, particularly in Mandeville, Columbus was to find it strange that during his first voyage he did not actually encounter any "hombres monstruosos." Manifesting his surprise, he even emphasized the unexpectedly "handsome" aspect of those *indios* whom he actually did find in what he thought was Gangetic Asia.[17] Obviously, "normal" people were not what a well-read European had any reason to expect to find in "India" in 1492. Columbus never did, in fact, cease to ponder the theme of the potentially inexhaustible diversity of his recently invented Indian humanity, for his was a Christian mentality that accepted nearly all the current notions of monstrous Asian anthropology. This was not a topic open to argumentation; even an incontestable authority like Saint Augustine dared not to doubt their existence, further observing that

> Whomever may be born "a man," which is to say a rational and mortal animal, and no matter how strange his shape and color may be, or also how peculiar in his movements and voice, or however he may otherwise

seem to be—and in regard to any other virtue, part, or natural quality belonging to him—no devout [Christian] person ought to doubt that he brings with him an origin in the first man [Adam].[18]

Since this pan-Adamic thesis was a cornerstone of medieval theology, the monstrous races naturally were to become the protagonists in some of the most interesting of the sculptural programs inserted into the tympanums of the Romanesque cathedrals built upon the pilgrimage routes leading to Santiago de Compostela in Spanish Galicia. A striking, but typical example is found on the west portal of the Cathedral of Vézelay in southern France. Here Christ appears, infusing the Apostles with the fire of the Holy Spirit before they embark upon evangelical missions expediting them to the far-flung, four corners of the earth. Invited to this grand ecumenical vision are all the inhabitants of the world, some of whom have strange, and even literally monstrous shapes. So what is the role of such monsters among this utopian congregation of diverse peoples who are universally eager to receive the *Evangelium?* Quite simply, they represent the offspring of Adam, all of whom, monstrous or not, have a God-given right to hear the Divine World leading them to their salvation.[19] So was it naturally to be for all men, even also, one day, with the Indians of the Americas (see Figs. 47ff.). They, too, deserved a timely "spiritual conquest."

This distinctly Christian evangelical tradition was to weigh upon the spirit of Columbus—just as it did upon so many other thoughtful writers during the period of the great overseas explorations belonging to the Renaissance. An indirect influence appears to have been exerted on Columbus's imagination by a recently published, Italian-language edition of Pliny's encyclopedic *Historia naturalis.* Pliny was a most widely read and highly respected pagan author; additionally, it was his exhaustive *Natural History* that happened to provide what was probably the most systematic description of the monstrous races known up to that time. It does not really matter whether Columbus actually handled these particular texts; much of what the Roman scientist wrote was later to appear, often with minimal alteration, in strictly Christian pseudo-anthropology. According to one largely canonic Plinian tradition, the worst deformity to be observed among these semihuman beasts was commonly represented as the appearance of a single organ where two normally belonged. A case in point are the cyclops, common already in Homeric mythology, and who possessed but one eye, hence their eponymous Greek name. These monocular anomalies also became one of the first native features attributed to *monstruos americanos.*

In spite of being obviously endowed with much common sense, at times Columbus imputes to the *indios* fantastic attributes that can only have originated in his previous reading materials, and a curious case in point is the American cyclops. Hence, on November 23, 1492, he writes about a certain island where, so he says, there are found certain "gentes con un [solo] ojo en la frente," meaning literally cyclopedian folk. Particularly thanks to his intimate knowledge of Mandeville's prognostications, he immediately equates them with the *caníbales,* evidently because the pseudo-Englishman had earlier described some cannibalistic Asian-Indian cyclops. These were endowed with a truly formidable aspect, namely, "they have the appearance of giants." Were that not sufficient, then we may further note how, according to Mandeville, "they only had but one eye in their forehead. These beasts would not eat any bread, nothing but flesh and fish." Mandeville's following observation about the monocular cannibal-giants was that, besides eschewing bakers' loaves, "more so than anything else, it is the flesh cut from men which they will devour with the greatest pleasure." Another fabulous type mentioned by Pliny (*Natural History,* VII, 2, 17) were the randy satyrs. Additionally notorious for having piglike tails, these mythical beings, as Columbus remarked in his 1493 letter to Luis Santángel, can be directly related to some Caribbean inhabitants of the island of Avan, "where people are born with tails."

On November 4, 1492, Columbus found himself on the island of Bohío (probably Haiti), and from his obviously faulty conversations with the locals he deduced that resident here were not only *cíclopes* but also other marginally manlike types with doglike snouts: "con hocicos de perros." The idea of such New World monsters—bug-eyed and hound-faced and, as shown here, cannibal *indios*—was still to prove attractive in 1530, when we find them depicted by an enterprising German printmaker (Fig. 12). As for those man-eating, dog-snouted Native Americans, the Old World quasi-canine equivalents—meaning the real reason for seeing any in 1492—can be none other but the *cynocephalloi.* Although these dog-men were first described by the Greek Ctesias, there were only to be made widely known to later generations through Pliny's descriptions (*Nat. Hist.,* VII, 2, 15). Nonetheless, Columbus's most immediate textual source was probably, once again, Mandeville. The would-be English knight vividly spoke (*Marvels,* II, 50) of some weird inhabitants belonging to the East Indian island of Bacermeran, a distant place where (according to the old Castilian translation that must have been known to Columbus), equally men and women,

> have the heads of dogs and so are called cynocephallic [*canefalles*], but they do have the ability to reason and [even have] good understanding. . . . These peoples are massive in their bodies and so are hardy warriors . . . and if they take someone in battle, they devour them directly. And because of this trait they do seem to be just like dogs.

Other European explorers believed that they, too, were able to discern on the American stage the presence of certain standard, or particularly Plinian, monsters. Among the few for whose beliefs we do have firm documentation, there is the governor of Cuba, Diego Velázquez. This is the gentleman who ordered, in writing, that Hernán Cortés should keep a sharp eye out for "los cinocéfalos y a los panocios" in his westward voyages, eventually leading him to conquer Mexico.[20] In the case of the latter beast, the panothians, we learn from both Ctesias and Negasthenes (however both as recorded by Pliny) that their monstrosity was due to a hypertrophy of a certain internal organ; this dysfunction directly contributed to their notoriously oversized ears. Although most ugly, such excess auricular accessories are, unquestionably, superbly useful in tropical regions, for they provide welcome shade from the sun's fierce rays (see Fig. 8: left center). Mandeville (of course) also mentions the *panocios*. Rather than in the tropics, he situates them in the mountainous regions of Scythia belonging to southern Russia, further noting (in the old Spanish translation probably read by Columbus) that these generally nomadic peoples "tienen orejas tan grandes que parecen mangas de tabardo, con las cuales se cubren todo el cuerpo."

Even though any definitive catalog of those Pliny-derived, monstrous American descendants would prove to be indeed lengthy, we may finally mention an apposite example put forth by a famous Englishman, Sir Walter Raleigh. In his last voyage to Guiana (largely motivated by the quest for a wholly mythical land called El Dorado), he mentions news he received of the peoples of Iwapanoma, described by Raleigh in his *Brevis et admiranda descriptio regni Guianae* (1594). He pictures them as being semihuman beings with their faces stuck in the middle of their chests (Fig. 13). In spite

13.

Jodocus Hondius, "Acephallic South Americans," from W. Raleigh, Brevis et admiranda descriptio regni Guianae . . . (Nuremberg, 1594).

of claims to other eyewitness sightings of such aberrantly acephallic *indios,* some of which were actually illustrated during the Renaissance, rather than South American the real locus for this type is non-geographical, or wholly literary.[21] Conforming to similar origins, one often finds these creatures depicted earlier in medieval art; besides a number of painted examples in manuscripts, other notable specimens are seen on the facade of the Italian cathedral of Ferrara and the choir stalls of the Cathedral of Toledo in Spain. The proper name for the headless creature is Blemmia, meaning that it is the same monster spoken of by Pliny, and afterward by a great medieval encyclopedist, Isidore of Seville (*Etymologiae,* XI, 3, 17), and both writers describe the Blemmiae as monsters native to Libya. Once again, but under wholly different geographical conditions—Indian—they are also to be found in Mandeville's spurious travel book (*Marvels,* II, 52). As explained here, these are peoples made ugly by dwarfish size and beastly habits. Above all, they are easy to spot from a distance, mainly because, and just as Columbus also supposed: "They have no heads whatsoever, and so they have their eyes placed upon their shoulders; their mouths are twisted like a horseshoe and put in the middle of their chests."

America Allegorized

Throughout the sixteenth century, particularly later in its more recondite or Mannerist phases, the educated European classes took great delight in allegory, or the metaphorical personification of abstract concepts. Much earlier, and particularly as used by Christian dogmatists, allegorical practice had became standardized in the form of wholly systematized series of mental equivalencies that would lend to either text or image two complementary senses. One significance was literal, clear, and explicit, whereas the other was taken to be *occulta* (hidden), and so it was much more profound in its potential applications. The original Hellenistic sense of *allegoria* was the substitution of one thing under a new guise; especially in its rhetorical applications, allegory literally provided a way of "speaking in another manner." Aristotle observed that the matter of allegory embraced the essential attributes of human thought. As further defined by later Aristotelians, the purpose of allegory was, by operating through illustrated metaphors, to make perceptible to sight—originally conceived as representing the figurative mind's-eye—a concept rendered otherwise invisible by its intrinsic nature. It was, therefore, only natural that *America* itself, that is once it opportunely turned up for close inspection by educated Europeans, would soon be treated as one among many other allegorical figures beloved in Mannerist and Baroque literature and art.

An emergent New World seemed to resolve in the European imagination a long felt cartographical omission, and so America was immediately given the role of *Pars Mundi Quarta,* so restoring a fitting sense of stability, through squareness, to a formerly tripartite, or triangular, allegorical representation of the parts of the world (see Figs. 3, 4, 5 and Figs. 9, 11). Thus there was born a new and symbolic image of a four-part world which was, however, to become subject to various iconographic combinations belonging to each successive era and to each different country. For instance, already in 1564 one finds, in a painting called the *Theater of the World* (*Theatrum Mundi*), the representation of the earthly parts as a quartet of imperial matrons.[22] Placed alongside the traditional triad of Europe, Asia, and Africa, this evolving image of America came to form an essential part of print series and geographical treatises establishing a new, four-part representation of the world. Either from those illustrated publications or from individual engravings, artists would then select an appropriate image of America to be employed for their own allegorical treatments belonging to a representation of this newly coined continent.[23] Various series of engravings depicting the "Four Parts of the World," all now necessarily showing America, began to appear in increasing numbers after 1500; among the older sets are those by Étienne Delaune, Joost Amman, Jan Sadeler, Theodore Galle, Crispijn van de Passe, and others.[24]

Obviously essential for the eventual standardization of such evolving allegorical figures were reports from Spanish chroniclers of the Indies, but these were themselves often influenced by those legends we discuss as contributing to the European preinvention of America. That imagery developed in the first half of the sixteenth century that is most representative of the concept of America as the "New World" properly belongs to the art of cartography.[25] For instance, in a new edition of Ptolemy's *Geographicae enarrationis* (1535), we see alongside a site-specific motto, *Terra Nova*, a group of exotic people illustrating the idea of this New Earth. Contextually depicted as being equally *indios* and *antropófagos*, these cannibalistic Indians (see, for instance, frontispiece and Figs. 12, 22, 26, 27, 50, 51, 52) are appropriately placed next to an equally monstrous animal. In the last half of the century, Abraham Ortelius published his famous *Atlas* (1570), the frontispiece of which displays a voluptuously recumbent America (see also our frontispiece), whose somnolent *deshabillé* is explained as follows by a Latin inscription:

> She is seated; as much forgetful of herself as of her chaste modesty, she would be completely naked, that is, were it not for a garland of feathers which gathers her hair, and if there were no gem to mark her forehead, and were there not little bells to embrace her shapely legs. In her right hand she grasps a club, and this is what she requires for her human sacrifices. Behind her hangs a hammock. Shortly she will stretch out upon it: the woman is exhausted by her man-hunt and so she wishes to surrender her body to sleep and dream. She well deserves her couch, which is a strange contraption for it is made like a net and fixed with nails to the four corners. Upon this woven material she rests her head and limbs.

As taken from Ortelius's *Theatrum orbis terrarum,* this evidently influential picture, and perhaps even more its provocative text, was a decisive factor in the conception of what many have considered the first important independent engraving of an *Allegory of the Discovery of America by Europe.* Composed by Stradanus (Jan van der Straet), this handsome print was published by Theodore Galle in 1589 (see the frontispiece). In a way consistent with Ortellius's description, the newly found continent of America appears as a nude woman voluptuously reclining in a hammock. She reacts, startled by the abrupt and otherwise unheralded entrance of another important, literally eponymous component in the European invention of America, Amerigo Vespucci. The Italian holds in his right hand a flag emblazoned with the cross of the Christians; in his left there is an astrolabe, pointing to the navigational science of an intrusive but technologically superior civilization. Both personages express in their faces the surprise that has been mutually triggered by a momentous encounter between two totally different worlds. The landscaped background of the Stradanus print further develops the theme with an appropriate display of physical attributes of the allegorized cultural clash: To the right one sees a strange native animal (probably an opossum) and a Brazilwood club; in the center, American cannibals are shown roasting a human leg on a spit, and on the far left side European brigantines bear yet more determined invaders toward these lethal shores.

Perhaps the most typical of these allegorical concoctions was one designed in 1594 by a Fleming, Martin de Vos, in order to become part of a triumphal arch erected in Antwerp to celebrate the *entrée joyeuse* of Archduke Ernest, the governor of the Spanish Netherlands. Jan Sadelaer made a drawing of de Vos's composition, and this *bozzetto* was in turn engraved by Adriaan Collaert, then to be adapted by other printmakers (see Fig. 15). Sadelaer's *America* shows a fearsome *India* endowed with Michelangelesque anatomy who, in the manner of an Amazonian cavalry woman, rides upon her unlikely (but indigenous) mount, a scaly armadillo. According to various chroniclers of the New World, the fierce aspect of the armadillo contrasts with its natural cowardice—and such *cobardía* was taken to be typical of Americans in general, no matter be they bi- or quadripedal. As additionally befits Americans, this aboriginal *guerrera* sets forth "as naked as the day she was born"; only a scrap of cloth covers the heroic loins of this majestic feminine representation of the New World. Bellicose in the extreme, in one hand she brandishes a battle ax while she grasps a bow in the other; on her back is a quiver full of arrows, presumably all tipped with quick-acting poisons. The background of Sadelaer's engraving, as in the Stradanus print, is similarly emblematic (and likewise its main thrust is *in malo*): Besides the usual array of exotic fauna, one see Indians hunting and, as is also their want, endlessly fighting with Spaniards. This widely circulated print was often copied in the seventeenth century; it inspired, for instance, decorations put upon a house in Wernigeroche, and was also used, in 1604, for the frontispiece of a German edition of descriptions by Hendrick Ottsen of his *Reise* to the Río de la Plata.

What really proved decisive for the canonization of a universally acceptable allegorical formula for America was the initial publication, in 1593, of Cesare Ripa's famous treatise, *Iconologia, overo Descrittione d'Imagini*. This was designed to be (according to its title page) "as much useful for the writer as to the painter"; accordingly, the 1611 edition (Padua) is copiously illustrated with allegorical figures, which soon after appear as pictorial motifs in innumerable Baroque paintings. This happened because Ripa's pioneering iconographic manual was subsequently issued in various languages and Ripa's *Iconologia* acquired such prestige that it soon became something like Scripture for both artists and poets working during the Baroque period (Fig. 14). As verbally fixed by Ripa in graphic detail, America is (and commonly was) to be very tangibly depicted in the guise of

a nude woman whose skin color is dark and tending towards yellow. She is to express fierceness in her expression. She ought to wear a veil: marbled with various colors, this cloth falls from her shoulders and crosses over her body and even entirely covers her shameful parts. Her hair must be shown to be straggly and in complete disarray. Falling completely around her body there will be additionally placed a beautiful, but wholly unnatural kind of ornament, for this must be represented as made from feathers in all possible colors. In her left hand she must carry a bow, and an arrow is to be put in her right; hanging at her side one places a bag (or quiver) full of arrows. Beneath her feet there is a [severed] human head, and this must be shown to be transfixed by one of the arrows I already mentioned. On the ground beside her there shall be painted some kind of a lizard or a crocodile; in either case, it

14.
"The Allegory of America,"
from C. Ripa, Iconologia
(Padua, 1611).

must be shown to be of enormous size. Since this part of the world has
been so recently discovered, Ancient Authors had written nothing at all
about it.[26]

As he claims, Ripa owes all those details of this unremittingly ferocious
imagery to the authority of a well-informed cartographer, Fausto Rughese.
The influential Italian iconographer is accordingly insistent that the proper
attributes of America are nakedness, a crown of feathers, bow and arrows, a
human skull underfoot, and an abundant, rapacious, and emblematic New
World bestiary, including the likes of the *caimán,* an enormous lizard that,
being *americano,* naturally devours rapaciously all the other indigenous animals, including humans.

Also wholly typical of late sixteenth century, Mannerist style is an engraving by Philippe Galle that refers to America. In this example, the forty-
third in Galle's series of the *Personifications* (1579–1600), a nude woman leaves
her hammock, now to stand defiantly upright. Feathers are woven into her
long thick hair, which falls over her shoulders and well below her waist. Followed by a gaudy parrot, the bellicose Brazilian strides resolutely forward
over a field strewn with trophies of war. Brandishing the now stereotypical

"Brazilian club" in her left hand, she carries in her right a recently severed human head. Her generic categorization is, of course, besides conventionally savage, additionally Amazonian. Another standard allegorical variation was the triumphal representation of America. This mode, obviously owing much to revived Roman iconography, may be seen in a certain print, a part of a set of playing cards designed by the Italian Stefano della Bella that was commissioned in 1644 by Cardinal Mazarin and called the *Jeu de Géographie.* Here an emblematic aboriginal lady is shown parading in a Baroque style chariot that is being pulled by a compliant pair of armadillos, saurian types not otherwise known as draught animals.

Almost as contrived is another print, by Hans Groenin (ca. 1610), which shows us the triumphant chariot of America being drawn by two New World felines (Fig. 15). Like the rest of her native sisters—at least such as those harpies were usually imagined and depicted by stay-at-home European artists—this lusty American Amazon proceeds equally unclothed, "according to Nature," and she also carries an equally obligatory bow and

15.

Hans Groenin, Allegory of America, ca. 1610.

arrows, for her intrinsic nature is consistently, inherently warlike. The wheels of her allegorical vehicle are labeled Perú, Cuba, Hispaniola, and so forth. Mounted imperiously upon her decidedly Old World-type war wagon, she transports money bags and also a chest filled with gold coins, all of which are motifs in perfect accord with the Latin inscription clarifying the print: "America auro et argento meos repleo." In the far background, once again we see European transports disgorging eager *conquistadores* who are met on the fatal shore by ferocious troops of Indian warriors. On the far left, any natives otherwise unengaged in self-defense are once again shown busy with their preferred task, the preparation of human steaks for yet another barbaric barbecue. Besides being notorious for its savagery and lawlessness, not to mention an atrocious American cuisine foreshadowing future "fast-food" horrors, even then America was viewed as the inexhaustible Land of Lucre. The one vignette in the entire composition that might pass for something like a journalistic slice-of-life is found in the exact center. Showing a palisaded native village, with a frenetic dance-party cavorting in the middle, we now recognize that the choreographed anecdote exactly copies a woodcut illustrating the Brazilian adventures of Hans Staden (*Wahrhaftige Historia,* 1557) in a place called Tammerka.[27]

We may conclude this brief survey of an often depicted topic, the *Partes del Mundo,* by making brief mention of what may represent the most spectacular of all the sculpted American allegorical figures. This late Baroque period example forged in solid silver was commissioned from Andrea Vaccaro in 1692 by the count of Santo Stefano, the Spanish viceroy in Naples, who sent it to Madrid as a gift to King Carlos II. Shortly afterward, in 1695, the Bourbon monarch donated this vigorously allegorical figure to Toledo Cathedral, along with the other three, canonical "Parts of the World."[28]

Having shown examples of the more fantastic extremes that representations of purportedly American types achieved in Europe under the allegorizing duress of either Mannerism or Baroque stylistic criteria, we may now approach the problem in another way, the strictly chronological one. After examining in detail the early evolution of such imagery, we can observe that only very occasionally do we ever find any depictions of Native Americans that might actually appear to have had any kind of "real world" inspiration. This means that, during the two-century long development of this kind of purportedly "American" iconography, only rarely were these native peoples ever really seen by the eyes of those European artists who increasingly came to illustrate them—nearly inevitably with a marked degree of anecdotal delight. A second conclusion is that the more crudely veristic sorts of imagery applied to Indian life generally belong to the years immediately following Columbus's voyages, with some rather more idealized (à la Michelangelo) renditions following a bit later.

Nonetheless, whatever the mode, truth is relative at best. As we will show, seemingly neutral artistic techniques, essentially meaning either verism (harsh naturalism) or idealism, pointedly applied either to Europeans or Americans, become a tacitly understood code, a way of making implicit value judgments. With few exceptions, the illustration of the Native American during the Renaissance was mostly a matter of art, an exercise of the imagination—or prejudice—and rarely that of scientific (or genuinely objective) ethnography.

First News of the American Indians

It is unquestionable that Europe as a whole only first received something like authentic reports concerning the existence of the lands lying to the west in the Atlantic Ocean after March 4, 1493. That was the date when the *Niña,* as commanded by Christopher Columbus, anchored in the port of Lisbon following successful conclusion of the momentous first voyage to the Caribbean. His arrival brought with him sensational news of unknown lands endowed with fabulous riches and inhabited by nude peoples hewing to exotic customs wholly distinct from European practices. Moreover, Columbus was actually accompanied by seven of those, never before seen or imagined, Native American *indios.* The surprise, even admiration, naturally stirred up by the presence in the Portuguese capital of such wholly "new" peoples from distant lands was briefly described in an entry included in the *Diario* corresponding to this triumphant day, where one reads how: "Informed that the Admiral had returned from the Indies, today many people from the city of Lisbon came to see him and the Indians, themselves objects of great admiration."[29]

To further his cause, it was Columbus himself who initially arranged publicity needed to finance future voyages. Even earlier, on February 15, 1493, he had sent off a long letter addressed to Luis de Santángel, one of the principal sponsors of his voyage, in which were included notes taken from the *Diario*. Presumably, other notices were sent off from Lisbon to his other financial backers in Spain, of which we have unfortunately since lost all record. Columbus then headed directly for the port of Palos de Noguer, where he received a communication sent to him earlier from the Catholic Sovereigns. From this, he was pleased to learn of his appointment as *Almirante de la Mar Océano y Virrey de las Indias,* as well as a formal invitation for him to be received at court, then temporarily situated in Barcelona. Setting out for the Catalan capital with his exotic American entourage in tow, Columbus aimed first for Seville. There, as was the case all along his triumphal passage through numerous cities and towns in Spain, the natural reaction of the populace was one of awe and surprise. According to Las Casas, already in Seville it was being remarked how

> his fame had began to take wing throughout Castile, and it became widely known that he had actually discovered those lands called *las Indias,* wholly novel places where there were many unusual peoples and things of great diversity. The man who had discovered it all came along this highway, bringing with him some of those *indios*. Not only did people come to see him from all the cities which lined his route [across Spain], but many others also came from great distances, emptying villages placed far from this highway. The roads were swollen with those who had come to greet him, and towns competed with one another in giving him a splendid reception.[30]

By means of his letter sent to the Spanish sovereigns, later widely published (see Figs. 16–19), Columbus had made himself personally responsible for spreading throughout Europe word of his great discovery. So doing, he originated what was to prove to be the enduring European image of the Native American as an *indio*—with all that term implied. This media event, probably the first significant one in history, served the immediate purpose of spreading unparalleled news of a "New World" in a uniquely dramatic fashion. The vehicle for its dissemination were innately superior to former means, either hand written or orally transmitted, for conforming to a new, and decidedly more impressive, technology of mechanical reproduction. Columbus's precocious media event occurred at an opportune moment, for just half a century before Guttenberg had developed the printing press, and the new invention had been operating in Spain since 1473. Even though the original holograph text of Columbus's *Carta* is lost, a published version has survived in various editions and different languages. Whatever the form of its various appearances, the overall impact of its contents is unmistakable. Amazed, like so many others, by its dramatic revelations, the historian Francisco López de Gómara was later to describe the news as representing the most important event since the creation of the world—that is, with the sole exception of the Epiphany of Christ.

We may now proceed sequentially to provide some details about the most significant illustrated publications initially dealing with this transcendental event, particularly those that treated in graphic detail the anomalous *indios americanos.*

The First Pictures: 1493

The *Carta* that Columbus mainly wrote for the *Reyes Católicos* appears to have suffered some minor textual alterations, probably mostly abbreviations, at the hand of its first editor. In the way it was first published in Spain, by Pedro de Poza, it only consisted of four folio pages. Besides describing the newly discovered lands, also spoken of here in some detail were *los indios,* those "marvelous," even fabulous, indigenous inhabitants naturally belonging to distant lands preordained to be *las Indias.* However, in order to become truly widely known, the astounding news must first be put into Latin, and this translation (from Columbus's quirky Castilian) was the work of an Aragonese priest, Leander de Cosco. Following its initial publication, in Rome on April 29, 1493, nine other editions of the Latin *Epistola* quickly followed, as issued copiously from presses in Rome, Paris, Antwerp, and also Basel. Given the demonstrated interest in its contents, it was only natural that Columbus's *Letter* was to be additionally translated into other vernaculars, with an initial German version appearing in Strasbourg in 1497. Soon there was even an Italian version, a *Lettera* rather oddly put into rhyming verse (Figs. 17, 18, 19), and this popularized doggerel became reprinted five times.

Our main interest naturally lies in those early versions of the *Carta* that are actually illustrated with woodcuts, a technology of precociously modern-age mass reproduction developed just half a century earlier to take the place of unique, and so expensive, hand-painted miniatures. For these purposes we may take as an apposite example the case of a Latin edition

16.

"The Island of Hispaniola,"
from De insulis inventis epistola
Cristoferi Colom *(Basel, 1493).*

produced in Basel (and probably in the print shop of Jakob Wolff von Pforz-
heim) in 1493. This twenty-page pamphlet *in octavo* contains seven woodcuts. The first line of text announces that the momentous subject is "De
insulis inventis epistola Cristoferi Colom." On the fourth page, one finds
the first known print actually describing itself as depicting the aboriginal
inhabitants of those newly "invented isles" (Fig. 16). Since the block print is
carefully labeled *Insula Hyspana,* one understands that the intention was to
represent the island then known as *la Española,* which today embraces Haiti
and the Dominican Republic. In the foreground, a typically Mediterranean,
or lateen-rigged, galley with banks of oars is shown, a nautically anomalous
detail that makes it immediately obvious that our anonymous Swiss artist
had absolutely no notion of the kind of ships that were actually needed
to sail clear across to the other side of the stormy Atlantic. Two outsized
European sailors approach the beach in a launch and offer objects for barter

to the natives, who are themselves equally outsized or disproportionate to their surroundings. The European wearing turbanlike headgear and who actually tenders the dubious gift has been often identified as representing Columbus. Nude *indios* hasten to the beach to reciprocate with an object presumably made of gold, for in his *Carta* Columbus often discusses (with undue optimism) the abundance of this coveted metal in the Indies. As is evidenced by another letter written to Luis de Santángel (February 15, 1493), it was (as mentioned before) particularly the nudity of the locals that fascinated Columbus:

> The people of this island and of all the others I visited live totally nude . . . just as their mothers bore them. However some women cover themselves in a certain place by means of a sheet of [woven] grass or with a piece of cotton which they have made for this purpose.[31]

Similarly the motif of an unequal exchange of gifts also figures in the same letter, just as it was portrayed in the print; according to Columbus, "Anything they might have, if you ask for it, they will never say no; instead they choose to please the person with that object, showing him so much affection as though they would surrender their hearts." The same print (Fig. 16), which has been (erroneously) attributed to Albrecht Dürer, was used again for yet another Latin version of the *Epistola* that was also published in 1493, and again in Basel, by Johann Bergmann von Olpe.

Also in 1493, on June 15, a first Italian translation of Columbus's *Lettera* appeared in Rome, which, however, contained a rather different kind of illustration portraying the same momentous initial encounter between Europeans and Americans (Fig. 17). This was the publication, consisting of eight pages *in quarto,* containing a contrived *vers libre* translation composed by the Florentine poet Giuliano Dati into ornate Tuscan rhyming schemes set in octaves. The pamphlet is known by the title placed at the end of the text in verse: *Storia della inventione delle nuove insule di Chanaria indiane tracte d'una epistola di Xpofano Colombo,* so uniquely making the objects of the "Invention" certain "New Islands Belonging to the Canary [Island] Indies." The boldly designed vignette illustrating the discovery of the New World by the Old is enframed, according to quattrocento taste, with irrelevant *grotteschi a candelieri,* four Cupids bearing a coat-of-arms, and it even includes the odd motif of an emaciated dog hotly pursuing a pair of terrified hares. In this

version of the initial encounter, or *Invenzione,* the major witness is none other than King Ferdinand, who sits upon a throne shown to be mysteriously floating above three caravels stealthily approaching the "Indic shores." The Spanish monarch points emphatically toward an island inhabited by naked and apparently timid natives; Columbus, with charter in hand, looks anxiously to his sovereign for approbation.

Although this is a trait that to our knowledge has not been contextually remarked upon previously, it may now be observed how there is a gross disproportion in scale between Europeans and Native Americans in the print invented in Rome in order to illustrate Dati's verses. Even though this peculiar giant-sized effect probably occurs here simply as a result of artistic convention (or the particular artisan's incompetence), nonetheless the essentially maladroit Roman print of 1493 was inadvertently to produce some unquestionable after-effects. One wonders in this case whether the outsized scale of every Native American appearing in this illustration, and as well in two other woodcuts obviously based on it (Figs. 18, 19)—which are, *nota bene,* the earliest prints purporting to illustrate, like a modern journalist's photograph, real Native Americans—contributed substantially to immediately forthcoming stories of various American giants. These oversized aboriginals were taken to be particularly conspicuous around Patagonia (see Fig. 23, dated 1505), for reasons we shall later have occasion to discuss in more detail.

The Roman printmaker's prominent display of a disproportionate re-

18.

"The Newly Found Islands," from C. Columbus, La Lettera dell'isole . . . (Florence, 1493)..

19.

"Newly Found Islands," from C. Columbus, Isole trovate nouamente . . . (Florence, 1495).

lationship between Indians and Europeans, with the latter ending up far smaller in size, is especially odd once we enumerate details showing this illustrator's otherwise close attention to Columbus's text. Once again we see Antillean Indians in that pristine state of nudity so often underscored by Columbus in his *Epistola,* and the print further includes a particular pictorial reference to the modesty of the native women, that is as being those virtuous maidens who "se cubrían un solo lugar con una hoja de yerba o una cosa de algodón que para ello hacen" ("cover themselves in a certain place by means of a sheet of [woven] grass or with a piece of cotton which they have made for this purpose"). Another departure from the pictorial format belonging to the print initially made in Basel, which reveals an even greater effort toward narrative fidelity uniquely belonging the Roman printmaker, is the depiction of the long hair belonging to the *indios,* two of whom carry poles. Since these natives are otherwise unarmed, we find further proof for a much more careful reading of Columbus's text on the part of the Italian illustrator, namely his acknowledgment of the reported fact that "they have no armament save for some weapons made from canes." Even the prominently displayed palm tree, in spite of the fact that it is situated like similar trees belonging to wholly conventionalized scenography commonly included in contemporary paintings depicting The Garden of Eden (see, for example, Fig. 1), can be shown to conform strictly to Columbus's text: "there are palm trees of six to eight different kinds, and they are a wonder to see due to their handsome misshapenness [*deformidad fermosa*]."

Even though Columbus says nothing in this *Letter* about the dwellings of the Indians, the Italian artist invented on his own initiative what he took to convey the idea of a properly primitivist, or proto-architectural structure, belonging to the New World experience. As initially pictured here, the schematic essentials of American primitivist proto-architecture are huts with thatched pitched roofs and with walls made rudely from untrimmed (and perhaps still living) tree trunks.[32]

On October 23, 1493, two other reprints of the versified Italian version of the *Letter* appeared in Florence. Both are eight pages in length, bound in quarto, and have only one woodcut illustration (Fig. 18). Both re-printings carry the same inscription in the upper part of the title page: *La lettera dell'isole che ha trouato nuouamente il Re dispagana.*[33] The enframing device, simple geometric motifs, is much less intrusive, but otherwise the composition of the print essentially remains the same as its immediate Roman predecessor. King Ferdinand, again seated upon his regal throne, now grounded more conventionally, still signals the next Indian island to be discovered, which is now set within a much broader and higher horizon. As before, besides depicted as timid giants towering over diminutive European sailors, all Indians are still shown to be quite nude, for this natural state has apparently already been solidly situated as an appropriately American mode. Once again the aboriginal ladies, with modest cotton aprons and long straight hair falling to their waists, and the men, still carrying their ineffectual *armas de las cañas,* timorously march off to the right, away from relentlessly approaching, albeit consistently miniaturized, Europeans.

This time, however, the native huts are described in even greater architectural detail than before, evidently all the better, once again, to convey that latent, now apparently canonic, subtext of specifically American architectural primitivism. Two very tall trees placed behind the distinctive native huts probably serve concretely to illustrate Columbus's mention of any number of "tall trees, diverse in a thousand ways, each seeming to touch the heavens." The tallest or most imposing figure appearing in the three caravels, the European shown nearest to the fleeing *indios* towering over him, may again be taken to represent Columbus himself.

The First Pictures: 1495

Two years later, on October 26, 1495, and again in Florence, two more editions of the Italian verse translation of the *Lettera* appeared, each illustrated by a single print. Whereas the first publication exactly repeated the woodcut just described (Fig. 18), a second pamphlet, entitled *Isole trouate nouamente per el Re di Spagna,* included a new picture (Fig. 19). With a simple framework of chain patterns and triangles, this print omits the Spanish monarch, perhaps simply because everybody knew by then that Ferdinand had never set foot in the Spanish Indies. The scale of the European invading fleet is now drastically reduced: Now we only find a single, boldly advancing, galleon with billowing sails. Nude as before, with characteristic waist-length hair, and all presently armed with those ineffectual *armas de las cañas,* now the conventionally giant-scaled, but notoriously fearful, Indians flee to the left. Even though those same rudely trimmed huts, now so obviously emblematic of New World primitivism, still remain in view, the "handsomely deformed" palm trees have been removed, their place presently taken by a poetic carpeting of flowers and lush native grasses.

Any number of students of the great discovery have remarked upon a surprising fact, that such a notable event as the revelation of wholly unknown lands, with consistently odd (perhaps even giant-sized) inhabitants, actually failed to produce any greater volume of publications dedicated to the unprecedented subject of a New World. It may be suggested that the scarcity of published commentary in both Spain and Portugal was due to a certain perception on the part of the authorities that this kind of publicity would prove awkward before physical domain by the Iberians over their newly found lands became much more firmly established. To support this thesis, one might cite a note attached by an Italian publisher, Angelo Trevignano, to the *First Decade* of Pietro Mártir de Anglería. According to Trevignano, anybody who rashly chose to reveal news about voyages to the *Indias* would be, at least in Portugal, punished with death.[34] A Spanish historian, Carlos Sanz, even explains this silence as representing state policy, adding that "certainly few in number were any Spaniards who actually wrote about those marvelous transoceanic discoveries then evolving with spectacular alacrity." His best guess is that "perhaps they submitted to the prudence of serious calculation, probably in defense of national interests."[35]

Whatever the motivation, in this early period there were unquestionably very few published references actually made in Spain about what was happening in America. A lone exception is represented by the publication, in 1502, of a different *Carta* by Columbus, one describing the generally futile course of his fourth voyage to the New World. It was only later, in 1511, that the first detailed and comprehensive treatment of nearly all the voyages made to the Americas appeared in print—and this time the author was not Columbus. At that date, but without any authorization from its author, Peter Martyr of Anglería, there appeared in Seville the pirated text of the first part of his monumental *Décadas de Orbe Novo*. Including numerous firsthand reports received from Spaniards just returned from the Indies, Peter Martyr's chronicles represent the first thoroughly detailed and unbiased history of the still-unfolding process of multiple European collisions with the Americas. These revelations began to appear as early as 1516, in the first authorized edition published in Alcalá de Henares, of the next series of Martyr's steadily unfolding *Décadas*. Publication of these *Decades* was, in fact, still underway in the mid-1530s, and additions and revisions only ceased with the death of their indefatigable compiler.[36] Although little mention was made of the *indios* in the early stages of the sporadic, and always unillustrated, publication of Martyr's successive *Decades,* the native peoples of the New World would soon acquire increasing prominence in later editions of this pioneering Americanist's magnum opus, from which we shall later quote.

The First Pictures: 1502

In the Bayerische Staatsbibliothek of Munich is a hand-drawn illustrated map of Portuguese origin; bearing the date 1502, it clearly shows the coasts of Brazil.[37] The descriptive intentions lying behind the creation of this map with illustrative vignettes (*à la mappaemundi*) are, however, more than narrowly cartographic. One of the pictures put upon it depicts both the dramatic scene of the killing of a white man and its immediate aftermath; as shown here, it was his fate to become a barbecued roast, à la Tupinamba (see Figs. 20 ff). Doubtlessly, the unknown European artist never actually saw this horror-inspiring, indeed sensationally portrayed, event, soon to become a staple of American iconography. Instead, as proves to be the case with nearly all of the illustrations of America disseminated during the Renaissance period, one must presuppose the artist's imposition of a current literary motif. It then follows that we must be dealing with a text that had been issued from a printing press, and so made widely accessible to an essentially popular audience. In this case, our known *locus classicus* functions rather like sensational news stories currently put into modern tabloids, likewise basely catering to a popular readership. As was the case with so many other contemporary artworks treating American exoticisms, this grisly vignette of a cannibal feast derives from one of the widely read letters written by Amerigo Vespucci. Describing his voyage of 1501–2 coasting Brazil, the Italian tells us that one of his fellow sailors was killed by Indians, roasted on a spit, and then devoured by his savage captors. Eventually published to great fanfare, European readers found Vespucci's tales thrilling stuff-and so did a host of European graphic artists (as can be seen in Figs. 12, 20–23, 25–29). According to the statement of a man who was to lend his name posthumously to two conjoined continents, once the unfortunate Lusitanian had been run down by the Brazilians,

> In an instant the other women grabbed him by the legs and started to drag him up the hill. The men ran toward the village-center with their bows and quivers and shot him full of arrows. Those of our men who were still on land were instantly seized with terror. Leaping into their launches, they immediately cut the anchor-ropes and fled; none thought to seize their arms. Those of us still on the ship let loose four cannon-shots, all of which missed their mark. Hearing the roar however, all the

Indians fled up toward the hill where their women were already at work, busy tearing the Christian to pieces; they quickly began to roast him over a roaring fire they already had started. In plain sight, they displayed to us various pieces torn from him—and then they ate them, one by one! Through sign-language and gestures, the warriors carefully showed us just how they had feasted upon him. All this weighed upon us greatly: with our very own eyes we had witnessed the horrible cruelty with which they treated the dead man, our former companion. For us, this was an intolerable outrage. All of the same mind, more than forty of us decided to leap upon the shore in order to avenge this cruel murder, this bestial and inhuman act. Our captain would not however allow us to do so, and we could only stand stunned in the face of such an affront. We reluctantly took ship from there, greatly shamed due to this order from our commander.[38]

The First Pictures: 1505

The year 1505 proves crucial for the spread of news—mostly sensationalized—about the New World known only for a dozen years in Europe. Strictly visual effects arising from the trans-Atlantic discoveries are now finally becoming quite apparent in Europe—these evidently mainly owing to Amerigo Vespucci. Born into a noble Florentine family, he later became tied to the Medici dynasty, whom he served as their commercial agent. In this capacity, he was first drawn to Spain around 1492; soon after, and in some unspecified way, he was invited to participate in some, perhaps four, of the early voyages of discovery made by Spaniards to the New World. Although mention was also made by Vespucci of a voyage in 1497, which apparently touched upon the coasts of Central America, this claim has been since contested because, had he actually done so, then one would have to believe him setting foot on the American continent even before Columbus is *known* to have done so. It is, however, known that, beginning in 1501, Vespucci offered his services to the crown of Portugal, and that under their flag he participated in at least two voyages, in 1501 and 1504, that actually did reach American shores. Still, a note of exaggeration remains: As Vespucci would have his many credulous readers believe (for he omits mention of the actual captains), he himself commanded all those trans-Atlantic expeditions recorded in his various letters.

Five of his lengthy reports were addressed to his protector, sponsor, and friend, Lorenzo de Pier Francesco de'Medici. Two of the Medici missives were published nearly immediately after their dispatch, and one, dealing with his second voyage and vividly discussing the cannibals of the Americas, became extremely popular once it was published with a highly significant title, *Mundus Novus* ("The New World"). It appears that the first edition in Latin, published in Paris, dates around 1504; this was already embellished with illustrations, which do not exactly match the text. By 1505, the Latin text has already been translated in vernacular languages, into German, Dutch, and even Czech, and a bit later also into French. Afterward, there were up to twenty-three different editions of the *Mundus Novus* in Latin, besides ten more in German. Vespucci's colorful New World was, in short, a Renaissance best-seller. Its popularity is easily explained. In comparison to the somber, sparse, even disjointed style of Columbus's often perfunctory journal entries, Vespucci's coherent, detailed, and often vivid narratives seem almost novelistic in composition—and even sensationalist in intention. Perhaps that was in fact his purpose; then, as now, sensationalism sells much better than objectivity. In short, Vespucci was the *second* essential European author-inventor of the American Indian image. Sir John Mandeville was the first.

Certainly it was only after 1504, following an initial publication of Vespucci's hugely popular *Mundus Novus* (and later including all those subsequent reprintings), that one consistently encounters a new iconographic commonplace adhering to New World depictions: the strictly melodramatic, or libidinal and anarchic, perception of America as the exclusive home of contemporary cannibal feasts and sexual orgies. At the very least, the chronology makes Vespucci an essential inventor of many of the most persistent aspects of the American myth—which is only fitting since the place is now named after him. This conclusion, perhaps only likely to occur to an art historian, is borne out by an examination of graphic details found in original prints vividly illustrating those provocative textual materials wrought by Amerigo Vespucci. It was toward 1505 in Strassburg (perhaps from the press of Matthias Hüpfull) that another variant of Vespucciana appeared with the title *De ora antartica per regem Portugallie pridem inventa* (Fig. 20). The frontispiece is made from two superimposed rectangular woodcuts. The uppermost shows four naked Indians who raise their arms and leap about in shock at the sight of the invaders' abrupt arrival; below

20.

"Naked Indians," from A. Vespucci, De ora antartica . . . inventa (Strassburg, 1505).

are three sailing ships and two launches, all crammed with Europeans eager to seize upon their American opportunities. The same print ensemble appeared in another edition (small quarto) of the same text, also published in Strassburg but now translated into German. As before, all the Indians are unclothed, a situation implicitly representing a certain "natural" state, figuratively moral as well as literally physical, consistently marveled at by Vespucci and his contemporaries. Accordingly, the Florentine exclaims that

> Everybody, one sex or the other, walks around stark naked. No parts of their bodies are covered up. They go about in this way until they die. They have big bodies, solid, well disposed and well proportioned. They are of a coloration which tends towards red, and I think this happens to them because, since they always run around naked, they have become tanned by the sun. They also have black hair in abundance.[39]

Another of the many Latin editions of Vespucci's letter, entitled *Epistola Albericus, de Novo Mundo,* was published in the distant Prussian city of Ros-

21.

*"Indian Man and Wife," from
A. Vespucci, Epistola . . . De
Novo Mundo (Rostock, ca. 1505).*

tock. Four folio-size pages long, it includes a single woodcut portraying an
Indian man and wife (Fig. 21). Since the male *indio* has long curly hair, and
an even thicker beard, one immediately knows that the anonymous Prussian artist had never left Europe. The American bride, here posed somewhat
like Botticelli's *Primavera,* has a similarly thick mane of curly locks tumbling
below her ample buttocks. Her irascible husband ostentatiously brandishes
an oversized bow and arrows. Besides commenting in his letters upon the
ubiquity of such Stone Age weaponry, Vespucci also made much ado about
the physical attractions of these well-endowed Amazonian ladies:

> Even though they parade about without a stitch, and even though they
> are libidinous, these women, just as I have said, betray no defect in their
> bodies. They are equally handsome and clean in their persons. Nor are
> they gross in form, as perhaps some might guess, and this is because
> they are so well fleshed. Similarly lacking is any apparent ugliness, which
> trait is mainly obviated by their attractive stature. One thing has, how-
> ever, seemed to us nearly miraculous, meaning that none among them
> has sagging breasts. By the shapes of their bellies or their waistlines,
> not even those who have given birth can be differentiated from virgins.
> They also seem virginal in those other parts of their bodies, of which,
> due to modesty, I shall make no further mention.[40]

Also in 1505, in either Augsburg or Nuremberg—and quite independent of any book text—a crude, but evidently very widely circulated, print was published whose subject was American cannibalism, and exactly as Vespucci had so vividly reported it in his *Mundus Novus* (Fig. 22). The foreground of the German woodcut shows five adult males and three females, one of whom suckles her babe. The sub-architectural setting of the Indians' cannibalistic orgies once again embraces the theme of an emblematic "primitive hut" belonging to contemporary Renaissance architectural theory, and such as it was already attributed to America (Figs. 17, 18, 19). Looming over the horizon in the distant background, two European sailing ships stealthily approach the savage American cannibal feast. In the foreground, a distinctly non-European motif enters the picture as an invidiously contrasting element: From a cross-beam hangs tasty cuts sliced from a human haunch that roast over a slow fire. It is meal time, and within their archetypal primitive thatched hut two aggressively feathered men and two sturdily voluptuous women feast from succulent human bits, a leg and an arm, just put upon their rude banqueting table, for yet another American savage symposium.

22.

Anon. German Artist, The American Cannibals (Augsberg [?], 1505).

Three males stand to the right; armed with bows and arrows, they are evidently ready to set off in hunt of more human prey. Besides the obligatory feather headdress, their costume also includes feather skirts, reaching to mid-thigh, and even more plumes fastened to their ankles and elbows. The faces and chests of all the men are shown decorated with circular motifs; rather than tattoos, these prove to represent an especially barbarous kind of jewelry. All this is explained by a lengthy caption composed in German:

> This picture presents to us the people and the island which have been discovered by the Christian king of Portugal and his subjects. These people are naked, handsome, wheaten-colored, and well formed in their bodies, in their heads, necks, arms, private parts. The feet of both men and women are somewhat hidden by feathers. The men have many precious stones set into their faces and chests. And no one owns anything; instead all things are held in common. And the men take to wife any woman who pleases them, no matter whether she be his mother, sister or friend; they will make no distinction. They also fight amongst themselves and they eat one another, including the wounded, and they will hang the flesh taken from them in order to cure it with smoke. They live to be one-hundred and fifty years old and they have no government.[41]

As becomes quite clear, this detailed caption, explaining the complete wherewithal of this crudely drawn, and evidently widely believed, German print was directly adapted, like a synopsis, from a dramatic statement drawn from Vespucci's *Mundus Novus*. In this particular discussion, Brazilian Indians

> have abundant black hair. Their manner of walking and playing is agile. They are endowed with emotionally candid and handsome faces which, however, they themselves choose to destroy. They perforate their cheeks and lips, nostrils and ears, but you ought not believe that these holes are at all small or that they will only drill one of them [into their faces]. Well, I have myself seen many of these [disfigurements], and just in their faces alone they might carve up to seven holes. Each one of these [perforations] may attain the diameter of a cherry. They stuff these cavities with different stones, all quite beautiful, cerulean, marble, crystal or alabaster, or with exceedingly wide bones, or some other manner of objects. These stones will have been intricately worked according to their

customs. Were you to see such unexpected things put upon a similar monstrosity, meaning a man who has just inserted some seven cut stones into his cheeks and lips, many being the size of half a palm-span, you would not cease to marvel at him. I have, in fact, often thought about these decorations, for I have also weighed them and saw that these seven stones came to some sixteen ounces. This measurement takes no account however of some other stones, which might dangle from each ear in a ring. This custom is only followed by the men, for the women never put holes in their faces, only in their ears. . . .

Neither do they have any kind of private property, for everything is held in common. They live together, but without any king; without higher authority, every man acts as his own lord. The men take many women, as many as they wish: the son has sex with his mother, brother with sister, and male to female cousin; even the casual passer-by may take seize whomever he may encounter. . . . And whomever may be taken captive by them in battle only survives until he is killed by his captors; then it is his fate to be served up as their nourishment. So it is among them: one to another, the victors feast upon the flesh of their victims. Human meat is common fare among them, and this is absolutely certain. Fathers have even been seen to devour their children and their wives. I myself once knew a man (with whom I actually once spoke), of whom it was said that he had, single-handed, eaten more than three-hundred human corpses. What is more, I myself once spent twenty-seven days in a certain town, and here it was that I saw human flesh salted and hanging from the rafters in the huts. They do this just as we ourselves commonly string up bacon, and other kinds of pig-meat, in order to cure it.[42]

Another important broadsheet was circulating in Germany at this time. This example was published in Nuremberg around 1505 with the title *Das sind die new gefunden Menschen* ("These are the Newly-Found Peoples") (Fig. 23). Likewise, this image is wholly text based: Once again, the eager illustrator has never actually seen his subject matter. This large woodcut shows three almost Lilliputian scaled, European ships entering the mouth of an untamed American river or strait. Groups of Indians, all immensely bigger in size than the minuscule European intruders, appear emerging from the tangled underbrush bordering the stream. On the right bank three towering natives, literal giants, may be understood to be portrayed in a by-now canonic manner; armed with staves and bows, they are adorned with feathers

23.

School of Nuremberg, These Are the New Found Peoples, ca. 1505.

attached to their heads and waists; six gemstones are stuck into the chest of the center warrior. On the far bank, two other groupings of American giants, arranged by sex, can be made out. While their women cower in a cave, a crowd of outsized feathered warriors brandish their weapons at the tiny fleet of intrusive foreign invaders. Given their huge scale, these tower-ing aboriginals must be giant Patagonians, specifically those described by Vespucci (in one of his more apocryphal moments) as having actually been seen by him during his second voyage to the *Mundus Novus*.[43] Accordingly, the river drawn by the German printmaker probably was meant to represent the Río de la Plata.

What is now taken to represent the very first oil painting including American subject matter was executed in Portugal toward the end of 1505, certainly the most decisive single year in the early history of a still-evolving American Indian iconography (Fig. 24). Now to be seen in the Cathedral of Viseu, this panel painting (measuring 134 by 62 cm., and presently at-tributed to a team of Portuguese artists, Vasco Fernández and Jorge Alonso)

24.

Vasco Fernández and Jorge Alonso, The Adoration of the Magi, 1505. Viseu Cathedral.

shows the initial Epiphany of Jesus as held in His mother's lap. In this scene of the adoration of the infant by the Three Magi, or Kings of the Orient, a splendidly costumed Native American oddly appears taking the place of Balthasar. From this, it appears that recently discovered inhabitants of the New World have now come collectively to represent the most exotic of all those "Gentile" peoples predestined to witness the divine manifestation of Christ to all those who still dwell in spiritual darkness upon the planet. Previously depicted as an exotic monarch from distant Black Africa, this new brand of gift-bearing Balthasar, with copper-colored skin, a long lance, and a crown of feathers, is now carefully rendered in the guise of a Tupinamba warrior from Portuguese Brazil. To explain the context of a timely substitution in 1505 of a Brazilian cannibal for a black Magus, one might mention, besides the impact of Vespucci's colorful epistles, a more strictly local event, the arrival in Lisbon of Alvarez de Cabral's fleet in 1500 from Brazilian waters.

Many years later, the iconographic innovation initially announced in the Portuguese panel with an American Magus was to become somewhat standard. For instance, one finds yet another ethnographically anomalous painting of the *Epifanía* executed a century and a half later in distant Andean regions and then placed inside the rustic church of Julí, erected upon the barren shores of Lake Titicaca in southern Peru. This example is the work of an amateur Jesuit artist, Diego de la Puente (1586–1663), who, responding to local traditions, chooses to turn Gaspar into a proud Inca emperor. As for the other two Magi, Melchior remains, as was customary, a *blanco*, or European, while Balthasar reverts to his traditional African negritude. In this way, a provincial and self-taught Jesuit painter makes a novel but timely point: He uses the Magi as a means to include representatives of the three major racial components of Christian Latin America in the middle of the seventeenth century: Indian, Negro, and European. The hypothesis may be supported by reference to a statement included by the mestizo historian Felipe Guaman Poma de Ayala in his *La nueva crónica y buen gobierno* (1616):

> In the time of the Inca Emperor Sinchi Roca there was born in Bethlehem the Infant Jesus; there Holy Mary, Ever-Virgin, gave birth, and it was there that the Child was adored by three kings, the three Magi, representing three races which God had placed in the world: Melchior was the [American] Indian, Balthasar a Spaniard, and Gaspar the Negro.

25.

"Naked Natives of the New World," from A. Vespucci, Van der nieuwer werelt oft landtscap . . . (Antwerp, 1508).

Guaman's characterization of the Magi as representatives of three essential racial components—red, white and black—of Latin America in his time was not unique and may, for instance, be observed in a few other art works displayed in Cuzco dating from the colonial period.[44]

The First Pictures: 1508

The first Flemish language edition of Vespucci's sometimes sensational account of his Brazilian adventures appeared around 1508. Published in Antwerp by Jan van Doesborch, it was entitled *Van der nieuwe werelt oft landtscap . . .* ("Concerning the Newest World or Landscape . . .") and contains several crudely conceived and executed prints. One of these shows two Indian couples, wholly naked (as usual) save for the women's uncut coiffure, falling heavily over their shoulders and down to their knees (Fig. 25). Ironically, both of the aboriginal ladies modestly cover their crotches with cupped hands according to the conventional *Venus pudica* pose initially formulated by Hellenistic sculptors and recently revived by Renaissance artists (as in Botticelli's *Primavera*). One warrior, with a gemstone stuck in his left cheek, brandishes a huge bow—actually an English "longbow"!—while another drags about an oversized club à la Hercules. The trees placed behind the two pairs of aborigines literally serve to make them sylvan folk, but really meaning in the negative sense of *selvatici-sauvages-salvajes*. Carelessly placed next to this print was another woodcut, but one that must belong to a wholly different context (and an earlier published book) for it depicted three Europeans, a youth, and old man and an aristocratic lady. Another woodcut from the same publication, one that was however actually intended to illustrate the Vespuccian materials, depicts two groups of Indians squaring off at lethal close range with their ubiquitous bows and arrows. As was so often the case, the intention here is to show (*in malo*) the mindlessly bellicose customs characterizing the savage Tupinambas of Brazil.

The First Pictures: 1509

In 1509, and again in Antwerp, the same publisher, Jan van Doesborch, published a broadsheet bearing an extract in Latin from Vespucci's letter dealing with his rampantly exotic *Mundus Novus*. The text on the flyer is illustrated with another crude print (Fig. 26). This example shows a nuclear family of Indian cannibals outfitted with the customary headdress, even though here the feathers now look like the spiky leaves of the maguey plant. The real significance of van Doesborch's picture is that it simultaneously conveys two readings, one positive and the other negative. The glowering Indian patriarch is, as usual, armed with both lance and arrow while, *à la Caritas Romana,* the anthropophagous matriarch suckles writhing twins at her fruitful bosom. The negative message, which is really the predominant one, appears at the left side of the composition. Behind the bellicose paterfamilias a bonfire blazes at the base of a dead tree, upon which are skewered a human head and leg: Another barbarous Brazilian barbecue is well underway. Although the formal layout is new, as displayed in the Antwerp woodcut clearly both the basic savage motifs and a characteristic thematic arrangement *in malo* are factors that must largely stem directly from an obviously influential, essentially Vespucci-derived German print of 1505 that we have already discussed (Fig. 22).

Yet another version of Vespucci's endlessly reprinted letter appeared in the same year in Strassburg, and this time as translated into Low German. The pamphlet in question, *Disz buhlin saget wie die zwe herre Fernandus . . . ,*

26.

"A Family of American Cannibals," from A. Vespucci, Mundus Novus . . . (Antwerp, 1509).

is illustrated with four prints that, at least artistically, show some slight improvement over the contemporaneous Flemish effort (Fig. 25). Among these, the most dramatically presented is one referring in specific detail to another sensational tale told by the Italian adventurer dealing with a horrific death at the hands of native savages of yet another supposedly guileless European sailor (Fig. 27). Since the aggressors were women in this especially notorious case, the topical theme now becomes both Brazilian and Amazonian. In the background one sees how several thoroughly naked native women, one of whom ducks into a cave with a great display of buttocks, are exchanging news of the exciting arrival of European men. The scene in the foreground shows a handsome young man dressed in the height of contemporary European fashion; accordingly, he is being eagerly admired by an aroused trio of completely naked and voluptuous young women. The resulting formal arrangement suggests to the bemused art historian that our illustrator was probably influenced by contemporary paintings of the sort produced by (for instance) Lucas Cranach or Peter Paul Rubens, *The Three Graces in the Judgment of Paris.* Now, however, the underlying purpose has nothing to do with either prized apples or any conventional celebration of female pulchritude (as previously represented by Aphrodite, Juno, and Minerva). Behind our fashionably attired Strassburger fop, complete

27.

"The Killer-Women of America," from A. Vespucci, Disz buhlin saget . . . (Strassburg, 1509).

with a fancy feather stuck into his felt beret, a frowning crone brandishes a weapon looking like the jawbone of an ass once wielded by Samson (Judges 15:16). Nonetheless, all of these gristly incidental details directly derive from Vespucci's text:

> Seeing how they [the Indians] seemed fearful, we thought first to dispatch towards them one of our crew, who happened to be a quite a bold youth. In order to back him up, we slipped into our boats while he approached the women. As soon as he drew near to them, they formed a circle around him. Staring intensely and touching him, the women appeared overcome with wonderment. Before we could get any closer to him however, we saw yet another woman who was coming down the hill with a big stick in her hand. Once she got right up to where our Christian companion was standing, she drew up behind him and, raising up her club, she dealt him such a blow that he was instantly left stretched out dead upon the ground.[45]

Another print from the same publication appears to represent a slightly earlier scene from the same narrative, a moment when the impetuous youth first rushed forward to hail the undraped dusky maidens, here initially shown to have been running toward the rocks for shelter (Fig. 28). His two companions, gravely conversing with one another in the foreground, seem to frown and shake their heads in dismay and disbelief at such a rash attempt to deal with notoriously savage and intractable cannibals. However, rather than being linked to the letter of any of Vespucci's various vignettes, this particular print instead seems to capture the broader meaning of the attraction exerted by this eagerly consumed text, namely the drama of a momentous encounter between two wholly opposed cultures, the European and the Native American, one clothed and civilized, or "noble," and the other naked and savage, or "ignoble." Viewed this way, the significant object of attention in the foreground plane is the outsized and very exotic plant. The endlessly strange, or unprecedented character of New World botany is a theme already apparent in the writings of the first of the sixteenth-century *cronistas de Indias*. Even today, as did Alexander von Humboldt nearly two centuries ago, Europeans still marvel at their first view of the exuberant vitality of nature in the American tropics. From this perspective, it is significant that the excited youth in the center of the picture is shown to be

28.

"The Seductive Women of America," from A. Vespucci, Disz buhlin saget . . . (Strassburg, 1509).

29.

"Shameless American Customs," from A. Vespucci, Disz buhlin saget . . . (Strassburg, 1509).

holding a freshly plucked flower in his left hand. He eagerly appears to offer this nosegay like a bouquet to the frightened native women, two of these are standing immediately in front of him. One has a bag hanging from a neck by a draw-string. Its probable contents, wholly gristly we assume, are indicated by an object held in the left hand of her companion: a human arm. As we must believe, our impetuous, also presumably amorous, youth is hastening to become the two Amazons' next meal.

Much better known, for being more frequently reproduced, is another print that shows nothing of the encroaching presence of European civilization; here we see only the Indians, a half dozen of them (Fig. 29). Four are shown in the foreground: a mother holding her squirming child in her lap and three men, all of whom are, as usual, completely unclothed. The fourth male, to the far right, is the one who has given this particular image an enduring notoriety. Firmly grasping his penis in his right hand with a curious overhand grip, he proceeds to urinate vigorously. The complementary background scene, besides displaying exceedingly strange (and most unlikely) exemplars of native architecture made from planks, including an anomalous wooden igloo, of which Vespucci made not the slightest mention, also includes the now-obligatory cannibalistic demonstration. In front of the two huts a table has been set up, and here two Indian butchers, one male and the other female, set about vigorously to chop up with a flint cleaver tasty portions sliced from a human arm and leg. In this example however, only one part of the pictorial narrative, the infamous motif of the Brazilian *manniken pisser* (now famous as a statue in Brussels) can be directly ascribed to Vespucci's text describing his first voyage to the New World. According to the peripatetic Italian, evidently the habits of all Native Americans

> are nasty, and they are particularly shameless in making water. I say this because, while speaking with us, they would do so [that is, piss], and without even turning their backs to us. Nor would they be at all embarrassed to bring forth such nastiness; in fact, none of this caused them the least shame or embarrassment.[46]

The First Pictures: 1513

One of the more interesting scholarly discoveries of the year 1929 involved an old map that turned up in the library of the Seraglio in Istanbul. It was soon determined to have been made around 1513 by a celebrated Turkish geographer, Piri Reis, who was already well known in Turkey for his *Book of the Sea,* a treatise dealing with the Mediterranean coastline. Closer inspection proved that the map from Istanbul was not originally of Islamic design, but instead must represent a copy made from one of the earliest European charts depicting the *Orbe Novus.* According to persistent tradition, the original model for the Piri Reis map, now lost and so otherwise unknown to us, had once been in the possession of none other than Christopher Columbus. The map of 1513 with Turkish inscriptions does unquestionably depict those parts of the New World that had been described in some detail by Vespucci (rather than Columbus), namely the Amazon and Orinoco regions. Nonetheless, Turkish traditions give the Piri Reis chart a different source: After supposedly leaving Columbus's hands, the lost original, probably only a fragment of what appears to have been a once-complete *mappamundi,* then passed directly into the possession of another Spanish mariner, an unnamed companion of the admiral during three of his four voyages to the New World. With the admiral's map still clasped in his hands, so the story goes, the hapless Spaniard was later captured in the Mediterranean by a celebrated Turkish commander, Gazi Kemal, and it was the latter who turned the purportedly Columbian *Urkarte* over to Piri Reis.

Among a variety of decorative and quasi-symbolic elements, just like those that had typically enlivened the medieval *mappaemundi,* various animals, also including a most incongruous unicorn, are now figuratively used by the Turkish cartographer to allude to the Amazon and Orinoco. Next to the unlikely unicorn, an obviously wholly mythological creature, was placed a semi-human figure who crouches upon some rocks. He too is wholly a creature drawn from myth; native only to the medieval European imagination, he is in fact an acephallic, or headless being, with his face incongruously stuck in the middle of his chest like a T-shirt emblem (see, for example, Figs. 12, 13). Bearing yet another name, this same fellow becomes one of those Blemmiae, of whom Columbus said that he had seen none, even though he was obviously expecting to find them in his purportedly Gangetic Indies. As we just saw, a century later Sir Walter Raleigh would state that the same kind of fabulous creatures did actually inhabit the very same regions depicted in the Piri Reis map, namely the Orinoco and Amazon river basins.

Whereas previously the task of illustrating Indians had been usually tied to one or another reprinting of texts by either Columbus or Vespucci, a wholly different, or nonfabulous kind of representation of Native Americans had been recently evolving in Germany. Beginning in 1513, a new Indian iconography was to be seen included within the format of an extensive iconographic program designed to honor the reigning Holy Roman emperor. The idea for the complex *Triumph of Maximilian I* came, in 1512, from the ruler himself, who passed it on to his private secretary, Max Treitz-Saurwein, for further development. The original idea embraced 109 miniature paintings (now housed in the Stuttgartner Staatsbibliothek), and these eventually gave rise, by 1519, to a compositional ensemble compris-

`30.

Hans Burgkmair, "Tupinamba Warriors," from The Triumph of Maximilian I, 1516–19.

ing 137 elaborately detailed woodcut prints. As finally published in 1526, half of these prints were the work of Hans Burgckmair the Elder, and the remainder occupied the talents of such distinguished German artists as Altdorfer, Beck, Huber, Schäuffelin, Springinklee, and even Albrecht Dürer. Directly behind Maximilian, who passes at the beginning of the suite under a magnificent and elaborately symbolic triumphal arch, there follows a lengthy and exceedingly colorful cortège. Among many pictures belonging to the diverse components of the imperial ensemble, we are most interested in the three woodcuts belonging to a festive group of American Indians (Figs. 30, 31).

Burgckmair's team created depictions of Native Americans aesthetically superior to any others executed up to that date. That said, the really odd fact is the inscription belonging to these prints, according to which these "Indians" are identified as being the "Kalekutsch Leute," meaning "Peoples from Calcutta [Kalikut]," a major city in *Asian* India. Nonetheless, as included in Maximilian's neo-Roman imperial triumph, Burgckmair's celebrants are clearly made out to be *American* Indians, and this specifically

New World identification is settled by the matter of their feathered skirts and headdresses, both of which had become, as we have seen, standard American features since at least 1509. As this provocative geographic translation additionally indicates, Columbus was certainly not the only European who continued to believe, and even as late as 1519 and 1526, that the Native Americans were really Asian Indians, and that, accordingly, the Caribbean really represented those fabled tropical seas, *las Indias,* situated adjacent to Taprobane. In any event, the presence of these newly rediscovered "Indian peoples" in a pictorial cycle celebrating an imperial triumph belonging to an Austrian Habsburg seems a significant premonition of so many others that would be produced by the Spanish Habsburgs, beginning with Charles V.[47]

The first "Indian" print in Burgckmair's *Triumph,* showing the imperial march begun with an enormous elephant guided by a turbaned mahout and followed by five similarly turbaned warriors, turns out to be wholly Asiatic in character. Nonetheless, the print directly following this (Fig. 30) does unquestionably depict Native Americans, specifically the bellicose (and ever-popular) Tupinambas from Brazil, about whom Vespucci had so much

31.

Hans Burgkmair, "Tupinamba Families," from The Triumph of Maximilian I, 1516–19.

to relate. These ten warriors, a squad, are all dressed in short feather skirts with their heads shaded by broad-brimmed hats ingeniously constructed from feathers. In case one missed the strictly New World aspect of their presence, they also are shown to be equipped with both war clubs and bows and arrows, for together these kinds of weapons had constituted standard features of Indian iconography since at least 1505.

Rather more complex is a print showing the next part of Maximilian's triumphant parade, which again has for its provocative protagonists the ubiquitous Tupinambas, now also including their undraped and ever-voluptuous women (Fig. 31). Once again the men's ethnic identity derives from their distinctive weapons, to which a few lances are now added, and of course by their routinely featured feathered apparel and headgear. It is the Tupinamba women who here make an important iconographic innova-tion, for they are shown carrying on their heads large baskets full of *maíz*. Never before had this basic staple in the Native American diet, Indian corn, been depicted by a European artist. Alas, some other, would-be ethno-graphic details are not quite so accurate; bringing up the rear, one of the Brazilian belles carries an African monkey perched upon her shoulder while another striding beside her leads a long-horned European ox, the now ex-tinct aurochs. An even more incongruous note is struck by a miniaturized Asian elephant who tags doglike at the heels of the Indian squad leader.

Unquestionably, the most important artist who collaborated (however briefly) in these propagandistic schemes of art served up at the express order of an Austrian emperor was Albrecht Dürer. But there is no doubt about this particular artist's interest in the ever provocative Tupinambas. While work-ing in 1515 on another order for Maximilian, a devotional book of hours, he drew a kind of unconscious doodle, which he placed alongside a text belonging to the Book of Psalms. For reasons still obscure to us, the great German artist sketched out, first, a wooden ladle, tipped upside down. Then, astride this commonplace dining tool, it occurred to him to put a minia-turized Brazilian *indio,* a feathered Tupinamba, who stands proudly upon the overturned spoon holding a shield and his now-emblematic war club.[48] The scripture apparently illustrated by Dürer's undersized but haughty New World warrior begins: "The earth is the Lord's, and the fullness thereof; the world, and [all] they that dwell therein" (Psalms 24:1). Perhaps for this intensely creative German artist, Native Americans have now collectively come to symbolize a newer kind of plenitude, one uniquely belonging to our planet in the age of expanding worlds belonging to the High Renaissance.

The First Pictures: 1519

Two maps making reference to the northern coasts of South America are contained in a copy of the *Miller Atlas* found in the Bibliothèque Nationale in Paris. One of these, which was composed around 1519, was the work of a Portuguese cartographer, Pedro Reinel. Beneath an inscription, *Ante Yllas* (Antilles), a group of four Indians may be seen, all of whom have decidedly black skins, which is a curious trait for this a date well before African slaves became commonplace in the American tropics. While one of these unlikely Native American blacks shoots an arrow, another brandishes a hoe of European design. Alongside the swarthy farmer there is placed a woman with another hoe, and she is accompanied by yet another Indian woman who crouches while she attempts to stick a pole into the earth. A landscape characterized by tall trees completes the ensemble. A more animated scene appears on another map made by Reinel with the help of his oddly named colleague, Lupo Homem ("Wolf Man"). This shows seven Indians in the primeval Brazilian rain forest collecting pieces of a native wood then known as *palo de Brasil*. Other Indians wearing feathered skirts and other characteristic accessories are shown to be working at similar arboreal tasks. To set the scene in a fashion thought to be typical of this exotic, literally "savage," landscape, wild animals and brightly colored birds inhabit the primeval American forest. An inscription helpfully explains that the inhabitants of Brazil are dark-skinned, adept at handling bows and arrows, and (according to a by-now obligatory coda) they notoriously feed upon human flesh.

Also in 1519 a twenty-four-page pamphlet, *Vivat Rex Carolus,* appeared in Cologne, the purpose of which was to exalt the recent coronation of Charles V as Holy Roman emperor. One result of Charles's accession was that he not only inherited the German crown but also that of Spain—including all of its recently acquired overseas possessions in the New World. Accordingly, it was thought most fitting to place on the title page the exotic figure of an Indian warrior. Ironically, most of the distinguishing traits of this American *guerrero* really belong to the familiar Renaissance type of the classical warrior, *a lo romano.*

The First Pictures: 1523

The *Letters* of Hernán Cortés, written to Charles V at various times and relating in great detail colorful episodes belonging to his amazingly rapid conquest of the sprawling Aztec Empire, were published in Europe with extraordinary rapidity. Obviously, this initial conquest of American terra firma was considered, and rightly so at the time, a hugely newsworthy event. In 1523, the complete correspondence between Cortés and his powerful Habsburg sovereign appeared in two different languages, Flemish and French, both as prepared in the Antwerp print shop of Michiel Hillen van Hocstraaten. Both editions used the same woodcut print for their frontispiece (Fig. 32). In the foreground, another archetypal Indian couple appears (a "type" also shown in Figs. 21, 25, 26). According to a standard iconographic formula employed in this period, the wife—standing by a tree, rather like evil Eve after the fall from grace in Eden—is completely naked, has a mat of hair falling below her waist, and carries a disheveled child in her arms. Her *indio* husband similarly conforms to a recently fixed American pictorial canon: Wearing a feather skirt and feather headdress, he aims his bow and arrow at a long-tailed parrot, a native *guacamayo,* perched in a tree scarcely a meter away from the tip of the intrepid hunter's curare-tipped arrow. In the near distance another Indian poles a canoe. In the far background, rising up behind the three natives, is a wholly incongruous motif, a thoroughly Europeanized, walled city, with domed- and gabled-buildings that make Aztec Mexico the New World projection of Antwerp. The best explanation for the unexpected urban vista is simple wish-fulfillment on the part of the illustrator and his publisher: Cortés's Nueva España is already destined to become the New Europe.

To sum up, during the first three decades of illustrations of the novel *res americanum,* between 1493 and 1523, the primary source materials for nearly all graphic representations of New World landscapes and Native American inhabitants would have been the woodcuts attached to published letters of either Columbus or Vespucci.[49] At this time, the standard, or already

32.

"An Indian Couple in New Spain," from H. Cortés, Briefen (Antwerp, 1523).

fixed, iconographic elements belonging to Native Americans are provocative nudity, incongruous feather outfits, primitive architecture, Stone Age weaponry, unrelenting bellicosity, and—most striking of all—revolting cannibalistic cuisine. These traits additionally demonstrate how, at this date, contemporary Europeans had no way to distinguish visually between the preagrarian cultures of the Tainos of the Antilles and the Tupinambas of Brazil, or even the highly sophisticated, and thoroughly urbanized, Aztecs of Mexico. Nonetheless, each geographically and culturally diverse type had actually been described in some detail by either Columbus, Vespucci, or Cortés. The underlying problem that produced this repetitiously simplistic, even caricatured, *indio* portraiture may be simply described as one of artistic failure. The bigger problem, explaining the failure, is that no trained (or professional) European artist, at least none that we know of who was active during the early phases of the conquest, ever actually laid eyes on his exciting American subject matter. This seems, in fact, to have been consistently the case—with the Englishman John White representing a notable exception, and then only as relates to *North* American scenery and ethnography—and it remained this way at least up to the 1640s (for example, Albert Eckhout, as in Fig. 52).[50]

Excepting perhaps only Dürer (and that only as a remote possibility), obviously none of our diverse group of largely anonymous European illustrators had ever seen in person any of the exotic peoples they drew in such lavish detail—and with such a near unanimity of negative interpretive contexts. While the contemporary texts they purported to illustrate with fidelity actually often did provide the means for establishing convincing ethnic differentiations between various American peoples, our European artists seem deliberately and uniformly to have dismissed those important particularizing details. One major influence explaining these odd departures from recently reported realities of America must have been, as it now appears, wholly textual in nature. Ironically, the literary sources decisively acting upon the developing canons of Native American iconography were, for the most part, not really those deriving from contemporary eyewitness reports. Instead, the really significant descriptions were drawn from late medieval fantasy, particular the kind enshrined in Mandeville's wholly fictitious, when not thoroughly plagiarized, *Marvels of the World.*

Moreover, besides generally ignoring various verbal particulars actually contained in contemporary reports reliably describing factual phenomena of the New World, the first illustrators of the *gestae americanorum* chose to hew to, or rather revert to, artistic norms belonging largely to Old World, and still largely medieval, routines of contemporary pictorialization.[51] The end result was that one picture fed off of another, and the most important initial component in this pictorial daisy chain of ethnic misrepresentations now appears to be the German broadsheet of 1505 (see Fig. 22). As treated by these Old World artists, the Native Americans were, in the end, just *indios.* Their New World—meaning that mysterious land running from pole to pole and so infinitely greater in size, richer in its variety of landscapes, and geographically and ethnically more diverse than anything to be found in Europe—was reduced to fit a largely conventionalized, still medieval and provincial, worldview. Accordingly, we must conclude that the all-inclusive term *Indian* had come merely to mean (as we would now say) the "Other," and such as the alienated stereotype had been long since canonized by the Hellenes' *barbaroi.*[52]

4

THE INFLUENCE OF
CLASSICAL MODELS ON
THE RENAISSANCE IMAGE
OF THE AMERICAN INDIAN

Humanist Impositions upon Latin America

Generally conforming to postulates of still evolving Renaissance aesthetics, a certain pictorial image of the American Indian began to evolve and spread throughout Europe during the sixteenth century. This was a period of humanistic scholarship, according to which, as much in art as in literature, the evocation of certain forms and themes prestigiously identified with the classical, particularly Latin-Roman, world became a predominant practice. Given various interests arising from the broader cultural context, once a time had opportunely come to interpret—and so to "invent"—the strange *Mundus Novus* of America, it seemed only logical that writers and artists alike would then equally resort to those ancient myths and figures that had been recently reinvested by the Renaissance with new life.

Understanding of a world as rampantly exotic as the Indies understandably proved difficult to achieve in the Old World. Accordingly, when it came time to interpret that *Mundus Novus* early in the sixteenth century, much of European society naturally turned for guidance to its newly canonized classical repertoire. Being men of their times, the explorers and *conquistadores* naturally tended to regard America through spectacles tinted by Roman classicism. Accordingly, we still call their part of the hemisphere "Latin America"—even though we seem presently to have forgotten the original, Renaissance humanist basis for the title. However, another kind of distorting optic was strictly medieval. One result is that the imagery of America textually transmitted by them to us frequently proves to have distanced itself from American realities. Similarly, European artists, especially since they nearly always remained at home in Europe, necessarily based their American imagery exclusively upon verbal accounts and texts, so further distancing their pictorial imagery from current trans-Atlantic visual realities. Either way, and whatever the particular artistic medium, it may be said that, from 1493 onward, these Europeans opportunely invented America within a Renaissance mold polluted by many lingering medieval trace materials.

In many kinds of visual imagery, either graphic or even architectural, arising from contemporary discussions of a newly formed sixteenth-century Spanish-American culture, we can easily perceive latent references to the prestigious world of classical antiquity. Even though the Indies offered unquestionably impressive pre-Hispanic architectural ensembles and urban models, many of which were comparable in scale and technique to contemporary European manifestations, these were all conveniently ignored by the *conquistadores:* The kind of city imagined by sixteenth-century Spaniards for the New World was to be decisively cast in a classical Renaissance mold. In practice, this meant that the kind of urban designs to become uniformly imposed throughout Latin America would be based upon a rectilinear and centrally focused plan, dominated by a *plaza mayor.* This centralized geometric motif was itself clearly derived from a canonic description of the classical *forum in quadrato* that was provided (ca. 50 B.C.) by the Roman architect Vitruvius (*De architectura,* v, 1).

An investigation of the writings of Carlos Cervantes de Salazar, who composed an elaborately allegorized pre-Columbian iconographic architectural program, offers a fascinating view into contemporary perceptions of the emerging Spanish-American city.[1] When, in 1559, this humanist author turned to consider a recently reborn Mexico City, arising phoenixlike directly over the ruins of Aztec Tenochtitlán, he viewed the magnificent spectacle through the prismatic lens of antiquity. Accordingly, he exalts the rebirth (*renacimiento*) in order to indicate to us the grandeur—past, present and forthcoming—of such a great and distinguished city, one without peer; as Salazar asserts, he has never seen "cosa más bella." This magnificently recast *ciudad novohispana,* originally constructed in the middle of a Mexican lake by Native Americans, becomes transmuted into a contemporary humanist product, reconceived according to Renaissance principles of painterly perspective and architectural antiquarianism, all allowing for the subordination of urban spaces within proportionate measure.

Voicing an enthusiastic allegiance to classical aesthetics, humanist writers and artists of the New World collectively express a sense of what we may call grandeur, *la grandeza.* In order to weigh the figurative value of these ambitious transoceanic re-creations of Renaissance Spain, the common pattern employed by colonial panegyrists was to compare these transplanted products with those of Europe, all the better to make patent the singularity of their American experience and achievement. This process may be representatively illustrated by the writings of a poet-clergyman, Juan de Castellanos (1552–1607), who, alongside rude soldiers, took a direct part in the complicated conquest of South America. Later, while overseeing construction of a new cathedral proudly rising high up in the tranquil Andean town of Tunja in Columbia, Castellanos set about writing his extended series of *Elegías de varones ilustres.* In one of his elegies celebrating local notables, the colonial poetaster refers to the Cathedral of Tunja, noting how:

> Capillas hay en él particulares,
> sepulcros de vecinos generosos,
> con tales ornamentos que podrían
> ser ricos en Toledo y en Sevilla;
> retratos y dibujos que parecen
> haber sido labrados por las manos
> de Fidias, de Cimón y Policleto,
> algunos de pincel y otros de bulto,
> príncipalmente la que dejó hecha,
> Pero Ruíz García, do su hijo
> Antonio Ruíz Mancipe se desvela
> en decoralla con preciosos dones,
> y ansí parece ya piña de oro.

[There are some private chapels included in it that contain the tombs of generous citizens; so richly decorated are these that they would appear lavish even in Toledo and Seville; these contain portraits and other designs, some painted and others carved, that would seem to have been wrought by the hands of a Phidias, a Cimon or a Polykleitos; most important among these is the chapel honoring Pedro Ruíz García, whose son, Antonio Ruíz Mancipe, vigilantly oversees its decoration with further precious donations, and just so that it might now seem to represent a golden fruit.]

Clearly Castellanos's earnest but somewhat clumsy aesthetic sense is wholly Renaissance in character. In the broader sense, this attribution seems confirmed not only by the general sense of rich grandeur, but much more specifically by those routine references (most likely drawn from Pliny) to Phidias and Polykleitos, so rooting the gaudily gilded *camarín* of the Ruíz family with different canons of classical austerity routinely denoted by two famous fifth-century Greeks—whose wholly pagan sculptures had been completely lost to sight for well over two millennia! There is also a formal equivalent to Castellanos's verbal imagery, the tiny detailed miniaturist techniques that one associates with quattrocento decorations, such as may also be perceived elsewhere in Castellanos's earnestly provincial verses. These effects are particularly apparent in a section where he imaginatively paints the improbable picture of a Botticelli-like aboriginal bride at a native wedding (*Las Elegías*, 1, 517ss.):

> Los cabellos cubrían las espaldas
> Tan largos que se vieron pocos tales,
> La cabeza con róseas guirnaldas,
> Rico collar de piedras principales:
> De rubíes, turquesas y esmeraldas,
> Una cinta de perlas y corales,
> Las muñecas y piernas con chaquiras
> Y entre ellas diamantes y zafiras.

[Her hair completely covered her shoulders, so long were these tresses that few alike have ever been seen; her head was decked with rosy garlands and she wore a necklace strewn with precious gemstones: rubies, turquoises and emeralds; she had a girdle of pearls and coral, and on her wrists and ankles were banderoles studded with diamonds and sapphires.]

Whether in New or in Old Spain, references to the classical world increasingly became formally conditioned by the commonplace use of a certain kind of generally stereotyped, graphic and literary language. To such routinized formalisms, which are equally abundant in literary as in pictorial compositions of the time, there were added equally conventionalized, or obligatory, mythological references. Rather than timely references to an indigenous, or pre-Hispanic pantheon, figures drawn from the Greco-Roman Olympus instead became routinely imposed upon literary production diligently composed in Latin America. Besides easily observing the misappropriated phenomenon in the poet of Tunja just cited, another kind of Old World appropriation occurs in the same colonial town—but as expressed in a wholly different artistic medium. In the provincial but opulent mansion of Juan de Vargas, the so-called *Escribano de Tunja,* there may be observed a fascinating pictorial cycle.

In this somewhat unlikely setting, one finds an astonishing array of familiar classical gods and goddesses— Jupiter, Minerva and Diana—placed alongside certain animals, none of which have anything to do with American natural history. We now know the immediate inspiration for this unlikely Hellenic epiphany in New Granada, a series of European prints designed by Leonard Thiry and engraved by René Boyvin. As depicted in these engravings, designated ancient pagan deities originally descended from a classical Olympus in order to parade through Rome during the Renaissance, thence moving north to Fontainebleau and, as captured on copper plates, eventually even end up displayed again in a walled colonial city situated far away in the distant Andes.

In sixteenth-century Latin America, an ideal vehicle for the spread of images of the pagan gods and mythological heroes proved to be (literally) ephemeral art. In the case of Nueva España, the most extraordinary manifestation made itself known in 1559. To mark the occasion of the momentous passing from this life of Emperor Charles V, a surrogate imperial tomb, or *tumulus,* was erected in his honor in Mexico City. The author of this complicated humanistic program was the same Cervantes de Salazar mentioned before. As one might expect, the results were not particularly masterful in the strictly artistic sense but, nonetheless, they represented a noteworthy example of the kind of Renaissance humanism that became fashionable in Spain slightly earlier during the reign of Charles V. This intellectual vogue was introduced into New Spain where, perhaps with a purity achieved nowhere else, there were defined certain key qualities essential to the new European intellectual life-style. These traits embraced the cult of secularism, where the layman becomes privy to the golden key of dead languages; the rise of the scholar, as much at home in sacred as in profane texts; the phenomenon of a man who mixes in equal measure adoration for Christ and a nearly obsequious respect for pagan antiquity. All these were found in the writings of Cervantes de Salazar, among other notable New World humanists.

In the imperial *tumulus* designed by Salazar there was much more than the customary pagan mythological references. As a product of the Spanish Renaissance, even a putatively secular monument must also include any number of references to medieval Christian traditions, particularly those appropriate to the funerary exigencies of the moment. Particularly interesting in the Mexican ephemeral monument was the figurative reincarnation of the dead emperor as, according to Salazar's written program, "Nuevo Hércules, Júpiter, Teseo y Apolo." For the art historian, perhaps even more significant is the priority of this funerary monument as representing the first thoroughly documented emblematic art work produced in the New World. It is known that Cervantes de Salazar had brought with him from Spain an illustrated edition of the famous *Liber emblemata* of Andrea Alciati ("The Book of Emblems," *editio princeps,* 1531) Following its initial employment in Salazar's Caroline funerary monument, Alciati's illustrated riddle book was to be used commonly as a standard rhetorical model among the intellectual elite of New Spain. For instance, Jesuit teachers decided to use this emblem book, which proves so useful in interpreting the so-called Mannerist mentality generally belonging to educated Europeans of the period, as a kind of textbook for seminary studies. Accordingly, in 1577, they applied to the Spanish viceroy, Don Martín Enríquez, for permission to publish in Mexico City their very own edition of Alciati's famous handbook.

Roman History as an American Model: López de Gómara

A paradigmatic historiographic model of the ancient world, especially that drawn from the writings of important Roman chroniclers, proved decisive in the composition of historical writings belonging to the period, including even those dedicated to dramatic events still unfolding in the New World.

Of course the capital of the ancient Roman empire still existed, was even being vigorously revivified under munificent papal patronage. Moreover, Latin, the language of the ancient *Caput Mundi,* was the recognized lingua franca of Renaissance humanism. For newly interested students of the history of ancient Rome, texts (many long forgotten) began to reappear and to be reread with ever greater interest and increasing comprehension. Among those ancient historical scriptures, evidently the most influential in Latin America were the so-called "Decades" by Titus Livy (*Ab urbe condita . . . :* "The History of Rome from its Foundations"). This seminal work was one we discussed as having served as the authoritative model for the narrative *Décadas* of Peter Martyr of Anglería, itself the first comprehensive history of New World settlements. Besides such retrieved texts, other influential models proved to be archaeological in nature, particularly including exemplars of Roman coinage and inscriptions. During the Renaissance, history was equally a literary and philosophical exercise. History itself was, moreover, figuratively taken to represent an exemplary reflective mirror in which the morality of different peoples, customs, individuals, and their exemplary leaders, could be held up for close inspection and invidiously compared to contemporary practice. All this was expressed in the *Praefactio* of Livy's standard history book, also including a certain sweeping statement, which was evidently taken to heart by nearly every European historian working during the Renaissance:

> In the dark dawning of our modern day, when we can neither endure our vices nor face the remedies needed to cure them, the study of History proves to be the best medicine for a sick mind. In History you have a record of the infinite variety of human experiences, plainly set out for all to see. And in that historical record you can find for yourself, and for your country as well, both examples and warnings. History displays equally fine things, which are to be taken as models, as well as base things, rotten through and through, which are to be avoided.

Since in this period one major impulse was the search for exemplary models, certain famous men and women mentioned in the standard ancient texts would be chosen as embodiments of representative virtues, which were, in turn, viewed as applicable to present day exigencies. It was accordingly believed that every city, each family or individual, should have an ancient hero who might be taken as a kind of secular patron saint. It was in this retrospectively moralizing context that, in 1559, Charles V would come to be characterized in the recently reconstructed capital of New Spain as representing a "New Hercules" or "Theseus Reborn."

This point may be concretely demonstrated by the only illustrated chronicle of the Indies that was ever published in Spain during the Renaissance. This was written by Francisco López de Gómara. We shall make particular reference to a reprinting—in 1554 in the Zaragoza print shop of Pedro Bernuz—of his *Historia General de las Indias y Nuevo Mundo mas la conquista del Perú y de México,* which now included a new, self-explanatory subtitle: "Now newly expanded and revised by the author, with a complete synopsis of each chapter and many illustrations [*figuras*] not appearing in previous editions." Although there was an earlier edition, also appearing in Zaragoza, as published by Agustín Millán, it is the 1554 *Historia General,* "agora [reimpresa] con muchas figuras" (see Figs. 33–36), that proves far more significant in the present context. This is, in short, the first history of America published in Spain to be accompanied by a wealth of purported American imagery. Previously, the norm was that reports about the New World would appear unembellished by graphic materials. Oddly, yet another illustrated chronicle of the Indies, the *Crónica del Perú* composed by Cieza de León, similarly illustrated with twelve woodcuts (see Figs. 39–45), was to appear simultaneously with the publication of Gómara's monograph, although it was printed far to the north in Antwerp.

The uniquely illustrated edition of Gómara's *General History of the Indies* arose from a peculiar, even somewhat droll, situation, which is characteristic of the curious nature of early book production in Spain. Much earlier in Zaragoza, a local publisher, Jorge Cocci, produced a lavished illustrated edition of Livy; as translated into Spanish by a monk, Pedro de la Vega, it was published as *Las quatorze décadas de Tito Livio* in 1520. As so often happened, the Zaragoza publisher had himself merely pirated an even earlier set of illustrations. As we now know, the original (but unintentional) source for the pictures explaining the texts in Gómara's *History of the Indies* were wood blocks that had been commissioned in 1505 by a publisher in Mainz, Jacob Schöffer, for a German translation of the Roman historical classic. Composed in what was an already archaic (or late medieval) style, Schöffer's woodcuts for the *Teutsche Livius* naturally betray none of the classicist preoccupations with accurate re-creations of ancient costume and settings that so preoccupied artists in Italy at the same time. The result is that, burdened by still lively medieval traditions, the actors belonging to a history of ancient Rome as conceived around 1505 in the Rhineland still are dressed according to contemporary Nordic custom. Such anachronisms are scarcely unique to Schöffer's workshop: The same visual confusion between ancient Rome and contemporary (or late medieval) Germany is found throughout Schedel's famous *Liber Chronicarum* (see Fig. 8).

A generation after the appearance in Mainz of a thoroughly medievalized, illustrated version of Titus Livy, Gómara's *Historia de las Indias*—the text of which is itself patently modeled after Livy—appears in Zaragoza in 1552. It was obviously an immediate success; in the following year yet another edition of the *Historia* immediately follows, with yet another printing, this time an illustrated version, coming just a year later. By 1554 however, although the text remains the same, the format and even the title of Gómara's American history are to be dramatically altered. Given implicit textual linkages between one and another historian, Livy the ancient model-author and Gómara his modern emulator, in 1554 the Spanish publisher seems to have thought that certain illustrative materials, perhaps equally pertinent to ancient and modern history, could serve just as well in either application. Accordingly, and we think somewhat ironically, Bernuz recycles the old Mainz illustrations made up for a German Livy and decides to collate them into a new version of Gómara's contemporary history of the Spanish Indies. This noteworthy, even paradoxical, adaptation results in what turns out to be one of the most exotic and arbitrary documentary falsifications known to American historiography. Those unremittingly anachronistic proto-Europeans concocted in 1505 for the Mainz Livy—ancient "Greeks" and "Romans," wholly opposed in actual appearances to the classical settings of their purported literary context—are resurrected and now proposed to illustrate dramatic scenes of the conquest and exploration of the New World during the Renaissance by contemporary Spaniards. This chronological anomaly naturally produces a double falsification: The provincial German printmakers from Mainz never saw either the ancient Roman world nor, of course, even the New World!

There is another contextual aspect that seems worth mentioning: a royal warrant (*real cédula*), dated January 2, 1554, ordering immediate confiscation of all copies of the 1553 edition of Gómara's *History of the Indies*. As one might now ask, exactly what was it in this book that warranted such a negative reaction on the part of the Spanish crown? Moreover, how is one to explain that such a censorious measure proved to be so ineffective? The success of the illustrated version of Gómara's *History of the Indies* was hardly due to the pictures, scarcely reliable in any event, but rather to the author's recently acquired notoriety. Gómara actually took a direct part in the great contemporary debate about American Indians, especially the controversy about a forthcoming working relation that Spain was obliged to establish with them. This is, in fact, a debate that has generated many important modern historical studies, particularly those by Silvio Zavala, John L. Phelan, and Lewis Hanke. The most pertinent questions belonging to this controversy had been raised as early as the beginning of the sixteenth century, and included the following issues. What was the essential nature of the American Indians? Exactly what cultural level had they achieved before the arrival of the Europeans? Were these Indians really those "slaves of Nature" who had been described by Aristotle? Exactly which rights or obligations did the Spanish crown possess according to the papal bull of 1537?

As is well known, there were two contrary positions. One was championed by Friar Bartolomé de Las Casas, an extremist defender of the Indians and their autonomous cultural identity and achievements. Minimizing the stain of human sacrifice and other such notorious moral defects, he chose to believe that, guided by their enlightened rulers, pre-Columbian Native Americans had been living in their very own Age of Gold. The opposite opinion, completely opposed to Las Casas's and largely propagated in the Spanish Indies by colonists and *encomenderos,* was implacably hostile toward all Indians, especially Aztecs. This second camp received in Spain its foremost intellectual support from Juan Ginés de Sepúlveda, a humanist scholar who argued, following Aristotle, that Indians were "slaves by nature." Accordingly, he affirmed that the best way to deal with them was to continue to submit them to the kind of political programs and religious indoctrination already employed by Spanish authorities in the Indies. This polemic not only raged within the exalted precincts of the Spanish court but equally impacted upon the American scene. The historian López de Gómara, as it turns out, was very much tied to the colonist party. He was, in fact, private secretary and chaplain to Hernán Cortés between 1541 and 1547 and, to compensate him for his rather polemical literary services, he was even paid five hundred pesos by the son of *El Conquistador,* don Martín Cortés.

López de Gómara's approach to historical writing was informative, pleasant to read, and tended very much to follow classical literary models. In practice, Gómara would attribute to Cortés elaborate discourses that were very much in the manner of Titus Livy's model rhetorical exercises, and these essentially fictive monologues served both parties to defend theses stated in other ways by Sepúlveda. The conclusions ultimately reached by Gómara through means of generous use of such rhetorical conventions were basically these: that the Mexican Indians were little more than liars and thieves, they were lascivious, lazy, and stupid, and so forth.

As was only natural, since Gómara's sympathies patently lay with the colonial usurpers, in an equally loud voice he sang praises of the superiority of European civilization in the face of Native American barbarism. There was yet another polemic in Gómara's book, an implicit condemnation of ongoing governmental policies, especially those that had been established by the Emperor Charles V to deal with the Indian problem in a moderate, even humane way. Given his not very veiled critique of the official position, the reason why the Spanish crown would have endeavored to suppress Gómara's partisan *History* in 1553 now becomes readily apparent. Nonetheless, such attempts at official censure ultimately failed, and prohibition of Gómara's *Historia* proved unsuccessful in particular, and so the anti-Indian position was tacitly to remain the dominant one in Spain through the end of the seventeenth century.[2]

The graphic imagery accompanying Gómara's chronicle represents a singular occurrence and deserves much more attention than it has previously received.[3] This ensemble comprises a total of just nineteen prints, even though, as we point out, there are frequent repetitions of pictures put in earlier chapters. Again, our attention is caught by the unusual recycling of imagery originally applied to illustrate the ancient world now used to re-create dramatic scenes of a subtly politicized American "new" world. At first glance, this application might seem wholly arbitrary; nonetheless, people in the sixteenth century would have taken a different point of view. When the moment arrives to analyze that other historical perspective belonging to the Renaissance, we shall try to explain how a certain significant relationship was then understood to exist between the American chronicle of López de Gómara and another perceived meaning, apparently opposed, derived from *The Decades* of Titus Livy. Following the order of their appearance in the *Historia de las Indias,* we will proceed to comment upon these

33.

"The Sabines in Italy = Columbus Defending His Thesis," from F. López de Gómara, Historia General de las Indias (Zaragoza, 1554).

prints in two ways: their original antique context, and a usually contrived American one belonging to its subsequent, Renaissance application.

The first print in López de Gómara's book corresponds to his chapter 15, making reference to Columbus's labors in preparation for his first voyage to the Indies (Fig. 33). Designed in two parts along a central vertical axis, it gives the impression that there were actually two separate, quite unrelated, scenes. As the image first appeared in the earlier German edition of Livy, it initially illustrated a scene (book 3, chapter 10) belonging to the ancient arrival of the Sabines in Italy. In the context of Gómara's historical account, the left-hand scene seems to make a new allusion to wholly different events occurring centuries later, namely discussions that Columbus had with influential persons belonging to the Spanish court, such as Cardinal Pedro González de Mendoza, in order that these worthies might present his petitions to the Catholic Kings. Because of their timely intervention,

the *Capitulaciones de Santa Fé* (referring to the military encampment built
in a grid plan before Granada) were eventually formulated, and the money
Columbus needed was then lent to him by Luis de Santángel. The next print
in the sequence was inserted into the sixteenth chapter of Gómara's history,
referring to the discovery of the Indies by Christopher Columbus. In the
German edition of Livy's *Decades,* this scene of a launch and a warship full
of disembarking troops was used to illustrate an episode from the Macedonian War against the Athenians by King Philip V, father of Alexander
the Great. The port in the German woodcut from which crowded warships are shown departing must be Brundisium, to which the consul Publius
Sulpicius went in order to embark in a fleet, commanded by the consul
Cornelius, which then set sail for northern Greece. In López de Gómara's
Historia the same scene now makes anachronistic reference to the departure
of Christopher Columbus in mid-1492 from the Andalusian port of Palos
de Moguer with three caravels and some 120 men, either sailors or soldiers.
However the same print appears again in the twentieth chapter of Gómara's
work, now referring to the second voyage of the famed *Descubridor de las
Indias,* which took place on September 25, 1493, and so an ancient Italian
port now becomes Cádiz.

A third print is found in Gómara's chapter 23, referring to the imprisonment of Columbus. It is exactly the same as the illustration found
in the German version of Livy (book 9, chapter 10), discussing the trial
of Pleminius and his transfer in chains to Rome. In this instance, there is
an understood functional analogy, albeit rather a generalized one. Reports
dealing with Columbus's failure as a governor had induced the Catholic
Kings to despatch Francisco de Bobadilla to take command in his place.
After hearing a number of complaints from the colonists, Bobadilla ordered
Columbus and his brothers, Bartolomé and Diego, to be placed under arrest
and immediately returned, in chains, to Spain. As soon as Ferdinand and
Isabella heard Columbus's explanations for his actions, they gave him a complete pardon. Nonetheless, they did strip him of his rank as *Gobernador de las
Indias.* In chapters 113 and 141 of the *Historia de las Indias,* the same woodcut
is used again, twice, to illustrate two other, later scenes of generic imprisonment, referring to the jailing of, respectively, the Inca Atahualpa and that
of Almagro, the infamous Spanish *conquistador* of Peru. The fourth print
belonging to Gómara's chronicle appears in three wholly different contexts
(Fig. 34). In the German Livy it was initially used to illustrate an episode in

34.

"The Siege of Bytheus = The Defense of Boriquén; (or) Attack on the Island of Cenú; (or) Discovery of Yucatán," from F. López de Gómara, Historia General de las Indias (Zaragoza, 1554).

the Macedonian War in which Lucius Quinctius laid siege to Bytheus with the aid of King Eumenes and the Rhodians. In Gómara's book, it appears initially in his chapter 44, dealing with the island of Boriquén (present-day Puerto Rico), which had been stoutly defended by the natives who had recently discovered that the intrusive Spaniards, rather than being immortal gods, could instead drown and die like mere mortals—or Indians. The print reappears twice more in the same *Historia de las Indias:* in chapter 69 it is used to depict Cenú, a place on the coast having a large and secure port formed by the mouth of a river, and again in a chapter dealing with the discovery of Yucatán.

The fifth print in the *Historia de las Indias* was taken from Livy's "First Decade" in the German version (book 9, chapter 2), where the picture originally referred to the terms of an armistice arranged by the Romans, putting nearly naked Samnites under the Roman yoke. It was reproduced in chapter 45 of Gómara's text, which, dealing with the discovery of Florida, makes the original Samnite connection extremely difficult to explain. Gómara's sixth print showing galleons and rowboats was first used in the German Livy in order to represent Aeolians requesting a truce from Lucius Cornelius Scipio while he was outfitting a great fleet to sail to Greece. In Gómara's *Historia,* the same print was to be used no less than three times, in his chapters 49, 92 and 108. In its first appearance, its usage makes sense contextually, as chapter 49 describes a fleet carrying some two hundred Spaniards toward the coasts of Yucatán as ordered by Francisco Hernández de Córdoba. Much less logical are the second and third employments of this same print, either to illustrate the discovery of the Strait of Magellan (as recounted in chapter 92) or to picture the discovery of Peru (in chapter 108). Gómara's seventh print was initially employed half a century earlier by the German publisher to illustrate Titus Livy's "Decade IV," referring (book 9, chapter 2) to the forced transportation of captive peoples to Peonia as ordered by King Philip of Macedon (Fig. 35). The German print illustrated a dramatic moment told by Livy when, refusing to comply with the order, a brave woman chooses instead to kill her children and grandchildren, while at the same time she and her husband hurl themselves into the sea. In Gómara's chronicle, the same print reappears to illustrate wholly different American anecdotes included in his chapters 58 and 198. The first occasion refers to Francisco Pizarro, shown embarking in two boats in order to establish the new town of Antigua in Darién (Panama), and the second use relates to Gómara's account of a harvest of pearls from the ocean, during which many men were drowned while diving in search of oysters.

Gómara's eighth print arose from Livy's *Decades* (book 1, chapter 3), describing a defeat inflicted by Gauls upon Romans led by Cornelius Bebius Pamphilus (Fig. 36). This vigorous battle scene seemed equally suitable to illustrate repeated accounts of bloody struggles taking place in the America between Indians and Europeans. Nonetheless, as used again in Gómara's book, Native Americans are now made to appear in the disguise of antique warriors—but these Roman "Indians" are anachronistically equipped with medieval European weaponry! Even more striking is the fact that the backgrounds of these battle scenes are filled with medieval cities which, of course, in no way approach the reality of American landscapes belonging to the New World. This same woodcut was reused for chapters 61 and 171 of

35.

"Philip of Macedon and the Collective Suicide of His Prisoners = Pizarro's Departure for Panama; (or) The Dangers of Pearl Fishing in Darien," from F. López de Gómara, Historia General de las Indias (Zaragoza, 1554).

Gómara's *Historia de las Indias,* where it could either refer to certain battles in the Gulf of Urabá commanded by Vasco Núñez de Balboa, or a wholly different combat, in which the Viceroy of Peru, Blasco Núñez Vela, was killed by the Indians.

The ninth print was originally used for the German Livy (folio 45) to illustrate an encounter between Hannibal and Eudamus, admiral of the Rhodian fleet; the latter, in spite of aid from the Syrians, was decisively defeated. The ancient naval battle is once again employed for chapters 62, 67, and 85 of Gómara's chronicle, either to recount the discovery of the *Mar del Sur,* or Pacific, by Vasco Núñez de Balboa, or to refer to a battle undertaken by Balboa against the Lord of Cuareca, or to illustrate discoveries and other battles—taking place much earlier in 1499—as commanded by Vicente Yáñez Pinzón. The tenth print belonging to Gómara's chronicle originally corresponded to the siege, and eventual successful capture, of the city of Samnium in 290 B.C. by the Roman general Fulvius (Livy, book 8, chapter nine). As repeated in the *Historia de las Indias,* in chapters 76 and 124, the same crowded image makes reference to the conquest of Cumaná, even though it would make much more sense to have had it relate to the taking of Cuzco. In any event, a besieged Native American city is (again) shown to be wholly medieval in appearance, so it (again) bears no real relation to either text, neither Gómara's nor Livy's.

Gómara's eleventh woodcut corresponds to the German edition of Livy's "Decade IV," where it was originally used to show the arrival with great acclaim of King Antiochus III in the port of Hyamea. In Gómara's

36.

"Gauls Defeating Romans = Attacks by Indian Troops Against Balboa and/or Núñez Vela,"
from F. López de Gómara, Historia General de las Indias (Zaragoza, 1554).

book, this image reappears in his chapter 95, where it is now used to refer
to the reception of a Spanish captain by an Indian monarch, Siripada, who
ceremoniously greeted him at the port of Borney. Nonetheless, the royal
personage dressed in wholly medieval fashion is shown in the act of arriving
(rather than departing), and so once again we see how difficult the adjust-
ment of details belonging a Roman historian must have been to more recent
American events recounted by Gómara. The twelfth print in Gómara's *History* first appeared in Livy's text in two wholly different contexts, one dealing
with the Asian Wars and the other with the first African War. In 1505 the
woodcut represented a hostile encounter between two enemy ships, and
according to its textual placement it must refer to a victory gained by the
Romans and their Rhodian allies over Polyxenidas and King Antiochus. It
was accommodated in 1554 to Gómara's chapters 103 and 175, where the
assigned narrative context now makes the illustration serve either a futile
search for the Spice Islands or a march inland toward Peru led by Pedro
Lagasca.

The thirteenth print in Gómara's *Historia de las Indias* corresponds to
Livy's "Decade III," and shows a troop of soldiers armed with lances and
milling around in front of the walls of a fortified city. In the Spanish
chronicle, this illustration was used twice by Gómara, in chapter 111, to
narrate the course of ferocious battles taking place on the island of Puná
between Pizarro and the Indians, even though there could never have been
there a city anything like the one used to picture an episode drawn from
Livy. Another print first appearing in the German Livy (Decade III, book 8)
also shows an army laying siege to a walled city put to the torch by its
desperate inhabitants who are pictured in the act of immolating themselves
in the holocaust, into which they carry their riches so that these may be
denied to the enemy. As inserted into Gómara's chapter 130, there is no
way that this picture can be related to the text, which merely discusses a
more or less peaceful agreement reached by the *conquistadores* Pizarro and
Almagro. Gómara's fifteenth print derives from Livy's "Decade IV" (book 7,
chapter 7), where the original purpose was to show Seleucus and his father
Antiochus laying siege to the city of Pergamon. Once transferred to chapter 135 in Gómara's chronicle, it is arbitrarily made to refer to a siege put
to Indians defending the citadel of Cuzco; as shown here, the mighty Inca
capital now acquires an unmistakably Gothic silhouette. Gómara's next two
prints are derived from Livy's "Decade III" (book 9, chapter 2), describ-

ing battles that took place in Spain between Publius Lentulus and Lucius Manlius. In Gómara's chapters 116 and 139, the same print is employed to illustrate either quarrels between the Inca leaders Huáscar and Atahualpa or discussions between Pizarro and Atahualpa, where the Inca emperor ends up treacherously ambushed by the Spaniard.

Gómara's eighteenth and nineteenth prints originally corresponded to Livy's "Decade III" (book 6, chapter 21 in the German publication), including an episode telling how the virtuous Scipio had ordered captive virgins to be protected against his Roman soldiers. This could, by taking certain liberties, be reemployed to fit in conveniently with an event narrated by the Hispanic chronicler in his chapter 170, dealing with the imprisonment of Almagro (with no virgins present). The actual historical source for a Peruvian scene taking place in the early sixteenth century, Gómara's final or nineteenth print, is Livy's "Decade I" (book 1, chapter 4, in the Mainz version), making reference to the murder of Amulius by Romulus and Remus. In the context of Gómara's *History of the Indies* (in chapter 170) an apposite example of ancient Roman treachery is now used to illustrate a contemporary misdeed, the cruelty of Francisco de Carvajal, a rebel who hounded to death all those loyal to the Spanish crown. That brings to an end our investigation of a particular (even peculiar) case study, showing how certain models abstracted from Roman history were, arbitrarily to say the least, imposed upon a wholly new historical context, the Spanish conquest of America. According to the terms belonging to a quite incoherent application, the typical, consistently discordant note struck here is images of American Indians appearing in the guise of ancient classical-era heroes, who are themselves dressed according to once current fashions belonging to late medieval Europe.

The Image of the Indian in Sixteenth-century Spanish Painting

This phenomenon of an overt imitation of classical literary models arbitrarily applied to American events taking place during the Renaissance was certainly not solely encountered in book illustration. That American iconography also had its place in Italian painting of the period is shown by frescoes, executed in 1588 by a Florentine artist, Ludovico Butti, who imaginatively applied imagery derived from the world of the Aztecs to the Hall of Arms in the Palazzo Medici.[4] Naturally, Spain would likewise participate in an artistic phenomenon current in this period throughout Europe. As has been shown by the investigations of Salvador Andrés Ordax, who has analyzed certain mural paintings displayed in the Palacio de Moctezuma in Cáceres (in Extremadura, the homeland of so many notable *conquistadores*), Spanish participation in the same kind of Renaissance American Indian iconography is unmistakable.[5] The unusual pictorial cycles found in this Extremaduran palace, unfortunately scarcely known and now badly preserved (so preventing reproduction), certainly deserve more attention (and hopefully physical restoration in the near future).

The exterior of this mansion presents the aspect of a fortress. Inside, passing through a portico, one finds a patio with three colonnades, and it is here, in the wings, that we find pictorial programs of great historical interest. As is now known through Ordax's research, the Renaissance aspects of the Palace of Moctezuma are to be specifically associated with an aristocratic family of Cáceres founded by Don Juan Cano de Saavedra. Cano was a veteran of the Spanish conquest of Mexico who, as a captain under the direct orders of Hernán Cortés, took part in the crucial battles of Tlaxcala, Tepeaca, and Otuma. Once the conquest was successfully completed, Cano married the only legitimate daughter of an Aztec ruler, Moctezuma II; his Indian wife had been baptized, so receiving her Christian name, Isabel Moctezuma. Their only child, Juan Cano, chose to return to his father's *patria chica,* Cáceres, where, sometime in the mid sixteenth century, he took up residence in a large medieval mansion situated in the Calle Empedrada. His son, the grandson of Juan Cano de Saavedra, was Juan de Toledo Moctezuma, who lived in Cáceres between 1559 and 1608. Don Juan married Doña Mariana de Carvajal, offspring of an even more important local aristocratic family, and henceforth the surname Moctezuma was to be dropped from the Cano family name, to which Carvajal was now added. It presently appears that it must have been this same Don Juan de Toledo who was responsible for a drastic reform of the old medieval building, carried out toward the turn of the seventeenth century, and therefore, for the commissioning of a uniquely Aztec pictorial cycle in Spain. The first-born son resulting from the union of Mariana Carvajal and Juan de Toledo himself married into the family of the dukes of Abrantes. It was the latter who eventually transferred title to the property, which was later to be designated a historical monument and part of the Spanish *Patrimonio del Estado.*

Although the building still displays some significant medieval features, particularly due to Juan de Toledo's addition of a central courtyard and wide halls, essentially it has now become a work characteristic of the late sixteenth century. At this time, sometime between 1597 and 1608, the exterior was embellished with coats-of-arms while series of paintings appeared around the courtyards; unfortunately, these have not survived in their entirety. Naturally, in neither its dimensions nor its artistic ambitions can this mansion in the dusty hinterlands of Extremadura be in any way compared to contemporary *palazzi* in Genoa or Florence. Nor, for that matter, can it be considered in any way comparable to the palace of the Marqués del Viso in La Mancha, which is notable for exhibiting an extensive fresco-cycle incorporating complicated and learned mythological themes *alla romana* that are unmatched elsewhere in Spain. To the contrary, even though an ambition to emulate contemporary pictorial cycles in Italy is readily apparent, the aesthetic level of the artistic program designed for the walls of two *salones* in dusty Cáceres still remains generally modest in conception and wholly provincial in execution.

The subject matter of one mural is conventionally *romano* whereas that of its neighbor is wholly *mejicano;* in either case, the overall intention was to exalt the often exotic heritage of the Moctezuma-Carvajal lineage. Ordax suggests that the specific impulse was to celebrate the marriage of Juan de Moctezuma, the great-grandson of the Aztec Emperor Moctezuma II, and Mariana Carvajal y Toledo, who had inherited the palace. Conforming to ubiquitous demands for politicized social rhetoric belonging to the mentality of the Renaissance, the conjoined Moctezuma-Carvajal lines are celebrated through an evocation of celebrated heroes and famous leaders of antiquity, equally drawn from ancient Roman and Aztec history. Subjects belonging to the so-called *Sala Romana* include a series of equestrian portraits of the emperors, among whom Julius Caesar, Augustus, Nero, Galba, Otho, Vitelius, Vespasian, Titus, Domitian, and so forth, may be recognized; each Roman portrait is enframed by heraldry belonging to the Moctezuma-Carvajal line. Considerably more original is the imperial iconography displayed in the adjacent *Sala Mejicana.*

Even though this cycle has unfortunately survived in a sadly deteriorated condition, its original format—and intention—remain fairly clear. Since the owners of the palace saw themselves as being directly related to Aztec emperors, it was only logical that reference should be made to exotic royal ancestors associated with a recently discovered America. As displayed in Cáceres, these imperial American ancestors become noteworthy moral exemplars; indeed, in their collective moral stature, they are wholly worthy of comparison with a series of nearly mythic Roman emperors. Given the poor state of preservation of the cycle, most of the names belonging to the sadly faded figures portrayed here have since become completely illegible; nonetheless, a few titles can still be read, so informing us of the presences of *los reyes* who once, before the advent of Spaniards, ruled over the Mexican states of (as spelled out here) *Otompa, Misteca, Tezcoco, Totolapa, Onalco,* etc. These Aztec rulers are represented in the Roman manner, *en buste,* but crowned in the contemporary regal European fashion. Obviously, our provincial Spanish decorator, whose name remains unknown, remained completely ignorant of Aztec dress and accessories. To the contrary, owing to the easy accessibility of contemporary engravings depicting the "Twelve Emperors"—particularly the equestrian-series by the Dutchman Stradanus that illustrated Suetonius's classic Roman history of the same name—the anonymous Extremaduran craftsman was much better informed about the proper appearance of notable ancient rulers majestically parading about on horseback.

Notwithstanding their low artistic level, these rather crude paintings represent a significant marker in the reception of American imagery in Renaissance Spain. Since they too, like those book illustrations we have just analyzed, reveal only the vaguest notions concerning the real appearances of Native Americans, once again we may speak of an imposition of traditional European iconography, which is applied with considerable arbitrariness and some obvious ignorance in order to deal with an unfamiliar situation for essentially political purposes.

The Persistence of Classical Imagery in the Ephemeral Art of New Spain

Classical subject matter and themes underwent a process of revitalization throughout the seventeenth century, a Baroque era in which mythological language attained new expressive heights. To illustrate the process *in nuce,* we may refer to an extraordinary example occurring in New Spain and belonging to the category of ephemeral art. The case in point is a pair of triumphal arches that had been commissioned, following an open competition, to commemorate the grand ceremonial entrance, on November 30, 1680, of a new viceroy, don Tomás de la Cerda, marqués de la Laguna and conde de Paredes, into the capital, Mexico City.[6] These were designed to be erected in the Plaza de Santo Domingo. Among the competitors, as authors of different "*Ideas*" (written iconographic programs), were two distinguished Mexican intellectuals, Carlos de Sigüenza y Góngora, and particularly, a celebrated Mexican nun-poet, Sor Juana Inés de la Cruz. Whereas Sister Juana Inés chose to submit an elaborately allegorized encomium of the Marquis de la Laguna, Sigüenza instead presented a most original program broadly dealing with the art of governing, a favorite theme in Baroque courtly rhetoric. Adding a new twist to familiar European modes, Sigüenza chose to look back upon the history of pre-Columbian Mexico; according to this author, the result should be that the viceroy's triumph would be "in no way inferior to the triumphs that made Rome great."

The central part of the northern face of Sigüenza's arch contained a dedicatory inscription and displayed portraits of previous Spanish viceroys, all of whom were shown seated upon different planets. Much more unusual were the flanking scenes, depicting exemplary Mexican leaders who had ruled long before the arrival of the Europeans. As presented here, these are Native American kings who may be proposed as worthy models to be emulated by current European-Spanish rulers. All of these were real historical figures, with the lone exception of a certain tribal god, Huizilopochli, who had been included because, according to legend, he had led his people to the promised land of Anahuac. Especially curious is the way that Sigüenza decided to characterize the Aztec deity by imposing upon him traits diversely belonging to two standard moral paradigms of European culture, namely Moses and Aeneas. Octavio Paz has shown how for this part of the endeavor the obvious literary models were the Bible and Virgil's *Aeneid;* accordingly, the end result was a typical Renaissance synthesis of classical antiquity and medievalizing Christianity. The process of humanist eclecticism works just as well for the Native Americans: Even specific details symbolically characterizing the supposedly Aztec figure of Huizilopochli were all derived from current European emblematic traditions. For example, displayed upon the arch is a disembodied arm placed next to a flowering branch seen emerging from the clouds, and both the verdant stalk and the nebulous limb were rather commonplace symbolic motifs found in many contemporary European emblem books. Nonetheless, upon the blooming emblematic twig a symbolic bird incongruously perched; named Huitzilin, it uniquely belonged to pagan Aztec mythology.

Other than the apocryphal Huizilopochli, all the other figures belonging to Sigüenza's scheme were notable Native American personages known from pre-Columbian historical chronicles. These worthies began with Acamapich, the first emperor of Mexico, for he was the one who liberated the Aztecs from Toltec tyranny. In a typically European fashion, however, next to the legendary monarch was placed the opportune symbol of "Hope" (*Spes*), just as this standard allegorical personification had been represented by Alciati and his many emblematic followers. As told by ancient Mexican legends, it was Acamapich who, with his own hands, had fashioned a humble hut out of reeds; from such emblematically modest beginnings grew the future metropolis called Tenochtitlán. The result was that the mighty Mexican capital need have no reason to feel envy before the most famous cities in Europe; it was above all else destined to become, Sigüenza claims, the "Roma del Nuevo Mundo."

Following Acamapich came a second Mexican emperor, Huitzilihuitl, who pursued the struggle initiated by his heroic predecessor for Mexican independence from the Toltec oppressor. Huitzilihuitl was eponymously related here to the mythic bird, Huitzilin; covered with priceless plumage, this avian augury becomes in Sigüenza's hands a symbol standing for a pair of typically Christian virtues deemed most necessary for rulers, namely *Clemencia* (Clemency) and *Mansedumbre* (Meekness). The third Aztec emperor in the historical series is Chimalpopocatzi; undergoing a magical change of gender, he is represented as a mother with her children stoutly defending Mexico City against the Toltecs. This composite figure symbolizes *Amor a la Patria.* Another virtue, *Prudencia,* was attributed to a fourth Aztec Emperor, Itzcoatl. This Nahuatl word (*itzcoatl*) may also designate a "razor viper" (*culebra de navajas*), long before taken by the Aztecs to symbolize Prudence. The strictly pre-Columbian part of Sigüenza's eclectic programmatic idea was completed by a bellicose ruler known as Moctecohzuma Ilhuicaminan, whose first name was interpreted to mean "Enraged Lord," and the last as "he who shoots arrows toward the heavens." The final title resulted from intercession of divine aid that this Aztec emperor had once received in battle, thereby helping him overcome his enemies. Accordingly, on the triumphal arch he was shown hurling a dart skyward; a Latin motto, *ibant,* meaning that his pious missiles "were going" upward, was included to allude to beneficial results forthcoming from his corresponding virtue of *Piedad* (Piety).

On the southern face of the triumphal arch, at the very top, one saw the present viceroy, the marqués de la Laguna, enthroned upon an eagle, long since employed as a standard Aztec symbol for Mexico itself. Similarly, an eagle throne would allude to the *aquila* symbol of the Habsburg dynasty. Alongside this symbolic conflation of pre-Columbian past and Hispanic present appeared an emblematic portrait of the sixth Aztec emperor, Axayacatzin. He was presented in the guise of yet another standard virtue currently attached to Baroque rulers, *Fortaleza*. Atlaslike, this representation of Mexican Fortitude carried upon his muscular shoulders the weight of a sphere representing "la bola del mundo mejicano." The next emperor in Sigüenza's complicated series is Tizoctzin, whom the Mexicans termed a peacemaker, *el Pacífico*. As befits his fame, for him there was painted an allegorical representation of *la Paz,* dolefully plucking a lyre and shown to be making a brave front against *la Guerra*. In order to defeat War and so approach Peace, Tizoctzin was shown gingerly picking his way across a thorny bramble patch. The name of the next Aztec emperor is Ahuitzotl, a Nahuatl word for a certain aquatic mammal, the nutria or otter. This furry reminder recalled an erroneous judgment on the part of the emperor, leading to the disastrous flooding of Mexico City and causing his own death by drowning. Since Ahuitzotl could have easily avoided such unlucky fate, had he but taken heed of certain good *Consejo,* accordingly his admonitory picture is placed next to one showing a group of worthy Aztec ancients expending Good Counsel to all comers.

This heavily allegorized recital of exemplary virtues belonging to the native Mexican people even includes a model derived from the very end of pre-Columbian history, in the sixteenth century. This historical-moral example is based upon the dossier of Motecohzuma Xocoyotzin (our "Montezuma"), whose exemplary virtues had even been sung by a notable conquistador-chronicler, Bernal Díaz del Castillo. In the triumphal arch erected in the Plaza de Santo Domingo, Motecohzuma Xocoyotzin, also known as Moctezuma, is celebrated as an exemplar of generosity. With these magnificent but didactic ends in mind, the Aztec emperor, wrapped in luxurious feather-robes, wrests jewels from the toothy mouth of a lion (itself never a native of Mexico); these precious stones would later be magnanimously distributed by the Indian chieftain throughout his kingdom.

Both regal lion and Aztec ruler collectively stand for two essential princely virtues, namely *Magnanimidad* and *Liberalidad.*

The culminating phases of pre-Hispanic Mexico continued on the triumphal arch with the figure of Cuitlahuatzin, Moctezuma's elder brother. Under the audacious guidance of *Audacia,* Cuitlahuatzin dared to oppose Cortés, inflicted a severe defeat upon the Europeans during the so-called *Noche Triste,* and even succeeded in (momentarily) ejecting all the Spaniards from the fortress-city of Tenochtitlán. In his emblematic portrait, the next-to-last Aztec emperor was shown covered in a mantle with a series of embroidered hands sewn upon it. The purpose of this manual motif was to suggest how Cuitlahuatzin's audacious resistance of recent memory evokes Plutarchian recollections of Alexander the Great, a famed emperor who blithely cut through a fabled Gordian Knot. Since the Greek had done this feat with the aid of his sword—which he held in his hands—thus the Aztec emperor-general bears a vaguely similar symbol, *las manos.* The final figure in the Aztec imperial series naturally belongs to Cuauhtémoc, the last of his line. Since he never flinched under Spanish torture, he was admired all the more by his European torturers for his steadfast *Constancia;* accordingly, like contemporary religious paintings of "Christ After the Flagellation," the martyred Cuauhtémoc is painted standing next to a firmly planted column carved from the hardest marble.

This brings to a close our brief survey of a unique, Baroque-period cataloging of various virtues belonging to Native American figures drawn from pre-Columbian history. According to perhaps heterodox opinions shared by an aristocratic coterie of colonial intellectuals who chose in this exceedingly contrived way to interpret those pre-Columbian notables, they were all worthy of imitation by contemporary *novohispanos.* According to Octavio Paz, the really significant factor leading to the composition of this exceedingly complicated scenario was the Jesuit upbringing of Carlos de Sigüenza y Góngora, for this kind of education had channeled his thinking along syncretistic lines, and so he naturally tries to make all cultures compatible. Recently endowed with these eruditely allegorized virtues so typical of Baroque rhetoric, Native Americans—now also including a majority population increasingly made up of mestizos and *criollos*—need in no way feel envious of ancient Roman grandeur. As many a benevolent colonial despot appears to have recognized, ethnic flattery succeeds where even *panem et circenses* might fail.

American Giants and Pygmies

This mental projection into the classical world occurring in the Spanish New World manifested itself in characteristic, often bizarre, ways. Marginal materials drawn from antiquity for New World situations included figures like the Giants and Pygmies that belonged wholly to the realm of mythological fable. Faced with an unprecedented American nature, apparently full of novel telluric forces, Europeans imagined that this kind of rampantly exotic landscape would have been the proper setting for gods and primeval beings who existed at the very beginning of earthly creation. Essential within this legendary cast of characters were the *Geantes,* those children of *Gea,* the Earth, born of blood flowing from the mutilated groin of her husband Uranus when he was castrated by Cronos. As told in the pagan classical texts, these were giants having an elevated divine origin but a lowly human condition. Their legend is tied to various combats they unleashed against the gods, in which they were soundly defeated. These were peoples of immense stature, plentiful body fur, and thick beards. Their overall horrific aspect was augmented by their legs, having the form of serpents, and by their legendary enormous strength. Nonetheless, they are not to be confused with the Titans, also having huge bodies and a prodigious strength. At the beginning of his *Theogony* (lines 183ff.), the ancient Greek poet Hesiod shows us the Muses, who sing of the birth of the gods, followed by the birth of mankind, and finally that of the Giants. This sequence was also portrayed by the Roman Ovid, in his *Metamorphoses* (I, 150–60). He adds that the Giants raised mountains upward from the earth toward the heavens, so desiring to conquer the celestial realms. It was all in vain: Jupiter blasted their plans with lightning bolts. According to Ovid, their's was an evil race, "despised by the gods and most avid for cruel slaughter." This dramatic subject matter naturally proved of interest to visual artists, and the most famous treatment of the *Gigantomachia* (struggles between the gods and giants) in classical art is the frieze on the Altar of Zeus in Pergamon belonging to the Hellenistic period.[7] Legends of the Giants never died out. Their grotesquely oversized figures reappear, for instance, in the *mappaemundi* belonging to the late Middle Ages, and during the fourteenth and fifteenth centuries they were even used to refer to the island of Taprobana (or Ceylon). As might be expected, the indefatigable Sir John Mandeville also claimed to have seen them in the fabulous East, in territory belonging to the Great Khan of Cathay.

According to a process we have already discussed in other contexts, these kinds of late medieval fantasies were easily moved from their original European (or pseudo-Asiatic) homelands into the recently discovered Americas. Accordingly, by the year 1500 maps by Alberto Cantino and Juan de la Cosa make brief verbal mention of islands belonging to either giants or (as was much more common) cannibals. As should be recognized now, the nature of the first documented appearance of any American colossus was wholly pictorial—but with no verbal inscription to acknowledge the fact of its unheralded epiphany. One result of our research is the conclusion that what was quickly to become a tradition of specifically American giants actually began with the first known depictions of the *indios de las Indias,* meaning those anomalous natives first revealed (quite naked) in original woodcuts composed upon the occasion of the initial publication of Christopher Columbus's often-reprinted *Letter* (Figs. 16–19). In the case of each of these four compositions, symbiotically feeding off of one another and sequentially published between 1493 and 1495, the Indians were always shown to be immensely taller than their intrusive European visitors, so much so that the latter end up consistently looking like (*avant la lettre*) Jonathan Swift's Lilliputians. That said, we may additionally point out how the first *verbal* representations of the same American giants were only forthcoming a few years *after* the appearance of four widely circulated prints, appearing in a context that might even be called journalistic. Is this, therefore, another case of what Oscar Wilde might have called "Art imitating Life?" a conundrum that in this case refers to certain illustrations, Art, generated by Columbus's verbal imitations of Life, such as it was initially stated by him to exist in America. Evidently this was the case, for other than some crude photography recently labeled as portraying an evidently apocryphal type like "Sasquatch" (a.k.a. Big Foot), to this day there are really no other pictures known of the Native American giants.

In any event, the first European explorer we know to have left a detailed *text* (versus picture) referring to them as such, "giants," was Amerigo Vespucci. In an account of his second voyage to American shores, he described how

we came to another island, and we found how this was inhabited by very large people. We immediately landed to find out if we could find any drinking water. Not seeing anybody, we believed the place to be unpopulated. However, going a bit further from our landing place, we discovered huge footprints in the sand. We thought that if their other limbs were of equivalent scale, then these must be men of enormous size. . . . We only encountered five women, two old crones and three young girls, who were however so big that we could only regard them with wonder . . . and they were of bigger stature than a tall man. They were, in fact, huge of body, like [the celebrated Italian giant] Francesco degli Albizzi, but much better proportioned, so much so that we were motivated to forcibly abduct the three girls, carrying them off to Castile as objects of wonder. While we were considering this plan, some thirty-six men, who were much bigger than the women, began to approach the landing place. Even though they were so well shaped that their sight inspired admiration, they nonetheless so alarmed us that we would have much preferred to remain on our ships rather then meet face to face such people. They were carrying outsized bows and arrows and also clubs. . . . They walked about as naked as all the others. This place is called the Island of the Giants.[8]

Those New World giants that most impressed Europeans were the ones supposedly inhabiting Patagonia. They were initially "discovered" (or invented) during Magellan's transworld expedition. With his five ships, the Portuguese captain decided to spend the winter of 1519/20 in the Bay of St. Julian. Notices of the outsized Argentines spread throughout Europe in the manner that they were originally reported by a supposed eyewitness, Antonio Pigafetta. According to the credulous Italian sailor, a typical Patagonian attained a height "so tall that none of us came to his waist." Moreover, "he had big facial features, which he painted red, putting yellow paint around his eyes." Nearly a century later, details supposedly belonging the initial Patagonian encounters by Magellan's men became considerably embroidered at the hands of Ruy Díaz de Guzmán. This chronicler wrote that when seven Portuguese soldiers landed on the frigid shores of southern Argentina they found, according to Díaz, several giants, beings "de monstruosa magnitud." Although the Europeans took three of them captive, two more succeeded in fleeing. At which point, says Díaz,

one of the giants was put upon the flagship. He was well treated by Magellan, made to sit down, and given things [to amuse him]. Nonetheless, he remained with a sad face, and showed fear upon viewing himself in a mirror. As soon as they recognized his strength, the sailors made him support a water-barrel on his shoulders, and this he carried about as though it were only a drinking mug. Then he thought to escape; eight or ten soldiers leaped upon him, but they were very lucky to be able to tie him down. The result was that the giant became so disheartened that he refused to eat and eventually died from sheer chagrin.[9]

The giants found around the Straits of Magellan were eventually dubbed Patagonians. The term *Patagón* is generally believed to come from the Spanish phrase, "el hombre de grandes pies" a man with big feet; nonetheless a French scholar, Jean-Paul Duviols, has pointed to a likely locus in contemporary popular literature, namely a medievalizing, anonymously authored novel entitled *Primaleón* (as it was eventually published in Seville in 1524). In this once very widely devoured chivalric romance, or *libro de caballerías,* there was specific mention made (on folio 142b) of an island inhabited by appropriately savage folk, all of whom were overshadowed by a giant actually named Patagón. Still, by 1524 this Andalusian author could himself have been informed of details of Pigafetta's dramatic narrative about the first circumnavigation of the globe, and so his picaresque reference to a King BigFoot probably was itself ultimately as much broadly pictorial as strictly Patagonian in its origins (see Fig. 23). About a much discussed "Big-Foot" (or Sasquatch) tribe, notoriously infesting northern California (and the popular press) during the later twentieth century, our Renaissance historians naturally have nothing to say. Still, the recurrence, 450 years later, of an unquestionably persistent, even pan–American, *patagón* motif is certainly provocative in itself.

Tales of the giants unquestionably endured for a long time in America. For instance, early in the seventeenth century (among other mythic notices analyzed by Enrique de Gandía) we find Friar Pedro Simón including the topic in the third chapter of his *Primera Noticia,* in which he speaks of certain *gigantes* who were known to be inhabiting the hinterlands of Peru. Their *sepulcros* (tombs) are described here as still being uncovered; when opened for inspection they were found to contain the enormous bones belonging to these giant beings. Much earlier (in 1554), Cieza de León not only discusses Peruvian giants but even illustrates them as fitting subjects for divine wrath (see Fig. 43). Yet another author, Sarmiento de Gamboa, actually claims to have seen *gigantes* around San Simón Bay. You did not have to be Spanish to buy into the outsized legend; even Protestants saw the American giants. In 1587, Cavendish the Englishman affirmed that he saw human footprints in the sand; these were, he says, eighteen inches long. However, according to two Dutch sailors, Van Noort and De Wert, in the vicinity of the Straits of Magellan they also saw several men who measured twelve feet in height. Among others making similar claims were Spielbergen and Marlborough in the seventeenth century, and Frézer, Shelvocke, Byron, Wallis, and Bougainville in the eighteenth.

We, however, know better. A modern Spanish historian (and debunker) of American myths, Enrique de Gandía, has analyzed local conditions that most likely contributed to the origin of these egregiously revived ancient legends. Among other pertinent factors, he notes the accidental discovery of different kinds of prehistoric animal remains, particularly fossilized dinosaur bones, which just might be confused with oversized human remains. Besides such paleontological *trouvailles,* there were of course nonphysical impulses, mainly transplanted European legends, either medieval or classical, and additionally a series of local fables belonging to Native American bardic traditions. The latter, exclusively verbal in character, would have been rejuvenated by the overheated fantasies of European conquerors, explorers, and colonists, either Spanish or northern European. Between New World mythic materials and Old World legends there was evidently a lively and longstanding symbiosis.

Subject matter touching upon the giants is not wholly unknown in Spanish colonial art; in fact, it makes its appearance as early as the end of the sixteenth century in South America. The most notable example is seen in painted decorations belonging to the mansion of Juan de Vargas, in Tunja (Colombia). Painted on the ceiling of his opulent reception hall is a huge coat of arms of the Spanish monarchy held aloft by two savages. These shield bearers are not, as one might first think at first glance, Indians. Instead, the anomalous *escuderos* represent a familiar pagan semidivinity from ancient Europe, Hercules. In an essentially allegorized fashion, Hercules had long since been intimately associated with the kings of Spain, for whom the athletic god came to represent a kind of dynastic patron saint. Ancient legend imputed to Hercules the foundation of various Spanish cities, most notably Cádiz (the ancient *Gadir*), and also the installation, in ancient Iberia, of a primeval Hispanic monarchial system. Moreover, as everyone knows, until relatively recently the Straits of Gibraltar, separating Christian Europe, Spain, from Islamic Africa, Morocco, were called the "Pillars of Hercules."

A poet resident in colonial Tunja, Juan de Castellanos, has left us a typically Baroque description of a legendary Iberian, Hercules-like giant belonging to the previously discussed iconographic program embellishing the mansion of Juan de Vargas in the same city. Obviously conforming to the same classicizing impulse, in part Castellanos's cumbersome verses read as follows:

> Salvaje más crecido que gigante,
> Y cuyas proporciones y estatura
> Eran según las pintan en Atalante,
> De hombre natural la compostura,
> En el hocico solo discrepante,
> Algo largo y horrenda dentadura.
> El vello cuasi pardo, corto, claro,
> Digo no ser espeso, sino raro.
> De nudoso bastón la mano lleva,
> El cual sobrepujaba su grandeza,
> Pues era como la mayor entena
> Y del cuerpo de un hombre la groseza;
> Y aqueste meneaba tan sin pena
> Como caña de mucha ligereza.[10]

[A savage grown bigger than a giant, he is one whose proportions and height are according to those used to paint Atlas. A normal man in composition, he was only outlandish in his muzzle, a bit too long and with horrid fangs. His fur was nearly brown, short and not dark in color; I mean it wasn't thick, just weird. He carries [like Hercules] a knotty club in his hand, with which to make boast of his grandeur for it was like the biggest of yardsticks. It was itself as thick as a man's body, and this he flourished as effortlessly as though it might have been a wand without any weight at all.]

Completely opposite to the Giants were, of course, another kind of legendary figures, the Pygmies. Since these undersized folk were rumored to have stemmed from a population of dwarfs that were believed to be roaming about in the southernmost regions of Egypt, then one supposes that something like a real historical inspiration for the pygmies actually existed in southern Africa, namely in the Bushmen, or Hottentots. Ctesias of Cnidus, a fourth-century B.C. physician, however claimed that the pygmies lived in the heart of India. According to this Hellenistic scientist, these diminutive Indians only measured two cubits in height and they had long beards; reaching nearly to their feet, their facial hair served as their only clothing. The standard, or original and rather brief, description of what may be called the Pygmy "life-style" came from Homer's *Iliad,* which suggests they dwelt instead alongside the Atlantic. At the beginning of Book III (verses 3–9), the bard pictures the noisy advance of the Trojans

> with a shouting and a din like that of birds. They filled the air with clamor, like the cranes that fly from the onset of winter and the sudden rains and make for Ocean Stream [the Atlantic] with raucous cries to bring death and destruction to the Pygmies, launching their wicked onslaught from the morning sky.

Ever omnivorous, Sir John Mandeville took his description of the pygmies from Homer, but considerably embroidered upon the picturesque but peripheral Greek anecdote of relentless struggles for food between these ravenous homunculi and the raucous storks. According to the fifty-fifth chapter of Mandeville's immensely popular *Book of the Marvels of the World,* each spring these dwarfish folk, with a dwarfish life span, had to reiterate ceaseless struggles along the seashores with angered birds in order to steal their eggs. Now, however, their geographical locus becomes China:

> This river, the Yangtze, runs through the middle of the land of the pygmies, who are men of small stature, for they are only three spans tall [two feet], but they are very handsome and well proportioned to their size. They marry when they are a year and a half old, and beget children; they usually live seven or eight years. If they live to nine, they are considered marvelously old. . . . Frequently they fight with cranes, having perpetual war with them; and when they kill one, they eat it. They do not work in tilling the land, or other heavy labor. . . . And these small men have great scorn for big men, and find them as much an oddity as we find giants. There is in that land a good city where a lot of these small men live. . . . The nature of the country is such that nothing but small things are engendered there. The Great Khan, who is lord of it, has this city looked after very well.

Later, Hellenistic or Roman-era Egyptian art shows the pygmies in either frescoes or mosaics, and usually at war with the storks or, occasionally, with crocodiles. As depicted in these scenes, pygmies are paragons of ugliness, deformed and endowed with outsized sexual organs. Besides occupying the attentions of classical poets, pygmies are also mentioned by Aristotle and by, especially, the exhaustive encyclopedist Pliny, whose works we know to have been widely consulted, and well past the Renaissance period. In his *Natural History* (VII, 26ff.), the Roman natural scientist goes much further than Ctesias when he emphatically asserts that their height never gets past three inches. That said, he recounts the familiar tale of their struggles with the storks. Centuries later and far to the north, the Pliny type of Pygmies reappear, somewhat incongruously, in Romanesque monumental art. For instance, on the facade of the pilgrimage church of Vézelay in France, they are shown making awkward attempts to mount a horse; since they are much too short to do the job right, they must make clever use of a ladder. Naturally, they also appear in late medieval cartography, where they are used to identify exotic African, or even Asian, localities (as in Mandeville).

They also, as perhaps now seems inevitable, turned up in America. Quite a few European explorers believed that they actually saw them in South America. For example, Federmann the German stated that he ran across them in Venezuela. Benalcázar, a Spaniard, gives his account of finding them in the kingdom of Quito. Other Old World explorers mention coming across pygmies in other places belonging to far distant south lands, some situating them in either the Río de la Plata, in Argentina, or in the Gran Chaco, in what is now Bolivia.[11]

In Search of the American Amazons

Whereas pygmies literally represented tiny subject matter in the European psychic conquest of the New World, other borrowed figures, some even washing up upon American shores, loomed much larger. Among a plethora of mythic personae belonging to the classical world, unquestionably the geographically most widely distributed figure in the Americas was the legend of the Amazons. They too were soon absorbed into the enterprising mythic picturing of the New World during the Renaissance (see the frontispiece, Figs. 13, 15, 27, among others). Whatever the historical period, luridness naturally enhances popularity of any given legendary type. Having excited the misogynist fantasies of classical pagan authors, the Amazons continued to obsess Christians no less during the Middle Ages. It was only natural that the enduring classical myth of certain incessantly bellicose femmes fatales would continue largely unabated into the Renaissance and that, therefore, it would similarly fire up the macho imaginations of the first explorers of the Americas. Thanks in part to the magnetism of this essentially misogynist legend, rapid discoveries were made of new territories, proof for the underlying mythic impulse being provided in the names of some of the more tempestuous of the South American rivers, still bearing the names of these ancient women warriors, one being the world's mightiest freshwater stream. That brilliant Spanish student of post-Columbian American legends, Enrique de Gandía, has observed how

> among all the myths attached to the conquest of America, there is none which is so confused, so deformed and so unfathomable as was the myth of the Amazons. There is none other so scorned, for being so misunderstood, nor is there another today more forgotten, for being so impossible in the first place. It is, nonetheless, the most authentic and most illuminating legend of all. This conclusion is not based upon what the name "Amazon" now evokes—a mere delusion entertained by *conquistadores*—but rather by what the mirage really represents in its historical context.

Based on the classical textual sources, it was known that the Amazons represented a community of bellicose women. They owed their intransigence to their descent from Mars and the Nymph Harmonia. Some put their realm in the foothills of the Caucasus. Others, however, chose to locate them much further to the west, in Thrace, where they were said to be governed by an exceptional woman who functioned like a queen. Surprisingly (to men at least), they lived with no need of men. For the Amazons, males could only be tolerated in the role of servants who, as ordered by their unsympathetic mistresses, carried out only the most menial labors. It was said that the Amazons denied, even liquidated, any male descent. Whenever male issue might be born to them, they would blind or cripple these boys, sometimes even kill them. They only had affection for their female offspring, the occasional result of very infrequent physical contacts with male strangers. As they preferred, their daughters were systematically trained for warfare.

Since the presence of a breast might hamper their ability to manipulate a bow, they underwent mastectomies as adolescents. Hence, according to the most common of interpretations, the Greek origins of their title: *a-* signifies negation, and *mazos* means breast; Amazons consequently deny, even extirpate their breasts. Another view would, nonetheless, have it that the tribe of proverbially irascible women got its name from a Semitic term, *amazo,* meaning "strong mother," a title that was also applied to that Hellenistic paragon of chaste female divinity, Diana of the Ephesians.

The cult of Diana (or Artemis) came to Ephesus from the Caucasus. Once situated along the Mediterranean in her new capital, she had a great temple raised in her honor. She was the goddess destined to be adored by the Amazons for she, like them, was both warrior and huntress. Diana was, as is perhaps only natural, not much liked by early Christianity, which was itself notably "patristic"; according to St. Paul, himself an exemplar of misogyny, "the temple of the great goddess Diana should be despised, and her magnificence should be destroyed, she whom all Asia and the world worshipped" (Acts 19:27). In pre-Pauline times the breasts of Diana, in her likeness as Artemis, wet nurse of nature, were interpreted as symbols of the clouds. Various Greek heroes (all males) fought against the Amazons, including Bellaphon, Theseus, and Hercules. It was Theseus who carried off Antiope the Amazon; immediately following, her spiritual sisters attacked Athens in order to avenge the offensive kidnapping. They were defeated. Elsewhere, meaning in barbarous places like Africa, Amazons were much more successful; in various efforts, they defeated the Numidian Atalantes, Ethiopians, and the dreadful Gorgons. Most famous of all Amazonian campaigns was the one carried out during the Trojan War in support of Priam. As commanded by their queen Penthesilea, who had already killed Achilles, the Amazons eventually reached Troy. In the end, they were eventually exterminated at the wrathful hands of Hercules, another splenetic male.

The artistic heat generated by this legend was enormous. For instance, Amazons appear in the relief sculptures of such important Hellenistic monuments as the temple of Apollo Epicurios, the mausoleum at Halicarnassus, and various others. Eventually their fame was projected into the Middle Ages, when the term *Amazon* was used to refer to exotic, barbarian peoples vaguely situated in the far corners of Asia, meaning specifically near to *las Indias,* and so their reputation became known to Columbus and his followers in the American Indies. The best-known text from the Christian era discussing Amazons in this fashion was produced by a famous Venetian traveler-trader, Marco Polo. Referring to certain "Male and Female islands," so labeled by him, here is how Polo established (in his *Divisament dou Monde*, chapter 190) a distinctively medieval and Asian-Indian adaptation of the venerable legend of the Amazons:

> Let us begin with two islands called Male Island and Female Island. Male Island lies in the Sea [Indian Ocean] some 500 miles south of Kech-Makran [Baluchistan]. The inhabitants are baptized Christians, observing the rule and customs of the Old Testaments. . . . But I assure you that in this island the men do not live with their wives or with any other women; but all the women live on the other island, which is called Female Island. You must understand in practice how men from the Male Isle go off to the Women's Island and there they will remain for three months, that is March, April and May, and this is because the women will never go to their island. During those three months the men go to that other island in order to live with their wives, at which time they take their pleasure with them. Each man goes to live in the house of his woman. At the close of this time period, they return to the Male Isle, where they earn their livelihood for the other nine months of the year. . . . They speak a language of their own. Male Island [likewise in the Indian Ocean] is about thirty miles distant from Female Island. According to their own account, their reason for not staying all the year round with their wives is that if they did so they could not live long. The sons who are born are nursed by their mothers in Female Island till they are fourteen years old, when they are sent to join their fathers in Male Island. When the men come to Female Island they sow the corn, which the women till and reap. The women also gather fruits, which grow there in great profusion. Otherwise, they have nothing to do except to rear the children. Such then are the customs of these two islands. As there is nothing else worth mentioning, we shall go on to tell of Socotra [much further west, at the mouth of the Red Sea].

The world traveler manqué, Sir John Mandeville, could no less avoid making timely reference to the sensational Amazons. Here the treatment is considerably more misogynist than was Polo's before him (even though the peripatetic Venetian may be supposed to have been his immediate literary model). In his *Book of the Marvels of the World*, Mandeville placed the legendary women warriors in Chaldea, a land which he calls the "land of

Amazoun," or realm of solitary women, "which we call the Maiden Land or the Land of Women: no man lives there, only women." They arrived at this militantly chaste condition, says Mandeville, because most of the Chaldean men were slaughtered in a battle. Next Mandeville explains that

> when the Queen and other ladies of that land heard the news that their King and his lords were slain, they marshalled themselves with one ac-cord and armed themselves well. They took a great army of women and slaughtered all the men left among them. And, since that time, they will never let a man live with them more than seven days, nor will they allow a boy child to be brought up among them. But when they want to have the [physical] company of men, they will go to that side of their country where their lovers live; they stay with them eight or nine days and then go home again. If any of them bears a child, and if it is a son, they keep it until it can speak and walk and eat by itself, and then they will send it to the father—or they kill it. If they have a girl child, they cut off one of her breasts and cauterize it; in the case of a woman of great estate, the left breast, so that she can carry her shield better, and, in the case of a girl of low degree, they cut off the right one, so that it will not hinder her shooting, for they all know very well the skill of archery. There is always a queen to rule that land, and they all must obey her. This queen is always chosen by election, for they choose the woman who is the best fighter. These women are noble and wise warriors; and therefore kings of neighboring realms hire them to help them in their wars. This land of the Amazons is an island, surrounded by waters, except at two points where there are two ways in. Beyond the water live their lovers, to whom they go [only] when it pleases them to have bodily pleasure with them.[12]

Since both these accounts place these sexually liberated ladies in the farthest reaches of Asia, or actually around India in the case of Polo, then the seeds were sown for the notion of a fabulous sexual Golden Age potentially avail-able to the first lusty European explorers of *las Indias,* as oddly reached by sailing west. Further proof for the currency of the Island of Solitary Women (Amazons) during the age of American discoveries is manifested in the *World Globe* (1492) of Martin Behaim (see Fig. 9). To reiterate, Columbus, as were other literate Europeans of his time, was unquestionably familiar with the Amazonian legend and, in fact, he searched them out obsessively.

Already on January 6, 1493, he noted in his *Diario* how he received news that toward the east "there was an island only inhabited by solitary women." Ten days later, he places these putative Amazons on the island of Martinique, which was, he claims,

> inhabited by women, five or six of them, without men, . . . but he was unable to go ashore, due to a shortage of water aboard his ships. Nevertheless, he says that it was a fact that there were [only] women there, and that at a certain time of the year men would come to the women belonging to that Carib island; the Island of Men, he also says, was distant from the Island of Women by some ten or twelve leagues. Moreover, if the women gave birth to a son, they would send it off to the Isle of Men; if it were a girl however, they would let it remain with them.[13]

As we have already noted on various occasions, we again may observe that Columbus had Mandeville very much on his mind; in this particular instance, he even appears literally to quote the fraudulent tourist-author.

In this context, another interesting testimony is that coming from the celebrated Italian chronicler resident in Spain, Pedro Mártir de Anglería. Trained as a critical humanist scholar, Martyr was not likely to accept these fantasies as easily as did Columbus; accordingly, he remains somewhat skeptical of reports, including Columbus's, circulating about New World Amazons. Nonetheless, rather than being particularly convinced by Columbus's statements, Martyr lends credence to what classical writers tell him — and they did speak of the existence of Amazons. In this spirit, the first historian of the Americas, who himself never set foot in *las Indias,* makes use of certain notices reaching his ears by way of mariners recently arriving in the Spanish court. He employs their eye-witness statements to make often-quoted classical texts more comprehensible, even immediate, for his Renaissance period readers and contemporaries. Concerning the matter of recent Amazonian apparitions in the Caribbean, Martyr composed the following, typically eclectic — ancient and contemporary — patchwork for his *Decades* (book IV, chapter 4):

> All round this island of Coluacana there are other islands, and there live certain women who have no traffic with men. Some believe that they must, therefore, live in the manner of the Amazons. Those who more

closely examine the matter might judge that these are Cenobite maidens who enjoy solitude, such as happens among us [with nuns], or as was the case in many references [in Latin literature] dealing with the ancient Vestals, those virgins who were consecrated to the goddess Bona. At certain times of the year, so I am informed, men pass over to the island belonging to the women, not however for connubial purposes, but instead as moved by compassion, in order to tend to their fields and gardens, by the cultivation of which these women are enabled to survive. It is however well known that there are yet other islands [in the Caribbean] which are inhabited by solitary women, but these had been raped [beforehand]. When they are young, so the mariners tell me, they cut off a breast so they can manipulate their bows and arrows with greater agility. And it is also said that men come there to couple with them, and that the men keep any male offspring they may give birth to.

Nonetheless, given his critical spirit, Martyr feels impelled to add at the end, "This I hold to be but a fairy-tale."

Notwithstanding this instance of humanist skepticism, it turns out that one can easily find repercussions of the widely spread legend cropping up in nearly all the writings of the conquerors and explorers of South America. One of the most detailed accounts of American Amazons we owe to a Dominican father, Gaspar de Carvajal, who landed in Peru in 1535, just in time to accompany Gonzalo Pizarro in his hapless expedition in search of the *País de la Canela* (Cinnamon Land). Leaving Pizarro before the end of his fruitless campaign, Carvajal chose instead to follow Francisco de Orellano and his fifty-six followers in their search for a river with an eastern outlet opening into the Atlantic. The course followed by Orellano's expedition was along a mighty Brazilian stream, presently known as the Amazonas. For Orellano and his men the end result was an odyssey of nine months of adventurous, mostly tortuous, and seemingly endless struggles through virgin jungle. In our mythic context, the most significant result was an identification made by the Spaniards of some warlike Native American women as representing the Amazons of hoary legend. Even Carvajal asserted that: "Las vimos con nuestros propios ojos!": We did see them, with our very own eyes! In Father Gaspar de Carvajal's *Relación* of the Brazilian venture, published initially in 1542, the American Amazons were even described as looking somewhat European:

These women are very tall and pale. Their hair is very long, and they twist it and wrap the braids around their heads. They are stoutly built and march about stark naked, with only their genitals being covered. Armed with bows and arrows, which they carry in their hands, they make war better than any ten male Indians.

With the aid of a male Indian who served them as an interpreter (one wonders how well), the credulous Spaniards were informed that the American Amazons were organized in no less than seventy different tribes, or *pueblos,* and that they all lived in stout stone houses, had fixed places of worship, and also much rich treasure, "ricos tesoros," always of interest to *conquistadores.* As Carvajal tells it, when Orellana asked if these women gave birth, the answer was that

> the Indian interpreter said, certainly, and then our captain asked how they could get pregnant, seeing that they weren't married, for there were no men living with them, and the Indian responded that these women did get together with men, but only during certain appointed seasons. He added that, when the mood hit them, certain *white* men [*blancos*], but ones without beards, would come to them from a certain neighboring province which belonged to a great lord, and so the [native] women arranged to share sport with these [white] men. . . . It is said that the ones that got pregnant with a male child would kill it or, perhaps, send it off to its father; if it were a girl however, with great rejoicing they would keep it to raise. It is further said that all these [different tribes of] women have a main leader, a mistress, to whom all must give obeisance, and her name is Coroní.[14]

If there could have been any tangible, real historical and local (eastern Andean regional), basis for this seemingly fabulous account, then informed opinion would have it that these second-hand stories of pseudo-Amazons might possibly represent a reflection of contemporary Inca religious customs. In this case, perhaps a real basis for Carvajal's American pseudo-Amazons were those Inca vestals called Virgins of the Sun, who resided in so-called Houses of the Chosen. Detailed accounts of these Indian vestals are, for instance, to be found in various places in the *Comentarios reales* (1609) gathered by Garcilaso de la Vega, "el Inca." Nonetheless, as eventually re-

ceived by most Spaniards, the story naturally became thoroughly colored by
traditions belonging to ancient legends already resident in the Old World.
Another apposite example would be the verses of a Colombian poet, Juan
de Castellanos, whom we have already cited in another context. As he spoke
of them in his *Elegía* xiv, the Amazons have already metamorphosed into
strictly Indian *guerreras:*

> E india varonil que como perra
> Sus partes bravamente defendía,
> A la cual le pusieron Amazonas
> Por mostrar gran valor en su persona.
> De aquí sacó después sus invenciones
> El capitán Francisco de Orellana
> Para llamalle río de Amazona.

> [Like a bitch, the mannish Indian woman-warrior bravely defends her
> own offspring, for which reason they are dubbed Amazonian, so to in-
> dicate the great courage belonging to their character. Whence it comes
> that Captain Francisco de Orellano would later draw from his imagina-
> tion the idea of calling his river the Amazon.]

You did not have to be Spanish to encounter an Amazon in America. In
1567, a German adventurer, Ulrich Schmidel, composed his *Tales of the Conquest of the Río de la Plata and Peru.* In the illustrated edition of 1599 (as
published by Ludwig Hulsius in Frankfurt-am-Main), one finds interesting
graphic depictions of certain aboriginals who have been given European
names, as *Carios* and *Scherves* (Figs. 37, 38). As told here, the adventurous
author and his Spanish companions had gone far up the River Paraguay.
Eventually they reached the realm of the Jarayes Indians, and it was here
that their king spoke to rightly amazed Europeans about the Amazons.
Naturally, the Old World adventurers went off immediately in search of the
legendary ladies. According to the German explorer-turned-author,

> These *Amazonas* are women, and their husbands only get to see them
> three or four times a year. If a wife finds herself pregnant with a male
> child, she sends him off to the man. If, however, her child turns out
> to be a girl, then she stays with the mother, who sears her right breast
> so that it cannot grow any further. The reason they do this is so that

37.

"The American Carians," from U. Schmidel, Wahrhafftige und liebliche Beschreibung . . .
Indianischen Landtschaffen und Insulen (Nuremberg, 1599).

the girls can better employ their weapons, particularly the bows. This is
because they are bellicose women who make incessant war against their
[male] enemies. These women live upon an island that is completely surrounded by water, and their's is a very large island. If you want to get to
them, you must go by canoe. However, on this island the Amazons have
neither gold nor silver; for that you must go to the mainland, which
is where the men live. There, one will find many riches. The Amazons
make up a great nation and they have a leader which must be called
Iñis.[15]

In short, here we find a résumé of nearly all of the standard topoi belonging
to the ancient European legend. Moreover, it even seems as though Ulrich
Schmidel had set about to turn himself into another John Mandeville, *re-
divivus.*

Not long afterward, in 1596, a celebrated English explorer, Sir Walter
Raleigh, broadcast the news in London of the results of a recent voyage

38.

"The American Scherians," from U. Schmidel, Wahrhafftige und liebliche Beschreibung . . .
Indianischen Landtschaffen und Insulen (Nuremberg, 1599).

made in his flagship, the *Discovery*, to distant Guiana. Further details were
given in his *History of the World* (1615), in which he dedicated a chapter to
the Amazons. His polemic purpose in describing them was announced in a
straightforward manner: "I also had a great desire to learn the truth regarding these woman warriors, for some believe in their existences, but others
not." As Raleigh was informed by a native *cacique,* the American Amazons
inhabited the province of Topago, situated some sixty leagues upstream
from the mouth of the Orinoco River. Flaunting his classical erudition, the
English buccaneer implicitly compares Topagan Amazons to some much
better known ones, those Amazons who, according to standard classical
texts, lived in Asia and Africa. According to Raleigh,

> The fact of their existence is collaborated in many historical accounts,
> and dealing with different periods and places. Those Amazons who are
> to be found [in America, are encountered] near to Guiana; they [are
> said] only to have contact with men but once a year, and for a period of
> only a month; this I understand to take place in April. At that time, all

the kings of the border regions and all the queens of the Amazons get together. Following an initial selection made by the queens, then the others may determine, by lot, their own [temporary] Valentines. During this month there are celebrated many banquets and dances, and everyone drinks their wine in great abundance. At the waning of the moon however, everyone must march off to their respective lands. If the Amazons find themselves pregnant, and if they do bear a child, and if it turns out to be male issue, they must send the offspring away to the father. If, however, it is a girl, she will stay with her mother, who brings her up. For every girl they bear, they send a present to the progenitor, for all of them have a great desire to increment the number of those of their own sex and their own class. I have not, however, found any confirmation for what is said concerning [the rumor] that they cut of the nipple of the right breast. I was also told by them that if they capture prisoners in any of their wars they may cohabit with them at any season; in the end however, inevitably, they kill them all. As they say, these women are very cruel and bloody-minded, especially with any who would intend to invade their territories.[16]

Even though by this date, at the beginning of the seventeenth century, the myth was largely discredited, nonetheless the famed English sailor feels obligated to repeat it—just as he bought the story of the American *acephalloi* (see Fig. 13). Further into the seventeenth century, a reactionary echo of this shopworn tradition was still being maintained by various Spanish authors, including, among others, Ruy Díaz de Guzmán and Cristóbal de Acuña. Even in the eighteenth century, much the same is stated by the Frenchman la Condamine, and also by certain Spanish scholars, such as Jorge Juan and Antonio Ulloa. These were, however, the last supporters of the myth of the American Amazons, and this mainly transpired due to their ignorance of some sixteenth century documents that had already severely criticized the putative existence of Native American women who, of course, had no relation whatsoever with the spectacularly fabulous Amazons derived from ancient Greco-Roman literary traditions.[17]

Cieza de León: Old World Illustrations for Hispanic Peru

In order to acknowledge significant departures to a general rule for this period—*un*illustrated chronicles of New World transactions—we must note the existence of publications by two important historians: Cieza de León and Antonio de Herrera. Their works do actually include some graphic materials pertinent to the theme that concerns us, namely early European pictorial reactions to, and a resulting iconography of the American Indian. As a rule, students of Latin American history rarely interest themselves in iconographical problems as such, and accordingly it is only by accident that one occasionally finds in their studies reproductions of authentic Renaissance period illustrations dealing with our subject. In such cases, unfortunately, the pictures are typically not analyzed by the authors, but only reproduced, and even the exact provenience of the prints is rarely indicated. It seems as though their publishers were only looking for attractive decorations for their volumes (as also seems the case much earlier with Lopez de Gómara's publisher: Figs. 33–36). One result is that modern readers remain largely unaware of the historical importance of the literary contexts originally attached to such imagery, namely as illustrations produced to enhance encoded messages embodied in various texts expressive of given rhetorical, even polemical ends.

Pursuing our subject in specific detail, we will first discuss the historical writings of Pedro Cieza de León. Born in Seville, at an early age this future chronicler left Spain for the Indies. Eventually he was to know at firsthand many of the western parts of South America, from Panama to Peru, where he actually took part in the civil war against Pizarro. Conscious early on of his mission as a historian, Cieza made a difficult journey to *Alto Perú* at the age of twenty-eight, precisely in order to inspect the most notable native monuments, including Cocha, Pucará, Vinaque, Tihuanaco, Ayaviri, among others. On his way toward these largely abandoned places, he was also able to interview people who had actually known the Incas. By 1550, he had already concluded a manuscript draft of his magnum opus, the *Crónica del Perú,* the first part of which was published in Seville in 1553. Its success was immediate; it was reprinted in Antwerp in 1554, and an Italian translation appeared in Rome the following year.[18] A major reason for the commercial success of Cieza's *Peruvian Chronicles* was an extensive series of woodcut prints accompanying his text in its Antwerp reprinting (Figs. 39–45). Whereas Spain had never been particularly noted for its bookish endeavors, even less for publishing finesse, Flanders had long since been famed for its elaborately rendered and dramatically conceived book illustrations. In this particular case, however, Cieza's illustrations, as designed by a wholly unknown Flemish engraver, turn out to be wholly informative and, accordingly, of scant aesthetic merit. Nonetheless, thanks to the foresight of his Antwerp publisher, this so-called *Príncipe de los cronistas de Indias* will be additionally remembered for leaving us with an uniquely attractive marker within this historical genre, making this volume stand out among the rest of the *crónicas americanistas* as much for its literary style as for complementary, but strictly graphic, information. Viewed this way, the only real competition to Cieza's *Crónica del Perú* turns out to be the anomalously illustrated publication, already amply discussed, by Francisco López de Gómara (Figs. 33–36).

The most interesting illustrations belonging to the *Crónica del Perú* are the first and the second prints in the series, both of which deal with urban planning and the building arts in early colonial Spanish America. Although many ground-plans of Latin American cities still exist (most of which are kept today in the Archivo de Indias in Seville), other than Cienza's there are no comparable depictions of actual daily urban life as it actually transpired in Spanish America in the mid sixteenth century (Fig. 39). Cieza de León's first woodcut shows us a mounted rider handing out instructions to stonecutters, behind whom we see the walls of a newly founded city rising, which already includes a Pantheon-like Christian temple. This authoritative equestrian has to be Pedrarias Dávila, who laid out the foundations of Panama City in 1519. Five years earlier Pedrarias had landed in Darién bearing instructions for the foundation of cities conforming to the classical grid plan popularized by various reprintings of Vitruvius's *De architectura*. Leaving Spain with Dávila was the celebrated *agrimensor*, or surveyor, Alonso García Bravo, and it was he who laid out, in 1523, the prototypical colonial urban plan for Mexico City. According to Cieza de León, given its tropical situation the choice for the site for Panama City was quite ill considered; as he explained, "It has been designed and constructed [arbitrarily, in the classical Roman fashion], running from east to west, and the result is that, once the sun rises, nobody can comfortably walk across the streets, for there is no shade whatsoever."[19]

As any architectural historian must recognize, notwithstanding an initial layout, *a lo romano*, the founders of the Panamanian capital ignored what Vitruvius had actually written (*De architectura*, I, 7) about proper urban orientation, for the Roman architectural theorist was careful to explain that a thoughtful engineer-foreman must lay out his plans in order to take careful

39.

"Pedrarias Dávila Directing the Construction of Panama City," from P. Cieza de León, Crónica del Perú (Antwerp, 1554).

account of the movement of the sun as well as the directions of the predominant winds. In the case of Panama City, notwithstanding its proximity to a river, a much better site could have nonetheless been found just half a league further away. Similar subject matter appears in the second print in the *Crónica,* showing us a master mason directing the work of stone cutters busy constructing a house in the city of San Sebastián de Urabá. According to Cieza's text, this town had been founded by Alonso de Heredia, brother of the *adelantado* Pedro de Heredia, governor of the coastal province called Cartagena de Indias (in present-day Colombia).[20]

In both prints, Spaniards are shown in a wholly positive context, as master builders, as bringers of urbanized civilization. In contrast, Native Americans will be pictured throughout the *Crónica* in a negative way, that is as barbaric peoples consistently given over to superstition and devil worship. Naturally, native religions—appearing here with all of their inevitably ugly divinities represented *al demonio*—caught the attention of all Chris-

40.

"An American Devil and His Worshippers," from P. Cieza de León, Crónica del Perú
(Antwerp, 1554).

tian chroniclers of the New World. Prominent among these was Cieza de León, who dedicated the fifteenth chapter of his *Crónica del Perú* to an essentially negative appraisal of the superstitious customs of the Anserma Indians. By his not so impartial reckoning, they were all "augurs" (*agoreros*), friends of witchcraft and superstition in general, and additionally, *caníbales* (Fig. 40). They are all, he further states, influenced by the devil, and so *el demonio* himself is shown working his wiles on a credulous Indian in Cieza's third woodcut. Since Cieza's anonymous Flemish illustrator-artisan had never ever seen *las Indias,* nor even *los indios,* he naturally reverts to native European customs, and so he shows the Devil decked with horns and bat wings. On the right side of the picture we see a group of five native gentlemen, incongruously bearded, who have already fallen under the malignant influence of the Peruvian demon. In short, there is nothing about these demonized onlookers that can be related in any meaningful way to Native Americans; one is better advised to find the real graphic sources

41.

"Devil Worship in Peru," from P. Cieza de León, Crónica del Perú (Antwerp, 1554).

for this thoroughly pejorative image in any number of illustrated, contemporary European publications dealing with the *artes maleficarum* currently demonizing inhabitants of the endlessly bewitched Old World.

The same kind of thoroughly Europeanized demonic subject matter is encountered in the fourth illustration for Cieza's *Peruvian Chronicles* (Fig. 41). Here we find ourselves at the gateway to an Indian temple. This is pictured as the site of gruesome human sacrifices, even the arena of cannibalism. Once again the essential deity of these American Indians is shown to be the Devil, who, in this instance, is shown perched upon an altar supported by a pair of harpies, horrific creatures much more native to the mental topography of classical European myth than to the aboriginal American landscape. In the nineteenth chapter of his *Crónica del Perú*, Cieza de León described in some detail just how cannibalistic Peruvian Indians offer human sacrifices to their Devil:

In these theaters [*tablados*] they have placed many bunches of woven rope. . . . At the very top of the stage they tie up Indians whom they have captured in their wars. They rope them together by their shoulders and will leave them hanging; from some of them they will rip out the hearts. These they will offer up to the gods. It is to the Devil that they are paying homage by means of these sacrifices. Immediately afterward, they will feast upon the corpses of those whom they have slaughtered in this fashion.

The fifth print shows a rather different scene, an Inca ruler graciously receiving homage from two of his crouching, and bearded, Indian vassals, curiously attired in what appears contemporary European dress. Cieza de León is himself astonished at the number of marvelous things that can be recounted about these Peruvian "reyes o emperadores," and about their immense wealth and great palaces. The Spaniard suspects that previously there must have been much civil disorder in Peru, and so he understands the natives to have been largely bereft of reason, even rather bestial. It is well known that they feasted upon human flesh, he says, and were much given to sexual promiscuity; all this was, of course, directly due to devilish influences. He tells us how this lamentable state of affairs was all abruptly brought to an end by Manco-Capa, Inca founder of the city of Cuzco, who erected fortresses, hostels, and temples. Cieza says he is not going to expound further upon the Incas since he has already written a book about them.

The sixth print in the *Crónica del Perú* belongs to chapter 42, dealing with towns in Ecuador, from Latacunga to Riobamba (Fig. 42). The Spanish historian is especially impressed by the magnificent pre-Conquest architecture of Mocha, now left wholly in ruins. Cieza is moved to lament that, since the Incas have fallen from power,

all their palaces and hostels, along with all the rest of their grand constructions, have been abandoned and so have fallen into total ruin. It has gotten so that nothing can be seen of them, except for their general outlines and a few parts still left standing. Nonetheless, since they had been crafted so excellently of stone with wonderful workmanship, these structures must be thought monuments clearly intended to last for centuries and through all the ages, without ever showing signs of wear.

42.

"The Inca Palace of Mocha," from P. Cieza de León, Crónica del Perú (Antwerp, 1554).

After what Cieza had to say about those Inca buildings, presently found in a state wholly "arruinados y parados," we can only marvel at the untrammeled imagination of our anonymous Flemish illustrator. In short, his woodcut has absolutely nothing to do with the Peru of the Incas. The architecture drawn here, besides being in no way *arruinada,* is completely classical in design, moreover wholly High Renaissance in style. Rather than Cuzco in Peru, what we have placed before us is instead a classicist architectural mise-en-scène brought about by papal munificence in cinquecento Rome.

Later the Spanish chronicler returns to consider the religious customs of the Peruvian Indians, and so the seventh woodcut illustrates his commentary on a most curious divinity worshipped by the ancient Inca peoples, namely an emerald of great size. The print presents a temple, into which are gathering a number of excited worshippers shown adoring a magic jewel displayed to them by a native priest seated upon an altar. As Cieza de León explained in his fiftieth chapter,

The lord of Manda resides, or was figuratively taken to be embodied, in a chunk of emerald, very big and so most valuable. This stone belonged to their ancestors, who held it in great esteem and venerated it. On certain days they would display it publicly, when they would adore it and pay reverence to it, as though there was enclosed within it some god of theirs. . . . And they say that this jewel is so big and so valuable that they could never be made to speak of it, even though the Spaniards have threatened even their lords and leading men to reveal its location to them. They will never speak of it, or so it is believed, even though they might all be killed for their silence.

Cieza de León gathered also some myths still current among the Peruvian Indians, among which was a legend dealing with those once ubiquitous American giants, of whom Cieza's Flemish publisher decided to include a typically fanciful illustration (Fig. 43). In chapter 52 of the *Crónica del Perú,* the credulous Cieza explains that the giants actually came to Peru on huge rafts, and their appearance was that of

men who were so big that the leg alone of any one of them, from the knee down, would be equal to the whole body of any normal man. Even though they were normal in structure and their limbs were in proper proportion to the huge scale of their extremely outsized bodies, their heads presented a monstrous sight, for they were so huge, with hair falling to their shoulders.

Cieza goes on to state that initially these giants seized women by force, but later they became simple *sodomitas* (buggerers). The horrific but inevitable result of such sexual license was, Cieza the God-fearing Catholic affirms, that they were eventually punished by divine wrath to a degree commiserate with the enormity of their sins: "les envió Díos el castigo conforme a la fealdad de su pecado." Moreover, as is shown in the print corresponding to this statement (Fig. 43), the actual vehicle of divine chastisement was an exterminating angel sent from on high; accordingly, the image owes far more to the Catholic Counter-Reformation than to native Peruvian religion.

Subsequent prints become more historical than eschatological in content, so the last prints are more documentary than propagandist in intention. The ninth woodcut, corresponding to materials presented in chapters 92 and 93 of Cieza's *Crónica del Perú,* shows a fateful meeting between

43.

"Divine Wrath Descends Upon the American Giants," from P. Cieza de León, Crónica del Perú (Antwerp, 1554).

Pizarro and the Inca emperor. In the background appears a city of typically Flemish aspect; nonetheless, according to its inscription, it represents Cuzco. Obviously, the Inca capital, today a typical South American *mestiza* city, did not look at all like this even in Cieza's time. Cuzco was initially founded as a religious center, and so its most important building was the Temple of the Sun, or Cori-Cancha, the symbolic center of the Inca Empire.

Given the macrocosmic signification of this great Native American city, it must be laid in a symbolic, macrocosmic fashion: from its navellike, *ompholos* center, four roads fanned out, corresponding to cardinal points of the compass, namely towards *antisuyu* (east), *collasuyu* (south), *cuntisuyu* (west) and *chinchasuyu* (north). On the microcosmic level, pre-Columbian Cuzco was distinguished by immense masonry buildings, made with spectacularly precise workmanship and grouped into regular sequences of city blocks, with either trapezoidal or rectangular shapes. The resulting *planificación urbana* featured more or less straight streets aligned upon irrigation canals and bridges. Hewing to a venerable Inca prototype, the colonial Spanish capital generally respected the arrangement of the old native buildings, and so the Christian city was literally raised up from megalithic pagan foundations.

Even though an architectural veneer expressive of the newly imposed dominion by European victors was to become its predominant visual aspect, in Cuzco, as much as in Mexico City, Spaniards still respected the original meanings of pre-Conquest urbanized spaces. Their original idea was to convert Cuzco, chartered as a *fundación española* on March 23, 1534, into the principal urban nucleus of the Viceroyalty of Peru. Later however, due to its perceived advantages as a commercial port, Lima on the coast was to become the grand colonial capital of Peru—so becoming increasingly subject to the kind of urban modernization that Cuzco has since largely escaped. Rather than upon a flat plain, the ancient Inca capital had been originally laid out upon a rising and unevenly contoured slope. As such, it was impossible to rearrange Cuzco according to monotonously regularized grid-plan designs recommended by Vitruvius and his Renaissance followers—who provided an ubiquitous and mind-numbing model employed for most other Hispanic urbanizations.

With the notable exception of a centrally situated *plaza mayor,* all the other city squares in Cuzco largely remained irregular and small scaled. Many colonial structures were built directly upon, and so were shaped by, their megalithic Inca foundations. Similarly, the parceling out of city lots was not to be apportioned as in other Spanish colonial cities, for the diminutive dimensions of ancient municipal blocks, with foundations too massive to be shifted, had to be maintained in Hispanic Cuzco. The Monastery of Santo Domingo was, to cite but one noteworthy colonial adaptation, raised within the sacred precinct of Cori-Cancha, the Inca Temple of the Sun.[21]

Cieza de León could not overlook the great lake known as Titicaca found in *Alto Perú,* described in chapter 103 of his *Crónica del Perú* (Fig. 44). He tells us that it is the biggest he has ever seen and also remarks upon its great depth. He explains that it is still called Titicaca due to a temple built upon an island of the same name found inside the immense inland sea. Cieza recalled a native myth to the effect that men belonging to regions bordering Lake Titicaca had lived in metaphorical spiritual darkness, that is

44.

"Lake Titicaca and its Temples," from P. Cieza de León, Crónica del Perú (Antwerp, 1554).

until there arose from an island a brightly shining sun. This heavenly apparition was regarded by them as a sacred object, and to commemorate this singular event, an Inca emperor erected upon the island a temple honoring the Sun. In spite of the outsized and opportunistic label, "TITICACA," it becomes readily apparent that high-gabled Flemish architecture placed around a small pond, incongruously filled with wooden rowboats carrying Netherlandish fishermen on holiday, has nothing much to do with that exotic Templo del Sol described in Cieza's text, purportedly illustrated by this crude but fanciful woodcut.

In an exhaustive discussion of the famous silver mines of Peru, appearing in chapter 109 of Cieza's *Crónica,* naturally the thorough historian must make prominent mention of the most celebrated—and wealthiest—of all, Potosí. Cieza's eleventh woodcut shows the colonial city, behind which steeply rises the hill of nearly pure silver, here labeled "Cerro de Potosí." It all began in 1547, when several Indians led by a Spaniard named Villarroel came across the nearly inexhaustible mother lode, and ever since that moment, in Spanish the word *Potosí* has come to signify endless riches. The abundance equally of gold and silver ores immediately attracted so many people that an initially ramshackle hamlet expanded quickly to become a real city with a population of 200,000. Potosí grew by accident, without plan. Toledo, the Spanish viceroy, soon put an end to the chaos, ordering the imposition in the flatlands below the silver hill of that stereotypical figure denoting modern urban planning, a grid plan *à la Vitruvienne*. Potosí was the first great New World gold rush, with all that would eventually come to signify for a still evolving, but uniquely American, get-rich-quick mentality.[22]

The twelfth woodcut in Cieza's *Crónica del Perú* deals with a completely different New World topic (Fig. 45). Discussing various animals uniquely indigenous to Peru, Cieza mentions (chapter 111) the most distinctive of all Andean species, *los llamas,* which name he cites as having always been used by the natives. He also observes how these camellike animals are well suited to the Indians, indeed are essential for their survival; uniquely adapted to the great elevations corresponding to the Andes, the llama serves as a beast of burden and provides his keepers with both meat and clothing. As our author is European, it was perhaps only natural that he would call them "sheep" (*ovejas*), even though, with superior hindsight, we now recognize llamas — as well as alpacas and vicuñas — to be related to the dromedary family. Obviously, study of American zoology was still in its infancy. The first serious speculations in detail about New World fauna come from Gonzalo Fernán-

45.
"A Herd of Llamas in Peru,"
from P. Cieza de León, Crónica
del Perú (Antwerp, 1554).

dez de Oviedo, who placed woodcuts of various uniquely American animals in his justly famous work called *Historia General de las Indias* (first published in Salamanca in 1547).

The intrinsically odd nature of the llama, to return to a particular point of concern to Cieza, also caught the attention of another important Spanish chronicler, Padre José de Acosta. In his *Historia natural y moral de las Indias* (book 4, chapter 26), Acosta attempts to deal with the interesting question of why certain animals are encountered in *las Indias* that are found in no other parts of the world. Since our author is a devout Christian, even a priest, he weights the novel biological question *filosóficamente,* applying to it various notions derived from Scripture. As he argues, all animals known today had been put into Noah's Ark, which is how it must be, for so it was told in the Book of Genesis. Still, how does one account for any subsequent zoological diversity, the anomalous llama being an excellent case in point? Acosta supposes that once Noah had disembarked his heterogeneous cargo, certain species of animals, whether by natural instinct or through heavenly providence, came to end up in entirely diverse places. Some sites proved so pleasing to certain breeds that they chose never to leave them. The inquisitive padre concludes that even if certain egregious beasts, for instance the llama, were once found in different places, they had since all died off. A further cause of speculation by Acosta might have been a contemporaneous near extinction of the Incas.

Even though this final digression about the llama really has nothing directly to do with our real subject matter, the picturing of (human) American Indians by Europeans during the Renaissance, as expounded by Father Acosta and illustrated in Cienza, it is a delight in itself, as are the rest of the illustrations in the extremely rare 1554 Flemish edition of Cieza de León's *Crónica del Perú.*

Antonio de Herrera's Episodic American Frontispiece

Since he was actually employed as a professional historian, Antonio de Herrera y Tordesillas represents a unique case among the various authors discussed here. Born in 1549, by 1596 he bore the prestigious title of *Cronista Mayor de Indias.* He began his literary career with several biographies of important personages, publications establishing his reputation as a historian well before he came to compose his magnum opus, the *Historia general de los hechos de los castellanos en las islas y tierra firme del mar océano* (Fig. 45). This ambitious work was published in 1601 in Madrid by the Imprenta Real (Royal Publishing House), and quickly became known in abbreviated form (à la Livy) as his *Decades.* Since a century of historical perspective allowed him the unique advantage of viewing earlier events in their real dimensions, Herrera turns out to be the most thorough historian of the Indies in his period. Unfortunately, due to his cumbersome prose, he does not turn out to be the most readable. Due, however, to his uniquely privileged titular position as "Principal Chronicler of the Indies," also paying him a handsome stipend, Herrera had a nearly unique access to not only standard published histories but also some firsthand reports, existing only in manuscript form in the State Archives and only intended for official inspection. Accordingly, Herrera provided the first summaries of certain important documents that only came to be published in full much later by Martín Fernández de Navarrete (in his *Colección de los Viages . . . ,* 1825–37).

As is indicated by the title of Herrera's work, this is basically an officially funded, narrative history of "The Deeds of the Castilians" in what had become Spanish America; consequently, this historian has scant interest in matters narrowly relating to Native Americans. In this context, we need only briefly discuss the lavishly illustrated frontispiece of his *Historia General,* for this is the most elaborately decorated *portada* of any such historical account published in Spain (Fig. 46). Engraved portraits of the major actors in the Spanish conquest of America—Hernán Cortés, Hernando Magallanes (or Magellan), Cristóbal de Olid, and Gonzalo de Sandoval—appear in four medallions, placed in each corner. Enframing the placardlike printed title are ten square vignettes schematically picturing characteristic episodes—land battles and naval exercises—illustrating the careers of Cortés and Magellan. For a later reprinting of the *Historia General,* in 1730, a radically different frontispiece was designed. Oddly enough, even though the text of Herrera's massive tome did not deal in any significant detail with the native peoples of Spanish America, the eighteenth-century *portada* displays a number of Indian motifs, all carefully labeled. Obviously, this change of ethnic emphasis, from *castellanos* to *indios,* was due to a shift of taste characteristic of the later period, later called an "Age of Enlightenment."

It was a different matter in 1601. Engraved vignettes occupying the left side of the composition refer to the martial deeds of Cortés. At the

46.

*Title page: A. de Herrera, Historia General de los hechos de los castellanos
(Madrid, 1601)..*

very top, next to a portrait of the conqueror of Mexico, appears a bird's-eye view of "la gran ciudad de México en la laguna." A complete explanation of this highly compressed scene appears in Herrera's text:

> Mexico City, or Tenochtitlán, although of great size, is completely sur-rounded by fresh water for it is situated within a lake. There are only three ways to enter it, by as many paved roads: One comes from the west and is half a league in length; another runs from the north and is a league long. There is no way to enter from the east, except by boat. . . . A great quantity of salt is prepared on the shores of this lake; there is much traf-fic in this material. More than a hundred thousand *canoas* are engaged in this commercial enterprise. Canoes are small boats made from a single log which have the appearance of a weaver's shuttle; the Indians also call them *achales,* which means house-boat. Spaniards who have lived in Cuba or Santo Domingo, becoming familiar with native language in those islands, instead choose to call them *canoas;* in the same way, they have applied any number of Carib names to many other things. In order to provide water for Mexico City, and also serving as means of transport and communication, there are some 5,000 canals running throughout the city; just as in the lake alongside, these canals are always filled with canoes. This lively commerce is well worth seeing.[23]

The next vignette, appearing on the left side of Herrera's title-page, is labeled "Aquí fué preso el Rey Quantimocco" and depicts the capture of the Aztec leader Cuauhtémoc by Cortés during his attack on Tenochtitlán. Herrera's published source for this particular episode was López de Gómara, who presented a most lively account of dramatic moments leading up the taking of the Aztec capital by the Spaniards. The earlier historian had put the following speech, a rhetorical model à la Livy of nobility under duress, into the mouth of the captive monarch: "I have done everything possible and whatever was necessary in order to defend myself and my people. It was all done so that we would not come to that condition and place in which I now find myself. Well, now you may do with me as you please. Kill me; that would be best."[24]

The next engraved episode—*El Rey de Mechocan visita a Cortés*—refers to the reception of the Spanish leader by the brother of Cazoncin, the Indian king of the province of Michoacán. News of the fall of Tenochtitlán and the subsequent collapse of Aztec rule sent shock waves throughout Mexico.

Cortés immediately began to receive delegations from native peoples who had formerly been unwilling subjects of the Aztec lords. The Spanish leader knew how to take best advantage of these visits; besides courting favor with his visitors by presents, he also intimidated them with displays of calvary, warships, and firearms. The ambassadors from Michoacán were just one of many Mexican tribes to be overawed by carefully orchestrated demonstrations of Spanish martial prowess.

The next picture — *El ejército castellano camina a las Ybueras* — depicts the march of the Spanish army to Higueras under the command of Cortés's favored lieutenant, Cristóbal de Olid. This scene calls for another, even more menacing, martial display of European technology. Besides an awesome exhibition of firepower from Spanish infantry and artillery, one also notes the presence of a recalcitrant Indian hanging from a gallows while yet another is shown to be set to roast upon a roaring bonfire. Finally, at the bottom of the page one arrives at the fifth picture — *México se reedifica* — referring to a more positive approach to pacification of New Spain, rebuilding the destroyed Aztec capital. According to López de Gómara, Cortés valued the prestige of the Aztec capital, which could now be turned to Spanish advantage, and he himself supervised designs for the reconstruction of Tenochtitlán as Ciudad Méjico. Leaving aside ample spaces for plazas, churches, and government buildings, all of which would be laid out in the Vitruvian manner, Cortés also supervised the construction of arsenals and fortifications to ensure a continuing Spanish hegemony over their newly subjected Indian vassals.

Four of the five engravings placed on the right side of the title page deal with the exploits of Ferdinand Magellan, and the last in the series depicts his momentous circumnavigation of the globe, leading to a dispute over the partitioning of the world. Herrera explained in his *Historia General* (book 5, chapter 14) how Magellan found the strait bearing his name in 1520, as is illustrated in the vignette placed beside his medallion-portrait: *Descubre Magallanes el estrecho.* Here we see the Patagonians, those largely fictitious Indian Big Foot-giants of the subequatorial regions, shooting arrows at diminutive European ships attempting passage of their straits; besides remarking upon their height, Herrera also noted their dexterity with their bows and arrows: "eran tan diestros en flechar."[25] Herrera's primary source for these episodes was Antonio de Pigafetta's eyewitness account of a momentous *Primer viaje alrededor del mundo.* Here, among other anecdotes, the

Italian sailor described the capture of the pathetic *gigante patagón,* whom the Europeans named Juan, and who shortly afterward expired from pure chagrin. The next vignette — *Magallanes pasa a la mar del Sur* — depicts an initial entry of the Europeans into the "Southern Sea," or Pacific Ocean. The current name would not have been so employed by Magellan and his sorely tried men; scarcely "pacific," their passage from east to west was stormy and they suffered greatly from scurvy.

Magellan was killed by Malays on the island of Mactan in the Philippine Archipelago on April 26, 1521. Nonetheless, the label belonging to the print that corresponds to this episode would instead attribute the demise of the Portuguese captain to murderous "Indians": "Muere Magallanes peleando con los indios." As Pigafetta recalled the actual event: "Recognizing the captain [Magellan], the natives concentrated their attack upon his person, knocking his helmet from his head twice. Nevertheless, being a stout hearted gentleman, he soldiered on bravely. . . . They fell like rain upon him, either sticking him with bamboo lances tipped with iron or lashing out at him with their swords. This scuffle lasted until, finally, our mirror, our light, our comfort, our peerless guide, fell dead at our feet."[26]

Leadership of the Magellan expedition was then taken over by a controversial figure, Juan Sebastián Elcano. Born around 1476 in Guetaria (Vascongadas), this intrepid Basque sailor previously captained his own ship in the African trade. Buried in debt, Elcano sold his boat and, attracted by profits promised in unfolding American adventures, went to Seville, the principal point of departure for the New World. Elcano signed on with Magellan, and was seconded to the *Concepción.* After Magellan's death, it was Elcano who was to carry on leadership of what was left of the expeditionary force. From the Moluccas to Seville, he steered westward in the single surviving ship, the *Victoria.* Elcano's arrival in Spain — *La nao Victoria llega a Sevilla, rodeado el mundo* — is shown in the next to last vignette. Nearly three years after having set forth, with only eighteen sailors surviving, the starving and scurvy-ridden remnants of Magellan's unprecedented expedition finally returned to the port from which they so optimistically departed so long before.

The last scene included in the frontispiece of the *Historia General,* in the lower right corner, seems out of place since it bears no direct relation with the deeds of either Cortés or Magellan. Nonetheless, it does fit the larger historical context for it refers an important event put at the very beginning of Herrera's narrative history, the political division of the world resulting from Columbus's discoveries of new worlds: *Dispútase en la partición del mundo.* The various disputing parties, wildly gesticulating and armed with a world globe and surveying instruments, are shown seated at a conference table awkwardly straddling a river, presumably the Tiber. The results of these excited negotiations were various papal bulls issued in 1493 by Alexander VI. Not long after Columbus arrived in Lisbon from his first voyage, João II, king of Portugal, tried to lay claim to the New World discovered by an intrepid Genoese sailor flying the Spanish flag. The most important of these papal decrees was the bull called *Inter Coetera* II, granting to Spain future dominion over all newly discovered lands, lying beyond Europe along a certain line traced from the Arctic to Antarctic poles, as somewhat arbitrarily placed "one hundred leagues west" of the Azores and Cape Verde. Other than Brazil, the tip of which just happened to fall within this line, Portugal was completely shut out of America.

Even though any references to *los indios* encountered in the series of engravings decorating the title page of Herrera's *Historia General* are mainly oblique at best, we have dealt with these vignettes at some length due to the early date of their conception and, additionally, because Herrera was one of the very few Spanish historians who actually chose to illustrate American subject matter. In any event, the very absence, except as vanquished victims, of *los indios* in this general history of Spanish America, is itself a vividly illustrative "negative proof" of their real significance in the eyes of their European masters.

Honorius Philoponus on an Apocryphal Apostle to the American Indies

To any discussions of illustrated books issuing from northern European presses treating American themes another should be added, especially as this interesting volume has not previously been discussed by scholars according to our specifically American art historical context. The publication in question is the *Nova typis navigatio novi orbis Indiae Occidentalis,* which was published in 1621, probably in Linz, Austria (Fig. 47).[27] According to a lengthy Latin subtitle, the real subject of the treatise was the evangelization of the "barbarous" peoples belonging to the "Western Indies of the New World." Its author was a Benedictine monk whose nom de plume is

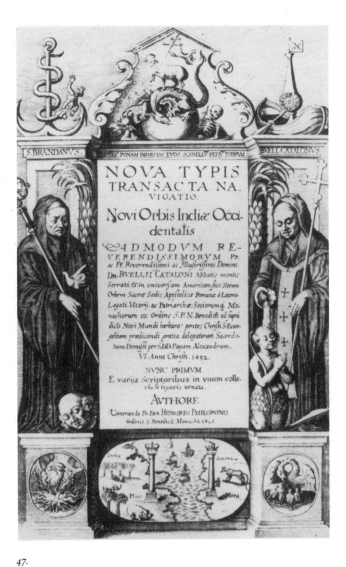

47.

Title page: H. Philoponius, Nova typis transacta navigatio Novi Orbis Indiae Occidentalis (Linz, 1621)..

Honorius Philoponus, or Philonus (1556–1627). As for the real name of the pseudonymous monkish author, no one really knows, but some have proposed Caspar Plautus, or Plautius. In any event, Philoponus-Plautius states that he had composed this most curious history of the imposition of Christianity upon the *Novi Orbis Indiae Occidentalis* within the solitude of his cell in the Seidenstetten Monastery.

In any traditional scholarly survey of the development of American historiography, this book would, if even mentioned, only be recognized to have scant significance; its author frankly states in his preface that he has largely relied upon notices coming from such standard publications as the histories of Pedro Mártir de Angleria and López de Gómara. For the art historian, particularly ones focusing upon American iconography, the principal novelty of this illustrated book will be found in its frontispiece and a few other copperplate engravings dealing with similar "Indian" issues. All the rest of Philoponus's graphic materials mostly only appear to repeat images belonging to a famous portfolio of New World prints, collectively called *America,* and published beginning in 1590 in Frankfurt by the de Bry brothers (and as will be later commented upon in some detail by us). The few designs that are completely original to Philoponus's text were conceived by Wolfgang Kilian; although he only signed one plate, portraying Columbus, all the other compositions not obviously stemming from the de Brys' publications are presumed to be his. Although Kilian (1581–1662) lived nearly all his life in Augsburg, he received his professional training as a printmaker in Venice, where he excelled at engraved copies of paintings by the great Italian masters.

The compositional format of Kilian's title page reprises a typical Baroque, pseudo-architectural motif, a niched altarpiece with a pedestal-socle. This commonplace device allows for illusionistic combinations of illustrative vignettes showing sculptures or paintings. The extended titular text, centrally situated, is presented in the form of an incised marble slab. This title-slab is flanked by trompe l'oeil portrait-statues of two famous monks, one essentially fabulous and the other historical. On the left is "S. Brandanus," the Irish monk famed for his mythic Atlantic voyages, and to the right is a Catalan Benedictine, Friar Bernardo de Boyl (or, as here, "Buell" in a Latin transcription), to whose indefatigable missionary labors the pseudonymous Philoponus dedicated his unusual book. In a gable at the top of the pseudo-retable is placed another simulated sculptural composition. Flanked by personifications of Death and the Devil, we see a world globe crushed under the weight of an enormous dragon. Above these familiar symbols of evil (here meaning barbarism or false religion), stands the triumphal figure of the mystic lamb, or Christ; the *Agnus Dei* in turn crushes underfoot the dragon of heresy. Placed on either corner are a pair of nautical symbols: a ship with a huge compass flying under the papal flag and an anchor with a serpent wrapped around it that has just seized a frog in its jaws. The metaphorical base of this allegorized missionary structure contains an oval vignette emblematically representing the Habsburg Empire. Several ships sail between the Columns of Hercules, inscribed with the motto *Plus Ultra* ("Yet Further") and resting solidly upon two continents, India and America, both home to "Indians," one land identified by elephants and the other with an armadillo. On either corner are placed two emblematic medallions, respectively containing a pelican and a salamander, symbolizing that self-sacrificing impulse necessary to bring glad tidings about the love of Christ to, and for, mobs of recalcitrant pagans situated in India-America.

This observation brings us back to the principal, sculpturelike figures of Saint Brendan and Friar Boyl. Both are characterized as being American missionaries; Brendan stands over a broken pagan idol, and Boyl is seen baptizing a kneeling American Indian. The Irish monk, who is believed to have died around 580, was (by some stretch of the imagination) often taken to represent a precursor of Columbus—a thousand years before. According to the familiar legend of Brendan's transoceanic voyages, he and fourteen other monks embarked upon an arduous Atlantic journey lasting seven years. Their most well-regarded anchorage was in the "Islands of the Blest" (*Islas de los Bienaventurados*). Whereas some (after 1493) took this mid-Atlantic archipelago to be the Antilles of the Caribbean, others took it to be the Canary Islands—which were themselves commonly dubbed the "Fortunate Isles" (*Insulae Fortunatae*) by innumerable prestigious authors, ranging from Plutarch to Pliny, and also including St. Isidore of Seville. Philoponus's illustrator, Kilian, obviously opted for the second, much more tradition location (as shown in Fig. 48). In any event, seven years after his departure, an angel appeared to Brendan, ordering him to return home to Europe in order to broadcast news of the visionary marvels he had encountered westward.[28]

Regarding the Benedictine monk on the right, the Spaniard Boyl or Buell, we do have an abundance of authentic historical documentation, even including writings from his own hand. It appears that he was born around 1445, most likely in Catalonia, but others say around Valencia or even in Aragón; it is however known that he was educated in Zaragoza, in the court of Ferdinand II, where he translated Latin texts belonging to the *Collationes* of Abbot Isaac. Since his youth, Bernardo de Boyl was employed by Ferdinand the Catholic, who named him his counselor and private secretary; in 1479, he was appointed *comisario de guerra* during a campaign to put Sardinia under Aragonese rule. In 1480, however, he became a hermit in the famous Catalan monastery of Montserrat; following a year of study, he took up holy orders. Named vicar-general of Montserrat, Boyl saw that his monastery required reform, a plan for which he presented to the Catholic Kings. Named Spanish ambassador to France, in Tours he came personally to know St. Francis de Paul, founder of the Minimite Order; he himself entered into this order. He returned to Spain as vicar-general of Minimites; in 1493, he founded in Málaga the convent of Santa María de la Victoria.

On the occasion of Columbus's second voyage to America, King Ferdinand ordered Boyl to go to the Indies as his pontifical vicar. He sailed in 1493 and remained for a year in the town of La Isabela, which had just been founded in La Española. Following some rancorous disputes with Columbus, Boyl returned to Spain. It seems the friar-monk was unable to adapt himself to the New World, especially to rough and disorderly *conquistadores* who already dominated the overseas colonies. The last straw for Boyl was his linguistic difficulties, frustrating all his attempts to convert the Indians. His brief American adventure over, he continued to be entrusted with sensitive diplomatic missions. Finally, following a recommendation of the Catholic Kings, Boyl was made abbot of Cuxá in Catalonia; here he was to die around 1506.[29] Even though Philoponus chose to call him a *patriarca,* Boyl was never that, nor was he ever appointed a bishop in America. Because of the notable failure of his American mission, in no way does he earn the title granted him here, as "the first American Apostle." Consequently, the way he is pictured in the *Nova typis,* in the act of baptizing a smiling and undersized American *indio,* represents purely rhetorical symbolism.

The first picture in Philoponus's book provides a curious portrayal of Columbus. As "Almirante de nauios para las Indias," or so states the caption, the Genoese discoverer is shown placed against an oceanic background; beside him are his nautical instruments and a wholly circular *mappamundi.* The latter refers to Columbus's famous statement that "el mundo es re-

48.

"St. Brendan and the Island-Whale," from Nova typis transacta navigatio Novi Orbis Indiae Occidentalis (Linz, 1621).

dondo y no llano," just as López de Gómara declared at the beginning of his often-cited book.[30] Nonetheless, by far Kilian's most original effort for Philoponus's odd volume is his second engraving (Fig. 48), picturing a thoroughly fabulous "Whale Island." Although it has been reproduced in various publications, its context in the *Nova typis* has never been specified. Even though Kilian probably did not have at hand any graphic model for this striking composition, its background is nonetheless composed just like arrangements typically seen in some much older, early-sixteenth-century maps of the Atlantic (see Figs. 9–11). To the east, the silhouette of the Iberian Peninsula and the northwestern shores of Africa can be made out; to the far west and south are the seven Canary Islands, also called here, according to hoary traditions, the *Insulae Fortunatae*. North of these fabled Isles of the Blest appears the equally apocryphal *Insula Sancto Brandano*. The literal centerpiece of the composition is an enormous, and zoologically impossible, whale surrounded by galleons under full sail. An altar table, with crucifix and burning candles, has been set up upon the back of a slumbering marine monster; kneeling reverently before it, in order to take part in the Holy Mass, are the doughty Irish saint and his devoted Celtic followers.

The oldest Latin manuscript recounting this adventure, the *Navigatio Sancti Brandanni,* dates to the tenth century (and is quoted from in Chapter 1). Adding odd bits of scriptural references and pagan legends, in the twelfth century Archbishop Benedeit further embroidered the poetic saga detailing adventures befalling the Irish monk during his prolonged search for the Earthly Paradise. As was told here, Abbot Brendan, carrying in his veins the blood of Irish kings, chose fourteen devout and stalwart companions, constructed his own post-Noah Ark, and went off to explore "the ends of the earth." Brendan's most evocative adventure is the one taking place on a certain Fish Island, which the credulous monks take to be an unknown chunk of land unmoored to the ocean bottom, and upon which they disembark, so to set up their liturgical goods in order to celebrate Easter Mass. Finished with their holy rites, the monks then lit a fire on the island in preparation for their midday meal. Fear is struck in their hearts as their island sanctuary begins to shake and quiver in alarming fashion. Brendan, however, has a handy explanation for them: "So you know, oh brothers, the reason for which you have experienced so much fear. It is because we have celebrated our sacred feast, not upon dry land but instead upon the back of a beast, a marine animal—one of the very biggest." [31]

In the twelfth century Honorius of Autun also wrote about Brendan's Isle in his *Imago mundi.* For Honorius, this was the Promised Land, a refuge uniquely apportioned to the saints; accordingly, for this northern European it is a place blessed with bright sunlight, plentiful springs, flowers and fruits. These felicitous traits constitute the same topographical topoi characterizing a *Paradisus terrestris* that had been around for centuries, at least in the minds of devout Christians; similarly, these were topoi Columbus was to apply centuries later to an American Eden he opportunely found at the mouth of the Orinoco. St. Brendan's Island was also known the "Lost Isle"; as soon as it was espied by sailors, it disappeared again. Next to the island of *Ante-ilha,* or Antillia, Brendan's Island was to resurface upon nearly all the *mappaemundi* designed during the Middle Ages—and even in some of the early Renaissance (see, for example, Figs. 3–7, 9–11). From the sixteenth until the eighteenth century, pursuit of this necessarily elusive island would provide the impetus for new adventurers; among those so moved were, beginning in 1526, Fernández de Troya, Hernán Pérez de Grado, Friar Lorenzo de Pineda, and even including Gaspar Domínguez in 1721.[32]

All of this legendary maritime substratum is present as late as the early seventeenth century in Kilian's magnificently evocative picturing of a monk-ridden Whale Island. Another motif points to different, but complementary, legendary materials. The foreground of Philoponius's print shows another vessel, a row boat. Two monks are reading while another rows them along; the steersman had light streaming from his face. Since Brendan is already shown elsewhere, leading the celebration of the Mass on the somnolent whale's back, it appears that Kilian here alludes to the presence of Saint Maclovius (Maclou or Malo), because the text of the *Nova typis* specifies that Malo was one of Brendan's seagoing companions.[33] In the event, St. Malo is a much better documented historical personage than is Brendan.[34] Towards the year 550, he established himself along the English Channel, in *Armorica* (Brittany), and eventually became bishop of Alet. The important French port of St. Malo today bears his name, from whence hardy Breton sailors, *les malouines,* much later sailed far south into the Atlantic to discover the Islas Malvinas, so called by the Argentines but better known to Britons as the Falkland Islands. Little by little, legend overtook the facts of Malo's life, and so it becomes a "fact" in 1621 that he actually accompanied Brendan in his visionary quest for the Earthly Paradise hidden within the Atlantic; accordingly both must have participated in the unlikely encounter with the rudely awakened whale.

The third print in the *Nova typis* depicts Pope Alexander VI receiving the dramatic news of the discovery of America from the Spanish ambassador in Rome. Immediately afterward the Bull of 1493 was issued by the Pope, donating *las Indias del Nuevo Mundo* to the Spanish *Reyes Católicos.* Departing completely from historical fact, Kilian makes this the moment when Bernard Boyl is named *vicario pontífico* at the request of Ferdinand and Isabella. Otherwise Philoponus's text followed López de Gómara, who transcribed the entirety of the momentous papal bull.[35] A fourth engraving again portrayed the Spanish kings, now showing them standing upon a seashore, bidding farewell to a fleet setting sail for the Indies. Among the departing sailors an outsized figure wearing liturgical garments, carrying a cross, and waving a flag emblazoned with the keys of St. Peter, stands out; this can be none other than Friar Bernard Boyl. According to its in-

scription, the fifth print depicts the dramatic arrival of the Spanish ships at
Insulae Canibalium, the Cannibal Archipelago. In this instance, it appears that
Kilian took advantage of two artistic prototypes; besides various splendidly
engraved graphic models to be found in the *Voyages* series of Theodore de
Bry, probably reference was also made to the crude woodcuts contained
in the account of Hans Staden, as published in Marburg in 1557.[36] Particularly the cannibalistic episodes, and even the kind of barrel-vaulted straw
huts depicted here, seem to point to earlier pictorial prototypes of the sorts
we have already discussed. In any event, such motifs had already, by 1621,
become iconographic commonplaces.[37]

The sixth print in the *Nova typis* made a different reference to the much
misunderstood Carib Indians. A native chieftain, or *cacique,* is shown standing upon a seashore in front of a temple dedicated to the Arawak winged
god-devil receiving tributes of fruit; on the right side a Spanish adventurer
graciously accepts an invitation to dine at the table of fearful American
people-eaters. The next print shows Benedictine friars destroying temples
and idols—both most un-American in appearance—supposedly belonging
to the New World pagans. Not surprisingly, the Indians react badly to such
monkish (and discourteous) iconoclasm, and proceed handily to slaughter
the intrusive European missionaries. Once again we have another Kilian
print that seems to be directly inspired by the precedent of de Bry's widely
circulated engravings appearing in the *Grandes voyages* and *Petits voyages* published in the last decade of the sixteenth century and collectively called
"America."[38]

Kilian's eighth print again deals with celebrated indigenous idols of
patently diabolic character, the most common of which was called *zemis*
by the locals (see the idol shown in Fig. 50), and about which extensive
descriptions were published much earlier in the sixteenth century. Referring to the Arawak Indians of La Española, Gonzalo Fernández de Oviedo
breathlessly writes (*Historia natural,* book 3, chapter 1) that

> I have only found among this generation of Indians one object which
> has been painted or sculpted, or made in bas-relief, since time immemo-
> rial; and nothing among them is so respected, so venerated, as is the
> abominable and most un-godly and sacrilegious figure of the Devil. It
> can be represented [by their artisans] in many different manners, whether

painted and sculpted or carved; it is always shown however with many hands and tails, all of which are deformed and frightening, and it is depicted with ferocious, doglike teeth and with huge jaws and outsized eyes. It has the flashing eyes belonging to a dragon or a ferocious serpent. It is shown in many diverse fashions, and even the least horrific of these must still inspire fear and awe. . . . To these idols they will give the name of *zemi,* and this is what they take to be their god.[39]

The tenth print in the *Nova typis* deals with forcible conversions of the Indians and illustrates textual materials drawn by Philoponus from the thirty-fourth chapter of the *Historia general* by López de Gómara. Kilian shows Friar Boyl raising a cross while he baptizes the natives, and the other two European figures in the print are Pedro Juárez de Deza, declared the first bishop in America, and also Alessandro Geraldini, an emissary from Rome who later became the second bishop of Santo Domingo in La Española.[40] Ferdinand and Isabella personally began the process of the conversion of the Americas in Barcelona by dragging to the baptismal font six Native Americans brought as slaves by Christopher Columbus to Europe in 1493. Mass conversion of the Indians in the Caribbean only succeeded once their idols were systematically smashed and their temples leveled by intrusive Spaniard iconoclasts. Kilian's print alludes to this transaction by showing tiny figures of laborer-friars who, with a cart and wheelbarrows, are starting to build new temples belonging to a newly imposed, all-American Catholic faith.

A whale that became an island in the Atlantic is not the only fanciful marine creature to be found in the *Nova typis* (Fig. 49). The other one—*el manatí*—is, however, a real American animal, even though Kilian succeeds it making it look like an apparition derived from some devil-ridden medieval nightmare of the Last Judgment. The initial mention of a manatee was published by Pedro Mártir de Anglería; in his *Décadas* (book I, cap. 8), he said that its name was actually invented by Spaniards since the creatures appeared to have hands—*manos*—at the ends of their short forelegs. Another of Philoponus's acknowledged textual sources was Fernández de Oviedo, who actually did see the strange Caribbean animal (as Kilian never did); in his long commentary on the manatee, he carefully points out that, even though it is much bigger than a shark, neither Pliny nor Albertus Magnus had ever heard of it. As described by Oviedo, "The head of this fish is like an ox's, only bigger; it has tiny eyes. Lacking arms, it swims by using two thick, heellike appendages; these are placed high up on its body, next to its head."[41]

However, given the curious anecdotal impetus of Kilian's composition, we know Philoponius's narrative to reflect directly a different textual source, an exotic narrative reported by López de Gómara in the thirty-first chapter of his *Historia general*. Gómara's anecdote concerns a certain Arawak *cacique,* Carameteji, who caught a young manatee. He kept the fish-like mammal in a pond for twenty-six years and even succeeded in taming it. Kilian's print is a faithful re-creation in its various piquant details of an observation made by Gómara, namely that the Indian's manatee would actually "romp on the shores with the boys and men; it displayed pleasure when they sang, and would even let them ride upon his back."

The *Nova typis* concluded with a negative interpretation of the effects of European culture as it had been imposed upon Native America by Spaniards. Contemporary accounts vividly reporting instances of Spanish cruelty, particularly as reported by de Bry and Benzoni (as their works will

49.

"An Indian Chieftain's Domesticated Manatee," Nova typis transacta navigatio Novi Orbis Indiae Occidentalis (Linz, 1621).

50.

"American Cannibalistic Orgies," Nova typis transacta navigatio Novi Orbis Indiae Occidentalis (Linz, 1621).

be later discussed), even had their effect on Philoponus, a monkish author sequestered in an Austrian monastery. Nevertheless, the seventeenth plate insists in turn on the cruelty belonging to the natives; here their generically bad customs are characterized by several variations upon the familiar, by now shopworn, theme of the Native American cannibal feast (Fig. 50). In this instance, a somewhat novel touch is provided by a big-mouthed *zemi-*idol being fed human parts in the upper left hand corner of the print. Oddly, a devilishly gluttonous sculpture supposedly unique to American savagery is sheltered within a fragile domed structure supported upon slim columns that could have only been imagined in Baroque Austria.

5

AN INDIAN EDEN LOST

The Entrance of an American Anti-Eden

Medieval allegory reveled in typology, a symbolic representation by signs of things to come, events prophesied or shadowed forth by the initial type. Thus, just as Eros has his Anteros, so must every purported Eden on Earth eventually have imposed upon it its very own preordained historical fulfillment, an antithetical Anti-Eden. For either inhabitants or their habitats, wherever they may be found, there are equally types and anti-types. For want of current geographical facts verifying its actual topographical existence (and we have recounted the many attempts to place the elusive *Paradisus terrestris* upon the medieval mappaemundi), we must now conclude that Eden was, and still is entirely, a state of the optimistic and ever-credulous human mind. But this seems an exclusively modern—and, therefore, cynically unimaginative—cosmographical assessment. However if you really believed in the Earthly Paradise, as Christopher Columbus certainly did, once you opportunely found a spot that fit the conventional

Edenic topographical formulas—soft and perfumed breezes wafting under cloudless skies, azure seas prettily plashing upon golden beaches, effortless floral fecundity, sweet bird-song, lush green hills, dusky and compliant maidens—then you knew (for a while at least) that you had finally found Eden on Earth.

The ever-optimistic and ever-deluded Don Quijote (Book 1, ch. 67) thought that he, too, had found Eden on Earth in the return of the Golden Age: "This must be the meadow where we shall encounter spritely goatgirls and elegant shepherds who, through mime, desired to renovate pastoral Arcadia upon this very spot." Alas, the real Edens (and even the Arcadias) on the real Earth never have physically lived up to (or effectively mimed) the grand expectations initially linking them to their immaculate mental prototypes. In the real Edens on Earth, mind rarely (if ever) triumphs over recalcitrant matter. If it's not the heat, then it's the humidity; if it's not the pesky mosquitoes, then it's the immeasurably alien locals.

In 1492, the American Indians, quite unaware that they had ever been lost (either physically or spiritually), remained oblivious to their fortuitous "discovery" and invention by Europeans during the Renaissance. In fact, all that one knew (until fairly recently) about this first, eventually fatal, encounter in an anomalously tropical Arcadia is what the Spaniards had told the world. Concerning the (opposing) aboriginal viewpoint, Renaissance Europeans really knew nothing. The original inhabitants of the New World neither called themselves by a single term, nor did they understand themselves to represent a collective body. The indigenous peoples of Mexico were wholly different from those of the Caribbean, nor was a sophisticated realm like the Peru of the Incas really anything like the Aztec Empire. Nonetheless, to conquistadores, all these richly diverse peoples were mostly all lumped together, as *indios*.

Be that as it may, the conclusion to be drawn in this final chapter is a given: The idea and the resulting, nearly perennial image of the Indians of the Americas must be entirely an European invention, meaning another work of art and largely malign artifice.[1] The most obvious surviving artifact is the very term Indian; due to Columbus's erroneous, egregious, and largely scripturalized geographical misconception of the world at large, he called the locals *los indios*. After all, who else lives in India? As is additionally apparent, to Columbus and his motley accomplices the term *India* was synonymous with nearly all of Asia, at least those tropical parts to be found east of the Indus River and south of Cipangu and Quinsay.

In his standard biography of Christopher Columbus (*Admiral of the Ocean Sea,* 1942), Samuel Eliot Morison bluntly stated that his adventurous hero had, in effect, single-handedly invented the concept of the Noble Savage. As he observed,

> To the intellectuals of Europe, it seemed that Columbus had stepped back several millennia, and encountered people living in the Golden Age, that bright morning of humanity which existed only in the imagination of poets. Columbus's discovery enabled Europeans to see their own ancestors, as it were, in a "state of nature," before Pandora's box was opened. The "virtuous savage" myth, which reached its height in the eighteenth century, began at Guanahaní on October 12, 1492.[2]

As Morison and other scholars have additionally pointed out, it was Pietro Martire d'Anghiera who, in his widely read *Decades de Orbe Novo,* mainly gave the idea currency in Europe. His *Decades* were often republished and translated and, according to Martyr's version of a pristine American Eden,

> It appears to me that our islanders [the Indians] on Hispaniola are to be made even happier once they receive [Christian] religion. They have lived in the Age of Gold: naked, without weights or measures, without death-giving money, without laws, without judges assigning guilt, without books. Being content with Nature herself, they live without any thought whatsoever for what the future might bring them. . . . They hold it to be certain that the earth, just like the sun and the water, represents common property, and, thus, that there must not be among them any thought of mine and thine [*meum et tuum*], which are the seeds of all evils; in that manner, they have contented themselves with so little in such a vast territory, where there is an abundance of land and where nobody ever wants for anything. For them, it is the Age of Gold. They do not enclose their holdings, neither with ditches, fences or with hedges; instead, they dwell in open gardens, without laws, with no books and no judges. By their very nature they venerate that which is correct. They hold to be an evil and perverse person whoever would take pleasure in doing an injury to anyone else.[3]

As it might appear to someone with a skeptical turn of mind, all those ubiquitous, supposedly modern concerns with ecological holistic thinking turn
out to represent just another result of the European invention of America
during the Renaissance. Just as in that period (as in Ripa's *Iconologia:* see Fig.
14), green is ever the color of *Spes* (Hope). However that may be, Peter
Martyr's enthusiastic discussion certainly does document a fact, namely that
the concept of the Noble Savage (as yet unnamed) was already, by 1510, a
long-standing topos and, additionally, that it was one that had been specifically attached to inhabitants of the Golden Age. Moreover, Martyr's nearly
automatic application of the antique notion to new materials, the Native
Americans, seems sufficient to disallow Morison's ingenuous claim that the
idea "began at Guanahaní on October 12, 1492." As with the idea of Eden
and Arcadia, this concept of the Edenlike existence of the inhabitants of the
Golden Age is easily traced to its classical sources. Therefore, at the very least
it may be presumed that vague premonitions of these ancient topoi were
very much in the minds of the first Europeans who invented the incongruous idea of the American Indians dwelling in a paradisiacal Golden Age.

There were, in fact, two opposing inventions of the American Indian
image after 1492, one "good" (Noble) and the other "bad" (Ignoble). Robert
F. Berkhofer has summarized the salient features of either attitude—as rhetorical conventions—relating to the native stock of the Americas as they
have been interpreted by Whites. On the one hand, the Good/Noble Indian

> appears friendly, courteous, and hospitable to the initial invaders of his
> lands and to all Whites. . . . Along with handsomeness of physique and
> physiognomy went great stamina and endurance. Modest in attitude if
> not always in dress, the noble Indian exhibited great calm and dignity in
> bearing, conversation, and even under torture. Brave in combat, he was
> tender in love for family and children. Pride in himself and indepen-
> dence of other persons combined with a plain existence and wholesome
> enjoyment of nature's gifts. According to this [positive] version, the
> Indian, in short, lived a life of liberty, simplicity, and innocence.

For every Edenic inhabitant there also exists his antithetical, Anti-Edenic
counterpart. On the other (left, or "sinister") hand, Berkhofer observes
how the Bad/Ignoble Indian broadly represents to disapproving white eyes

"nakedness, and lechery, passion and vanity," and these wholly undesirable traits

> led to lives of polygamy and sexual promiscuity among themselves, and constant warfare and fiendish revenge against their enemies. When [Indian] habits and customs were not brutal, they appeared loathsome to Whites. Cannibalism and human sacrifice were the worst sins, but cruelty to captives and incessant warfare ranked not far behind in the estimation of Whites. Filthy surroundings, inadequate cooking, and certain items of diet repulsive to White taste tended to confirm a low opinion of Indian life. Indolence rather than industry, improvidence in the face of scarcity, thievery and treachery added to the list of traits on this side. Concluding the bad version of the Indian were the power of superstition represented by the "conjurers" and "medicine men," the hard slavery of women and the laziness of men, and even timidity or defeat in the face of White advances and weaponry.[4]

Either way, good or bad, there was a classical (and also a derivative, medieval) textual precedent. The idealization of "savages"—"wild folk," as derived from the Latin *silvaticus,* an inhabitant of the forests—belongs to the larger topic of "primitivism." Primitivism is both a broadly cultural and largely achronological and nongeographical theme since the characterization arises from the concept of an ideal (meaning largely imagined), original or primordial, state that supposedly once applied to all mankind everywhere. Therefore, in the Renaissance present of the Columbian discoveries, primitivism could be reapplied to savages discovered in places isolated from the technological advances and purported benefits of modern European civilization. If the primitivist designation is applied in the positive sense, the standard, quite ancient topos is the Golden Age. In a negative sense, the now-traditional terms of definition, representing another, wholly modern invention never used by the ancients, are those of "hard primitivism."

The Classical Pedigree of the American Noble Savage

The earliest textual references to the positive sort of Noble Savage corresponded to the blissful inhabitants of the *Elysion pedion* or the *Insulae*

Fortunatae. As was told in the classical texts, both those insular proto-Edens were functionally analogous and well worth seeking westward, across the vast and darkening Ocean Sea. Other mythical tribal equivalents discussed by the pagan authors were the Hyperboreans, who lived "beyond the North Wind."[5] Less mythical for ancient writers were the Scythians, real savage peoples living in southern Russia who provided living models for hard primitivism *ante litteram*. Of course, with art historical hindsight we know a bit better today, for at least being familiar with the highly sophisticated artifacts of the Scythians, especially their gold work. Of them Herodotus (*Histories,* IV, 48) said that "no one could claim that they have any of the arts of civilized life"; as a result, "in most respects, I do not admire them."[6] The same kind of ethnographic information could, however, lead to an entirely different conclusion—no matter whether the targets were Asians or Americans. According to Justin's discussion of the Scythians (*Historiarum philippicarum epitoma,* II, ii),

> Justice is served by the tribe's inherent respect for it, not by laws. Theft is the most serious crime in their eyes, since, if they were permitted to steal, what would men, whose flocks and herds are in the woods unprotected by a roof, have left? They shun gold and silver—just as the rest of mortals seek it. They live [only] on milk and honey. . . . This moderation shows the justice of their way of life, for they desire nothing they do not possess. Indeed, the desire for riches exists only where there is a use for them. Would that the rest of mortals had similar moderation and regard for others' property! If so, there would not have been waged so many wars throughout the ages in all lands, nor would martial weapons destroy more men than does the natural course of fate. How wonderful indeed it would seem that Nature gave to the Scythians what the Greeks, by the long teaching of their sages and the precepts of their philosophers, were unable to attain; [the result being] that civilization may be surpassed by comparison with barbarism. In this case, so much more does ignorance of vice accomplish for the latter, the Scythians, than does knowledge of virtue for the former, the Greeks.[7]

Of all the Noble Savages of antiquity, all essential textual prototypes for the Renaissance invention of American "Indians," other than the geographically very distant Scythians doubtlessly within Europe itself the most discussed group were the Germans (*Germani*). The sylvan-dwelling Teutons first appear in their ennobled barbarian role in Julius Caesar's *Chronicles of the Gallic Wars* (51 B.C.). They then epitomized (as they have since, repeatedly) hard primitivism, particularly the kind characterized by predatory belligerency and wanton destructiveness wreaked upon usually terrified neighbors. Their better qualities were a hardy life-style and a healthy lack of interest in material possessions, traits likewise early attributed to Native Americans. As one reads in Caesar's *De bello gallico*, 1, 2,

> The customs of the Germans are entirely different [from the Gauls]. They have no Druid-priests to control religious observances [and] the only beings they recognize as gods are things that they actually can see, and by which they are obviously benefitted, such as Sun, Moon, and Fire; the other gods they have never even heard of. They spend all their lives in hunting and warlike pursuits, and inure themselves from childhood to toil and hardship. Those who preserve their chastity longest are most highly commended by their friends. . . . They attempt no concealment, however, of the facts of sex: men and women bathe together in the rivers, and they wear nothing but hides or short garments of hairy skin, which leave most of the body bare. The Germans are not agriculturalists, and they live principally upon milk, cheese, and meat. No one possesses any definite amount of land, nor has any private property. . . . They are not, therefore, anxious to acquire large estates, nor are they strongly tempted to dispossess the weak [and thus they avoid] becoming too fond of money—a frequent cause of division and strife.

Besides being precocious communists, alas, the Germans were also rapacious and bloodthirsty; much later, the same attributes were to become "American" traits. According to Caesar,

> The various tribes regard it as their greatest glory to lay waste to as much as possible of the land around them and to keep it uninhabited. They hold it a proof of a people's valor to drive their neighbors from their homes, so that no one dares settle near them. . . . When a tribe is attacked or intends to attack another, officers are chosen to conduct the campaign and are invested with powers of life and death. . . . No discredit attaches to plundering raids outside the tribal frontiers; the Germans say that they serve to keep the young men in training and prevent them from getting lazy. When a chief [*dux,* "a leader"; in modern German, *Führer*] announces in an assembly his intention of leading a raid and calls for

volunteers, those who like the proposal, and who approve of the man who makes it, stand up and promise their assistance amid the applause of the whole gathering. Anyone who backs out afterward is looked upon as a deserter and a traitor, and no one will ever trust him again.[8]

A century and a half later, a much more complete ethnographic description was provided by Tacitus in his *De Origine et situ Germanorum*. With Tacitus, the equivocal dichotomy in the German character, oscillating between selfless nobility and feral barbarism, is even more sharply etched. He remarks how Germany is known for "its forbidding landscapes and unpleasant climate; it is a country that is thankless to till and, for anyone who was not born and bred there, dismal to behold," being, "in general, covered either by bristling forests or by foul swamps." For an urbanized Roman distressed by a sense of the increasingly effete customs of his own countrymen, the most laudable quality of the rustic Germans was their enthusiasm for battle and their great valor and soldierly loyalty. According to Tacitus (*Germania,* xiv),

> On the field of battle it is a disgrace to a [German] chief to be surpassed in courage by his followers, and, to the followers, not to equal the courage of their chief. To leave a battle alive after their chief has fallen means lifelong infamy and shame. . . . The chiefs fight for victory, the followers for their chief. Many noble youths, if the land of their birth is stagnating in a long period of peace and inactivity, deliberately seek out other tribes which have some war in hand. For the Germans have no taste for peace; renown is more easily won among perils, and a large body of retainers cannot be kept together except by means of violence and wars. . . . A German is not so easily prevailed upon to plow the land and to wait patiently for harvest as he is to challenge a foe and earn wounds for his reward. He thinks it is tame and spiritless to accumulate slowly by the sweat of his brow what can be gotten quickly by the loss of a little blood. When not engaged in warfare, they spend a certain amount of time in hunting, but much more in idleness, thinking of nothing else but sleeping and eating. Thus dawdling away their time, they show a strange inconsistency—at one and the same time, they love indolence and hate peace.[9]

One might think that such preferred preoccupations as warfare or sloth would make for an Ignoble Savage, be he European or, later, American. Not so; according to Tacitus, in all other respects,

They live uncorrupted by the temptations of public shows or the excite-
ments of banquets. Clandestine love-letters are unknown to men and
women alike. Adultery is extremely rare. . . . No one in Germany finds
vice amusing, or calls it "up-to-date" to seduce or be seduced. . . . Good
morality is more effective in Germany than good laws are elsewhere. . . .
They develop that strength of limb and tall stature which excite our admiration. . . . The young master is not distinguished from the slave by
any pampering in his upbringing. They live together among the same
flocks and upon the same earthen floor.[10]

The same sorts of ancient European cultural values could, and would eventually be just as easily applied to the Native Americans. This point may
be quickly demonstrated by reference to the much later example of James
Fenimore Cooper, a white American author who established the Indian as a
significant literary type in world literature during the Victorian era. Eleven
of his immensely popular novels featured Indians; in so doing, he was not
at all deterred by the fact that he himself directly knew little (or nothing)
about the Native Americans. He commented, Tacitus-like, in the middle of
the nineteenth century concerning the Red Men and, in his fictionalized
accounting, they seem to become pseudo-Teutons:

Few men exhibit greater diversity, or, if we may so express it, greater antithesis of character, than the native warrior of North America. In war,
he is daring, boastful, cunning, ruthless, self-denying, and self-devoted;
in peace, just, generous, hospitable, revengeful, superstitious, modest,
and commonly chaste. These are qualities, it is true, which do not distinguish all alike; but they are so far the predominating traits of these
remarkable people as to be characteristic.[11]

Cooper and his immensely popular *Last of the Mohicans* (1850) of course
represent a much later development in the evolution of a concept that initially began in pagan antiquity. As Cooper's appraisal certainly shows, it did
not in any way end in the classical period; in fact, the idea of the Noble Savage did not necessarily diminish, but rather was drastically changed during
the Middle Ages. In this shape, it was made ready for application to newly
discovered-invented Native Americans after 1492.

The Medieval Pedigree of the Indian Noble Savage

During the medieval period, the preferred virtues inherent to a savage life-style were naturally those which could be appraised as venturing toward a specifically Christian ideal. For the Roman authors, what really mattered was *virtus,* a Latin word having its roots in *vis* and *vir,* or "power" and "manhood." In the succeeding Christian era, the important thing was "virtue," suggesting then (as now) passive moral qualities largely resting upon "purity," specifically physical virginity, and thus celibate monks and nuns became approved role models during the Middle Ages. Christian virtues were certainly not those Teutonic, proto-macho, traits of intermittent drunken sloth, occasional gluttony, sudden bursts of bellicose ferocity, and consistent attributes of martial discipline and blood loyalty that pagan and effetely urbanized Roman aristocrats had found so appealing.

St. Jerome (*De gubernatione Dei,* IV, 14) effectively summed up the new, largely negative, early medieval attitudes toward the barbaric but hardy Germanic tribes:

> For since all the barbarians are, as we have already said, either pagans or heretics, let me speak first of the pagans, since their guilt is first: the Saxons are cruel, the Franks faithless, the Gepidae inhuman, the Chuni shameless; in short, the life of all barbarian tribes is vice.[12]

As Jerome suggests, during the Christian era (officially at least) those traits that were prized much more highly than previously were the contrary values of timidity, self-denial, innocence (equally of sex and of material goods), and an ascetic devotion to a higher, spiritual, and largely dematerialized, ideal.

In the case we have chosen for study, it is particularly interesting that the place where those specifically medieval Christian kinds of ascetic values, Noble Savagery, were supposed to be most highly esteemed by rude savages was none other than *India,* a geographically real, rather than mythical, land. This is especially useful to know since, as has been shown in these pages in numerous ways, *las Indias* was exactly the name for that fabled land toward which Columbus thought he was approaching late in 1492 and, for that matter, thereafter in his subsequent voyages. Moreover, nearly all of the peoples of Asian India were praised by the medieval writers in terms by which they represent ethnic types approaching what we would call Noble Savages.[13] As was also demonstrated here at great length, these particularly Noble Indians of tropical Asia were additionally all taken by the medieval writers to be dwelling very near to, if not directly within Eden. The Indians' purported geographical proximity to Paradise certainly reinforced their virtuous status and saintly attributes in the eyes of their pseudo-anthropologizing European exegetes.

One of the most lauded Indic peoples were the "Camerini, who live in the East." According to the anonymously authored (ca. 359) *Expositio Totius Mundi et Gentium* (articles iv–vii), not only is the fabled homeland of the Camerines *Eden,* but their Edenic lifestyle is (by inference) exactly that which had earlier been attributed to the happy inhabitants of the pagan Golden Age:

> Moses called their country Eden. . . . The men who live in the said country are extremely pious and good, and among them is to be found no evil, either of body or soul. . . . They say that a kind of [mannalike] bread rains down on them day by day, and that they drink wild honey and pepper. . . . They are, moreover, without government, ruling themselves. As no evil is found among them, so they have neither fleas nor lice nor bedbugs, nor anything else which is harmful. Their clothes cannot become soiled, but, if it should happen, they wait for a cleaning by the sun's fire, for burning makes things better. They also have various precious stones, emeralds, pearls, jacinths, agates, and sapphires in the hills. . . . Living, therefore, in such great happiness, they know not how to labor, nor are they wearied by any weakness or disease.[14]

Much better known among the inhabitants of India were the Brahmins (whom we met earlier). In the version of the *Gesta Alexandri* that had been told by the Pseudo-Callisthenes, we are perhaps somewhat surprised to read that the Brahmins of India pass their entire lives exactly in the manner as did those Indians who greeted Columbus in 1492! As would have been known to any casual reader of the various versions of the *Deeds of Alexander the Great* (including Columbus, according to Las Casas), all Indians, eastern or western,

> dwell in a state of nature, living in nakedness. There is no four-footed beast among them, no agriculture, no iron, no building, no fire, no

bread, no wine, no clothing, nor anything pertaining to the productive
arts or to pleasure. . . . Worshipping God and possessing wisdom [*gno-
sis*]—and this they have to no small degree—and even though they are
not able to comprehend the reasons of Providence, yet they pray unceasingly. And when they pray, they look to Heaven instead of to the
East. And they [only] eat the fruits of the trees, upon which they happen, and wild vegetables, and they [only] drink water. Being wanderers
in the woods, they sleep on beds of leaves.[15]

As this version would have it, Alexander the Great, being a naturally wise
ruler, of course desires even *more* wisdom. Acceding to his request for sage
counsels (for which vegetarian Indian gurus are still famed, at least among
privileged but rebellious contemporary youths conventionally subscribing
to counter-cultural lifestyles), the Brahmins grandly announce,

Desiring wisdom, Alexander, you have come to us. Therefore, we Brahmins grant your request, the more willingly as wisdom is the kingly
power in our life. . . . The philosopher is not ruled, but he rules because
no man has power over him. . . . Our food is the medicine of health. We
live without wealth in accordance with nature, and death is the termi-
nation of our life, as it is of all. But if some mortals, having learned false
doctrines, shoot at us with vain arrows, they do not hinder our freedom.
It is the same thing to lie and to believe too rapidly. . . . Slander is the
mother of War and gives birth to Passion, because of which men fight
and make war. . . . Courage is to combat the rigors of the climate with
naked body and to destroy the desires of the belly and . . . not to be conquered by desire in the hunger for reputation and wealth and pleasure.
Conquer these desires first, Alexander, slay these. For, should you conquer these, you will have no need to fight against external foes. . . . Love
of Money, Love of Pleasure, Death by Treachery, Fornication, Murder,
Wrangling—by those and many others are mortals enslaved. . . . But we
Brahmins, since we have already won the inner battles, we do not fight
in external wars.

If there is a familiar pattern for the Brahmin way of life (that is, before the
omnipresent rise of drop-out communes in post-Columbian Vietnam-era
America) then that would be the European but pre-Christian Stoics. Ac-

cording to the European invention of the vegetarian, pacific, and Brahmin code of conduct, at least as recounted by the Pseudo-Callisthenes,

> We rest in view of the trees and of heaven, and we listen to the melodious voices of the birds and to the eagle's call, and we are roofed over with leaves, and we live in the open air, and we eat fruits and drink water. We sing hymns to God, and we gladly accept the future, and we listen to none who are not of profit to us. Such is the life of us Brahmins, not speaking many words, but keeping silence. . . . When hunger approaches, we dispel it with nuts and vegetables furnished by Providence. And when thirst approaches, we go to the river, trampling gold underfoot, and we drink water and relieve our thirst. . . . It is clear to all [of us] that to desire gold is foreign to nature. For every desire of man [ideally] ceases when he takes his fill, since this abstention is in accordance with nature. But the love of money is insatiable, because it is contrary to nature.[16]

Thomas Aquinas had conceded that if any pagan (in India or in the Indies — or anywhere else) had never heard of doctrinal details of the Christian faith, then his paganism was not, after all, a sin. Dante tackled the same moot question in his *Paradiso* (XIX, 70–78) — and then he decided to put the problem squarely in India:

> Che tu dicevi: "Un uom nasce all riva
> Dell'Indo, e quivi non è chi ragioni
> Di Cristo, ne chi legga, ne chi scriva;
> E tutti i suoi voleri ed atti buoni
> Sono, quanto ragione umana vede,
> Senza peccato in vita o in sermoni.
> Muore non battezzato e senza fede:
> Ov'è questa Giutizia che il condenna?
> Ov'è la colpa sua, se ei non crede?"

You said that: "Here's a man born on the banks of the Indus River — where there's no one to explain Christ, and none who reads and no one who writes; and all his desires and all his acts are good ones, and he shows as much human reason as any man, and is additionally blameless in life and speech. Nevertheless, he dies unbaptized and, therefore, 'faithless.' So where's the Justice now in condemning him, and where's his guilt—if he is not, after all, a 'believer'?"

Such, in sum, were the utopian, quasi-Christian traits traditionally ascribed to the Gangetic Indians by various Christian authors writing in Europe after the fourth century, when the pious legend appears to have been initially invented. This picture of prelapsarian innocence and anti-materialism is clearly common to nearly all the initial European impressions (previously quoted) of the Edenic inhabitants—"Indians"—of the New World that had been inadvertently invented in 1492.

The Entrance of the American Ignoble Savage

Nevertheless, just as soon as the initial, Brahmanic-Indian impression of the locals invented by the Europeans became eroded by the harsher facts of reality in the Caribbean, trouble began brewing in Paradise, and Pandora's box began to open. In short, Columbus discovered the living existence of the Anti-Brahmins of the Caribbean, namely the cannibals. They too have their own classical-medieval literary pedigree.

As we saw earlier, Columbus admitted their presence in the *Diario* record of his first voyage. At that time however, he was still able to relegate them to the background of his demanding exploratory tasks. However, on subsequent voyages, the cannibals—the genuinely Ignoble Savages of the Caribbean—crept evermore into the foreground of the consciousness of the bewildered European explorers of the New World. But that consciousness was there already: People primed with presuppositions, positive or negative, *do* find what they expect to find. Columbus was, as we already know, one of those people who are particularly given to presuppositions.

Our knowledge of the details of Columbus's second voyage late in 1493 largely derives from a report written by Dr. Diego Alvarez Chanca, the admiral's secretary and another avid reader of *The Travels of Sir John Mandeville*. According to the "Chanca Letter," on the island of Guadaloupe,

> We went on land many times, going about the dwellings and villages which were on the coast. There we found a great quantity of men's bones and skulls that were hung up around the houses, like vessels to

hold things. . . . We asked the women, who were held captive on this island, who these people were. There replied that they were the Caribes. After they understood that we abhorred that race for their evil custom of eating human flesh, they were greatly relieved . . . for, as a subjected race, they went in terror of them, even here, where they all were in our power. . . . The customs of this race of Caribs are bestial. . . . One and all, they make war on all the other neighboring islands, and they go by sea in the many canoes which they have. . . . These people raid the other islands and carry off any women they can, especially the young and pretty ones. They keep them in bondage and use them as concubines. . . . These women also say that they are treated with a cruelty which appears to be beyond belief.

The Caribs even eat their male children, which they take from them; they only raise [to maturity] those children who belong to their natural wives. As for any men whom they are able to capture, such as are still alive, they march them to their houses in order to cut them up for meat, and those that are dead, they eat them later. They say that the flesh of a man is so good that there is nothing quite like it in the whole world. This certainly seems to be the case: from the evidence of the bones which we found in their houses, they had gnawed off everything that they could. Nothing was left on them, except whatever was too tough to chew. In one house we found the scrawny neck of a man cooking in a pot. They cut off the penises of the boys they capture, and then [as eunuchs] they employ them as servants until they are fully grown. Then, when they wish to make a feast, they kill them and eat them up, even though, as they say, the flesh of boys and women doesn't really make such good eating. Of these boys, three came running up towards us, and all three of them had been castrated.[17]

Even though the "Chanca Letter" remained unpublished for centuries, Dr. Alvarez Chanca (or his companions) did pass the gristly word on to Peter Martyr. In his private correspondence (the *Epistolae,* eventually published in 1530), Martyr announced to an aghast friend as early as 1494 that

I know that you don't doubt that there are Lestrigonians or Polyphemuses who feed upon human flesh. Listen up now, and be careful that your hair doesn't stand up straight up from sheer fright! When our sailors recently departed from the *Insulae Fortunatae,* which some are want to call the Canaries, they then headed for Hispaniola, for that is the name by which they call the island which they have just colonized. Then, pointing their bows a bit to the south, they began to come across islands filled with fierce men called "cannibals" or "caribes." Even though they are naked, these are brave warriors. They take full advantage of bows and arrows and mainly spears. They have boats made of single logs which they call *canoas;* with these canoes, they pass over in a mob toward neighboring islands where peaceful men dwell. They attack the villages of their neighbors and they eat raw any men whom they catch. They castrate the children, just like we do with chickens. Once they have fattened them, they cut their throats and eat them. . . . When our men entered into the cannibals' houses—which are round and made from vertically implanted logs—they found the salted legs of men hanging from the rafters, and these were treated just like the way that we cure the meat of swine. They also found the head of a recently killed boy, still filled with blood, and also some pieces from the same youth, put into pots and ready to be cooked, along with meat from ducks and parrots, and some other pieces of human flesh were already roasting on the spit.[18]

Cannibalism, a very specific manifestation of generic *sauvagerie,* rapidly became the most shocking attribute of the increasingly Ignoble Savage of the Americas. As a recent critic of the fateful Columbian venture, Christopher Sale, remarks, "a myth was perpetrated and the cannibal became the dominant image for Europeans of the people of the Indies." But the myth, like all such, was nothing new: "For centuries Europe had read about strange tribes of man-eaters in the nether regions of the world—*anthropophagi* were standard in the highly popular 'reports' of world travellers such as John Mandeville." As Sale also observes, the refurbished myth

> permitted the denigration, and thus the conquest and exploitation, of peoples whose lands were seen as increasingly desirable in European eyes. It is always convenient to regard foreign populations as inferior, more convenient still to regard them as animalistic, or bestial, especially when you have [already] decided to enslave or eliminate them.[19]

An American Invention of Cannibalism During the Renaissance

Cannibalism was also the specific subcultural attribute of the aborigines of the Other World that, as might be expected, some European illustrators found most noteworthy. In a crude woodcut (Fig. 22), a German print of 1505 (cut either in Augsburg or Nuremberg), which we previously discussed as perhaps representing the earliest European depiction of American Indians pretending to some ethnographic accuracy, cannibalism becomes the foremost collective characteristic of the newly described peoples of these, as-yet-unnamed Americas.[20] Obviously, this German artist was not an eyewitness since he erroneously shows the male Indians to be heavily bearded. In any event, the several lines of text placed below this horrific image neatly sum up the earliest European impressions of, and opinions about, the savages so recently uncovered by Columbus. Those were allegations, to repeat, that

> the people are thus naked, handsome, brown, well formed in body, in their heads, necks, arms, privy parts; the feet of the women and men are slightly covered with feathers. The men also have many precious stones [placed] in their faces and breasts. No one owns anything, but all things are [held] in common. And the men have as wives [all] those that please them, be they mothers, sisters or friends; therein they make no difference. They also fight with each other. There also eat each other, even those who are slain [in battle], and they hang the flesh of them to smoke. They live one hundred and fifty years. And they have no government.

This schematic, but densely comprehensive statement is a complete ethnographic invention. As invention, it has two obvious textual sources. The first deals with "the Indies," that is, the tropical islands that had always been in Asia, and as such, they were those insular Edens that were so persistently sought by Columbus. According to a fanciful description (ca. 1356) of the island of Lamory (Sumatra) appearing in the *Travels of Sir John Mandeville:*

> In that land it is extremely hot; the custom there is for men and women to go completely naked. They scorn other folk who go clothed; for they say that God [in the Garden of Eden] made Adam and Eve naked. . . . In that land there is no marriage between man and woman; all the women of that land are held common to every man . . . and, in the same way, the land is all common property. . . . for all things are common, as I said, corn and other goods too; nothing is locked up, and every man is as rich as another. But they have an evil custom among them, for they will eat human flesh more gladly than any other kind. Nevertheless, the land is abundant enough in meat and fish and corn, and also gold and

silver and other goods. Merchants bring children there to sell, and the people of the country buy them. Those that are already plump they eat; those that are not yet plump they feed up and fatten, and then they kill and eat them. And they say that human meat is the best and sweetest flesh in the world.[21]

As it must now appear, Sir John Mandeville has once again, and largely single-handedly, invented a majority of those presuppositions so essential for the specific, and still persistent character of the European invention of America and the Native Americans. The other textual source informing the hard primitivist context of the German print was written in the early sixteenth century, and it specifically supplied the ethnographic details paraphrased in the caption attached to the woodcut. As opposed to the popular and rampantly exotic folklore contained in *Mandeville's Travels,* written well over a century *before* any announcement of the European invention of America, the subject of the second published source of the German print was "America" itself—so named (eventually) after its author, Amerigo Vespucci.

Appearing late in 1504, Vespucci's descriptions of the *Mundus Novus* provided eager European readers with, besides the first particularized news since Columbus's *Carta* of the New World, a wealth of crude, but mostly provocative illustrations. The modern reader of these early descriptions of America, as now eponymously named for their author, Amerigo Vespucci, can now appreciate how these ostensible eyewitness reports are little more than recycled Mandevilliana. Besides containing many more vivid details than did Columbus's much earlier pamphlet, and with no less than twelve Latin editions and thirty-seven more in the vernaculars by 1510, Vespucci's much longer account obviously was considerably more widespread than was Columbus's. Its illustrations were also more striking (see again Figs. 12, 20–21, 25–29). Given its demonstrable influence, the strictly ethnographical section again deserves quotation at length in order to convey the richness of its minutiae, in effect establishing in very concrete terms the basic— and perennial—traits of the exclusively white man's image of the American Indian. Many, often contradictory subthemes are woven into this extended description.[22]

Vespucci begins by raising a timeworn—and obviously very much Mandeville-derived—picture of the Noble Savage, saying:

First then, as to the people [of the New World]. We found in those parts such a multitude of people as nobody could enumerate (as we read in the Apocalypse), a race, I say, so gentle and amenable. All of both sexes go about naked, covering no part of their bodies. Just as they spring from their mother wombs, so do they go [naked] until death. They have indeed large, square-built bodies, and are well formed and proportioned, and in color they verge upon reddish. This condition, I think, has come to them, because, going about naked, they are colored by the sun. They also have hair that is plentiful and black. In their gait, and when playing their games, they are agile and dignified. They are comely, too, of countenance, which they, nevertheless, themselves destroy; for they bore holes in their cheeks, lips, noses and ears.

Following his somewhat Michelangelesque anatomical introduction, a humanistic trait also appearing in many later European prints depicting Native Americans (see, for example, Figs. 21, 25), Vespucci immediately launches into his real thesis (also probably Mandeville-derived), the Ignoble Savage. According to the widely read Italian explorer,

They have another custom, which is very shameful and beyond all human belief. Their women, being very lustful, cause the private parts of their husbands to swell up to such a huge size that they appear deformed and disgusting. This is accomplished by a certain device of theirs, the biting of certain poisonous animals. In consequence of this practice [not otherwise explained], many lose their sexual organs, which break off through lack of attention, and thus these men remain eunuches.

Having briefly announced this incredible and shameful custom, all the more tantalizing because of the lack of explanatory details, Vespucci now reverts to motifs arising from the traditional theme of the Noble Savage of the Age of Gold:

They have no cloth, either of wool, linen or cotton, since they need it not; neither do they have goods of their own, but all things are held in common. They live together, without king and without government, and each is his own master.

Unfortunately, this kind of precocious socialism also contains the pernicious seeds of sexual misconduct, even incest:

They marry as many wives as they please, and son cohabits with mother, brother with sister, male cousin with female, and any man with the first woman he meets. They dissolve their marriages as often as they please, and they observe no sort of law with respect to them.

Now Vespucci feels he must once again bring up the classic image of the Noble Savage, living in philosophical harmony with nature:

Beyond the fact that they have no church, no religion, and are not idolaters, what more can I say? I say that they live according to nature, and are what may be called "Epicureans" [i.e., in the manner of Lucretius's prehistoric peoples], rather than Stoics. There are no merchants among their number, nor is there any barter.

Having said that, there follows yet another reversion to the pernicious image of the "hard primitive" life-style of the Ignoble Savage, addicted to both mindless warfare and to the disgusting gourmandizing customs of unchecked cannibalism. According to Vespucci,

The [Indian] nations wage war upon one another, without art or order. The elders, by means of certain harangues of theirs, bend the youths to their will, and so they inflame them to wars, in which they cruelly kill one another. Those whom they bring home as captives from war they preserve. They do this not to spare their lives, but instead so that they may be slain for food, for they eat one another. The victors eat the vanquished and, among other kinds of meat, human flesh is a common article of diet with them. Nay, be assured of this fact: the father has already been seen [by me] to eat his children and wife. I knew a man, whom I also spoke to, who was reputed to have eaten more than three hundred human bodies. And I likewise remained twenty-seven days in a certain town, and here I saw salted human flesh suspended from beams between the houses, just as, with us, it is the custom to hang bacon and pork. I say, furthermore, that they themselves wonder why *we* do not eat our enemies, and why *we* do not use as food their flesh—which, they say, is most savory. Their weapons are bows and arrows and, when they advance to war, they cover no part of their bodies for the sake of protection; they are much like beasts in this matter. We endeavored, to the extent of our power, to dissuade them and to persuade them to desist from these depraved customs. They did promise us that they would leave off.

With this unlikely promise in hand, Vespucci abandons the loathsome business of an anthropophagous diet and opens up a new topic of obvious pleasure to him. This is the fleshy delights that were constantly being paraded before him for his own, evidently libidinous, ocular inspections:

> The women, as I have said, go about naked and they are very libidinous. Nevertheless, they have bodies that are tolerably beautiful and cleanly. Nor are they so unsightly as one, perchance, might imagine. Inasmuch as they are plump, their ugliness is the less apparent, which [facial defect] indeed is, for the most part, concealed by the excellence of their bodily structure. It was a matter of astonishment to us that none was to be seen among the women who had a flabby breast, and that those who had borne children were not to be distinguished from the virgins by the shape and shrinking of the womb. In the other parts of the body, similar things were seen, of which, in the interest of modesty, I make no [further] mention. When they had the opportunity of copulating with Christians, urged on by excessive lust, they defiled and prostituted themselves.

Following this gratuitous erotic digression, Vespucci brings his often self-contradictory discourse to its improbable final conclusion:

> They live one hundred and fifty years, and rarely fall ill and, if they fall victims to any disease, they can cure themselves with certain roots and herbs. These are the most noteworthy things I know about them.

Perhaps not surprisingly, whether American or elsewhere, cannibalism had long since been considered one of the worst attributes of the hard primitivist life-style. In short, like so many other uniquely "American" features of European Renaissance descriptions, cannibalism is another standard literary topos, additionally meaning that it has a long pedigree all of its own within European legendary culture. According, for instance, to a Hellenistic author, Stobaeus (*First Eclogue,* viii, 38ff.),

I shall begin to unfold in my poem the original condition of human life. . . . This was a time when men lived like beasts [when] the flesh of their fellows was men's food, and Law was humbled and Brute Strength was enthroned with Zeus, and the weak was food for his better. And when Time [Kronos or Saturn], the father and nurturer of all things, changed mortal life again [in the Golden Age] . . . then were discovered cultivated fruits, the food [grain] given by chaste Demeter, and there was discovered the sweet stream of Bacchus [or wine]. And Earth, till then unsown, was now plowed by yoked oxen, and cities were turreted and roofed houses built, and they changed their savage way of life for civilization. And law decreed that the dead be left concealed in tombs, and ordered that the unburied dead should be buried—and not be left before men's gaze as a reminder of their impious meals of earlier [cannibalistic] days.[23]

In spite of Stobaeus's prediction, and despite a passing promise made to Amerigo Vespucci, the American Indian—at least as he was traditionally reinvented in the European mind—was not soon to discard his impious and undainty diet of supposedly savory human flesh. Viewed in retrospect, it would appear that Renaissance Europeans equally envied and resented the Age of Gold premise attributed to Native Americans. As a Roman poet, Catullus, once sang, "Odio et amo," I love you and I hate you. The obvious reaction, what we would call today a psychological defense mechanism, was in turn to create Ignoble Savages, and that was most easily done by making them, according to the classical label, *anthropophagi,* people-eaters.

Defining "Just Wars" Against the American Wild Men

The next step was to put the American wild man into a previously conventionalized wilderness. For this move the Old Testament provided the sanction: "The land is the Garden of Eden before them, and behind them is a desolate wilderness [*solitudo deserti*]" (Joel 2:3). Clearly the ceremonial cannibalism practiced in so many places of the New World came as a profound cultural shock to the *conquistadores.* This was especially true once some of the aghast Europeans realized that they themselves were intended as a main course! Bernal Díaz del Castillo reports an unsettling incident with the "treacherous Cholulans" in central Mexico:

Cortés then asked the *caciques* [Indian chiefs] why they had turned trai-
tors . . . seeing that we had done them no harm, but had merely warned
them against certain things as we had warned every town through which
we had passed: [namely] against wickedness and human sacrifice, and
the worship of idols, and eating their neighbors' flesh, and sodomy. All
we had done was to tell them to lead good lives and to inform them of
certain matters concerning our Holy Faith, and this without compul-
sion of any kind. . . . Their hostility was plain to see, and their treachery
also. . . . So, in return for our coming to treat them like brothers, and
to tell them the commands of our Lord God and the King, they were
planning to kill us and to eat our flesh—and they had already prepared
the pot for us, with salt and peppers and tomatoes! [24]

With historical hindsight, that proffered feast seems only fitting. When
Cortés landed in 1519, it has been estimated (as best as can be done without any reliable census) that there were about 25 million Indians living in
central Mexico; thirty years later, it is supposed that only a third remained.
By 1605 (according to similar modern estimates), less than a century after
the start of the physical and spiritual *conquista de la Nueva España,* perhaps
barely a million Mexicans had survived. This same pattern, probably up
to a 95 percent extermination rate, as some now believe, applied to all of
Spanish America.[25] Whatever the real figures, or even the real causes, this
was unquestionably a time of unrelenting horror for indigenous American
peoples. One result of the mass extinction of native cultures was that, by
the middle of the seventeenth century, the depopulated Americas had become largely European, even if only by default. One large part of the New
World reinvented in the image of the Old World was called New Spain,
and another New England. A good deal of this was accidental, largely due
to the introduction of European diseases, for which the natives had no acquired immunity. There is absolutely *no* evidence of a Nazi-type policy of
Endlösung ("final solution") being deliberately practiced by the Spanish colonial authorities. However that may be, clearly the traditional, classical-to-
medieval, European imagery of cannibalistic practices (and also "sodomy")
newly associated with Native American cultures allowed many Spaniards to
entertain less than Christian thoughts about their newly won subjects. Such
notions eventually demolished the previous Golden Age interpretation and,
additionally, ejected the "treacherous" Native Americans from their wholly
fictional Eden.

Certainly Hernán Cortés—among many other *conquistadores* who have left no written records behind them to describe their medieval sense of mission as the *milites Christi* ("Knights of Christ")—saw himself as a noble champion of Christendom waging a wholly just, "holy war" (*guerra santa*) against the savage infidel. Before 1492, the hated "infidel" in Spain was a *Musulmán* (Muslim); immediately afterward, in America, he was an *indio*. Certainly, Cortés could not easily tell the difference between one and the other; consequently he always refers to Aztec temples as "mosques" (*mezquitas*). So moved, the Latin motto Cortés inscribed on his coat-of-arms affirmed that "the Judgment of the Lord overtook them; His strength supported my sword arm." *Judicium Domini apprehendit eos, et fortitudo ejus corroboravit brachium meum.* The reasons for his righteous outrage—the barbarous religious practices of the Aztecs—were angrily listed in Cortés's *First Letter* (1519) to Emperor Charles V in Spain:

And they have another horrible and abominable custom which is truly worthy of punishment, one which, until now, has not been seen anywhere else. And this is that, whenever they wish to request something from their idols, and in order that their petitions might find greater favor, they take children, girls and boys alike, and even men and women of mature age, and, in the presence of those idols, they take them— still living!—and they cut their chests open and, out of them, they rip out their hearts and entrails. They burn the said entrails and hearts in front of the idols and offer them up to them in the form of smoke. This has been seen by several of us, and those that saw it say that it is the most terrible and frightening thing that they have ever seen. The Indians do this so frequently and so often that, as we have been informed, and which has already be seen at first hand in just the little bit of this land that we have already been in, there must be no year in which they do not probably kill and sacrifice fifty souls—that is, in each one of their mosques. . . . According to the breadth of this land, which seems to be very big indeed, and because of the many mosques which they have, at least in those parts which we have discovered and have actually seen, then there is probably no year in which they do not actually kill and sacrifice in this way some three or four *thousand* souls. . . . In addition to that which we have recorded above for Your Majesty about the children, men and women which they do kill and offer up in their sacrifices, we have also learned and been informed of the unquestionable fact that they are all buggerers [*de cierto que todos son sodomitas*], and that they all practice that abominable sin.[26]

More details on this sacrificial custom, "horrible y abominable y digna de ser punida," were later provided, albeit in a more objective and genuinely anthropological manner, by Fray Bernadino de Sahagún in his *Historia general de las cosas de Nueva España* (1577):

> The second month [of the Aztec calendar] was called *Tlacaxipeoaliztli*. On the first day of this month, they celebrated a festival in honor of the god *Totec*, who is also called *Xipe*; this was when they killed and flayed a number of slaves and captives. . . . When the masters of these captives took their slaves to the temple, where they were to be killed, they dragged them by the hair. As they pulled them up the steps of the *Cu* [temple], some of these captives would faint—so often their owners had to drag them by the hair as far as the block where they were to die. As soon as they had dragged them to the block—which was made of stone and three *palmos* high, more or less [or about two English feet], by almost two in width—they threw them down on their backs; five men held them, two by the feet, two by the arms, and one by the head. Then, all at once, the priest who was to kill him would come up and strike him a quick blow on the chest with both hands. Holding a flint knife shaped like the iron of an anchor, he cut a hole, and into this incision he would thrust one hand and tear out the heart, which he then offered to the Sun. Later, he put it into a bowl or a jar. After having thus torn their hearts out, and after pouring their blood into a gourd, which was then given to the dead slave's master, the body was then thrown down the temple steps. From there, it was taken by certain old men, called *Quaquaquilti*, and was carried to their *calpul* [chapel] where they cut it to pieces and distributed it to be eaten [by the general populace].[27]

The specific grounds for a "just war" to be waged against the newly invented pagan infidels of the New World were, however, already well in place—and even *before* Cortés landed in Mexico. According to a Dominican priest, Tomás Ortiz, whose remarks, a veritable catalog of infamies, were recorded in the 1515 edition of Peter Martyr's widely read *Decades*, it had become already common knowledge that the Native Americans

> eat human flesh on the mainland. They are sodomites, more so than any other species known. There is no justice among them. They walk about naked. They know neither love nor shame. They are crazed and stupid. They will not hold to the truth, unless it is to their advantage. They are inconstant. They have no idea of what good advice might be. They are

most ungrateful and are only fond of novelties. Esteeming drunkenness, they have wines they make, like beer and cider, from various herbs and fruits and grains; by also drinking distillations drawn from other plants, which they devour, they get intoxicated. They are bestial and only take pride in being abominable by their vices. Youths show neither obedience nor any courtesy toward their elders, nor do sons to their fathers. They are neither fit for doctrine nor for bearing punishment. They are treacherous, cruel and vengeful, and they never forgive. They are enemies to religion. They are braggarts and thieves. They maintain neither faith nor order. Husbands exhibit no loyalty toward their wives, nor wives to their husbands. They are spell-casters and prophesiers, also as cowardly as rabbits. They are filthy: they feed upon lice and spiders and raw worms, wherever they may find them. They have neither the manners nor the wits of men. . . . The older they get, the worse they become. Until they reach the age of ten or twelve years, it seems that they just might prove susceptible to some breeding and a sense of virtue. Nonetheless, getting older, they only turn into brutish beasts. In short, I mean to say that never did God raise such a people, cooked in vices and bestialities and having no trace whatsoever of kindliness or social order.[28]

It now seems somewhat ironic that the various Spanish priests who wrote about the "horrible and abominable" Aztec religious practices, especially Sahagún, the precocious anthropologist, failed to acknowledge its central functional analogy with Catholicism. In short, both religions are *deipophagous,* meaning "god-eating." The principal difference is that Catholics digest a transubstantiated wafer of bread, the miraculous Host, representing rather literally the *Corpus Christi.* The Aztecs, having no wheaten bread and suffering from a protein-poor diet, instead partook of a decidedly untransubstantiated meal of *carne humana,* human meat: *De gustibus non disputandum!* In any event, the image of the bad, cannibalistic Indian became a staple of debates in Spain during the sixteenth century.

One of the Indians' more vocal opponents was Juan Ginés de Sepúlveda, who righteously wrote a *Tratado sobre las justas causas de la guerra contra los Indios* in 1548. In 1550, Sepúlveda again sought to justify the Spanish domination of Native American cultures by recycling familiar, early medieval speculations about the exotic and generally "monstrous" races infesting the fabulous Asia pictured by Mandeville, to which the Spaniard now adds a rather later medieval motif, the *hombre salvaje.* Sepúlveda begins his racist polemic by invidiously comparing Spanish gifts of prudence, talent, magnanimity, temperance, humanity, and religion with those [belonging to the] little men [*homúnculos,* the Indians]. In them, you will scarcely find traces of humanity. . . . But, if you deal with their virtues, if you look for temperance or meekness, what can you expect from men who were involved in every kind of intemperance and wicked lust—and who used to eat human flesh? And don't think that, before the arrival of the Christians, that they were living in tranquillity and in the Saturnian peace of the poets [i.e., the Golden Age]. On the contrary, they were making war continuously and ferociously against each other, and with such rage that they considered their victory worthless if they did not satisfy their monstrous hunger with the flesh of their enemies. This represents an inhumanity in them which is all the more monstrous since they are so distant from the unconquered and wild Scythians—who also fed upon human flesh. These Indians [as opposed to the "hard primitive" Scythians celebrated by the classical historians] are so cowardly and timid that they scarcely withstand the appearance of our soldiers. Often many thousands of them have given ground, fleeing like women before only a very few Spaniards, who did not even number a hundred.[29]

In many ways, the most significant of the early Spanish histories of the Americas was written by a proud *mestizo* (half-breed), Garcilaso de la Vega, "El Inca." He was born the son of a Spanish *hidalgo* and an Inca princess-mother at Cuzco in 1539, and died in Spain, at Córdoba, in 1616. He read classical Latin and was fluent in both Castilian and Quechua, the native tongue of the Andes. In 1609 he published his *Primera parte de los Comentarios reales que tratan del origen de los Incas* (the second part, posthumously published in 1617, only deals with post-Conquest Peru and mostly repeats materials found in other Spanish *cronistas de Indias*). In this exhaustive (and truly pioneering) ethnographic work, which is consequently of more than local interest, he very clearly employs the familiar metaphors of "hard primitivism" in order to describe the life of the indigenous population before the coming of both the Incas and the Spaniards. In discussing "como vivían antes de los Incas," Garcilaso implies that the primitive Indians conformed to certain patterns of behavior considerably more barbarous than those that had been attributed to the savage *Germani* by Tacitus:

> In that first age of ancient paganism, some Indians spoke scarcely better than tame beasts do, and others did much worse than do wild beasts.

Beginning with their gods, we would say that they had put them in conformity with all the other simplemindedness and crudities which they were accustomed to employ. That is how it was for the majority of them, just as is seen in the vileness and primitiveness of the objects which they used to adore. . . . They did not know, as did the pagan Romans, how to personify their gods, as Hope, Victory, Peace, and other allegorical figures of this sort. This was because they did not raise their thoughts towards invisible things; instead, they only adored what they could see . . . and thus they worshipped weeds, plants, flowers, all kinds of trees, high peaks, great rocks, and even the cracks in these; they also paid homage to deep caves, pebbles and little rocks.

For this haughty Roman Catholic humanist, animistic nature worship is obviously beneath contempt; as he continues, this is a biologically minimalist life, and just as Thomas Hobbes might have described it (and as will be quoted here later),

In the manner of their dwellings and towns those pagans displayed the same barbarism which they had in their gods and sacrifices. Even the most politically minded had their towns laid out without any plazas or any ordering of streets, and none even of houses; instead, it must have looked like a corral for wild animals. . . . Some lived in caves beneath the ground, in the crevices of crags or in the hollows of trees. . . . Other peoples, who were never conquered by the Inca kings, are still found living in that ancient rustic mode, and today these are the ones that are the hardest to reduce, either to the service of the Spaniards or to Christian religion. Because they have never had any [theological] doctrine, they are completely irrational. They have hardly any language by which one can understand another, even within the same tribe. In this way, they live just like animals of different species, without being joined and without any communication, except perhaps with their individual wives.

As described by the Europeanized Inca, the despicable effects of this hard primitivist life-style are still visibly apparent in all surviving aspects of precivilized, meaning pre–Inca and pre–Spanish, life in Peru:

In many provinces, in the manner that they dressed themselves and covered their bodies, the Indians were so simple and crude that their

costume still inspires laughter. In yet other places, in their mode of eating and kinds of food, they are so bestial and barbaric that such extreme
animality really must be admired. . . . Even in the hot lands, which are
the most fertile, they planted little or nothing at all; they keep themselves alive with weeds and roots and wild fruits and also by some beans,
which either grow wild or which require little help in that land. Like
all the rest, they attempted nothing more than the maintenance of their
natural life; they were content with very little.[30]

Even though "se contentaban con poco," it is abundantly obvious that Garcilaso de la Vega finds this in no way an admirable life-style. Within such
an unrelentingly hard-primitivist context, it is perhaps only natural that
this half-breed humanist historian must also dwell upon the ubiquitous
phenomenon of cannibalism:

In many provinces, they were exceedingly fond of human flesh. They
were so greedy for this treat that, even before an Indian died whom
they had killed, they would drink his blood directly from the wound
they gave him. They did the same thing while they were cutting him
up: they sucked up his blood—and they even licked their hands so that
they wouldn't lose even a drop! They even celebrated public slaughters
of human flesh: from the guts they made sausages and salamis. These
they stuffed with human meat so that they wouldn't waste any. Pedro
de Cieza [de León] says the same thing [in the twenty-sixth chapter of
his book, *Crónica del Perú,* 1553], and he saw it with his own eyes.

This passion grew so that even their own children—at least those
born of foreign wives that had been captured in their wars—were not
excused from the slaughter. They had taken these women as concubines.
The children which they produced together were treated generously—
that is, until they got to be twelve or thirteen years old: Then they ate
them right up. . . . For these purposes, they used to make a kind of monastery of boys, so that they could eat them all up, and none were excused
because of their parentage. . . . These peoples were so outlandish in their
lust for feasting upon human flesh that [metaphorically speaking] they
even buried their own dead inside their own stomachs. Once someone
expired, all of his relatives would get together—and then they ate him,
cooked or roasted, depending on whether the remaining flesh was much
or little. He would be cooked, if the meat was meager; if there was a lot
of it, then he became a roast.[31]

51.

"*Cannibals of the New World*," from S. Grynaeus, *Novus Orbis Regionum ac Insularum
veteribus incognitarum (Basel, 1532).*

The image of the generally hard primitivist and specifically cannibalistic American soon became nothing less than a cartographic emblem of
the New World. In Simon Grynaeus's world atlas, including the "New
World, Its Regions, and the Islands that were Unknown to the Ancients"
(*Novus Orbis Regionum ac Insularum veteribus incognitarum:* Basel, 1532), the
new kind of all-inclusive and north-oriented *mappamundi* became current
(Fig. 51). At the four corners of Grynaeus's planisphere allegorized representations of the now-canonic four continents appear. America, *Terra Nova,*
lies just to the east of Zipangri. Its historiated emblematic representation—
clearly labeled "Canibali"—appears at the lower left corner of the newly extended world map. The cannibals' "primitivist" hut—quintessential American proto-architecture, which is typically shown to be constructed from
still living leafy boughs—appears at the far left. Like a bloody banner, a
severed human head is impaled at the peak of the rustic *bohío,* and a human
leg dangles gruesomely over its entrance. In the center of the picture three
American Indians prepare their savory human feast upon a rustic banqueting table; one of the naked butchers wields a most unlikely, *iron* (meaning
European) cleaver. To their right, various succulent human steaks are shown
roasting upon a grill and turned upon a spit shaped like a crank. Another
anthropophagous comrade brings in the next load of stiffened *carne humana,*
strapped across the back of an overloaded and vexed (European) horse.

This gruesome cannibalistic image of the Americas remained in force long afterward. One of the artists employed in Brazil by Prince Maurits of Nassau was Albert Eckhout, who was commissioned to create a gallery of life-size portraits of the indigenous inhabitants of the new Dutch colony. This commission, in short, makes Eckhout notable for being one of the few, if not really the first known, professionally trained European artists to travel to the New World for the express purpose of accurately (even "scientifically") capturing the distinct appearance and ethnography of Native Americans. One of these truly singular pictures was his 1641 oil painting, *A Brazilian Woman of the Tapuya Tribe* (Fig. 52).[32] The nude woman looks

52.

Albert Eckhout, A Brazilian
Woman of the Tapuya Tribe,
1641. Copenhagen, Danish
National Museum..

calmly at her European viewers and stands in a nonchalant posture belonging to those traditional in Baroque state portraiture. The other bits of exotic paraphernalia are rendered with objective, nearly ethnographic exactitude. Cannibalism is casually introduced by Eckhout in his majestic painting as just another, typical and passing incident in *la sauvagerie brasilienne*. One has to look rather carefully in order to see that this majestic matron, daintily crossing a jungle stream, is holding a severed human forearm at her right side while a man's foot awkwardly sticks out of the neatly woven straw basket suspended from her head.

The Eternal "Wildness" of America and the Americans

Cannibalism was just the most sensational aspect of the "wildness" of the American savages. In fact, in all their other negative aspects (that is, as perceived and reported by early Europeans) they fit right into another pre-established pattern of ignoble savagery that had long since become standard in medieval European folklore. In this case, after the twelfth century, the conventional literary topos was that of the *silvaticus* of Latin letters, or *wilder Mann,* as he was known in Germany, or *hombre salvaje,* as he was called in Spain. Whatever he was dubbed, long before Columbus had invented his New World counterpart, in Europe the Wild Man was a conventional figure, who shakily existed at some ill-defined, pseudo-ethnographic point situated somewhere midway between tentative humanity and outright animality. His predecessors were those "monstrous races" that so fascinated medieval minds, and these heterogeneous types were eventually collapsed into this single figure. Finally, the European wild man, states John B. Friedman, "became conflated with aboriginal peoples found in the New World."[33] The pre-Columbian European wild man was woefully lacking in civilized *scientia,* or even in human will—and so were his newly acquired American brethren.

Like the more human types belonging to the pseudo-historical theories of hard primitivism, the hairy and bearded European wild man pursued a life of bestial self-gratification. Only directed by animal instinct, he of course remained balefully ignorant of God and organized, specifically Christian religion. Like his putative prehistoric prototypes, isolated from all civilized human contact in the present-day world, he hunted animals and gathered plants for his minimal biological sustenance. This bestial state of affairs is neatly summed up by Richard Bernheimer, the foremost historian of the imaginary wild men supposedly infesting Europe's medieval forests, and this scholar states that the meaning of his post-Edenic *solitudo deserti* is

> not a simple concept; it has sociological, biological, psychological, and even metaphysical connotations. "Wildness" meant more in the Middle Ages than the shrunken significance of the term would indicate today. The word implied everything that eluded Christian norms and the estab-lished framework of Christian society, referring to what was uncanny, unruly, raw, unpredictable, foreign, uncultured, and uncultivated. It in-cluded the unfamiliar as well as the unintelligible. . . . Wildness em-bodied not only a task but a temptation, to which one exposed oneself by plunging into the great wild unknown. . . . The derivation is, of course, from the Latin *silva* [forest]. The names given to the [European] wild man—*homme sauvage, salvage man, huomo selvatico* [and *hombre salvaje*]— indicate, therefore, not only his inner character, but also the nature of his habitat.[34]

The savage American Indians were always described as living in the un-tamed forests, the sylvan "wilderness," the postlapsarian *"solitudo deserti"* of the Scriptures, and, according to their inescapable status as "pagans," they automatically "implied everything that eluded Christian norms." Both Roman and medieval writers routinely described barbarians and wild men in analogous terms; by their reckoning, they were all creatures enslaved to brute instinct and unchecked passion. To their city- or monastery-dwelling European critics, the mythical wild men of the Middle Ages were incapable of sedentary existence. Ignorant of self-discipline and enemies of sustained labor, nomadic, confused and chaotic, they were hostile to all the accepted norms of medieval Christian *humanitas*. All these negative designations were afterward to be consistently applied to the Native Americans: The unlovable European wild men had merely moved their untamed habitat to a savage "new" continent. From this global perspective, cannibalism was just the most revolting attribute of a life-style made already all too familiar by the popular medieval culture of the first European visitors in the New World. Not surprisingly, in popular literature written much later in English the Native Americans used to be commonly called "savages," another enduring (if not endearing) eponym preestablished in European conventional thinking, just like "Indians." In either case, a preconception seems to have created an image by coining a phrase, and the invented image in turn became "fact": *Semper nomen est omen.*

Having dealt in detail with delusions entertained by Spaniards confronting a *Mundo Nuevo,* it seems only fair play to expose similarly fallacious thinking about Native Americans as conceived by Anglo-Saxon minds. The English, of course, mostly settled north of the Caribbean. Regardless of supposed barriers of language and religious orientation, they, like the Spaniards, more often than not thought of the indigenous "savages" (*silvatici*) in the traditional terms belonging to the medieval European wild man. To demonstrate this point, only one representative text by an early English colonist need be examined, Edward Waterhouse's *A Declaration of the State of the Colony [of Virginia] and . . . a Relation of the Barbarous Massacre* (1622). Waterhouse's observations effectively illustrate the general tendency of his fellow European settlers to read hostility, treachery, and cunning—in short, wild man "savagery"—into the alien character of the Indians. In his case, the trigger was the "barbarous massacre" of 1622, ignited by the murder of a greatly respected Indian of the Powhatan confederacy and leading that group to a well-coordinated and effective attack on the white settlement at Jamestown. Whatever the causes, the long-term result was an understood agreement among the Europeans: The English were now free to hunt down (literally) Indians wherever they might be found. As Waterhouse righteously declared (so recalling recent memories of certain Anglo-Saxon rationales broadcast for various neo-colonial misadventures),

> Our hands, which before were tied with gentleness and fair usage, are now set at liberty by the treacherous violence of the savages. So that we, who hitherto have had possession of no more ground than their waste, and our purchase at a valuable consideration to theire owne contentment gained, may now, by right of Warre, and law of Nations, invade the [Indian] Country, and destroy them who sought to destroy us; whereby wee shall enjoy their cultivated places, turning the laborious Mattocke into the victorious Sword (wherein there is more both ease, benefit, and glory) and possessing the fruits of others labours. Now their cleared grounds in all their villages (which are situate in the fruitfullest places of the land) shall be inhabited by us, whereas heretofore the grubbing of woods was [for us] the greatest labour.

Having stated an appropriate profit motive, acquisition of "the fruitfullest places," Waterhouse provides the appropriate (and precociously modern) means to a given end: *total war,* employing starvation, thereby leading to a coldly deliberated genocide:

> Victorie may bee gained many waies; by force, by surprize, by famine in burning their Corne, by destroying and burning their Boats, Canoes, and Houses, by breaking their fishing Weares, by assailing them in their huntings, whereby they get the greatest part of their sustenance in Winter, by pursuing and chasing them with our horses and blood Hounds to draw after them, and Mastives to teare them.

Following his well-thought-out catalog of an immediate means of ethnic extinction, Waterhouse (whom one presumes to have been a professed Christian) finally provides the appropriate justification—pure racism—informing his sympathetic readers that the Indians, as they all know,

> are by nature sloathful and idle, vitious, melancholy, slovenly, of bad conditions, lyers, of small memory, of no constancy or trust, . . . by the nature of all people [they are] the most lying and most inconstant in the world, sottish and sodaine, never looking what dangers may happen afterwards, lesse capable then [white] children of sixe or seaven yeares old, and less apt and ingenious.[35]

Besides cannibalism (admittedly rarely mentioned in the English accounts), one of the best inducements for those tacitly accepted programs of total war and genocidal pogroms were the many published reports of the excruciating tortures that Indians routinely, and notoriously, inflicted upon their terrified white prisoners. Since these accounts are legion, only one, particularly detailed, eighteenth-century report need be repeated here. According to the published *Journal of Captain Thomas Morris, of His Majesty's* XVII *Regiment of Infantry* (London, 1791),

> The usual modes of torturing prisoners [by Indians] are applying hot stones to the soles of the feet, running hot needles into the eyes, which latter cruelty is generally performed by the women, and shooting arrows, and running and pulling them out of the sufferer, in order to shoot

them again and again: this is generally done by the children. The torture is often continued two or three days, if they can contrive to keep the prisoner alive so long. These modes of torture I should not have mentioned, if the gentleman who advised me to publish my journal, had not thought it necessary. It may easily be conceived what I must have felt at the thought of such horrors which I myself was to endure. I recollect perfectly what my apprehensions were. I had not the smallest hope of life; and I remember that I conceived myself as if I were going to plunge into a gulf, vast, immeasurable; and that, in a few moments after, the thought of torture occasioned a sort of torpor and insensibility.[36]

Captain Morris obviously survived his horrific experience. The result was another publication telling Europeans just how unspeakably "savage" the American natives were. It was reports like this one that had earlier caused an eminent British political philosopher, Thomas Hobbes, to consign the Native Americans en masse to the lowest ranks of subhumanity. As notoriously revived in the twentieth-century, subhumanism became a popular topic among the modern *Germani*, who termed this condition *Untermenschheit*. As was much earlier affirmed in Hobbes's influential treatise, *Leviathan, or The Matter, Forme and Power of A Commonwealth Ecclesiastical and Civil* (1651),

> For the savage people in many places of America, except the government of small Famillies, the concord whereof dependeth on natural lust, have no government at all; and live to this day in that brutish manner, as I said before.

"That brutish manner, as I said before," was exactly this one, illustrating a Lucretius-like perception of the lower depths of the human race, now concretely exemplified by the "brutish manners" of the savage Americas:

> Whatsoever therefore is consequent to a time of Warre, where every man is Enemy to every man; the same is consequent to the time, wherein men live without other security, than what their own strength, and their own invention shall furnish them withall. In such condition, there is no place for Industry; because the fruit thereof is uncertain; and consequent no Culture of the Earth; no Navigation, nor use of the commodities that may be imported by Sea; no commodious Building; no Instruments

of moving, and removing such things as require much force; no knowledge of the face of the Earth; no account of Time; no Arts; no Letters; no Societie; and which is worst of all, continuall fear, and danger of violent death; *and the life of man [is] solitary, poore, nasty, brutish, and short* [emphasis ours].[37]

This negative evaluation of the Native Americans as rampantly Ignoble Savages was a commonplace, so much so that only two more (much later) instances need be mentioned. This denigrating description of the North American Indians, who were all too frequently seen as a race whose life is literally "solitary, poore, nasty, brutish, and short," proves to be a truly enduring topos. It is, for instance, once again encountered in Mark Twain's caustic Wild West travel diary of 1872, *Roughing It.* Contrary to Hobbes's sweeping philosophical devaluation of untamed American savagery, entirely formed on the basis of secondhand accounts and merely mentioned in passing as an illustration of a larger situation common to *all* backsliding mankind, Twain's vividly scathing comments are presented in the highly particularized form of an eyewitness report. According to the American humorist,

I refer to the Goshute Indians [in Nevada Territory, who] were small, lean, "scrawny" creatures; in complexion a dull black like the ordinary American Negro; their faces and hands bearing dirt which they had been hoarding and accumulating for months, years, and even generations, according to the age of the proprietor; a silent, sneaking, treacherous-looking race, taking note of everything, covertly, like all the other "Noble Red Men" that we [do not] read about, and betraying no sign in their countenances: indolent, everlastingly patient and tireless, like all other Indians; prideless beggars—for if the beggar instinct were left out of an Indian he would not "go," any more than a clock without a pendulum; hungry, always hungry, and yet never refusing anything that a hog would eat, though often eating what a hog would decline . . . savages, who when asked if they have the common Indian belief in a Great Spirit, show a something which almost amounts to emotion, thinking whiskey is referred to; these Goshutes are, who produce nothing at all, and have no villages, and no gathering together into strictly defined tribal communities—a people whose only shelter is a rag cast on a bush to keep off a portion of the snow. . . . The Bushmen [in Africa]

and our Goshutes are manifestly descended from the selfsame gorilla, or
kangaroo, or Norway rat, whichever animal-Adam the Darwinians trace
them to.

Following this vitriolic diatribe, obviously pure racism (but uniquely risible
as such), Twain begins seriously to question the validity of what we may
call the standard literary image of the Noble Savage:

> The disgust which the Goshutes gave me, a disciple of Cooper and a wor-
> shipper of the Red Man . . . —I say that the nausea which the Goshutes
> gave me, an Indian-worshipper, set me to examining authorities, to see
> if perchance I had been over estimating the Red Man while viewing
> him through the mellow moonshine of romance. The revelations that
> came were disenchanting. It was curious to see how quickly the paint
> and tinsel fell away from him and left him treacherous, filthy, and re-
> pulsive—and how quickly the evidence accumulated that wherever one
> finds an Indian tribe he has only found Goshutes, more or less modi-
> fied by circumstances and surroundings—but Goshutes, after all. They
> deserve pity, poor creatures; and they can have mine—at this distance.
> Nearer by, they never get anybody's.[38]

Lacking the humorous intention, very much the same thing had been commonly stated in Europe a century or more before. Among our other apposite examples of literary *opprobia* we may add the vitriolic comments of a
Dutchman, Corneille de Pauw, who (besides never venturing toward the
Americas) chose to publish in French, so potentially attracting a much wider
audience for his polemics. According to his *Recherches philosophiques sur les
Américains* (1768):

> A brutish insensibility forms the basis of the character of all [Native]
> Americans; their indolence prevents them from being attentive to any
> instruction; they know no passion strong enough to move their souls, to
> transcend their nature. Superior to animals [only] in the use they make of
> their hands and their tongues, they are nevertheless truly inferior to the
> lowest Europeans. Deprived [innately] of both intelligence and perfecti-
> bility, they can only obey the impulse of their instincts. . . . America was
> discovered nearly three centuries ago; since that time, [Native] Ameri-
> cans have constantly been brought to Europe. Attempts have been made
> to give them all sorts of education and culture, but never has one of them

succeeded. . . . The true western Indians cannot connect their ideas, for they do not think upon what they have said nor what they will say next. They do not think, and they have no memory. This defect is also common to Negroes. . . . They [both] regress instead of developing, and so completely forget what they have learned that one is obliged to give up all attempts at educating them, and to abandon them to their fate.[39]

A Black Legend of Aghast Christians Versus Cannibal Wild Men

Since this sort of racist rant can be easily found and cited ad nauseam—it is after all a textual commonplace since the Renaissance—we may instead stop to pose a timely question: Just how "Christian" were the European Christians who actually dealt with Native Americans newly invented in their Old World image and prejudices? To examine this question, we may return to the areas around the Caribbean, where Columbus first invented the need for this inquiry. Using Occam's razor, the most simplistic reduction of what one takes to be a characteristically Christian attitude toward the Indians (or anybody else) is "love thy neighbor." If so, then we must see if the European Christians actually put that benign injunction into practice. Since we have already heard the presumably typical recommendations of a presumably Christian Englishman, Edward Waterhouse—who precociously recommended the "final solution" (and some three centuries before the same idea occurred to Adolf Hitler, who gave it a name, *Endlösung*), we may turn to the Spanish sources. These allow us to see what—in practice, as opposed to theory—actually happened during the initial stages of the Spanish colonization of *las Indias*.

The earliest premonitions of the depredations to be increasingly put by Europeans upon the Native Americans were first published by the earliest historian of America, Peter Martyr d'Anglería. In his *First Decade* he was already observing how

once the chieftains of the islands—who had hitherto lived quietly and content with their little, which they thought quite abundant—began to perceive that our men were fastening foot within their provinces and to bear down their rule upon them, they took the matter so seriously that they thought of nothing else but by which means they might utterly destroy the invaders and forever abolish any memory of their name, because that kind of men, the Spaniards I mean, the ones that followed the Admiral [Columbus] in his voyages were, for the most part, wholly undisciplined, and had regard for nothing but idleness, sport, and their liberties. Additionally, they would by no means abstain from doing injuries: they [the Europeans] ravished the island women right before the faces of their [Indian] husbands, fathers, and brethren. By means of their abominable misconduct, they troubled the minds of all the inhabitants.[40]

A few years later, after the Spaniards had firmly settled upon those Edenic islands, the Iron Age European conquerors began to use the natives as slave laborers, and then Martyr exclaimed that:

It grieves me not a little that these simple poor souls, who were never brought up to labor, do now daily perish from intolerable exertions in the gold mines. They have thereby been brought to such desperation that many of them kill themselves. They have no more interest in the procreation of children: it has gotten so bad that a woman with child, perceiving that she shall bring her issue forth only to have it made into a slave for the use of the Christians, will now use medicines to destroy her conception. . . . The number of the poor wretches is amazingly reduced. They were once reckoned to number about 1,200,000; but as to what they may actually be now, that I hate to contemplate.[41]

Diego de Landa, later promoted to bishop of Yucatán, reported the following in a document of 1566 (which was not, however, to be published until the end of the nineteenth century):

The Indians took the yoke of servitude grievously. Even though the Spaniards held the towns comprising the country well partitioned, there were some among the Indians who kept stirring them up, and very severe punishments were inflicted in consequence, resulting in the reduction of the [indigenous] population. Several principal men of the province of Cupul they burned alive, and others they hung. Information being laid against the people of Yobaín, a town of the Chels, the Spaniards took the leading men, put them in stocks in a building and then set fire to the house, burning them all alive with the greatest inhumanity in the world. I, Diego de Landa, say that I saw a great tree near the village, upon the branches of which a [Spanish] captain had hung many women, with their infant children being hung by their feet. At this town, and at another two leagues away, called Verey, they hung two Indian women, one a maiden and the other recently married, for no other crime than their beauty, and because of fearing a disturbance among the [Spanish] soldiers on their account; also further to cause the Indians to believe that the Spaniards were indifferent to their women. The memory of these two women is kept both among the Indians and the Spaniards on account of their great beauty and the cruelty with which they were killed.

A provocative piece of evidence corroborating de Landa's grisly, but long unpublished, account is found in Las Casas's well known *Brevisima Relación,* which even includes a print appearing to illustrate this very scene (see Fig. 58). In any event, the results of these atrocities were inevitable; according to Landa,

> The Indians of the provinces of Cochuah and Chetumal rose, and the Spaniards so pacified them that, from being the most settled and populous, it became the most wretched region of the whole country. Unheard of cruelties were inflicted, cutting off their noses, hands, arms, and legs, and the breasts of their women; throwing them into deep water, with gourds tied to their feet, thrusting the children through with spears, because they could not go as fast as their mothers. If some of those who had been put in chains fell sick, or could not keep up with the rest, rather than stop to unfasten them, they would instead just cut off their heads among the rest. They also kept great numbers of women and men captive in their service, with similar treatment.

As recent history shows us all too well, even an atrocity (especially when it is called "pacification") has its apologists. One of those was (again) Diego de Landa, who observes that,

> In their defense, the Spaniards urge that, being so few in numbers, they could not have reduced so populous a country, save through the fear of such terrible punishments. They offer the example from the [biblical] history of the passage of the Hebrews into the Land of Promise, committing great cruelties by the command of God. On the other hand, the Indians were right in defending their liberty and trusting to the valor of their chiefs, and they thought it would so result as against the Spaniards.[42]

Buried in the Spanish state archives for centuries, the details of Diego de Landa's *Relación de las cosas de Yucatán* remained a secret. Another such report was also only intended for the eyes of Spanish officials but, somehow (historians are still unsure by which means), it began to circulate in manuscript. However it happened, Bartolomé de Las Casas's *Brevísima relación de la destrucción de las Indias* (completed around 1542) was eventually translated into Flemish (1578), French (1579), English (1583), and German (1597). The title of the French version tells how it was then meant to be read, particularly in the Protestant countries: *Miroir des tyrannies et cruautés des Espagnoles.* Now we just call it the Black Legend (*la leyenda negra*), and that trope represents, mostly in the political sense, not only a "Mirror of the Tyranny and Cruelty of the Spaniards" but also a metaphorical but certainly damaging fall from grace for imperial Spain during the strife-torn period of the Protestant Reformation and Catholic Counter-Reformation.

The Leyenda Negra

Whatever one's position on the issue, for our purposes it becomes necessary to review in some detail the context and components of a certain fantasy that perpetuated, and has done so for some centuries now, an askew appreciation of the realities of Spain's fundamental contributions to the Europeanization of America. The so-called *Leyenda Negra* still distorts, to one degree or another, any profound historical understanding of the Hispanic background of America.[43] Additionally, it has especially affected, which is of particular interest to us, the evolving European image of the Native American. As the term indicates, under this blanket heading there are included a whole series of "blackening" distortions of Spanish achievements, whether in America or even in Europe itself, since the post-Columbian period. Like every enduring legend, especially one based upon a largely negative evaluation of now distant events, the Black Legend represents a widely accredited historical picture, one, however, it may be argued, largely without foundations. Viewed objectively (as best as one can presently), either the facts themselves were patently false, or real events had been falsified or distorted to a considerable degree.

Once a legend of such magnitude had been wrought, it was essential that it be continually nourished by repeated recitations of its conventionally fixed, often truly stereotypical attributes. Once assigned, such set traits prove difficult to eradicate, and to militate against them only earnest re-evaluations or tardy apologia can be retrospectively produced. In his classic, often reprinted study on *La Leyenda Negra,* Julián Juderías has called this anti-Spanish myth an absurdity with tragic connotations. He observes that

> it arose from memories of the past and a disdain for the present, due to which, whether we like it or not, we Spaniards are bound to be, either individually or collectively, thought of as cruel and intolerant, *aficionados* of barbarous spectacles and the enemies of every manifestation of real culture and progress.

As is well known today, the Black Legend was invented, with a certain amount of deliberation, during the course of the sixteenth century. It did not pertain to actions by the Catholic Kings, even though Ferdinand and Isabella were the ones who had actually introduced the Inquisition into Spain toward the end of the fifteenth century. In retrospect, it is clear that the legend could only have fully matured and acquired its set, even stereotypical character during the long reign of Philip II (1556–98). Clearly, it needed to have materialized at that time when an originally Germanic Habsburg Empire was becoming transformed into an awesome *imperio nacional español,* additionally turning Spain into the first all-powerful, and so universally resented, national entity of modern times. As the em-blematic leader of this monolithic political abstraction, Philip II came to be known to northern Europeans — especially Protestants — as the Devil In-carnate of the South, *el demonio del Mediodía.* For those who know Spanish history, it seems only characteristic — actually rather ironic — that the anti-Spanish legend would have originated among Spaniards, some of whom created it consciously, whereas others, acting impulsively from motives of spite and envy, acted largely without deliberate design. Whatever the motivation, the long-term effects have proved often devastating.

The foundation stone of the Black Legend is a polemical, and eventu-ally widely circulated, text by a Dominican friar, Bartolomé de Las Casas; published in Seville in 1552, its inflammatory title was *Brevísima relación de la destrucción de las Indias.* This not really so "Very Brief [an] Account of the Destruction of the Indies" was to be opportunely exploited by anyone hos-tile to Spanish ambitions and, in the second half of the sixteenth century, this could include nearly everybody living north and east of the Pyrenees. A major feature accounting for its enduring appeal was that all these irredeemably black deeds had actually been denounced by a Spaniard who was himself a man of the cloth; hence, so it was understood, neither the veracity nor the legitimacy of his provocative data need be questioned.

Another Spaniard who contributed to the early evolution of the Black Legend in the sixteenth century was a former employee of the Inquisition, Reinaldo González Montes, who left Spain and converted to the Lutheran heresy. Yet another was Antonio Pérez (1540–1611), former private secretary and confidant of Philip II. Once the full scope of his criminal intrigues, including arranging for the assassination of an innocent man (Juan de Escobedo, secretary of Don Juan de Austria), were eventually uncovered, Pérez was incarcerated. Somehow he managed to escape from prison, and in 1594, under the nom de plume of Rafael Peregrino, he published in London his scurrilous *Relaciones,* an incendiary *feuilleton* that was eagerly devoured throughout Europe.

Constant features of the Black Legend were a series of standard accusations. In the foreground there was always an ad hominem condemnation of Philip II, inevitably for his policy of recalcitrant Catholicism and sometimes for a purported engineering (some said by poisoning) of the death of his son Carlos in 1568. The other essential component, although much less focused, was the already proverbial stigma of cruelty attributed to all Spaniards. This denunciation en masse would be supported *en détaille* with specific references to either the practices of the Spanish Inquisition or to various events associated with the Iberian colonization of America. Even though the Black Legend was endowed with certain invariable and endlessly belabored traits, relative emphasis on one or another shifted with the evolving historical circumstances. In the seventeenth century, for instance, it was the savagery and hypocrisy of the Iberians that became the predominant traits *in malo,* whereas, in the eighteenth century, Spaniards were attacked, according to current rationalist postulates, for their exalted religiosity, then dubbed "fanaticism."

New features belonging to a nineteenth-century version of the legend were accusations of thoroughly despotic powers attributed to the Spanish monarchy and, on the lower ends of the global equation, the backwardness and ignorance supposedly characterizing the Spanish people *in toto.* Given the time frame, it was naturally the last topoi that were to be trumpeted in 1898 by a newly prominent national entity, *los norteamericanos.* These peoples were themselves thereafter to become increasingly notorious in Spain and Latin America as the *imperialistas del siglo* xx. In this context, the most tangible result was a so-called "Spanish-American War" which put a decisive end to a decidedly moribund *imperio ultramar español.* Now bereft of any traces of that once-feared overseas Spanish Empire, for the most part Spain's Black Legend is presently consigned to oblivion. Ironically, a Spanish Empire that began in America, the first upon which the sun never set, was terminated four centuries later by other transplanted Europeans, an aggressive group now, in 1898, unilaterally calling themselves "Americans," so denying the honorific title to citizens of such unquestionable Native American nation-states as Bolivia, Brazil, Colombia, Ecuador, Guatemala, Mexico, Peru, Venezuela, etc. Some good has however emerged from all this: The truth of the matter of an extended *leyenda negra,* determining the origins of those ancient and now wholly obsolete anti-Hispanic myths, may now be examined with rather more objectivity than was possible during the emotionally heated moments of their birth during the Renaissance.

The Controversial Career of Fray Bartolomé de Las Casas

It is not easy to deal with the controversial figure of Friar Bartolomé de Las Casas, because those who have studied the man and his times generally fall into two diametrically opposing camps, either *lascasistas* or *antilascasistas.* He was born in Seville, probably in 1484, in an archetypal *barrio popular sevillano,* la Triana. He died in 1566 in Madrid, in the Dominican monastery of Atocha, at the ripe old age of 82. His future affiliation with the American enterprise was something like a paternal legacy; in 1493 his father, Pedro de Las Casas, took part in Columbus's second voyage to the New World. Upon his eventual return to Seville, Pedro received from Columbus the gift of a young Indian slave. Now nine years old, his son must have been as much impressed by his father's tales of the Caribbean as he was enthralled by his youthful Taino companion. Nine years later, his father once again sailed to the New World, this time in an expedition led by Nicolás de Ovando. On this occasion he was accompanied by his son, Bartolomé. Now eighteen, the young Las Casas, who had already attended the University of Salamanca, where he picked up rudiments of classical learning and certain techniques of legalistic argumentation that were markedly to characterize his later writings, acted like any other Spanish adventurer in the New World. Like the rest, bent on speedily acquiring his personal fortune, Bartolomé acquired his own Indian slaves, worked them in mines and assiduously attended to the cultivation of his evidently lucrative estates. His dormant conscience was, nonetheless, finally awakened in 1515, when he took part in the Cuban campaign led by Pánfilo de Narváez, and then he chose to renounce his share of the lavish booty due an expeditionary participant.

Upon his return to Spain in 1517, Las Casas endeavored to effect a change in official policies regarding the American natives. He argued for treatment of the Indians as rational beings, following a position already initiated in 1511 by Friar Antonio de Montesinos. From that moment on, his multifaceted personality was going to reveal itself in varied directions. Among other appointments, acting in the roles of *consejero de gobernantes y reyes* and *abogado defensor de la causa india,* Las Casas presented lengthy suits in defense of the *derechos* of the Indians. He quickly became known as a polemical writer and staunch opponent to whomever did not support his views. Although his voice was not the only one raised in support of the Indians, it certainly proved the most persistent. It was first publicly heard in 1525, when he founded the Consejo de Indias, and continued to be heard until 1542, the date of the establishment of the so-called "Leyes Nuevas." The most prominent traits of his personality, as recognized then and now, were generosity, arbitrariness, and impetuosity.

Certainly foremost in the career of Las Casas is his pro-Indian position. Whereas this benevolent stance seems, in retrospect, very much in line with our contemporary attitudes, such strident multiculturalism was nearly unique in his time, the Renaissance. Opposing a new political order that was slowly but surely being imposed in the New World, it was Las Casas who mainly championed the cause of political and cultural recognition for autonomous Native American communities; this distinction was, in fact, only to be conceded in the twentieth century. Las Casas only admitted one concession to the spirit of his time, and that was in regard to the evangelical mission of the Spaniards. He, too, accepted that native cultures should be drastically transformed by the absolute imposition of Christianity; it was, after all, for their own good. But this was only natural; he was a member of the Dominican Order.

Although, as was mentioned, Las Casas was not alone in advocating *derechos indios* at this moment, what made the future bishop of Chiapas notorious in his own time was his transformation into one of the first propagandists of attitudes really belonging to the modern era. He fought tirelessly and endlessly to have his obdurate opinions on controversial subjects become accepted by the Spaniards during the age of the Renaissance and, further, to have them made public policy by the Spanish crown itself. His compatriots would be *made* to listen to arguments for the rights of the Indians presented by this fiery polemicist. Lewis Hanke has observed that the other European nations sent explorers to the Americas in order to gain for them overseas empires. In the case of Spain, however, "no other European people, before or since the conquest of America, plunged into such a struggle for justice as developed among Spaniards shortly after the discovery of America and persisted throughout the sixteenth century."[44]

In his sober analysis of Las Casas's career, Hanke succeeded in pointing out both the positive qualities and the defects of the Dominican's efforts as an historian. As he concluded, Las Casas's greatest deficiencies were a lack of discipline and balance, and these faults often led him to interpolate bizarre materials, some of which may often seem to have little relation to the historical reality of the New World. His greatest lapse was in objectivity. This was a negative factor that was emphasized long ago by, among others, the Basque historian Altolaguirre:

> He became so impassioned in his treatment of relations existing between Spaniards and Indians that he seized upon the greatest blunders committed by Spaniards and, building upon these indiscretions, he formulated the most bitter censures against the *conquistadores*. He lent credence in his writings to secondhand information, biased by hatred and rancor. He took anything which reached his ears in order to denigrate Spanish colonists, and without seeking to separate the true from the false. Instead, expanding upon these *habladurías,* and re-telling them as it suited him, he used them in order to present the conquerors as heartless and impelled by bloody instincts; it was these traits which made them commit the greatest cruelties and the most horrendous crimes against the unhappy Indians. As he concluded, the latter were just *corderos* [lambs], wholly incapable of doing any harm against their greatest enemies.[45]

The final assessment of Las Casas's value as an admittedly polemical historian falls to meticulous and objective—for being neither Spanish apologist nor Protestant polemicist—modern historians like Lewis Hanke. As Hanke observes, "the detractors of Las Casas have shrewdly exploited his [frequent] numerical errors without ever disproving his essential truths." Nonetheless, Hanke's overall conclusion is that "no one today would defend the statistics Las Casas gave, but few would deny that there was considerable truth in his main charges."

The Legacy of the Brevísima relación de la destrucción de las Indias

We have already cited this publication as representing the cornerstone of the Black Legend and, additionally, as the first to appear along these lines. No other book like this proved to be so effective, and accordingly none other did so much damage during the prolonged anti-Spanish campaigns. This is, moreover, by far the most famous of the various treatises produced by Las Casas. Written in haste in 1542, its composition was concluded in Valencia on December 8th. Friar Bartolomé, who was usually never fond of brevity, was concise (*brevísimo*) in his *Brevísima relación*. This was a report addressed to the current king of Spain, Philip II, and it took the form of a memorandum reporting on serious problems occurring in America. We cannot, of course, believe that Las Casas would have written this book with any conscious intention of defaming Spain. That was not his intention, but it certainly was the motivation for various foreigners who would later use the *Brief Relation* to advance their own causes, many of which were completely opposed to the original purposes of Las Casas. Moreover, we are not dealing here with a historical narrative as such, rather with multiple allegations of serious operational improprieties in dealing with native peoples. One motive for the great polemics stirred up by this treatise has always been the charge, as advanced by Spanish authors, of its apparent lack of veracity and the great exaggerations arising from this fault.

For instance, according to a notable scholar, Ramón Menéndez Pidal, Las Casas verged on paranoia and his emphatic conclusions must have been dictated by a kind of mania or obsession. He observed that, even when dealing with regions with which he was quite familiar, Las Casas will often slip into unwarranted hyperbole. For example, he mentions some "30,000 rivers" that supposedly descend from the Cibao Mountains and, likewise, he guesses the length of the island of Cuba to be comparable to the distance from Valladolid to Rome. Always more commented *in malo* was what Las Casas had to say about the indigenous populations, for he generally tends to overpopulate—drastically—Native American landscapes. Accordingly, for Las Casas, Yucatán was a land full of "infinitas gentes"; Nueva Granada becomes the most populous region in the whole world; Honduras was "un paraíso" and, likewise, its lands were the most crowded with indigenous peoples that one could find anywhere in the world. Tied to his geographical fantasies were his numerical exaggerations, one result being the surmise in his *Brevísima relación* that the number of Indians killed by the conquerors must exceed some 24,000,000. Regarding this conclusion, a French scholar, Robert Ricard, recalls that,

> since it is unquestionable that in no way could Las Casas have been made privy to an official census of those Indians who actually had their throats cut [by Spaniards], one must therefore proceed with caution when dealing with his calculations. But he would have it backwards too: in his *Destruyción,* he manipulates figures in the millions with an offhanded slovenliness. Once those figures, appearing in many different places in the *Destruyción,* are mutually compared, it becomes readily apparent to one's eyes that, due to their internal contradictions, populations in the millions, more or less, could never really have been correctly arrived at.

It never occurred to Las Casas to ponder the single great cause, the real one, leading to the rapid depopulation of America. Nonetheless, it was a clearly evident fact, of which Spanish authorities were themselves well aware, and even within a few years after the beginning of the process of colonization. From the third decade of the sixteenth century, naturally foremost in the eyes of observant Spaniards was the effect of contagious diseases brought over by white men from the Old World, against which the Indians had no natural immunity nor any antibodies.[46] Among other causes that had early been posited to explain the decimation of native peoples one was the designation of the Indians as belonging to an "inferior" race; this factor, it was then explained, made them incapable of resistance to the stress presented by common European maladies. Another aspect of the degenerative complex, also soon made manifest, was *el mestizaje,* the mixing of the races, for the conquistadores quickly took up with native women for the lack of any serviceable *españolas blancas.* Yet another factor was a battery of vices imported from the Old World, probably the most widely spread, certainly the most widely condemned by Spaniards, being drunkenness.

In keeping with the character of a propagandistic memorandum, to which subliterary genre Las Casas's text properly belongs, its author often resorts to his personal presence as an eyewitness; as he was wont to exclaim, "Una vez vide . . ." (Once I myself saw . . .). Much more common, since the writer is preoccupied by his one-on-one desire to persuade the king himself, is that he will speak in a vague and imprecise tone. The basic format of the different chapters in the *Brief Relation* turns out to be the same: The Spanish *conquistadores* arrive in each different region in order uniformly to perpetuate the most serious moral offenses while at the same time they commit the most incredible physical atrocities. Over a forty-year long stretch, it is as though they were all the same protagonists, monotonously carrying out massacres without number. As various scholars point out, for each supposedly distinct anecdote, Las Casas's description becomes the same as the preceding, including the employment of certain phrases that are nearly identical in one and another case.

This little book, which was to prove so effective in the hands of Lutherans, was published — without license — by Las Casas in 1552 in the Sevillian print shop of Sebastián Trugillo. Las Casas's provocative *libellus* was made readily available throughout Europe, was even shipped to America. Curiously, as we have discovered, *grotteschi* patterns that decorate the handsomely designed frontispiece of the *Destruyción* in its 1552 printing manifestly copied decorative motifs still seen today on the lavishly embellished Renaissance-style staircase of the Augustinian monastery of Actopán founded in Nueva España itself.[47] Presumably, Las Casas saw (perhaps drew) these ornamental devices in the handsome church built not far from Mexico City.

Outside the Hispanic sphere, certain extrinsic circumstances, mainly of a political and religious nature, were to provide for the *Destruyción* a readership never foreseen, and most likely never desired, by its zealous author. For instance, the Dutch were intent upon dismantling Spanish dominion over their provinces; since their population was primarily Protestant, naturally they would not tolerate further Iberian domination over the Low Lands for primarily religious reasons. In this situation, Netherlanders opportunely saw in Las Casas's texts the means to unleash a concentrated campaign of defamation and derision against their Catholic enemies. The key year, marking the real installation of the *Leyenda Negra,* was 1578, when a Dutch translation of the *Brevísima relación* appeared. In a reprinting of 1579, the Netherlandish title becomes significantly altered, with its Spanish equivalent being *Espejo de la tiranía española, en que se cuentan los hechos criminales, escandalosos y horribles que los españoles han perpetrado en Las Indias* ("The Mirror of Spanish Tyranny, in Which Are Recounted Criminal, Scandalous and Horrible Deeds Perpetrated by Spaniards in the Indies"). The gist of this inflammatory title—*Miroir de la tyrannie . . .*—was exactly repeated in a French translation published in Antwerp in the same year. By the close of the sixteenth century, editions of the *Brevísima relación* followed one after another, almost without interruption, and also including further translations into Latin and German. One result was that nearly anyone literate in his own language was able to digest at his leisure the appalling recitations of Padre Las Casas.

Among these translations, noteworthy is a German text that appeared in Frankfurt in 1597, as published by an expatriate Dutchman, Theodore de Bry. This version was unique in being illustrated; its seventeen, vividly conceived engravings provided a strictly visual equivalent to the verbal recitations of reiterated atrocities. For mainly doctrinal reasons, de Bry had become an implacable enemy of Spain. Fleeing from the Spanish Netherlands, this committed Protestant publisher once again established his already successful firm in Germany. By conceiving of a mechanically produced book as a beautifully illustrated objet d'art, de Bry came to enjoy huge commercial success. In nearly all the de Bry publications one did not really need to read the texts; the handsome plates anticipated their content, and so even an illiterate was able immediately to seize upon the propagandistic essentials. His editorial, and additionally polemical, policies were to be faithfully hewed to by his inheritors. The same principles and format naturally applied to his hugely successful edition of Las Casas's *Miroir de la tyrannie espagnole,* so allowing a reading (or just browsing) public, mostly Protestants, to become instantly apprised of its contents, an almost cinematic resumé of uniquely heinous Iberian operations in the New World.

One need only review a listing of the many editions of the *Mirror of Spanish Tyranny,* most of which were illustrated, in order to document the unquestioned commercial and propagandistic success of this vividly polemical tract. During the period preceding the Peace of Westphalia in 1648, bringing the Thirty Years' War to a somewhat indecisive close, Las Casas's treatise was reprinted, in various languages, up to twenty-six times, and ten of these editions were illustrated with de Bry's most expressive engravings. In the seventeenth century alone, there were the Latin versions of 1614 and 1664, as well as impressions in other, more "living," languages: German (1613, 1665), French (1620, 1623, 1630, 1642, 1697), English (1625, 1656, 1689, 1699), Italian (1626, 1630, 1636, 1640, 1643, 1644, 1645, 1657), Dutch or Flemish (1607, 1609, 1612, 1620, 1628, 1638, 1643, 1644). Its singularly enduring—polyglot and pan-European—*Nachleben* as a triumph of politically engaged publishing naturally conditioned its enormous spread across the continent, and so its persistent employment as a sectarian weapon. In short, Las Casas's often distorting "Mirror" was itself precociously something like the twentieth century "media event." Rómulo Carbia, who enumerated all these various editions, also observed that,

> as it were, just as soon as the artillery would fall silent, then the printing presses would began to grind away once again, and once again Las Casas's tract, sometimes with its familiar engravings, seventeen of them, or sometimes without any illustrations at all, started on its march once more.[48]

Thanks to the kindness of a Mexican colleague, Guillermo Tovar de Teresa, who has loaned us his copy of a Latin edition of Las Casas's treatise that was printed in Heidelberg in 1664 with the title *Regionum Indicarum per Hispanos olim desvastatarum accuratissima descriptio,* we have access to the entire series of celebrated engravings belonging to this self-styled "Most Accurate Description of the Lands of the Indians Now Laid Waste by the Spaniards." These we may now proceed to discuss in some detail, making specific reference to their exact textual situations and thus to their "literal" functions.

In the introduction to his work, Las Casas begins with an idyllic eulogy of Edenic life-styles belonging to rustic, pre-Columbian inhabitants of the New World. His was a largely idealized vision of the Indian, which, pushing the very limits of objectivity, he shapes to make a rhetorical counterpart to a complementary, nevertheless largely diabolic, image of the Spanish *conquistadores.* His manner of initially describing those newly discovered American aborigines draws heavily upon tropes belonging to the ancient Age of Gold, beloved by generations of secular European poets who had invented the pseudo-Edenic theme millennia beforehand; as he pictures them,

Among all these diverse peoples, *a toto genero,* whom God had created, these were the most simple, a folk without either evil intentions or double-dealing, making them most obedient and faithful to their natural lords, and also to the Christians, to whom they now serve. They are the most humble, most patient, most peaceful and tranquil peoples, without either spitefulness nor resentment, neither quarrelsome nor contentious, without anger nor hatred, never desirous of vengeance; in this, they are like no others in the world. At the same time, they are the most delicate folk, weak and tender in compliance and less able to suffer labor and who are, therefore, most easily brought down by any sort of illness. There are among them neither sons of princes or nobles; nor will there be found among them—such as exist among those of us [Europeans] who are brought up with gifts and a delicate life—any who might prove to be more delicate than are these gentle folk, even though there are among them those who stem from the laboring classes. They are additionally peoples given to great poverty, for they own much less than we do, nor do they have any wish to possess earthly goods. Nonetheless, they are not given to pride, nor are they ambitious nor covetous. Their food is such that not even the Holy Fathers in the Wilderness would seemed to have pursued a more straightened, less pleasurable and impoverished, life. Customarily, their clothing is just their own skins, with their private parts covered, and when they might choose to cover themselves with a cotton blanket, it will be but a square of cloth measuring a yard and a half or two in width. Their beds are put upon matting and, most often, they sleep in hanging nets; in the language of Hispaniola, these are called *hamacas.* In this too they are hygienic and without pretension. Of lively intelligence, so they are most capable of, and are truly open to receive every kind of good doctrine; thus, they are most fitting to receive our holy Catholic faith and so to become endowed with virtuous customs. For this, they present less obstacles than any other of the peoples in the whole world created by God.[49]

In order to appreciate just how far Las Casas went in his eulogies of the Native Americans, it would be sufficient to compare them with that rather more negative (or, if you wish, realistic) picture that had been drawn of the Indians by a fellow Dominican, Tomás Ortiz, whom we have quoted earlier in this chapter and whose statements were published in Peter Martyr's *Decade* VII.[50] But let us now return to what Las Casas would have us believe. Following that idyllic picture drawn of Indians in the introduction to the

Brevísima relación, the Dominican announces the arrival of Europeans in the Caribbean, following which the rapacious intruders fall upon the unsuspecting locals, here called "tame sheep." The comportment of the Spaniards, according to Las Casas, was

> like the cruelest of wolves, tigers and lions, who have gone hungry many days. And they have not acted in any other way in these parts for some forty years, and they are still doing so today. Right to the present day, the only thing they do [to the natives] is tear them apart, kill them, torture and torment them, decimate them by pulling out their guts, and by other new and varied cruelties, none of which have before been seen, or read, or even heard about. These methods, a few of which will be mentioned below, have been employed in such manner that, whereas there had originally been on the island of Hispaniola some three millions of peoples whom we saw, today there remain of the natives no more than two hundred persons.

Following this initial accusation, Las Casas offers an explanation for the notorious depopulation of the mainland, or *tierra firme.* There, he says, due to the cruelty, "tyranny and infernal operations" of the Spaniards over a period of forty years, some twelve, perhaps even fifteen, millions of natives have been done away with. The motivation for the slaughter is simple:

> The reason why so many souls have been killed and destroyed by Christians in such infinite numbers has only been due to their conquerors' ultimate goal, gold. These have only wished to bloat themselves with wealth in just a few days, thereby to arrive at a high station which in no way corresponds to their real origins. They were enabled to do so by their insatiable greed and ambition, which must be the greatest ever known to the world, and by reason of the felicitous and extremely rich nature of these lands, filled with peoples so humble, so patient and, therefore, so easy to dominate.

Las Casas Depicts Some Spanish Atrocities

Keeping with the narrower purposes of this investigation, a step-by-step analysis of the evolution of European delineations of American Indians, we may now present detailed commentaries on the seventeen engravings

53.

Plate 1: "Spanish Atrocities in Hispaniola," from B. de Las Casas, Regionum Indicarum per Hispanos olim devastatarum (Heidelberg, 1664).

ordered by Theodore de Bry, and as designed by Jodocus de Winghe, to illuminate key passages in the *Brevísima relación* (Figs. 53–58). These images also provide the first extensive documentation of the final aspect of American Indian iconography; now, besides the Noble and Ignoble Indian tropes, we additionally have the figure of the "Doomed Indian." This iconographic type, however, only again becomes predominant after around 1876, and then mostly in English-speaking America.

The first chapter in Las Casas's book deals with the island of Hispaniola. As the first Caribbean region to be settled by Spaniards, it naturally became the bridgehead for future operations on the continent. Las Casas's discussion of this island treats it as a place where techniques characterizing all subsequent atrocities practiced by Spaniards were first deliberately rehearsed. From the outset, he claims, these "estragos y crueldades de los españoles" spared neither pregnant women nor ancients nor infants (Fig. 53).

Accordingly, the first engraving in his broadside shows an enraged *conquistador* repeatedly smashing an innocent babe against a rock while another Spaniard crouches to fan the flames of a lurid barbecue of locals hanging from a gallows. This horrific premonition of Auschwitz was described by Las Casas as follows:

> Spaniards would take babies from their mothers' breasts; swinging them by their feet, they then bashed their brains out upon the crags. Other infants were thrown upside-down into rivers; laughing, sporting and falling into the water, the Spaniards would then cry, "boil the corpse of this one." Yet other infants would be speared together with their mothers, along with any others the Spaniards might come across. They made some gallows, which were almost high enough to allow the feet of the Indians to touch the ground; hanging them in rows of thirteen, so they said to honor and make reverence to our Redeemer and the Twelve Apostles, they then set fire to wood placed underneath and so burned them all alive.[51]

The next part of the text directly inspired the next print in de Bry's inflammatory series (Fig. 54). Las Casas, whose statement explains all the gory details shown by our Flemish engraver, says that

> some other Indians, whom they wished to keep alive, would have both their hands cut off, which the Spaniards then hung around their necks, telling them then to "take off with these letters." This meant that they were to carry the news to those people who had escaped earlier into the hills. Here is how they usually killed Indian lords and nobles: they would make grills out of stakes suspended upon forked sticks. They tied them to these and then lit a slow fire below them. Screaming from their torments, from which there was no hope of release, they all went mad, little by little.[52]

The next chapter deals with native kingdoms that had been in la Española, particularly one which had been governed by two Indian *caciques,* Behechio and his sister Anacaona. The gruesome graphic contents copied in the third print are explained by Las Casas:

> The Spanish governor who ruled over Hispaniola arrived here one day with seventy calvary and three hundred infantrymen; the horsemen

54.

Plate 2: "More Spanish Atrocities in Hispaniola," from B. de Las Casas, Regionum Indicarum per Hispanos olim devastatarum (Heidelberg, 1664).

alone would have been sufficient to lay waste to the entire island—and the continent too. Under a pledge of safety, more than three hundred Indian lords came to meet the governor at his request. Duping them, the Spanish captain had most of them put into a big thatched house. Once they were all inside, he ordered the hut put to the torch, and so he burnt them all alive. As for the other lords, along with any number of other Indians, they were all run down with lances or put to the sword. As for the lady Anacaona, in order to pay her special homage, they had her hung.[53]

In a chapter discussing events on Cuba, Las Casas makes mention of another *cacique*, Hatuey (Fig. 55). The Dominican states that, even though Hatuey managed to flee from Hispaniola, eventually he fell into the hands of implacable Spaniards. It is the ghastly torture which they subsequently inflicted

55.

Plate 4: "The Torture of Chief Hatuey in Cuba," from B. de Las Casas, Regionum Indicarum per Hispanos olim devastatarum (Heidelberg, 1664).

upon him, finally ordering him burnt at the stake, which becomes the centerpiece of the fourth print. As Las Casas explains the scene,

> While Hatuey was being tied to the post, a Franciscan who happened to be there, himself a holy man, told him some things, about which he had never been informed, concerning God and our religion. The scant time allowed by executioners for this [religious] instruction only permitted the chieftain to be told that he might go to heaven, where he would find glory and eternal repose; if not however, then he must go to hell, where he must suffer endless torment and pain. Thinking about this for a moment, the Indian asked the friar if Christians went to heaven. The reply was that, yes, they did, but only if they were good. Without much further thought, the chief then announced that he was only desirous of going to hell, since that was where good Christians were not, since he had no further wish to see any more of these cruel peoples.[54]

The fifth print depicts another Spanish governor of the *tierra firme,* in this case probably Pedrarias Dávila. Las Casas's text informs us that this Spanish captain was exceptionally cruel, and so he ordered the following punishment to be inflicted upon a brave Indian chief:

> Among numberless evil deeds committed by this governor during the period of his appointment, one stands out: A certain *cacique,* or lord, gave to Dávila the sum of 9,000 *castellanos;* he did so either voluntarily or out of fear (which is more like the truth). Not satisfied with this amount, the governor seized said chieftain. They tied his back to a pillar and seated him upon the ground; stretching out his legs, they placed his feet into a fire. This was done to make him cough up more gold. The chief sent [messengers] to his house and these returned with 3,000 more *castellanos.* The Spaniards [nonetheless] again began to torture him. But he would give them no more gold, either because he had no more or because he did not wish to capitulate again. They kept on torturing him in this manner until the marrow ran out of the soles of his feet. This was how he died.[55]

Another chapter dealing with Nueva España (present-day Mexico) provided the various anecdotes illustrated in prints 6, 7, and 8 in the *Brevísima relación.* The first of these concerns an infamous massacre at Cholula, and the text corresponding to the sixth engraving reads as follows:

> All the native chieftains, and there were more than a hundred of them, were ordered by the Spanish captain to be tied to stakes rammed into the earth in order to be roasted alive. Nonetheless, one of these chiefs, probably the greatest or king of that land, managed to unloose himself and escape. He gathered up another twenty, thirty, or even forty men in a huge temple, called by them *Duu,* which they had there [in Cholula]. This building was like a fortress and the Indians successfully defended it for most of the day. Nonetheless, the Spaniards, who rarely showed any mercy to unarmed Indian peoples, set fire to the temple, and there the defenders were all burnt up while they cried out the following: "Oh, evil men! What have we done to you? Why are you killing us? So, go then to Mexico City. Go to where our universal lord, Moctezuma, will avenge us, wreaking vengeance upon you all."[56]

Next came the equally horrific massacre of Tepeaca, which de Bry (for reasons unknown to us) chose not to illustrate. Then the Spaniards set out on the final stage of their determined march to the Aztec capital, Tenochtitlán, which is the subject of the seventh print, which is also one of the very few in the *Miroir de la tyrannie* that shows no Native American blood being spilt. The initially pacific encounter between Spaniards and Aztec leaders was described by Las Casas:

> From Cholula the Spaniards marched toward Mexico City. The great king Moctezuma sent them thousands of gifts, and he ordered lords and peoples to make *fiestas* for them along the route. At the entrance to the causeway leading into Mexico City, which is two leagues in length, he sent to greet them his own brother, who was accompanied by many great chieftains who brought immense tribute, gold, silver and clothing. Carried on a litter covered in gold, along with all his great court, he himself graciously received the Spaniards at the city gates and then he accompanied them to quarters he had ordered prepared for them in various palaces in the city.[57]

The eighth print reverts to another scene of untrammeled slaughter, and in this case the subject is an infamous massacre that took place within the Great Temple of Mexico City (Fig. 56). Las Casas describes the bloody scene (for which, uniquely, we also happen to have an Aztec eyewitness account, also quoted later):

> In the nearest part of these palaces there were to be found over two thousand children belonging to the Aztec lords and representing the flower of the nobility of Moctezuma's entire empire. Towards them the leader of the Spaniards went with a band of armed men, and he sent out other squads into all other parts of the city where these festivals were being celebrated. The captain ordered that his men were all to pretend that they had only gone as spectators to the festivities, but that at a certain moment they were to fall upon the Indians. Once the Indians felt safe and had became intoxicated, the captain then gave his order: *¡Santiago y a ellos!* and then the Spaniards began to cut open those naked and delicate bodies with their unsheathed swords, and out poured that generous life-blood. They left not one alive; the rest of the Spaniards did the same in the other city squares.[58]

The scene presented in the ninth print deals with an expeditionary force led into Guatemala by Pedro de Alvarado, the result of which was destruction of the Quiché kingdom. The text illustrated by this engraving recounts how

56.

Plate 8: "A Massacre in the Great Temple of Tenochtitlán," from B. de Las Casas, Regionum
Indicarum per Hispanos olim devastatarum (Heidelberg, 1664).

the natives then crafted some deep holes in the middle of the roads.
These were covered by grasses and plants so there would seem to be
nothing there. Into these [Spanish] horses would supposedly plummet,
there gutting themselves upon sharpened and fire-hardened stakes which
filled the pits. Since the Spaniards were warned to watch out for these,
horses only fell into them once or twice, no more than that. Still, the
Spaniards took their revenge. They made it a rule that any Indians they
captured alive, whatever their gender or age, would be thrown into these
pits. It made no difference whether they grabbed pregnant or recently
delivered women, children or old folks. Anyone they could lay hands
on they pitched straightway into the booby traps; so many were they
that bodies of the Indians, run through by their own stakes, actually
overflowed the edges of the holes. It was a sorrowful sight, especially
the [slaughtered] women with their children. All others seized by the
Spaniards were slaughtered with lance and knife, or they threw them to
ferocious dogs, which tore them to pieces and feasted upon their bodies.

57.

Plate 10: "Cannibalistic Acts of the Spanish Mercenaries," from B. de Las Casas, Regionum Indicarum per Hispanos olim devastatarum (Heidelberg, 1664).

> Whenever they would stumble across a chieftain, they honored him by roasting him in the flames.[59]

A seemingly obligatory "American" cannibalistic anecdote also appears in the Las Casas's polemic; illustrated by the tenth print it is taken directly from the same chapter in the *Brevísima relación* referring to Guatemala (Fig. 57). As told by Las Casas,

> Alvarado had a certain habit. When he was preparing to make war upon certain native peoples or provinces, he would take along with him as many as he could manage of already subjected Indians. These [mercenaries] would be employed to make war on other Indians. Since he would give no food whatsoever to the ten or twenty thousand natives he dragged along with him, he permitted them [the *indios*] to eat any

Indians they might capture on their own. That is how he happened to be in attendance at one of their regal and most solemn butcheries of human flesh, at which occasion, and in his very presence, they were seen busy killing children and roasting them entire; when, however, they also butchered a man, it would be just for his hands and feet, which they took to be the tastiest snacks.[60]

In the case of the eleventh engraving illustrating the pamphlet put out by de Bry, the *conquistador* being vilified turns out to be Gonzalo Jiménez de Quesada. This image, showing the Spanish commander torturing a stalwart Indian king named Bogotá (who posthumously bequeathed his name to the capital of a modern South American nation), was inserted in a chapter dealing with the conquest of Nueva Granada (present-day Colombia). As was his custom, Las Casas described the scene as thought he himself had actually been an eyewitness to the cruel occurrence:

> They gave him the rope treatment. They splashed burning tallow onto his belly. To each foot they applied a red-hot horseshoe fastened to a stick, and his neck was tied to another pole. Two men held him by the feet and in this way they set fire to his feet. The tyrant [Jiménez de Quesada] would drop by from time to time to tell the chief that, unless he gave them gold, he was going to die very slowly from this torture. And the order was complied with, and they did kill that lord with their torture.[61]

In the twelfth print belonging to the *Brevísima relación,* the protagonist is, as Las Casas puts it, an "ill-fated" [*malaventurado*] Spaniard. This man, an inspector-general, went across Mexico, from Michoacán toward Jalisco. The Dominican says that Jalisco was then a state "as densely populated as a bee-hive," and so large that it was nearly seven leagues long (or forty kilometers in length). Just as we see in de Bry's print, this "otro tirano" committed the usual European villainies, namely:

> He burnt the villages, made the chiefs his prisoners, then tortured them, as well as enslaving all the remainder. He carried off an infinite number of natives in chains. Recently delivered mothers were made to carry loads belonging to the evil Christians. Since, due to their labors and their weakness from starvation, they could no longer carry their own

58.

Plate 13: "Spanish Atrocities in Yucatán," from B. de Las Casas, Regionum Indicarum per Hispanos olim devastatarum (Heidelberg, 1664).

babies, these were left by the sides of the road, where great numbers of them perished.[62]

The thirteenth plate refers to Yucatán, yet another Indian kingdom described as being once populated with "infinitas gentes" (Fig. 58). Alas, there fell upon Yucatán a certain Spanish governor, "embustero y tirano," who unleashed his war dogs and set them upon the unfortunate Indians. This episode, or one very like it, was similarly recounted by Diego de Landa (as quoted earlier). As Las Casas describes the gruesome actions depicted in the print:

> The melancholic Spaniards were coming with their fierce hounds, hunting down Indians, women and men alike, in order to set their dogs upon them. A sickly Indian maiden recognized that she was incapable of escaping from the dogs. Not wishing to have them tear her to pieces, as

they did to the others, she took a rope and tied her one-year old infant from her foot. Then she hung herself from a limb. But she was not quick enough: the dogs arrived and tore her baby to bits. Just before he died, however, a friar baptized him.[63]

Las Casas carries on and on in this way, not sparing any prominent Spaniard from his devastating accusations. In the fourteenth print his target is a famous leader of the conquest of Peru, Francisco Pizarro. His entry into the city of Tumbala (or Túmbez) had as its sequel a series of horrific crimes, most prominent being a series of terrible tortures inflicted upon the Inca emperor Atahualpa. This Inca noble wished to have his authority recognized by the European intruders, but his petition to Pizarro was in vain, and as Friar Bartolomé explains, Atahualpa

> responded that in all this land [of Peru] not a single leaf on a tree could move without his permission; therefore, if his peoples joined together it would be believed that he had ordered their organization. He [Atahualpa] said that he was their prisoner and that they [the Spaniards] should kill him. It was all in vain: the Spaniards condemned him to be burnt alive. Afterward, some Spaniards pleaded with their captain to have him hanged, and so he was both hung and burnt.[64]

In the print corresponding to these accusations the torture of Atahualpa takes place in the foreground; in the background is displayed a sort of "picture in a picture," showing Spaniard lancers and riflemen warding off a mob of enraged natives.

The fifteenth print shows yet another horrific torture scene. In this case the unfortunate recipient was Catzonzin, ruler of the Tarascans in Mexico. This torment had been ordered by Nuño Guzmán, "tirano insensible y cruel," and, according to Las Casas, this Spanish leader

> set fire to said king because he was famed for being very rich in gold and silver. So that he [Catzonzin] would provide them with much treasure, the [Spanish] tyrant began to subject him to various kinds of torture. They put his feet into manacles, stretched out his body and tied his hands to a post. They placed a brazier under his feet. From time to time, a lad armed with a brush soaked in oil would sprinkle drops of this on his skin so that this would toast nicely. At the middle of his body another

cruel man was stationed; his job was to point a loaded cross-bow at his heart. At the other end of his body there was yet another; it was he who let a terribly fierce dog snap at him which, if unleashed, would have completely torn him to bits. These were the ways he was tortured by the Spaniards in order to make him reveal the treasures they sought. This went on until a certain Franciscan found out and Catzonzin was allowed to be released into his hands. Nonetheless, he eventually died from these ordeals.[65]

With another geographical leap, plate 16 returns us to Nueva Granada. Once again the protagonist is a notorious villain, but this is one, Jiménez de Quesada, whom we saw in malevolent action earlier. According to Las Casas, in this case the bloody deeds, faithfully recounted in meticulous detail by the Flemish engraver, necessarily include the following:

The Spanish captain marched many leagues across this land. He seized as many Indians as he could, but none would tell him the name of the chief who had succeeded Bogotá. To make them talk, either men or women, he might choose to cut off the hands of some or he might throw others to dogs, who would tear their bodies apart. In this way, he managed to kill and destroy many male and female Indians. One day, four hours after sunrise, he attacked a number of Indian chiefs (or captains) and a great many ordinary folk. All believed that they were in a state of peace, for this had been assured to them by the Spaniards, who had given them their word that they would receive from them neither evil nor pillage. Because of this pledge, they came down from the mountains where they had hidden themselves, returning to the plain where their village is situated. And so it was that, careless for being confident in a promise given, a great number of people, women and men alike, were able to be seized. Jiménez ordered that their arms be stretched out upon the ground. Then he himself cut off their hands with his cutlass. Then he told them that this punishment was done to them because they had refused to identify the whereabouts of the new lord who had taken over rulership in that kingdom.[66]

In spite of its high numbering, the subject depicted in plate 17 was actually inspired by anecdotes belonging to some of the earlier chapters in the *Brevísima relación,* dealing with actions on Hispaniola, specifically with the fifth kingdom on that island, ruled over by the *cacique* Higüey. Las Casas additionally refers here to an aged native queen, Higuanamá, who was, he affirms, hanged by "los españoles rapaces," who then placed her subjects in slavery. On this occasion the Flemish engraver seems to have departed from the text, for he chose to put two scenes of torture in the foreground; on the left is a flagellation scene and, beside it, a native writhing in torment from having molten lead generously poured upon his naked back. Perhaps ironically, given the mostly Protestant purposes put to these prints, one points out how both Indians are posed (as in nearly all the other plates) in ways that exactly correspond to wholly conventionalized poses belonging to notable Catholic martyrs, pious unfortunates depicted voluntarily undergoing the most abominable tortures for the sake of their Roman faith slightly earlier in Counter-Reformation art. Explaining the eventual fate of Higüey's subjects, Las Casas states that

> the treatment given to, or care taken by the Spaniards for these Indians was to send the men to the mines to extract gold, which proved for them an intolerable labor. As for the women, they placed them on plantations, which are farms, where they made them dig up the fields and prepare the ground, even though that was work better given to the strongest and most sturdy men.[67]

One purpose motivating this detailed analysis of the engravings selected by de Bry to illustrate Friar Bartolomé's inflammatory pamphlet has been to demonstrate that this magnanimous soul was often wanting in what today might be called minimal objectivity. According to some modern Spanish detractors of the Renaissance *Leyenda Negra*, Las Casas represents the antithesis of an objective historian, and so particularly Ramón Menéndez Pidal would classify him as "paranoica." In Las Casas's *Brevísima relación* not one Spaniard is spared from a collective charge of "la infamia," and all merely seem headless puppets; as he would have it, all the daring deeds performed by the *conquistadores* were nought but simple misdeeds.

To repeat a point probably sufficiently reiterated, as Las Casas consistently intends to make clear in his often monotonously interminable catalog of horrors, these were nearly all atrocities that he himself had seen with his very own horror-struck eyes: "Yo vide todas las cosas arriba dichas y muchas otras infinitas." Since this is stomach-turning stuff, only one of the many detailed accounts provided by Las Casas need be cited in order to give our readers another final instance of the bloody and tragic flavor of the contents of this historically significant book, the precursor of innumerable examples of a supposedly modern genre, atrocity literature. This particular example deals with a part of what transpired in Peru in 1531, such as this series of "items" were reported to Las Casas by an eyewitness, a Franciscan friar, Marcos de Niza:

> Item: the Spaniards gathered together a great number of Indians and locked them up in three houses, as many as each would hold. Then they set these on fire and burned up all those people who were inside, even though they had committed not the least wrong against the Spaniards. And it happened there that a priest named Ocaña grabbed a boy from the fire in which he was being burnt alive. Another Spaniard came along and snatched him from the hands of the priest and threw the boy right back into the fire, where, along with the rest, he was quickly reduced to cinders.
>
> Item: I affirm that I myself saw, before my very own eyes, how the Spaniards had cut off the hands, noses and ears of Indian men and women. There was no cause for this; they did it just because it pleased them to do so. I saw this happen in so many places and parts [of Peru] that it would take a very long time to tell it all. And I saw how the Spaniards would let their dogs loose on the Indians so that they would rip them into pieces. I saw them set the dogs upon a great many other people. I additionally saw them burning a great many houses and villages; so many that I am unable to tell you the number of them. It is likewise the truth that they would take babies from their mothers' breasts and would smash as many of them into pieces as they could. I saw other unlawful and cruel deeds, and all with no provocation whatsoever, which all filled me with horror, along with innumerable others that I saw and which would be too long in the telling of them.
>
> Item: I saw how they called to the chiefs and leaders of the Indians to come to the Spaniards in peace, and how they promised them their safety. Once they arrived however, then they burned them. And, in my presence, they burned two; one was in Andón and the other in Túmbala. And I wasn't able to stop them from burning them all alive, no matter how much I preached to them not to do it.[68]

At the very least, one understands now why Las Casas's work would have been delayed ten years in finding its publisher in Spain, and why even then it would have necessarily been issued without a publishing license. This is also understandable since other kinds of corroborating evidence (some cited here) indicate the essential veracity of Las Casas's precociously modern atrocity journalism.

Attempting as impartial an evaluation as possible of Las Casas's book, we must admit, in short, that Spaniards perpetrated outrages and cruelties during their initial adventures in the Indies; these hardy *conquistadores* were, after all, merely men and not angels. That notwithstanding, viewed objectively their achievements in such adverse conditions are certainly worthy of recital alongside the greatest moments known in the history of mankind. For the sake of fairness, brief mention should be made to a more historically balanced judgment rendered by a modern Colombian, Martín Mexía Restrepo:

> Many of the misdeeds attributed to the Spaniards were in fact due either to the hardness of the times or to certain notions of criminal justice then common to all European nations. For instance, had the task of the conquest of Latin America fallen to them, would the English, French, or Germans have proceeded with any less severity? What we do know about their lesser degree of participation in the great American adventure tells us, in fact, quite the opposite. Any history of their [English, French or German] corsairs, pirates, and filibustering expeditions—which fell upon colonies founded by Spaniards like wild beasts in order to rob, rape, kill, burn, and commit any number of other, truly hideous crimes—will serve immediately to dispel all traces of the illusion. Even though we are today truly moved by, for example, the story of the death of Atahualpa [at the hands of the Spaniards], nonetheless it is not proper to judge men living in a distant historical period by the standards of ours, taken to be another more advanced one; even worse is judging men belonging to a single nation as though men from any of the others might have behaved any better.[69]

Contributions of the Italian Benzoni to the Black Legend

Following Las Casas in the crucial evolutionary stages of the Black Legend, an Italian, Girolamo Benzoni, made the next signal contribution. By means of an often reprinted book, *Historia del Mondo Nuovo,* first published in

Venice in 1565 and later translated into Latin in 1578, Benzoni was to offer further anecdotal accounts of Iberian villainy complementing those advanced previously by Las Casas. Contrary to the Dominican's polemic, Benzoni's narrative—besides inserting the usual, truly appalling listings of various Iberian misdeeds—offers many references to truly heroic accomplishments performed by the *conquistadores* in their admittedly difficult enterprises. Although the Italian reports many similar incidents of "Spanish cruelties," of which—like Las Casas—he often affirms that he was himself an eyewitness, it is interesting to note that current scholarship (particularly the publications of Carbia, Duviols, and Keen) assumes Benzoni's apparent total ignorance of the contents of Las Casas's infamous *Brevísima relación*. Accordingly, since it appears that Benzoni's textual sources did not include Las Casas, perhaps he actually *did* witness (at least some of) the atrocities he records in an almost journalistic, or somewhat dispassionate manner.

In a dedication to Pope Pius V, attached to the first edition, we learn that Benzoni was born in Milan in 1518 and that, after traveling overland through Germany and France, he finally arrived in Spain in 1541. Shortly afterward, he found himself in the Canaries; here, conveniently avoiding a prohibition against foreigners traveling to the Indies, he managed to secure passage to the Caribbean. The Italian adventurer first landed in Cubagua, on the northern coast of Venezuela, whence he set out for Santo Domingo, Cuba, Nicaragua, and various other places along the southern and western shores of the Caribbean. He also spent considerable time, between 1547 and 1550, in vast Viceroyalty of Peru, but mostly in present-day Ecuador.

Following a fourteen-year-long sojourn in America, in 1556 Benzoni found himself once again in Spain; nine years later, he published his book in Italy. His *Historia del Mondo Nuovo* clearly proved to possess great commercial potential for it was quickly republished in various translations. There were, for instance, two versions in Italian, the second one being illustrated with eighteen woodcuts (1565, 1572); many more in Latin (1578, 1581, 1586, 1594–96 [the de Bry edition], 1600, 1610, 1612, 1617, 1644); French (1579, 1600); German (1579, 1532-23, and, as republished by Theodore de Bry, in 1594, 1597, 1613, 1618); Flemish and/or Dutch (1610, 1663, 1704, 1707, 1727); and there was even a partial English translation, as *Briefe extractes . . .*" (1625, in *Purchas his Pilgrimes*). For reasons soon to be obvious, there was, however, to be no *published* Spanish version, at least not until 1967; nonetheless, since García de Icazbalceta attests to having seen it, we do know that a translation—remaining only in manuscript—of Benzoni's *Historia del Nuevo Mundo* did actually exist in the eighteenth century. This lacuna has been recently resolved for Spanish speakers by means of an excellent paperback edition, edited by Manuel Carrera Díaz and reproducing the eighteen prints belonging to the 1572 edition, which was published in 1989 by Editorial Alianza in Madrid.

Benzoni states that his primary motivation was to write about the "rare and strange things" he saw in the New World. Whereas some of these discussions actually do rest upon experiences occurring during Benzoni's extensive travels, the rest of it, particularly nearly all the historical data, was derived (actually plagiarized) from then-standard historical publications, such as those written by, among other authors recently identified, Pedro Mártir, Fernández de Oviedo, and López de Gómara. Although Benzoni's narrative was usually dismissed in the nineteenth century as mere plagiarism, particularly by Spanish historians, recent scholarship has carefully separated the actually witnessed wheat from the purloined historical chaff, which are both indiscriminately mixed together in the *Historia del Mondo Nuovo*. To cite one example of the more balanced recent view, Benjamin Keen recognizes Benzoni's often contradictory purposes. Whereas the Italian mentions numerous examples of early Spanish misconduct in the Indies, particularly their interminable slaving raids on peaceful Indian tribes, Benzoni did take pains to characterize the so-called "Leyes Nuevas" of 1542, which attempted to halt Indian servitude, as a welcome "legge sacratissima y gloriosissima, granted by a divine emperor," Charles V. On another occasion, Benzoni praises the president of the Audiencia de Guatemala, Alonso Hernández de Cerrato, and adds that "I can personally testify that there never was in all the Indies a better judge." Likewise, the Italian generously congratulates Spanish viceroy Antonio de Mendoza for his prudent application of those New Laws in Mexico. And so forth; in short, the verdict on Benzoni's intentions must remain mixed.

Nonetheless, there is not much doubt about the uses posthumously put to his book by his Protestant publishers, most notably Theodore de Bry. In this case, the secondary intentions, unquestionably realized successfully by those publishers, were designed to impress any literate European—meaning anyone who might *already* have been disposed to read of these things—with the enormity of the repetitive series of atrocities routinely inflicted upon Native Americans by Spaniards. Even though he occasionally treats of the genuinely heroic aspects of Iberian enterprises in the Americas, for Benzoni was himself a participant and so himself likewise a "hero," he never ceases to rail at the flimsiness of various legal arguments advanced by Spaniards in order to justify their conquest of these native peoples. In particular, the Italian repeatedly argues that the behavior of many *conquistadores* contradicted the evangelical spirit of papal bulls. Among these, particularly important was the *Sublimis Dei,* by which Paul III again "donated" America to Spain in 1537, noting however that

> the Indians are truly men [and so] the said Indians, and all other peoples who may later be discovered by Christians, are by no means to be deprived of their liberty or the possession of their property . . . nor should they be in any way enslaved. . . . The said Indians and other peoples should be converted to the faith of Jesus Christ by preaching the word of God and by the example [as, one would hope, illustrated by Spaniards] of good and holy living.

Benzoni observed, as did Las Casas independently, that, rather than providing salutary examples of Christian virtues, far too many Spaniards instead behaved like savage brutes bereft of any spirit of generosity or compassion.

Alas, to make his points even more dramatic, Benzoni tended (as Las Casas rarely did) to put in the mouths of the natives certain rhetorical statements that they are unlikely to have ever uttered. However, just as Las Casas always did, the Italian describes in loving detail strings of atrocious tortures applied by Spaniards to compliant Native Americans, and he describes their zealous persecutors as cruel beings who were only impelled by motives of vengeance. Like Las Casas, he mostly denounces a by-now notoriously insatiable Spanish hunger for gold. This is a bit ironic, inasmuch as at the beginning of his quasi-travel book, Benzoni admits that his first act in the New World was to enlist in an expedition led by Jerónimo de Hortal, the express purpose of which was to seek out *"Eldorado,* a term which means 'the land of great wealth,' and one understood that, in just a very short time, we should all get quite rich." Alas, Lady Luck did not smile upon the garrulous Italian adventurer: shipwrecked twice, he was to lose all his wealth in Cuba. Understandably disgruntled, Benzoni does echo an ubiquitous theme also belonging to Las Casas's writings, namely the *injusta guerra* practiced by Christian Spaniards against Native American Indians.

Whatever his particular motivations, Benzoni certainly painted verbal pictures of atrocities, particularly the wholesale enslavement of native peoples, that do seem very much in the vein of Las Casas's graphically evocative word-of-mouth exhibits. In the event, true or false, the emotional impact left on northern European readers by one and the other author would have been very much the same. One, rather typical example cited by Benzoni relates to the early years of the Spanish takeover of Hispaniola:

> The natives found themselves oppressed in a truly intolerable manner; they were forced to do all sorts of hard labor and suffer all manner of pain. Bereft of any hope of recovering their ancient liberties, they wept and lamented, desiring nothing but their own death. There were many among them who, acting from pure desperation, came to kill their children and would then go and hang themselves in the forests. They explained that it was far better for them to die by their own hands than to live so miserably, as enslaved by such pitiless thieves and ferocious tyrants. Making use of certain herbs, to evade giving birth [to slaves] Indian women would make themselves abort; afterwards, they would do as their husbands had already done: they too hung themselves from the trees. Some of them flung themselves from cliffs into the sea, others leapt off of high mountains; yet others drowned themselves in swift rivers while some others allowed themselves to die slowly from starvation. There were some others who would either commit suicide with their flint knives or who would run themselves through their chests or sides with sharpened sticks. In sum, of more than two million Indians who had been living on that island, between those who committed suicide, those who expired from exhaustion, or those who were victims of the Spaniards, today there scarcely remain any, perhaps no more than one hundred and fifty souls.[70]

In sum, could there have been presented any more tragic—or effective—picture by which to impress—or outrage—Europeans, and especially at a certain moment in time when these designated readers, Protestants for the most part, fancied Spain and its awesome and enviously wealthy overseas empire to represent their preferred object of destruction?

The Persistence of the Black Legend in
Northern European Editorial Campaigns

Unquestionably, Germany became that part of Europe that most busied itself with production of images dealing with the American Indians during the sixteenth and seventeenth centuries. Alas, here as elsewhere, the end results were usually distorted to a greater or lesser degree. Although their numbers were obviously reduced in proportion to the Spaniards, there actually were some Germans who participated in the great American adventure. Among eyewitness German authors who have left behind published accounts of their adventures in the New World, often vividly written and even more vividly illustrated, most notable were Nicholas Federmann, Philipp von Hutten, Ulrich Schmidel, and Hans Staden. There was an important precedent set in Germany for this publishing phenomenon. In 1494, just one year after Columbus's return to Europe following his first voyage to the New World, Sebastian Brant was to publish his famous satire, *Das Narrenschiff* ("The Ship of Fools"), in which—Emblem 66: "Alle Länder erforschen wollen"—he was to allude to the astonishing news of distant isles, previously unknown, rich in gold and populated by naked folk. As he put it in rambunctious Teutonic meters, long after the age of Ptolemy, Pliny, and Strabo,

> Doch hat man noch gefunden viele
> Der Länder hinter Norwegen und Thyle:
> Wie Island und Pylappenland,
> Die vordem man noch nicht gekannt.
> Man hat seitdem von Portugal
> Und von Hispanien überall
> Goldinseln gefunden und nackte Leut,
> Von denen gewußt man keinen Deut.

> Since then more countries far away
> We've found: past Thule, past Norway,
> As Iceland and Lapland,
> Which ancient writers never scanned.
> They've found in Portugal since then,
> And in Hispaniola, naked men,

And sparkling gold, and islands too
Whereof no mortal ever knew.[71]

Hans Joachim König has carefully studied quantities of so-called *Americana,* meaning a corpus of diverse printed materials dealing with the New World that appeared in Germany during the Renaissance.[72] As he observes, in their eager production of Americana, publishers in the Germanic lands were far in advance of other European countries, especially (even though somewhat curiously) Spain. In part, this activity was only natural since Germany was an acknowledged leader in the newly founded print industry, and had been so since 1460 when Guttenberg produced the first published *incunabulum.* The influence exerted by German printers—likewise of book illustrators trained in the north—in the spread of this technological advance was only natural, and their impact was especially noticeable in the Mediterranean countries. Following the precocious pattern set by Brant, German publishers exhibited a special dedication to broadcasting topical new items relating to the astonishing New World, "whereof no mortal ever knew."

According to König, between 1492 and 1650, up to twenty-two different kinds of Americana were issued by busy printing presses in Germany alone. Besides a few books (most notably those written by von Hutten, Schmidel, and Staden) and also some geographical and cartographical compilations, by far the greatest quantity of this material appeared in the form of printed ephemera, particularly broadsheets and gazettes, to which media common folk were particularly addicted during the sixteenth and seventeenth centuries. Consequently, rather than constituting "learned" materials, in both form and content Americana in the Germanic north came to be treated as something like a folk art. Publishers soon came to learn however that the greatest commercial success, and greatest item return, became attached to compilations of voyages. These travelogues, some of which actually were wholly genuine, would instruct a marginally literate reader at the same time that they delighted and titillated him with racy anecdotal accounts of barbarous customs belonging to strange and mostly savage folk living in dank forests lurking on the other side of the Atlantic. The inherent attraction of such *fremde Volk* was that they were designed and presented as creatures even stranger than contemporary Germans. As ambitious editors quickly came to realize, the more fantastic the story—and the more dramatically composed those folkish illustrations that usually accompanied it—the more likely the eventual commercial success of one's perhaps hastily concocted publication.

König underscores the nature of some other difficulties encountered at this time in providing a truly objective, or realistic, perspective on the complex nature of those unprecedented American actualities:

> In Americana put out in Germany during the Renaissance missing is that fundamental debate, which was pursued so rigorously in Spain at this time, concerning Indian culture, its putative inferiority or superiority. On the other hand, German perspectives on the American Indian reveal the same lack of understanding and, particularly, an inability to appreciate the markedly different qualities of Indian culture, especially such as these might represent the results of a different kind of historical evolution, or even as phenomena perhaps having value in their own right. Basically, such misunderstanding came about because the fundamental concepts and norms belonging as much to the authors as to their printers and publishers—and surely their public too—were really ones belonging to the Middle Ages, a period characterized by its own notions of the Marvellous, including the *Wilder Mann* fantasies and beliefs in barbarian frenzy, and, above all, those ubiquitous and deeply rooted assumptions about the basic defects of anything, or anybody, "non-Christian."

A fundamental role in the creation and spread throughout Europe of American travel and adventure books was played by a certain German family enterprise of printers, publishers, and copper engravers. At the head of this dynasty stood an imposing figure, of whom we have already made mention, Theodore de Bry. He came from a wealthy and well-established family originating in Liège, now part of Belgium but then forming part of the Spanish Netherlands. In 1570 the de Bry family was collectively accused by Spanish authorities of being sympathizers with the Protestant reform movement. Forced into exile, they lost both their wealth and their status. Theodore the patriarch later claimed that all that remained to them was their art. Naturally, they were resentful, and the natural result, soon to be tangibly expressed, was a profoundly felt malevolence against both Spaniards and Catholics, one and the same in the eyes of any embittered de Bry.

They established themselves anew in Frankfurt, where Theodore restarted his publishing business, which he personally directed from 1590 until

1598, the year of his death. He was succeeded in this highly successful commercial venture by his sons, Johann Theodore and Johann Israel. One of his daughters married Matthieu Mérian, a justly celebrated Swiss engraver, who took over the strictly graphic aspects of the family business, so assuring the highest quality for its important, indeed essential, illustrative components. Early in the seventeenth century, the business was moved to Oppenheim, a small town in the Rhenish Palatinate. Due to the fame and prestige of the publishing enterprise, in 1618 the prince elector commissioned the composition of a lavishly produced volume on the *Hortus Palatinus* ("Palatine Gardens") of Heidelberg from the House of de Bry. Under similar auspices, they also produced a notable emblem book with exotic alchemical subject matter, the famous *Atalanta Fugiens*.[73]

A shrewd businessman with wide-ranging interests, Theodore de Bry also proved to be a publisher endowed with both ambition and great vision. Besides his other informative enterprises, bucolic and alchemical among others, he additionally planned two highly ambitious series of travel anthologies, with texts and pictures conjoined, dealing with notable Renaissance voyages and overseas explorations. Issued in two parts, his first effort, the lavishly illustrated *Grandes voyages,* dealt with the West Indies, or America, while a complementary series, called the *Petites voyages,* was dedicated to the East Indies, or Asia. The massive American anthology, which represented a unique attempt to provide a comprehensive vision on the grand scale of the New World for all interested European stay-at-home world travelers, was the more successful of the two works.

The unifying theme of the *Grandes voyages,* embracing a typically Renaissance global viewpoint, was the recent European conquest of America and included much documentation concerning those initial, startling contacts between Europeans and Native Americans. The very first volume in the series, lavishly illustrated with engravings—like all the ones following—dealt with the recently inaugurated British colony of Virginia (also including the Carolinas), and it was simultaneously published with Latin, German, French, and English texts.[74] The entire series of de Bry's *Voyages* was implicitly directed toward a very different kind of public than that which consumed the previous glut of mostly crudely printed Americana ephemera. In this case, de Bry's targeted consumers were ideally members of the European aristocracy, particularly rulers of the German principalities and duchies; accordingly, various volumes were dedicated to these princelings and bore their distinctive heraldry. The greatest attraction of the series as a whole were, as is only natural, the engravings, which immensely impressed—and increased—the generally well-placed de Bry clientele.[75]

Besides being a prolific publisher, de Bry was also a hands-on editor; it is, therefore, worth mentioning the selection process that implicitly shaped the final character of the *Voyages*. As is now apparent, the de Bry family generally responded to editorial criteria that were clearly of a ideological, meaning specifically doctrinal, character. In this light, it becomes significant that nearly all of the authors chosen by the de Bry dynasty to be reprinted in the *Grandes voyages*—including Ribault, Laudonière, Le Moyne, Jean de Léry, and Hans Staden among others—just happened to be identified with the Reformed Protestant faith. The only notable Catholic authors represented in the American *Voyages* were Girolamo Benzoni and Bartolomé de Las Casas; nonetheless, as we have just seen, these in turn must have been chosen because·they provided a critical, even lurid view of Spanish operations in America, and particularly of the "black" effects of a forced Catholic evangelization of the entire New World.

All of these wholly politicized points were made especially (literally) vivid as they were illustratively portrayed by the workshop of industrious and highly accomplished copperplate engravers captained by Matthieu Mérian. Their highly refined techniques additionally allowed for much more aesthetically pleasing compositions, which were additionally much more detailed than had been possible before with the cruder medium of woodcuts. The addition, uniquely made possible by copperplate engraving medium, of many more pictorial details naturally encouraged a much greater amount of narrative embellishment, on occasion even considerable polemical digression. A typical example, indebted in this case to neither the accounts of Las Casas or Benzoni, is another engraving, entitled "A Spanish Attack on an Indian Village," just one among many other inflammatory prints appearing as generic atrocity imagery in the provocative, thirty-five volume de Bry collection called *America (sive, Collectiones peregrinationum in Indiam Occidetalem)* (Fig. 59). As should be apparent at this point, for Theodore de Bry & Co. often historical authenticity was not the major concern, and this bias even finds an interesting formal expression, *en détaille,* in the prints designed by Mérian & Co.

Accordingly, as routinely depicted in the de Bry graphic presentations (for instance, Fig. 59), Spaniards would typically be figuratively character-

59.

"A Spanish Attack on an Indian Village," from Th. de Bry, America, sive Collectiones peregrinationum in Indiam Occidentalem (Frankfurt, 1594).

ized by means of harshly naturalistic modes that had became fashionable toward the very end of the sixteenth century. Nonetheless, the artistic treatment of Native Americans, as counterpoised ethnographic types, hewed to a rather different canon of representation, namely those heroic modes of idealization, what might be called "noble nudity," that had been popularized by followers of Michelangelo since the *beginning* of the sixteenth century. Because they were shown to be idealized, so were these typically tyrannized Indians implicitly understood to be good. Since the graphic treatment of the Spaniards was rampantly naturalistic, so were they meant to be viewed, according to that same commonplace pictorial code, as belonging to lesser social classes, or even lower levels of humanity, and so they were implicitly viewed as bad.

In short, throughout his extensive graphic oeuvre, de Bry anatomi-

cally recasts his oppressed Americans in the prevailing, meaning culturally prestigious, Michelangelesque mold. Thus Native American Indians
are henceforth repeatedly endowed by sympathetic European engravers
with those heroic physiques and pathos-ridden postures once exclusively
characterizing antique gods and suffering classical heroes, while their modern European conquerors and oppressors, Spaniards dressed in the vulgar
contemporary fashion, are implicitly converted into the new barbarians,
the *European* Ignoble Savages. One need only compare the Mérian-de Bry
graphic production with that belonging to earlier illustrated publications,
appearing under the authorship of Hans Staden or by Jean de Léry and John
White—all as illustrated (or burdened) with schematically rendered, simply
presented, and "boring" woodcuts—to quickly perceive the nature of some
radical artistic and rhetorical changes in underlying character.[76]

A tenaciously waged editorial campaign censuring Spain through the
medium of hallucinatory scenes, and purporting to expose endless horrors
wrought by iniquitous Iberian *conquistadores,* is generally apparent throughout the *Grands voyages,* and especially so in a number of prints luridly illustrating Sections IV (1594), V (1595), and VI (1596). These pictorial materials all
happen to correspond to a timely reprinting of Benzoni's *Historia del Mondo
Nuovo,* to whose text we have already referred. These provocative engravings were not, however, specifically composed by the Mérian-de Bry entourage in order to illustrate an opportune reprinting of Benzoni's broadside.
Owing to the research of a French scholar, Jean-Paul Duviols, we now recognize the original source—and functions—of these illustrations.[77] Nearly
all of them, it seems, had first appeared in a polemical treatise published
in Antwerp in 1587, Jan Verstegan's *Theatrum crudelitatum haereticorum nostri
temporis* ("A Theater of Cruelties Belonging to the Heretics of Our Age").
Ironically, this sectarian diatribe was originally manufactured—by Catholics—to denounce atrocities supposedly perpetrated in France somewhat
earlier by *Protestant* Huguenots! So this particular "Theater of Cruelties"
fundamentally had nothing whatsoever to do with America. As originally
produced by French Catholics, it has even less to do with Spanish Catholic
atrocities supposedly being played out on the far side of the Atlantic. The
overriding theme is merely the endlessly illustrated topic—alas, one fast
becoming more current in real life than in art—of man's inhumanity to
man. But serious treatment of that hoary theme would take at least twenty
volumes of this size to explore, let alone exhaust.

Other Accounts of European Atrocities —
Two Indian and the Other French

Although mostly ignored until fairly recently, there were also a few surviving written accounts provided by the Indians describing the ferocious
brutality of their newly arrived European conquerors. One such account,
originally transcribed in Nahuatl, then translated into Spanish, documents
the slaughter of peaceful Aztecs who were celebrating a native fiesta inside the sacred precincts of the main temple of Tenochtitlán (now Mexico
City) in 1520. This tragic encounter was also described, and illustrated, by
Las Casas (see Fig. 56). As described by an Aztec eyewitness, the infuriated
Spaniards

> ran in among the dancers, forcing their way to the place where the
> drums were being played. They attacked the man who was drumming
> and cut off his arms. Then they cut off his head, and it rolled across the
> floor. They attacked all the celebrants: stabbing them, spearing them,
> striking them with their swords. They attacked some of them from be-
> hind, and these fell instantly to the ground with their entrails hanging
> out. Others they beheaded: they cut off their heads, or split their heads
> to pieces. They struck others in the shoulders, and their arms were torn
> from their bodies. They wounded some in the thigh and some in the
> calf. They slashed others in the abdomen, and their entrails all spilled to
> the ground. Some attempted to run away, but their intestines dragged
> as they ran; they seemed to tangle their feet in their own guts.
>
> No matter how they tried to save themselves, they could find no
> escape. Some attempted to force their way out, but the Spaniards mur-
> dered them at the gates. Others climbed the walls, but even then they
> could not save themselves. Those who ran into the communal houses
> were safe there for a while; so were those who lay down among the vic-
> tims and pretended to be dead. But, if they stood up again, the Spaniards
> saw them and killed them. The blood of the [Aztec] warriors flowed
> like water and gathered into pools. The pools widened, and the stench
> of blood and guts filled the air. The Spaniards ran into the communal
> houses to kill those who were hiding there. The Spaniards ran every-
> where; they invaded every room, hunting and killing.[78]

Another such account belongs to the *Annals of Tlatelolco,* written in Nahuatl
in Latin letters around 1530. As opposed to the preceding, it is written

in a manner that catches (even in translation) the powerful rhythms and distinctive phraseology of native lyric poetry:

> And all this happened among us. We saw it. We lived through it with an astonishment worthy of tears and of pity for the pain we suffered. On the roads lie broken shafts and torn hair: houses are roofless, homes are stained red, worms swarm in the streets, walls are spattered with brains. The water is reddish, like dyed water; we drink it so, we even drink brine; the water we drink is full of saltpeter. The wells are crammed with adobe bricks. Whatever was still alive was kept between shields, like precious treasures, between shields, until it was eaten. We chewed on hard wood, brackish fodder, chunks of adobe, lizards, vermin, dust and worms. We eat whatever was on the fire; as soon as it is done, we eat it together, right by the fire.
>
> We had a single price; there was a standard price for [sex with] a youth, a priest, a boy and a young girl. The maximum price for a slave amounted to only two handfuls of maize, to only ten tortillas. Only twenty bundles of brackish fodder was the price of gold, jade, mantles, feather plumes; all valuables fetched the same low price. It went down further, when the Spaniards set up their battering engine in the market place. Now, Cuauhtémoc orders the [Spanish] prisoners to be brought out; the guards don't miss any. The elders and chiefs grab them by their extremities — and Cuauhtemoc slits open their bellies with his own hand.[79]

We will close these gristly accounts with another written by an essentially uninvolved European. Jean Esquemeling, a French buccaneer from Saint-Mâlo, much later described the desolation in Hispaniola that resulted from the improvident Spanish exploitation of the land. In rather approving terms, he also commented upon the means and the results of the total decimation of the peaceful Arawaks, once dubbed noble and ethical children of the Golden Age. His point of departure is a comment, appearing in his book *De Americaenesche Zee-Rovers* (1678), about the abundance in those parts of fierce and untamed dogs. The tough French pirate wondered "whence and by what accident came so many dogs into these islands." The answer is that these were the same beasts that Las Casas had described as being universally employed "to hound" the defenseless Indians. As Esquemeling tells it,

The Spaniards, having possessed themselves of these isles, found them much peopled with Indians. These were a barbarous sort of people, totally given to sensuality and a brutish custom of life, hating all manner of labor, and only inclined to run from place to place, killing and making war against their neighbors—not however out of any ambition to reign, but only because they agreed not with themselves in some common terms of language. Hence, perceiving that the dominion of the Spaniards laid a great restriction upon their lazy and brutish customs, they conceived an incredible odium against them, such as never was to be reconciled, more especially because they saw them to take possession of their kingdoms and [former] dominions. Thereupon they made against them all the resistance they were capable of, opposing everywhere their designs to the utmost of their power, until the Spaniards, finding themselves to be cruelly hated by those Indians, and nowhere secure from their treacheries, resolved to extirpate and ruin them, every one, especially since the Spaniards saw that they could neither tame them by the civilities of their customs, nor conquer them with the sword.

The Indians, it being their ancient custom to make the woods their chiefest places of defence, at present made these their refuge whenever they fled from the Spaniards that pursued them. Thereupon, those first conquerors of the New World made use of dogs in order to range and search the intricatest thickets of woods and forests for those [Arawaks], their implacable and unconquerable enemies. By this means, they forced them to leave their ancient refuge and to submit to the sword, seeing that no milder usage would serve turn. Thereupon, they killed some of them, and, quartering their bodies, placed them in the highways, to the intention that others might take warning from such a punishment not to incur the like danger. But this severity proved to be of ill consequence: instead of frighting them, reducing their minds to a civil society, they conceived such horror of the Spaniards and their proceedings that they resolved to detest and fly from their sight forever. And hence the greatest part died in caves and subterraneous places of the woods and mountains.

In those places I myself have seen many times great numbers of human bones. The Spaniards afterwards, finding no more Indians to appear about the woods, then endeavored to rid themselves of the great number of [hunting] dogs they had had in their houses, whence these animals, finding no masters to keep them, betook themselves to the woods and fields, there to hunt for food to preserve their lives. Thus, by degrees, they became unacquainted with the houses of their ancient

masters and, at last, grew wild. This is the truest account I can give for
the multitudes of wild dogs which are seen to this day in these parts.[89]

Is this, after all, "the truest account" one could have given at that time?
Whatever the truth of the matter, many Europeans unquestionably believed
so, and had done so since the end of the sixteenth century. So did the supposedly outraged illustrators of texts very much like this one in tone and inflammatory detail (see Figs. 53–59). All that remains unquestionable in this
particular case is a fact of chronology: Esquemeling's atrocity-ridden anecdotes only appeared after those widely distributed and largely sensational
pictures of Hispanic black deeds in the Indies had been commissioned—
and widely published—by Theodore de Bry.

Homo Lupus: *Aristotle on an American Tragedy*

How can we understand, let alone condone, this kind of behavior? In short,
we cannot even begin to imagine it—not unless *we* have found ourselves,
once or more, unwilling eyewitnesses, sometimes even direct participants
in similar, and very recent, episodes of collective insanity and unchecked
blood lust.[81] Recent experience shows that this kind of cruelty, these sorts of
bloodbaths, this racist-inspired slaughter, was, and still is, in no way any kind
of exclusive province of Spaniards—nor of any other kinds of European, or
Asiatic, or African peoples. The problem transcends national boundaries. It
seems the inherent and collective fault of the human race itself. Such rapacious inhumanity, Christian or Islamic or otherwise, nearly always arises in
situations that are unchecked, either by internally applied moral standards
and ethical restraints or by externally imposed and implacably enforced laws.

Is it necessary again to remind the reader that there was *never* any con-
certed plan by Europeans to exterminate the indigenous populations of the
New World? It all happened by chance, according to fate, a kind of gratuitous, precociously genocidal Kismet. The near extinction of the Indians
in the New World was mainly due to diseases unwittingly imported by
infected Europeans from the Old World. Still, particularly in Mexico, the
Indians were grossly abused by the near-slavery imposed upon them by the
neo-feudal *encomienda* (or forced-labor) system of the earliest Spanish colonial governments. Additionally, the Spaniards might be legitimately faulted

for their neglectful governmental apparatus, but then so too could *all* the
other colonial European governments at that time be so maligned. The
viceregal system in Spanish America was ponderously legalistic and paper
choked, and thus inhumanly rationalized, rather like a contemporary urban
grid plan. It was, additionally, unquestionably neglectful at best and, at the
lowest bureaucratic levels, miserably corrupt as a rule—which is still the
pattern today in most parts of Latin America.

Even though it was generally understood to be a lost cause, many
Spaniards (not just Las Casas!) really tried to improve the ever-worsening
lot of the *indios*. One of these few, superior civil servants was a model judge,
Don Alonso de Zorita, who was forced into an impoverished early retire-
ment in 1556 after twenty years of ethically exemplary service. He described
the miserable plight of the Indians—in this case as strangled by bureaucratic
indifference—in an outraged report he sent across the Atlantic, directly to
King Philip II:

> Who shall tell the sum of miseries and hardships these poor unfortu-
> nate people suffer, without help or aid from any quarter?!? Who does
> not turn his face against them?, who does not persecute and vex them?,
> who does not rob them and live by their sweat!?! Since I cannot tell it
> all, but have told enough to make clear the need for a remedy, let me
> be silent concerning the innumerable crimes that I have personally seen
> and verified, or that I have heard of from trustworthy persons.
>
> Their ancient kings and lords never ruled in this way, never took
> the Indians from their towns, never disrupted their way of life and labor.
> I cannot believe that either Your Majesty nor the members of Your
> Majesty's Council either know or have been informed of what is really
> taking place [in America]. If they knew of it, they would, surely, take
> steps. . . . Very extensive lands have become depopulated in our time.
> The wishes of Your Majesty and his Royal Council are well known, and
> are made very plain in the laws that are issued every day in favor of the
> poor Indians, and which are designed for their increase and preserva-
> tion. But these laws are not obeyed and so they are not enforced. Hence,
> there is no end to the destruction of the Indians, nor does anyone [here]
> care what Your Majesty decrees. . . . Indeed, the more laws and decrees
> that are sent [from Spain to America], the worse is the condition of the
> Indians. This is due to the false and specious interpretation that Spanish
> [local] officials give to these laws, twisting their meanings to suit their
> own purposes. . . .

We have a multitude of laws, judges, viceroys, governors, *presidentes, oídores, corregidores, alcaldes mayores,* a million lieutenants, and yet another million *alguaciles.* But this multitude is not what the Indians need, nor will it relieve their misery. Indeed, the more such men [bureaucrats] there are, the more enemies do the Indians have. . . . These Spaniards care for one thing alone, and that is their own advantage. They do not give a damn whether these poor and miserable Indians live or whether they die, even though the whole being and the entire welfare of the country completely depend upon them.

God has closed the eyes and darkened the minds of these Spaniards. They see with their eyes what is happening, yet they do not see it. They perceive their own destruction, yet they do not perceive, and this is all because of their callousness and heartlessness. . . . These officials have not seen the Indians' sufferings and miseries because they are quite content just to sit in the cool shade and to collect their pay. . . . These officials control a major part of the wealth of this land. *That* is what blinds them, and that is what makes them say what they say and do what they do [and don't do]. . . . I would say much more on this subject, but to tell it all would only weary the reader.[82]

One last, most wearisome, observation follows in order to close these retrospective, and sometimes melancholic, meditations upon the enduring implications of the European invention of America and its native inhabitants half a millennium ago. Inhumanity, whether expressed through bureaucratic negligence or by murderously hands-on savagery, seems, perhaps paradoxically, the enduring, fundamental, and transcendent trait of *humanitas* in general. And—what irony!—all of these gristly catalogs of inhumane colonialist horrors actually transpired in what has been commonly called an Age of Humanism. As it appears, a certain elitist mental condition, still coloring our definitions of the Renaissance in Europe, did not really need to be exported, and then applied to America after all. The noble experiment was never tested in its ideal laboratory, America. Just *talking* about all those lofty humanistic ethical principles—in Europe—was apparently considered sufficient in itself.

It was human nature, *humanitas,* that had opportunely invented during an optimistic Age of Humanism in Europe the idea, indeed the very *need* for Utopia. Utopia was not merely the literary creation of Sir Thomas More. It really existed. It was, in fact, the rediscovered, originally pristine,

Eden in the West, deluded Columbus's *el Paradiso terrenal*. This historical phenomenon, Renaissance Humanism, was the same high-mindedly imaginative faculty that had similarly assigned the thoroughly conventionalized Arcadian scenography of the Golden Age to the Western Eden's unexpected inhabitants. Not long after, it was that same kind of culturally molded mind set that was, eventually and inevitably, to invent an Anti-Eden in the very same place, making it into Hell on Earth. The new Inferno was imposed equally upon gradually disappearing aborigines and, nearly as quickly, upon a mass of newly imported drones, black slaves ripped from the green heart of Africa. After all, had not the Bible (Genesis 1:28) — had not, therefore, *God Himself?* — promised to the True Believers of the Old World absolute "dominion over every living thing that moveth upon the earth?"

As we can now easily see, five hundred years after the fact, it was an inherently and perennially "hard primitivist" human nature, Christian zeal, and superior European technology that brought near-extinction to the displaced peoples of an easily invented, then quickly discredited, and now nearly wholly despoiled, Paradise on Earth. History usually only writes ineptly its own minidramas; certainly the European invention of America during the Renaissance was one of those. As this massive event demonstrates, history occasionally deigns to compose (for our potential enlightenment) a rather grandly scaled tragedy, one reerected in the ancient Greek mode. As was the case way back then, in any properly invented tragedy the real lesson is *hubris*. Hubris signifies, according to classical theory of dramatic composition, an inevitable humpty-dumpty Great Fall that was, and still is, always due to a single fatal flaw, the lack of critical insight.

The same philosopher, Aristotle (384–322 B.C.), who, in his *Poetics,* had provided for the Renaissance a classic definition of *tragedia,* its means and its goals (and also a loose definition of "natural slavery" that could be opportunely applied — and misapplied — by *encomenderos* to justify their reliance on forced Indian labor), also supplied the philosophical basis for what became a standard topos during the period of the endlessly inventive European conquests of the New World. After 1492, the common motto among the European critics of human nature was "homo homini lupus": Man is like a rapacious wolf, a savage beast, to his fellow men. The predatory feral pattern was, like everything else concerned with the European invention of America during the Renaissance, "nothing new under the Sun." As Aristotle put it so long ago (*Politics,* I, 2),

> Man, when he is at the goal of his [social and ethical] development, is the best of all animals: but he is the worst of all when he is detached from customs and justice. Injustice, given weapons, is the most oppressive thing there is; and man is given weapons at birth, which are meant to serve prudence and goodness, but which can easily [are usually!] turned to the opposite ends. Man, without goodness, is the most wicked and savage of animals, the most subject to lust and gluttony.[83]

If Aristotle ever needed an historical verification, then that was supplied in abundance during the sixteenth century, and particularly during the European invention and subsequent conquests of native peoples and cultures found throughout the conjoined Americas. Inhabitants of the Edenic landscapes in the Americas were first taken to be blissfully lost in a defenseless Golden Age first imagined by ancient European poets. Then came the Age of Iron, another invention of America in the European mould. That one, of course, is the one today prevailing. As the rapacious Renaissance pattern of *homo homini lupus,* particularly enjoying in America a scripturally licensed "dominion over every living thing that moveth upon the earth," has since changed more in terminology than in real substance, then there is—hopefully—a lesson to be learned here.

But enough of historical lessons, either learnt already or still to be envisaged. Now, somewhat better informed of some forgotten mythic origins of the image of America and the Native Americans in classical and (especially) medieval Europe, we may bring to a close this often rhetorical investigation of certain aspects of the Renaissance image of Native Americans by pointing out to our readers a most interesting phenomenon. In short, as we hope to have made clear in various ways, such as it was implanted in the sixteenth century, the European vision of the objects, peoples, and events belonging to the novel New World of America was really very much deeply influenced, indeed decisively shaped, by any number of illusions, or apocryphal traditions, belonging to the medieval Old World. That said, we can only hope now that any successor images meant to be eventually applied to those American "Indians," whether noble or even ignoble in purpose, might begin to improve considerably in both accuracy and in fundamental intention upon the original models, so laboriously excavated, then displayed here for our mutual edification.

NOTES

Chapter One

1. Since the Columbian bibliography is immense (and ever-expanding), for the specific question of Columbus's consistent quest for Indian shores, one need only refer to the rich documentation assembled in P. E. Taviani, *Christopher Columbus: The Grand Design* (London, 1985). For his frequent conflation of *las Indias* and *el Paraíso terrestre,* as put down in his own hand, see D. West and A. Kling, eds., *The "Libro de las profecías" of Christopher Columbus: An en face edition* (Gainesville, 1992), and note particularly pp. 154–45, announcing a universal evangelistic process, to be funded by "gold and silver," that implicitly spreads from the recovered Earthly Paradise, a place probably consistently identified throughout these texts with certain "islands," sometimes specifically identified with "Tharsis and Ophir," and apparently all standing for "the Promised Land."

2. See the posthumous publication of Bartolomé de Las Casas, *Historia de las Indias,* 2 vols. (México, 1951), which additionally contains, vol. II, 47–61, the author's extensive and erudite speculations, *à la* Columbus (whom Las Casas took at his word), on the geographical particulars of the Earthly Paradise in the New World, as newly rediscovered by a now-famous Genoese navigator.

3. Bartolomé de Las Casas, ed., *Cristóbal Colón: Diario, Relaciones de viajes* (Madrid, 1985), 159–60.

4. Ibid., 198–204.

5. Pedro Mártir de Anglería, *Décadas del Nuevo Mundo* (Madrid, 1989), 13–14.

6. Ibid., 32–33.

7. Ibid., 77.

8. Ibid., 79.

9. Ibid., 88. Martyr also mentions (p. 60) Columbus's designation of the Gulf of Paria as the newly recovered site of the Earthly Paradise. The chronicler's conclusion: "Basta ya de estas cosas, que me parecen fabulosas. Volvamos a la historia [del descubrimiento de América] de que nos hemos apartado."

10. *Kyng Alisaunder,* as quoted (p. 86) in M. M. Lascelles, "Alexander and the Earthly Paradise in Medieval English Writings," *Medium Aevum* V (1936): 31–47, 79–104, 173–88.

11. L. S. Dixon, "Giovanni di Paolo's Cosmology," *The Art Bulletin* LXVII (1985): 604–13.

12. For these stereotyped literary topoi, see E. R. Curtius, *European Literature and the Latin Middle Ages* (New York, 1963).

13. *The Travels of Sir John Mandeville: Facsimile of Pynson's Edition of 1496,* M. Seymour, ed. (University of Exeter, 1980) (unpaginated: at the end); for a modern English transcription, see *The Travels of Sir John Mandeville,* C. W. R. D. Moseley, ed. (Harmondsworth, 1983), 184–85.

14. Dixon, "Giovanni di Paolo's Cosmology," 609.

15. On these two charts, see G. H. Kimble, *The Catalan World Map of the R. Biblioteca Estense at Modena* (London, 1934); T. G. Laporace and R. Almagia, *Il mappamondo di Fra Mauro* (Venice, 1956). In any event, the *Este Map* (Dixon's Fig. 1) figuratively locates Eden, as identified by diminutive figures of Adam and Eve, as being situated "in the South."

16. Dixon, "Giovanni di Paolo's Cosmology," 608.

17. For the latest summary of research in the early history of cartography, see D. Woodward, "Medieval *Mappaemundi,*" in J. B. Harley and D. Woodward, eds., *The History of Cartography I: Cartography in Prehistoric, Ancient, and Medieval Europe and the Mediterranean* (Chicago, 1987), 286–370; J-G. Arentzen, *Imago Mundi Cartographica: Studien zur Bildlichkeit mittelalterlicher Welt- und Oekumenekarten unter besonderer Berücksichtigung des Zusammenwirkens von Text und Bild* (Munich, 1984)(with extensive bibliography). For the specific context of this chapter, re-creating Columbus's more fanciful cartographic projections, an especially useful introduction is J. B. Harley, *Maps and the Columbian Encounter* (Milwaukee, 1990).

18. For the *Bianco Mappamundi,* see L. A. Brown, *The Story of Maps* (New York, 1979), 128, 140; A. Nordenskjöld, ed., *Facsimile-Atlas to the Early History of Cartography* (New York, 1973), 51–53; see also Arentzen, *Imago Mundi,* 216, 220. Another quattrocento *mappamundi,* later in execution but also from Venice, would serve just as well for these comparative purposes. In effect, the *Leardo Mappamundi* (ca. 1452) is a near duplicate of the earlier *Bianco Mappamundi* of 1436; on the former, see P. Durazzo, *Il planisfero di Giovanni Leardo* (Mantua, 1885); J. K. Wright, *The Leardo Map of the World, 1452 or 1453, in the Collection of the American Geographical Society* (New York, 1928); Harley, *Columbian Encounter,* 19–21.

19. For a firsthand encounter with the wide variety of ideas held about Paradise during the Middle Ages, particularly its significance, see the primary documents as-

sembled in J-P. Migne, ed., *Patrologia Latina* (Paris, 1844–82), vol. 219, cols. 67–79, "Index de Paradiso terrestre" (many entries). A bibliography of more recently published interpretations of these patristic sources and other, more secularized literary materials would prove far too extensive to list here, but most will be found in our comprehensive bibliography.

20. L. Baransky-Job, "The Problem and Meaning of Giovanni di Paolo's 'Expulsion from Paradise,'" *Marsyas* VII (1959): 1–6.

21. *San Isidoro de Sevilla: Etimologías,* L. Cortés y Góngora, ed. (Madrid, 1951), 339; see also Arentzen, *Imago Mundi,* 107–12 ("Isidor-Karten").

22. Bede, *Hexameron,* as given in Migne, ed., *Patrologia Latina,* vol. 91, 43.

23. Augustine, as cited in G. Boas and A. O. Lovejoy, *Essays on Primitivism and Related Ideas in the Middle Ages* (New York, 1978), 46.

24. *St. Augustine: The City of God,* G. C. Walsh, S. J., et al., eds. (Garden City, N.Y., 1958), 318; for more of Augustine's strictly allegorical interpretations of "Eden," see also pp. 286–88, 306–9; for the strictly cartographic implications, see Arentzen, *Imago Mundi,* 107–12.

25. Ernaldus, as in Boas and Lovejoy, *Primitivism,* 72–73.

26. *St. Peter's Apocalypse,* as quoted in E. Gardiner, ed., *Visions of Heaven & Hell Before Dante* (New York, 1989), 1–12.

27. *Saint Paul's Vision,* as quoted in ibid., 28–31.

28. For more particulars on Isidore's often copied world map, see W. M. Stevens, "The Figure of the Earth in Isidore's 'De Natura Rerum,'" *Isis* LXXI (1980): 268–77; A. de Egry, *O Apocalipse do Lorvão* . . . (Lisbon, 1972), 135–37 & lam. XVII; Arentzen, *Imago Mundi,* 55–57, 107–12.

29. On the *Hereford Mappamundi,* see L. Bevan and H. W. Phillott, *Medieval Geography: An Essay in the Illustration of the Hereford Mappa Mundi* (London, 1873); K. Miller, *Mappae Mundi, IV: Die Herefordkarte* (Stuttgart, 1896); G. R. Crone, *The World Map by Richard of Haldingham in Hereford Cathedral* (London, 1954); A. L. Moir, *The World Map in Hereford Cathedral* (Hereford, 1977).

30. For this important world map, see W. Rosien, *Die Ebstorfer Weltkarte* (Hannover, 1952); see also Arentzen, *Imago Mundi,* 138–64 ("Ebstorfer Karte"), 267–74 ("Christus-Figur").

31. For mention of this obscure *Relation,* see S. Sebastián, *Iconografía medieval* (San Sebastián, 1988), 19; Arentzen, *Imago Mundi,* 213ff. The story of Enoch and Elias in India seems mainly to have been given substance by the transcriptions of Petrus Comestor (*Historia Scholastica,* 30), a work that was cited by Columbus in those arguments (see note 3 above) about his own *Paraíso terrenal* up the Río Orinoco.

32. Hugh of St. Victor, as quoted in Boas and Lovejoy, *Primitivism,* 160–61.

33. *Book of Juniorus the Philosopher,* in ibid., 138–39.

34. This follows the synopsis of the *Iter ad Paradisum* given by Lascelles, "Alexander and the Earthly Paradise," 36–38. For more on the vastly important (and I think somewhat underrated) effects of the strictly medieval apotheosis of the Alexander-in-India legend, see F. Pfister, "Das Nachleben der Überlieferung von Alexander und den Brahmanen," *Hermes* LXXVI (1941): 143–69; D. J. A. Ross, *Alexander Historiatus* (London, 1963); J. Brummack, *Die Darstellung des Orient in den deutschen Alexandergeschichten*

des Mittelalters (Berlin, 1966); W. J. Aerts, ed., *Alexander the Great in the Middle Ages* (Nijmegen, 1978).

35. "Prester John's Letter," as quoted in Boas and Lovejoy, *Primitivism*, 161–64; see also F. M. Rodgers, *The Quest for Eastern Christians: Travels and Rumor in the Age of Discovery* (Minneapolis, 1962).

36. *Deeds of Alexander*, in Boas and Lovejoy, *Primitivism*, 140–46. By later (ca. 1357) saying very much the same thing about the Brahmins, it was Sir John Mandeville who really popularized the idea in his *Travels;* see Moseley, ed., *Travels of Sir John Mandeville*, 178–79, "The Isle of Bragman," where the Brahmin inhabitants, "even if they are not Christian, nevertheless, by natural instinct or by law, they live a commendable life, are folk of great virtue, flying always from all sins," etc.

37. J. W. McCrindle, ed., *The Christian Topography of Cosmas* (London, 1897), 18–19. The authentic (or verifiable) reference here is to the Copts of Ethiopia and to the Nestorian Christians of India; both sects still practice their heterodox religions in those places. For more on Cosmas the cartographer, see Arentzen, *Imago Mundi,* 37–45.

38. For these travelers' reports, see E. N. Adler, ed., *Jewish Travellers in the Middle Ages: Nineteen Firsthand Accounts* (New York, 1987); C. Dawson, ed., *The Mongol Mission. Narratives and Letters of the Franciscan Missionaries in Mongolia and China in the Thirteenth and Fourteenth Centuries* (London, 1955); O. and E. Lattimore, eds., *Silk, Spices, and Empire: Asia Seen Through the Eyes of its Discoverers* (New York, 1971).

39. *Travels of Sir John Mandeville*, 182ff.

40. On this phenomenon, see R. Wittkower, "Marvels of the East," *Journal of the Warburg and Courtauld Institutes* V (1942): 159–97; idem., "Marco Polo and the Pictorial Tradition of the Marvels of the East," in *Oriente Poliano* (Rome 1957), 155–72; J. B. Friedman, *The Monstrous Races in Medieval Art and Thought* (Cambridge, Mass., 1981).

41. We shall be quoting from a standard English version: R. E. Latham, ed., *The Travels of Marco Polo* (Harmondsworth, 1959); see also L. Olschki, *Marco Polo's Asia: An Introduction to His "Description of the World"* (Berkeley, 1960).

42. Latham, ed, *Travels of Marco Polo*, 40.

43. M. M. Pickthall, ed., *The Glorious Koran* (London, 1956), 35, 320, 327.

44. Lorenzo de'Medici, as quoted in McClung, *The Architecture of Paradise: Survivals of Eden and Jerusalem* (Berkeley, 1983), 40.

45. Latham, ed., *Travels of Marco Polo,* 255. "Adam's Peak" in Ceylon was mentioned, and named as such, a thousand years before Marco Polo's passage through these tropical regions; in this case, the chronicler was a Chinese visitor to Ceylon, Fa-Hsien (A.D. 391–414); for his travel diary, see Lattimore, eds.,*Silk, Spices, and Empire,* 35–45. The tradition proves to be amazingly tenacious; a much later (between 1338 and 1353) medieval European traveler, self-described as "a most curious wanderer of all the provinces of the Indies," who did clearly place the site of the Earthly Paradise in Ceylon, was Giovanni de'Marignolli; see Friedman, *Monstrous Races*, 196. Borrowing from these authors, "Sir John Mandeville" (see note 50) very specifically located the Earthly Paradise in Ceylon, and it is he who really most popularized the concept thereafter.

46. Latham, ed., *Travels of Marco Polo,* 257.

47. Ibid., p. 258.

48. S. Baring-Gould, "The Terrestrial Paradise," in *Curious Myths of the Middle Ages*

(London, 1869), 250–65; the author described the map (p. 253) as being by Lambertus Floridus, and "preserved in the Imperial Library in Paris." Baring-Gould cites, p. 257, another *mappamundi* ("in a MS. volume in the library of Corpus Christi College, Cambridge"), "whereon Paradise is figured as an island opposite the mouth of the Ganges."

49. *Eiriks Saga*, as quoted in ibid., 260–63; on 264–65, the inquisitive author cites eight more, considerably later treatises discussing the "real" geographical situations of the Earthly Paradise; these curious works date between 1629 and 1842.

50. *Travels of Sir John Mandeville*, 135.

51. Odorico, *Viaggio*, as quoted in its entirety in M. Komroff, ed., *Contemporaries of Marco Polo, Consisting of the Travel Records to the Eastern Parts of the World* (New York, 1989), 227.

52. What follows immediately summarizes the examples given by A. B. Giamatti, *The Earthly Paradise and the Renaissance Epic* (Princeton, 1966), 17–32. For the application of traditional "Golden Age" terminology in various ways to the Native Americans, see G. Costa, *La leggenda dei secoli d'oro nella letteratura italiana* (Bari, 1972), 71ff., "La scoperta dell'America."

53. *Navigatio*, as quoted in Boas and Lovejoy, *Primitivism*, 158–59; for another version, see Gardiner, ed., *Visions*, 81–128; for the whale-island, "Jasconius," see pp. 91–92.

54. On this early Renaissance *mappamundi*, see the brief mentions in Nordenskjöld, *Facsimile-Atlas*, 36, 44, 100, where it is just cited as an anachronistic example of medieval cartographic practice.

Chapter Two

1. Las Casas, ed., *Cristóbal Colón: Diario*, 159–60.

2. For the meaning of the terms *art* and *artifice*, specifically as understood in Renaissance poetic and rhetorical practice, see H. Haydn, *The Counter Renaissance* (New York, 1960); see also S. K. Heninger, *Sidney and Spenser: The Poet as Maker* (University Park, Penn., 1989), esp. chapter 2, "A Model for the Art of Imitation." For some shrewd observations about how "la óptica del Almirante [Colón] es predeterminada por una tradición artística," see E. W. Palm, *Los Monumentos Arquitectónicos de la Española* (Santo Domingo, 1984), 8ff. Palm very usefully notes the patent analogies with the literary tropes of landscaped medieval poetry, for which see also C. V. Langlois, *La Connaissance de la Nature et du Monde au Moyen-Ages d'après quelques écrits français à l'usage des laïcs* (Paris, 1927); D. Pearsall and E. Salter, *Landscapes and Seasons of the Medieval World* (New York, 1973); J. M. Steadman, *Nature into Myth: Medieval and Renaissance Moral Symbols* (Pittsburgh, Penn., 1979); for specifically medieval "paradisial gardens," see D. Pearsall and E. Salter, *Landscapes and Seasons of the Medieval World*, especially chapter 3; for their recreation in a Mexican monastery, see J. F. Peterson, *The Paradise Garden Murals of Malinalco: Utopia and Empire in Sixteenth-Century Mexico* (Austin, Tex., 1993). For some likely patristic and/or popular sources for Columbus's *óptica*, see L. Olschki, *Storia letteraria delle scoperte geographiche: Studi e ricerche* (Florence, 1937).

3. Las Casas, ed., *Cristóbal Colón: Diario*, 58.

4. Ibid., pp. 60–61. For the "scientific"—versus "poetic," as pursued here—signifi-

cance of Columbus's (and other explorers') descriptions of the Indies, see R. Romeo, *Le scoperte americane nella cosienza italiana del Cinquecento* (Milan, 1954); A. Gerbi, *Nature in the New World, from Christopher Columbus to Fernández de Oviedo* (Pittsburgh, Penn., 1985); S. Greenblatt, ed., *New World Encounters* (Berkeley, 1993); M. Zamora, *Reading Columbus* (Berkeley, 1993).

5. Las Casas, ed., *Cristóbal Colón: Diario,* 100–101.

6. Ibid., 113–14.

7. Sidney, *The Countesse of Pembroke's Arcadia,* vol. I, 19.

8. *The Four Voyages of Columbus: A History in Eight Documents,* L. C. Jane, ed. (New York, 1988), 5–7.

9. Curtius, "The Ideal Landscape," in *European Literature,* 183ff.; for more on the medieval literary *paysage moralisé,* overflowing with "moral symbols," see the authors cited in Chapter 2, note 2 above.

10. Homer, *The Odyssey* (New York, 1971), 120.

11. Horace, as quoted in Boas and Lovejoy, *Primitivism,* 293.

12. Homer, *The Odyssey,* 99.

13. For a broad, but provocative discussion of the specifically Virgilian contributions to the post-medieval and generally "elegiac" interpretations of landscape subjects during the Renaissance, see *"Et in Arcadia ego:* Poussin and the Elegiac Tradition," in E. Panofsky, *Meaning in the Visual Arts* (Garden City, N.Y., 1955), 295–320; see also "A Humanist Dreamland," in F. Saxl, *Lectures* (London, 1957), 215–27; for the strictly literary mechanics of the Renaissance Arcadia, see G. Costa, *La leggenda dei secoli d'oro nella letteratura italiana* (Bari, 1972), where Arcadia is correctly identified as just another mise-en-scène of the Golden Age.

14. Curtius, *European Literature,* 186, 195.

15. *The Four Voyages of Columbus,* 7.

16. Las Casas, ed., *Cristóbal Colón,* 69.

17. Tertullian, as quoted in Boas and Lovejoy, *Primitivism,* 18–19.

18. Columbus's *Carta,* as given in *The Four Voyages of Columbus,* 7–9; this passage represents a summary of longer descriptions now only known from Las Casas's transcriptions of the lost *Diario;* for which see the initial entry of October 11, 1492—in Las Casas, ed., *Cristóbal Colón,* 43–44—telling of the first landing by the Europeans, on the island of Guanahaní, now generally thought to be Watling Island in the Bahamas.

19. *The Four Voyages of Columbus,* 9.

20. Sir Thomas More, *Utopia* (Harmondsworth, 1965), 40, 67.

21. Ibid., 80, 84.

22. Mártir, *Décadas,* 38. This to me seems the original source for a statement by Shakespeare—*The Tempest,* II, 1, 148–64—usually attributed to Montaigne (who, likewise, must have read Peter Martyr; see also note 57 below).

23. This phrase, "mine and thine," as used by these Renaissance authors, is observed in Haydn, *The Counter Renaissance,* 483, 503–4, 508–9, citing Peter Martyr as the earliest instance. However, for an antecedent, ca. 1490, in Lorenzo de'Medici's *Selve d'amore,* see Costa, *La leggenda dei secoli d'oro,* 50. For an even earlier one—by a hardy Asian traveler, Odorico da Pordenone—see the next note.

24. Odorico, in M. Komroff, ed., *The Contemporaries of Marco Polo, Consisting of the*

Travel Records to the Eastern Parts of the World (New York, 1989), 222. Given that this particular phrase, *meum et tuum,* became so current in Renaissance letters, it really deserves a searching analysis by a much more qualified student of philology and European letters than we can pretend to be. It scarcely seems possible to me that Odorico, a humble Franciscan monk, could have "invented" it all by himself. However, for any such occurrence *after* 1520, one may then believe that the immediate source for the usage was Peter Martyr.

25. For more on the topic of the Golden Age, using different materials and contextual emphases, see Costa, *La leggenda dei secoli d'oro;* B. Gatz, *Weltalter, goldene Zeit und sinnverwandte Vorstellungen* (Hildesheim, 1967); H. Levin, *The Myth of the Golden Age in the Renaissance* (Bloomington, Ind., 1969); E. Lipsker-Zarden, *Der Mythos vom goldenen Zeitalter in den Schäferdictungen Italiens, Spaniens, und Frankreichs zur Zeit der Renaissance* (Berlin, 1933).

26. Porphyry, as quoted in Boas and Lovejoy, *Primitivism,* 94–95.

27. Isidore, as quoted in G. Arciniegas, *Amérigo Vespuccio y el Nuevo Mundo* (Madrid, 1990), 144.

28. *Virgil's Works* (New York, 1950), 274–75. Virgil's motif was first, but decisively, "Christianized" by the Emperor Constantine the Great; henceforth, Virgil himself was seen as the pagan, but fitting, *"vaticinatore del cristianesimo";* Costa, *La leggenda dei secoli d'oro,* xxi, with further bibliography on pp. 232–34.

29. D'Étaples, as quoted in J. B. Ross and M. M. McLaughlin, eds., *The Renaissance Reader* (New York, 1960), 85–86.

30. *The Four Voyages of Columbus,* 70–71.

31. Hesiod, *The Homeric Hymns and Homerica* (London, 1964), 10–11 (with Greek text).

32. For the likely "invention" by Hesiod of the perennial topos of "The Age of Gold" (along with four other, equally symbolic "Ages"), see J. G. Griffiths, "Archaeology and Hesiod's Five Ages," *Journal of the History of Ideas* XVII (1956): 108–19.

33. Hesiod, *The Homeric Hymns,* 14–17 (with Greek text).

34. Ovid, *The Metamorphoses of Ovid* (Harmondsworth, 1961), 34–35.

35. Isidore, as quoted in Boas and Lovejoy, *Primitivism,* 68.

36. *The Metamorphoses of Ovid,* 33–34.

37. Ambrose, as quoted in Boas and Lovejoy, *Primitivism,* 42.

38. Boethius, *The Consolation of Philosophy* (New York, 1943), 33.

39. Tacitus, *The Annals of Imperial Rome* (Harmondsworth, 1964), 129.

40. For "Edenism" and "Arcadianism" (usually however appearing under different names) as a leitmotiv in later American historiography, see especially H. N. Smith, *Virgin Land: The American West as Symbol and Myth* (Cambridge, Mass., 1970). For more details on these self-fulfilling expectations, see G. Chinard, *L'exotisme américaine dans la littérature française au XVIe siècle* (Paris, 1911), whose first chapter, for example, shows how quickly Europeans were to identify "the Indies" with the *Insulae Fortunatae;* another link (not cited by Chinard) is Columbus himself: "Forsè il Paradiso terrestre è quel luogo che i classici chiamano 'Insole fortunate'" ("Postilla," as cited in Costa, *La leggenda dei secoli d'oro,* 72).

41. *The Four Voyages of Columbus,* 118.

42. Las Casas, ed., *Cristóbal Colón,* 9–11.

43. Ibid., 15.

44. Ibid., 11.

45. Schedel, as quoted in P. Hermann, *Conquest by Man* (New York, 1954), 84–85. For what we take to be Schedel's direct, and likely (for being relatively recent and, additionally, repeatedly translated) textual source, see *Travels of Sir John Mandeville,* 128– 29: "Those men who live right under the Antarctic Pole are set foot against foot to those who live right below the Arctic Pole, just as we and those who live at our Antipodes are foot against foot. It is like that in all parts. Each part of the earth and sea has its opposite, which always balances it. And understand that, to my way of thinking, the Land of Prester John, Emperor of India, is exactly below us [etc.]."

46. Las Casas, ed., *Cristóbal Colón,* 15.

47. *The Four Voyages of Columbus,* 66.

48. Ibid., 56–57.

49. Ibid., 74.

50. Las Casas, ed., *Cristóbal Colón,* 119.

51. Mártir, *Décadas,* 77.

52. *The Four Voyages of Columbus,* 82.

53. Ibid., 97.

54. Las Casas, ed., *Cristóbal Colón,* 15–17.

55. *Travels of Sir John Mandeville,* 134, 136–37.

56. Ibid., 127.

57. Michel de Montaigne, *Selected Essays* (New York, 1959), 137–52, "Of the Cannibals." On this author's New World textual sources, mostly López de Gómara and Jean de Léry (among others identified as likely in our text), see G. Defaux, "Un Cannibale en haut de chausses: Montaigne, la différence et la logique de l'identité," *Modern Language Notes* XCI (1982): 919–57; F. Lestringant, "Le Cannibalisme des 'Canibales,'" *Bulletin de la Société des Amis de Montaigne* IX/X (1982): 27–40; G. Nakam, *Les "Essais" de Montaigne: Miroir et procès de leur temps* (Paris, 1984), 329–51. See also note 22 above.

58. Lucretius, *On the Nature of the Universe* (Harmondsworth, 1970), 199–202.

59. Ibid.

60. This ethnographic shift from "soft" to "hard" primitivism (an academic way of defining the ubiquitous process of "familiarity breeds contempt") describes a familiar pattern; in fact, it may be called the leitmotiv of nearly *all* European colonialism; for the persistently "hard" European interpretations of (only) the American Indians, see (among other pertinent titles cited in further chapters) R. F. Berkhofer, *The White Man's Indian: Images of the American Indian from Columbus to the Present* (New York, 1979); B. Bucher, *Icon and Conquest: A Structural Analysis of the Illustrations of De Bry's "Great Voyages"* (Chicago, 1981); R. Drinnon, *Facing West: The Metaphysics of Indian-Hating and Empire Building* (New York, 1990); G. Gliozzi, *La scoperta dei selvaggi: Antropologia e colonialismo, da Columbo a Diderot* (Milan, 1971); R. H. Pearce, *Savagism and Civilization: A Study of the Indian and the American Mind* (Baltimore, 1965). Viewed from a much broader cultural perspective, all this invective simply represents prejudices automatically applied by "agriculturalists" to their historical ancestors, the "hunter-gatherers," and probably since the Neolithic era;

see P. Farb, *Humankind* (New York, 1980), 83ff. For the broader historigraphic picture, see R. Nisbet, *History of the Idea of Progress* (New York, 1980).

61. "Insensible aux stupides hommes des premiers temps, échappée aux hommes éclairés des temps postérieurs, l'heureuse vie de l'age d'or fut toujours un état étranger à la race humaine," Rousseau, in a preliminary draft of the *Contrat Social* (ca. 1755), as quoted in A. O. Lovejoy, *Essays in the History of Ideas* (New York, 1960), 15.

Chapter Three

1. Pérez, as cited in J. H. Elliott, *El Viejo Mundo y el Nuevo, 1492–1650* (Madrid, 1972), 28. For the concept of an opportune "invention" of the New World by Europeans in the Renaissance, see E. O'Gorman, *The Invention of America* (Bloomington, Ind., 1961). For a more detailed analysis of the enduring theme of "wonderment-marvel" experienced by Europeans in the face of myriad American *mirabilia,* see S. Greenblatt, *Marvelous Possessions: The Wonder of the New World* (Chicago, 1991).

2. Humboldt, as quoted in G. Giraldo Jaramillo, "Humboldt y el descubrimiento estético de América," *El Farol* (Caracas), no. 181 (1959): 10–19.

3. For this point, besides others publications we have already cited, particularly see A. Milhou, *Colón y su mentalidad mesiánica en el ambiente franciscanista español* (Valladolid, 1983). For the essential Columbian text proving his "messianic mentality," see West and Kling, eds., *Libro de las profecías.*

4. For what follows in the broader sense, see J. Phelan, *El reino milenario de los franciscanos en el Nuevo Mundo* (Mexico City, 1962); for the Mexican "Solomonic" architectural motif in particular, see S. Sebastián, "La significación salomónica del templo de Huejotzingo," *Traza y Baza* III (1973): 62–71. For the essential medieval psychological precedents, see N. Cohn, *The Pursuit of the Millennium: Revolutionary Millennarians and Mystical Anarchists of the Middle Ages* (London, 1978).

5. *Cristóbal Colón: Textos y documentos completos* (Madrid, 1982); see also (among others commenting on Columbus's American Eden) J. Manzano Manzano, *Colón y su secreto* (Madrid, 1976), 222–24; C. Kappler, *Monstruos, demonios y maravillas al fin de la Edad Media* (Madrid, 1986), 102–3.

6. León Pinelo, as cited in H. Capel, *La física sagrada* (Barcelona, 1985), 96–98.

7. M. Eliade, *Mitos, sueños y misterios* (Buenos Aires, 1961), 37–41.

8. A. Milhou, "El indio americano y el mito de la religión natural," in (no editor named) *La imagen del indio en la Europa moderna* (Seville, 1990), 171–96; H. White, "The Noble Savage: Theme and Fetish," in F. Chiapelli, ed., *First Images of America: The Impact of the New World on the Old* (Berkeley, 1976), 121–25; for a broader "scientific" context, see also M. T. Hodgen, *Early Anthropology in the Sixteenth and Seventeenth Centuries* (Philadelphia, 1964).

9. *Colón: Textos,* 29–31 (December 12, 1492).

10. Bartolomé de Las Casas, *Historia de las Indias* (Madrid, 1927), *Biblioteca de Autores Españoles,* vol. 95, I, ch. 2, 22.

11. For the Mandeville-Columbus connection, as observed by a shipmate, see

A. Bernáldez, *Memorias del reinado de los Reyes Católicos* (Madrid, 1962), 270, 307, 315, 319; cf. Milhou, *Colón*, 11; we cite here a new translation in Castilian, also reproducing the old woodcuts: *Juan de Mandeville: Libro de las maravillas del mundo* (Madrid, 1984).

12. For what immediately follows, see particularly W. R. Jones, "The Image of the Barbarian in Medieval Europe," *Comparative Studies in Society and History* XIII (1971), 376–407; see also Milhou, *Colón*, 160–62.

13. Amerigo Vespucci, *El Nuevo Mundo: Viajes y documentos completos* (Madrid, 1985), 62.

14. For these and other cannibalistic culinary memorabilia, see Hans Staden, *Verdadera historia y descripción de un país de salvajes desnudos, feroces y caníbales* (Barcelona, 1983).

15. So noted in Kappler, *Monstruos*, 185–86.

16. H. Schedel, *Liber Chronicarum cum figuris et imaginibus ab initio mundi* (Nüremberg, 1493). For the Schedel-derived prints appearing in Mandeville's *Marvels*, see *Mandevilla: Libro;* for an analysis of same, see S. Sebastián, "Lo maravilloso y lo monstruoso en el grabado valenciano del Protorrenacimiento," *I Coloquio de Arte Valenciano* (Valencia, 1989), 1–12.

17. *Colón: Textos*, 144, "Carta a Santángel."

18. St. Augustine, *La Ciudad de Dios* (XVI, 8, 1–2), as in *Obras completas* (Madrid ["B.A.C."], 1965), vol. 17, 211.

19. E. Mâle, *L'art religieux du XII siècle en France* (Paris, 1966), 330; J. B. Friedman, *The Monstrous Races*, 77–81.

20. Velázquez, as first published in J. Fernández Navarrete, *Colección de documentos inéditos para la historia de España* (Madrid, 1842–95), vol. I, 403; for a broader perspective, see also L. Weckmann, "The Middle Ages in the Conquest of America," *Speculum* XXVI (1951): 130–41.

21. For more on this particularly monstrous *topos*, see B. Bucher, *La sauvage aux seins pendents* (Paris, 1977) 23; see also an important exhibition-catalog: K-H. Kohl, ed., *Mythen in der Neuen Welt: Zur Entdeckungsgeschichte Lateinamerikas* (Berlin, 1982) 22, fig. 12.

22. H. Joris-Zavala, "L'allégorie de l'Amérique," in *Mémoire d'une Amérique* (La Rochelle: Musée du Nouveau Monde, 1980), 101–4.

23. F. J. Pizarro Gómez, "La iconografía del Nuevo Mundo y su repercusión en las artes españolas y portuguesas," in *Actas del V. Simposio Hispano-Portugués de Historia el Arte* (Valladolid, 1990).

24. For commentaries and reproductions of this imagery, see K-H. Kohl, ed., *Mythen der Neuen Welt,* 326ff.

25. Mª. Sanz Hermida and A. M. Armand, "La alegoría en geografía: Estudio iconológico de los frontispicios de los Atlas holandeses de los siglos XVI y XVII," *Actas del Congreso del CEA* (Cáceres, 1990); see also G. Antei, "Iconología americana: La alegoría de América en el Cinquecento florentino," *Cuadernos de Arte Colonial* V (1989): 5–33.

26. Cesare Ripa, *Iconologia, overo Descrittione d'Imagini delle Virtù, Vitii, Affetti, Passioni humane, Corpi celesti, Mondo e sue parti* (Padua, 1611) [facs. ed. New York, 1976], 359–60. It may also be mentioned that, shortly after the first illustrated edition (1603) of Ripa's universally consulted allegorical handbook, certain (often erratic) descriptions of Native American, particularly Aztec, gods and myths begin to appear in European mythological

treatises, a notable example being the substantial revisions, after 1605, put to Vincenzo Cartari's *Imagini degli Dei* (orig. Venice, 1571). Unfortunately, these interesting ethnographical developments within European culture of the Baroque period lie outside the scope of the present investigation (and also our mutual expertise).

27. Staden, *Verdadera historia,* 93.

28. E. Santiago Páez, "Algunas esculturas napolitanas del siglo XVIII en España," *Archivo Español de Arte* XL (1967), 126.

29. *Colón: Textos,* 135 (March 6, 1493).

30. Las Casas, *Historia,* I, 336.

31. *Colón: Textos,* 141.

32. Ibid., 141–42. For the classical sources of the idea of "primeval" architecture appearing in Italian art at this time, also including these "proto-American" structural features, see J. F. Moffitt, "Leonardo's *Sala delle Asse* and the Primordial Origins of Architecture," *Arte Lombarda* 92/93 (1990): 241–48 (with complete bibliography on the "primitive hut" problem); idem., "Vitruvius in a Carolingian Eden: The Genesis Cycle from the *Moûtier-Grandval Bible,*" *Source* XII, no. 1 (1992): 7–12 (showing a much earlier, medieval application of the same motif).

33. H. Honour, *The European Vision of America* (Cleveland, 1975), cat. no. 1.

34. For Trevignano's remark, see H. Harrisse, *Biblioteca Americana Venustissima . . .* (Madrid, 1960), 304.

35. C. Sanz, *El gran secreto de la Carta de Colón* (Madrid, 1959), 113.

36. For the historical context of Peter Martyr's *Decades,* see E. O'Gorman, *Cuatro Historiadores de Indias: Siglo XVI* (Mexico City, 1972), 11–44; for the strictly pictorial effects at this time, see R. E. Alegría, *Las primeras representaciones del indio americano, 1493–1523* (Puerto Rico, 1978), 11–36.

37. C. Sanz, *Mapas antiguos del mundo (siglos XV–XVI)* (Madrid, 1962), 60–61 and fig. 9.

38. A. Vespucci, *Nuevo Mundo,* 60.

39. Ibid., 62.

40. Ibid.

41. For the source for the German artist's pictorial motifs in Vespucci's correspondence, see ibid., 60–63 (letter to Pier Francesco de Medici); and also so noted by Alegría, *Primeras representaciones,* 66. We shall again mention this German print in Chapter 5.

42. Vespucci, *Nuevo Mundo,* 61–62.

43. Ibid., 99–100; the Isla de los Gigantes described by Vespucci can probably be better identified with Curaçao.

44. Guaman Poma, as quoted in T. Gisbert, "Los Incas y los Reyes Magos," *Traza y Baza* VII (1973): 39–43. According to Gisbert, another painting of a similar *Epiphany,* with yet another Indian Magus, may be seen in the Peruvian parish church of Ilabe in Puno province. For another example of the "Indian Magus," see P. Verger, *Fiestas y danzas en el Cuzco y en los Andes* (Buenos Aires, 1945), fig. 47.

45. Vespucci, *Nuevo Mundo,* 106.

46. Ibid., 80.

47. For a lavishly illustrated and eruditely commented survey of a wealth of other-

wise unaccessible Austrian Habsburg imagery dealing with America and Native Americans, see F. Polleross, ed., *Federschmuck und Kaiserkrone: Das barocke Amerikabild in den habsburgischen Ländern* (Vienna, 1992).

48. E. Panofsky, *Vida y arte de Alberto Durero* (Madrid, 1982), 193; H. Honour, *European Vision,* cat. no. 5; Alegría, *Primeras representaciones,* 77; W. C. Sturtevant, "First Visual Images of Native Americans," in F. Chiapelli, ed., *First Images of America,* 420–23.

49. According to Ricardo Alegría, "La asociación entre la imagen clásica de la vida durante la llamada Edad de Oro y la vida de los indios desnudos, en contacto con la naturaleza, se manifiesta claramente en estas primeras representaciones de los aborígenes americanos.": *Primeras representaciones,* 90.

50. John White's eyewitness drawings were later, shortly before 1590, made into engravings illustrating the first volume of the *Grands Voyages* published by Theodore de Bry, who is discussed by us in his role as an important Protestant propagandist in chapter 5. For an inexpensive facsimile edition of the première de Bry volume with White's pictures, see *Thomas Hariot, A Brief and True Report of the New Found Land of Virginia: The Complete 1590 Theodore de Bry Editions* (New York: Dover, 1972). For the original drawings, unknown to the general public before our century, see P. Hulton and D. B. Quinn, *The American Drawings of John White, 1577–1590* (London: British Museum, 1964), exh. cat.

51. For a recent analysis of a case illustrating the conceptual gulf frequently existing between a source text and its illustration in Renaissance graphic art, see J. F. Moffitt, "An Airborne Rescuer from the North in El Paso: 'Ruggiero' or 'Perseus'? 'Hippogriff' or 'Horse'?" *Journal of the Rocky Mountain Medieval and Renaissance Association* IX (1990): 79–99.

52. For a definitive analysis of American "Otherness" at this time, see T. Todorov, *The Conquest of America: The Question of the Other* (New York, 1992).

Chapter Four

1. For what follows in general, see S. Sebastián, *Album de arte colonial* (Tunja, 1963), figs. 15–18; idem., "El empleo y actualización de los modelos europeos en México y América Latina," in *Simpatías y diferencias: Relaciones del arte mexicano con el de América Latina* (México, 1988): 113–25; for an accessible introduction to Alciati's important emblem book, see S. Sebastián, ed., *Alciato: Emblemas* (Madrid, 1985). See also note 6 below.

2. As so noted in G. Baudot, *Utopía e Historia en México,* (Madrid, 1983), 495.

3. The Biblioteca Universitaria de Valencia contains two contemporary copies of the Spanish translation of Titus Livy (both Zaragoza, 1520), and additionally another of the work cited here by Francisco López de Gómara (Zaragoza, 1554); these rare *incunabula* are the sources for our illustrations. For a much more accessible (but unillustrated) editions of these two works, see Francisco López de Gómara, *Historia general de las Indias* (Barcelona, 1966); *Livy: Rome and the Mediterranean: Books XXXI–XLV of The History of Rome from its Foundations,* H. Bettenson, ed. (Harmondsworth, 1976).

4. For the Florentine fresco cycle, see S. Heikamp, *Mexico and the Medici* (Florence,

1972), 20–21; H. Honour, "Wissenschaft und Exotismus," in K-H. Kohl, ed., *Mythen in der Neuen Welt*, 34, figs. 27, 28.

5. See S. Andrés Ordax, "El Palacio Moctezuma en Cáceres," *Memorias de la Real Academia de Extremadura* I (1983): 83–85; idem., "Los frescos de las salas romana y mejicana del Palacio de Moctezuma de Cáceres," *Norba* V (1984): 97–115; C. García Sanz, "La imagen del indio en el arte español del Siglo de Oro," in *La imagen del indio en la Europa moderna* (Seville, 1990): 417–32.

6. For what follows (besides note 1 above), see the brilliant cultural dissection of Baroque Nueva España by Octavio Paz, *Sor Juana Inés de la Cruz, o Las Trampas de la Fe* (México, 1985), 203–11 (Sigüenza), 212–41 (Sor Juana); for the original source materials for the former author's allegorical program, see Carlos de Sigüenza y Góngora, *Triunfo Parthénico* (rpt.: Mexico City, 1960), 278–79; for more on this author, see also I. A. Leonard, *Don Carlos de Sigüenza y Góngora: A Mexican Savant of the Seventeenth Century* (Berkeley, 1929). We are additionally indebted to Dr. Helga von Kügelgen for allowing us to see an unpublished manuscript of her lecture, "The Way to Mexican Identity: Two Triumphal Arches of the 17th Century," presented at the International Congress of the History of Art, in Washington D.C., 1986.

7. See F. Vian, *La guerre des Géants. Le mythe avant l'époque hellénistique* (Paris, 1952).

8. *Vespuccio: El Nuevo Mundo: Viajes y documentos completos* (Madrid, 1985), 100.

9. A. Pigafetta, *Primer viaje alrededor del mundo* (Madrid, 1985), 42; see also E. de Gandía, *Historia crítica de los mitos y leyendas de la conquista americana* (Madrid, 1929) 39; J-P. Duviols, *L'Amérique espagnole vue et rêvée* (Paris, 1985), 59.

10. See M. Germán Romero, *Juan de Castellanos: Un examen de su vida y obra* (Bogotá, 1964), 365.

11. For some of these accounts of encounters with American Pygmies, see Gandía, *Historia crítica*, chap. 2; see also J. Gil, *Mitos y utopías del descubrimiento* (Madrid, 1989), III, 89ff.

12. *Juan de Mandeville: Libro de las maravillas del mundo* (Madrid, 1943) I, 146; see also Gandía, *Historia crítica*, ch. 6 (also quoting Marco Polo and Peter Martyr).

13. *Colón: Textos*, 119.

14. Carvajal's *Relación* has often been republished; we are following extracts gathered in E. Rodríguez Monegal, *Noticias secretas de América* (Barcelona, 1984), 114–19.

15. *Ulrico Schmidel: Relatos de la conquista del Río de la Plata y Paraguay, 1534–1554* (Madrid, 1986), 69.

16. Raleigh, as quoted in D. Ramos, *El mito del Dorado: Su génesis y proceso* (Caracas, 1973), 552–53.

17. Gandía, *Historia crítica*, 81–82; Duviols, *L'Amérique espagnole*, 47–53. For more on the American (and elsewhere) "Amazons," see R. Henning, *Wo Lag das Paradies: Rätselfragen der Kulturgeschichte und Geographie* (Berlin, 1950), "Die Amazonen-Sage," 83–95; G. Speck, *Myths and New World Explorations* (Edmonds Wash., 1979), "The Amazons," 33–48.

18. P. Cieza de León, *La Crónica del Perú* (Madrid, 1984); see also F. Esteve Barba, *Historiografía indiana* (Madrid, 1984), 413–15. To date, study of the illustrated Antwerp edition of Cieza's *Crónica del Perú* remains preliminary, but it is the as-yet unpublished re-

search of our colleague and friend, Luis Tovar, to whom we are greatly indebted for what follows; see also his *Lo medieval en la Conquista y otros ensayos americanos* (Madrid, 1970).

19. Cieza, *Crónica,* ch. 12.

20. Ibid., ch. 8.

21. M. A. Durán, *Fundación de ciudades en el Perú durante el siglo XVI* (Sevilla, 1987), 121–30. For another recent study, taking a much broader view of urban planning in the Hispanic world, see Bonet Correra, A., *El urbanismo en España e Hispanoamérica* (Madrid, 1991).

22. M. Ballesteros Gaibrois, *Descubrimiento y fundación de Potosí* (Zaragoza, 1955); C. Prieto, *La minería en el Nuevo Mundo* (Madrid, 1969), 116–17.

23. A. de Herrera, *Historia general de los hechos de los castellanos en las islas y tierra firme del mar océano* (Madrid, 1936), vol. V, 204–5.

24. F. López de Gómara, *Historia general de las Indias* (Barcelona, 1966), vol. II, 270.

25. Herrera, *Historia general,* vol. V, 339–42.

26. A. Pigafetta, *Primer viaje,* 110.

27. For the recent literature on this rare publication, see F. Polleross, ed., *Federschmuck und Kaiserkorne: Das barocke Amerikabild in den habsburgischen Ländern,* (Vienna, 1992), exh. cat. no. 8:19.

28. L. A. Vigneras, *La búsqueda del Paraíso y las legendarias islas del Atlántico* (Valladolid, 1976), 25ff.; see also P. Tuffrau, *Le merveilleux voyage de Saint Brandan à la recherche du Paradis* (Paris, 1925); for the Canary Islands as the *Insulae Fortunatae* discussed by various classical authors, see J. F. Moffitt, "Filostrato, sus *Imágines* y la imagen de las Islas Canarias en la Antigüedad," in *Homenaje al Profesor Dr. Telesforo Bravo* (Universidad de la Laguna, 1990), vol. II, 437–60.

29. For a substantial bibliography dealing with Abbot Boyl, see the entries gathered by J. Castañeda, as in the *Diccionario de Historia Eclesiástica de España* (Madrid, 1972).

30. Gómara, *Historia general,* vol. I, 10.

31. Archbishop Benedeit, *El viaje de San Brandán* (Madrid, 1983), 18.

32. A. Ballesteros Gaibrois, *Génesis del descubrimiento* (Barcelona, 1947), 231–33.

33. Honorius Philoponus, *Nova typis transacta navigatio novi orbis Indiae Occidentalis* (Linz, 1621), 12–13.

34. P. Lestienne, *Saint Malo ou Maclou: Sa vie et son culte* (St. Malo, 1954); see also L. Réau, *Iconographie de l'art chrétien* (Paris, 1958).

35. Gómara, *Historia general,* vol. I, 38–41; see also Philoponus, *Nova typis,* 22–24.

36. H. Staden, *Verdadera historia;* it also includes some fifty sixteenth-century illustrations.

37. Of the series of engravings from the *Nova typis,* only the fifth, "Insulae Cannibalium," has been recently published, with however no further clarification about its intrinsic significance given here; see Duviols, *L'Amérique espagnole,* 100; Polleross (as in n. 27).

38. Theodore de Bry, *Americae, pars IV,* plate 16 (more details on this important work will follow in the next chapter); for the series as a whole, see B. Bucher, *La sauvage aux seins pendants* (Paris, 1977).

39. G. Fernández de Oviedo, *Historia general y natural de las Indias* (Madrid, 1959), vol. I, 112. We know of no surviving art historical examples of Arawak "Devils."

40. Gómara, *Historia general,* vol. II, 59.
41. Oviedo, *Historia,* vol. II, 63–65.

Chapter Five

1. For the European invention of the idea of the American Indian, above all see the various essays gathered in (no editor named) *La Imagen del Indio en la Europa Moderna* (Seville, 1990); see also some outstanding and easily accessible monographs consulted by us (among many other studies cited in our bibliography): R. F. Berkhofer, *The White Man's Indian* (New York, 1979); R. Drinnon, *Facing West* (New York, 1990); B. Keen, *The Aztec Image in Western Thought* (New Brunswick, N.J., 1985); R. H. Pearce, *Savagism and Civilization: A Study of the Indian and the American Mind* (Baltimore, Md., 1965); R. Wauchope, *Lost Tribes and Sunken Continents: Myth and Method in the Study of American Indians* (Chicago, Ill., 1962).

2. S. E. Morison, *Admiral of the Ocean Sea: A Life of Christopher Columbus* (New York, 1962), 226; for the various meanings of the *bon sauvage* in European thought, see G. Cocchiara, *L'eterno selvaggio: Presenza e influsso del mundo primtivo nella cultura moderna* (Milan, 1961); H. N. Fairchild, *The Noble Savage: A Study in Romantic Naturalism* (New York, 1928); R. Gonnard, *La légende du bon sauvage: Contributions à l'étude des origines du Socialisme* (Paris, 1946). Even though many people still think that the concept of the "Noble Savage" was exclusively a product of the Age of Enlightenment, nonetheless see J. B. Friedman, *The Monstrous Races,* chapter 8, "Monstrous Men as Noble Savages," showing that a major source (as previously pointed out here) for the idea was the medieval "Alexander Legend" as it was set in exotic India.

3. Mártir, *Décadas,* 23, 38 (Déc. I., caps. 2, 3). Again (as in chapter 2, note 22), we see this quotation as the basis for a much discussed passage in Shakespeare's *The Tempest* (II,1, 148–64).

4. Berkhofer, *White Man's Indian,* 28.

5. For the classical period texts relating to these barbarian peoples, see Boas and Lovejoy, *Primitivism,* 404–14.

6. Herodotus, *The Histories* (Harmondsworth, 1965), 257; for other ancient texts relating to the Scythians, see Boas and Lovejoy, *Primitivism,* 315–33.

7. Justin, as quoted in Boas and Lovejoy, *Primitivism,* 328.

8. Julius Caesar, *The Conquest of Gaul* (Harmondsworth, 1958), 35–37.

9. Tacitus, *The Agricola and the Germania* (Harmondsworth, 1970), 113–14.

10. Ibid., pp. 117–18. For the ongoing Noble Savage myth in *modern* German history, see J. F. Moffitt, *Occultism in Avant-Garde Art: The Case of Joseph Beuys* (Ann Arbor, 1988), 83 ff.

11. Cooper, in his Introduction to the revised (1850) version of *The Last of the Mohicans* (originally issued in 1828), as contextually quoted in Berkhofer, *White Man's Indian,* 92. It has been recently remarked (Drinnon, *Facing West,* 160) that of all Cooper's Indians, "from *The Pioneers* (1823) to *The Deerslayer* (1841), all but a handfull were stock merciless savages."

12. Jerome, as quoted in Boas, *Essays on Primitivism and Related Ideas in the Middle Ages* (New York, 1978), 132.

13. This idea is neatly developed in Friedman, *Monstruous Races*, chapter 8, "Monstrous Men as Noble Savages [in India]."

14. *Expositio*, as contextually quoted in Boas, *Essays*, 138–39.

15. Pseudo-Callisthenes, as quoted in Boas, *Essays*, 140–41. As reported by Friar Bartolomé de Las Casas, Columbus similarly subscribed to these traditions, and the Spanish historian accordingly quotes the admiral as praising the Native Americans as forming part of a nation "a quién mejor no la pueda comparar, que a la nación que los antiguos y hoy llaman y llamamos Seres, los pueblos orientales de la India [gangética], de quién por los autores antiguos [¡y los medievales!] se dice entre si quietísimos y mansísimos," etc. Immediately following, Las Casas usefully lists a number of *autores antiguos* who wrote "to the same effect" about the Asian Indians; his bibliography includes such standards as Pliny, Solinus, Mela, Strabo, Virgil, Boèthius, St. Isidore, Ammianus Marcellinus, etc. (Las Casas, *Historia de las Indias*, vol. I, 202–3).

16. Pseudo-Callisthenes, as given in Boas, *Essays*, 141–43.

17. Chanca, as quoted in *The Four Voyages of Columbus*, 311–33.

18. Pedro Mártir de Anglería, *Cartas sobre el Nuevo Mundo* (Madrid, 1990), 41–42 (*Epistolae*, CXLVI, December 5, 1494).

19. C. Sale, *The Conquest of Paradise: Christopher Columbus and the Columbian Legacy* (New York, 1990), 132–35.

20. For this particular print, see B. Schuller, "The Oldest Known Illustration of South American Indians," *Heyde Foundation Indian Notes* VII (1930): 484–97; W. C. Sturtevant, "The First Images of America," in F. Chiapelli, ed., *First Images of America*, 417–54; for the later communality of the real ethnographic subject of the German print, "cannibalism," see B. Bucher, "Die Phantasien der Eroberer: Zur graphischen Representation des Kannibalismus in de Brys America," in K-H. Kohl, ed., *Mythen der Neuen Welt*, 75–91.

21. *Travels of Sir John Mandeville*, 127.

22. Américo Vespucio, *Cartas* (Madrid, 1983), 46–49.

23. Stobaeus, as quoted in Boas & Lovejoy, *Primitivism*, 216; another, more jocular, reference to primitivist cannibal cuisine is found in Athenaeus's *Deipnosophistae* (XIV, 660–61); see ibid., 213–15; for more on the theory and general practice of anthropophagous feasting, see M. Harris, *Cannibals and Kings: The Origins of Cultures* (New York, 1978); R. Tannahill, *Flesh and Blood: A History of the Cannibal Complex* (New York, 1988), chapter 4 being exclusively devoted to the infamous Native American Cannibals.

24. Bernal Díaz del Castillo, *Historia Verdadera de la Conquista de la Nueva España* (Madrid, 1985), 167 (cap. 83).

25. For the decimation of the Native Americans, largely through exposure to European diseases—measles, influenza, typhus, pneumonia, tuberculosis, diphtheria, pleurisy, scarlet fever, whooping cough, cholera, dysentery, bubonic plague, gonorrhea, typhoid, alcoholism, smallpox, etc.—see A. W. Crosby, *The Columbian Exchange: Biological and Cultural Consequences of 1492* (Westport CT, 1972), 35ff.; W. H. McNeill, *Plagues and Peoples* (New York, 1976), 176ff. Unquestionably, these Old World plagues allowed for the most devastating aspect of the European invention of America: depopulation.

26. Hernán Cortés, *Cartas de la conquista de México* (Madrid, 1985), 36 (Carta I).

27. *A History of Ancient Mexico by Fray Bernadino de Sahagún: The Religion and Ceremonies of the Aztec Indians,* (Glorieta, N.M., 1976), 52.

28. Mártir, *Décadas,* 440–41 (Déc. 7, cap. 4).

29. Ginés de Sepúlveda, as quoted in L. Hanke, *All Mankind is One: A Study of the Disputation Between Bartolomé de Las Casas and Juan Ginés de Sepúlveda in 1550 on the Intellectual and Religious Capacity of the American Indians* (Carbondale Ill., 1974), 84.

30. Garcilaso de la Vega, "el Inca," *Comentarios reales: El origen de los Incas* (Barcelona, 1968), 77.

31. Ibid., 83–85.

32. On Eckhout and his ethnographic portraits, see H. Honour, *The New Golden Land: European Images of America from the Discovery to the Present Time* (New York, 1975), 79–83; E. van den Boogaart, "The Slow Progress of Colonial Civility: Indians in the Pictorial Record of Dutch Brazil, 1637–1644," in *Imagen del Indio,* 389–403.

33. Friedman, *Monstruous Races,* 197.

34. R. Bernheimer, *Wild Men in the Middle Ages: A Study in Art, Sentiment, and Demonology* (New York, 1970), 19–20.

35. Waterhouse, as quoted in S. M. Kingsbury, ed., *The Records of the Virginia Company of London* (Washington D.C., 1906–35), vol. III, 556–57, 562–63.

36. Morris, as quoted in S. Rifkin, ed., *The Savage Years* (New York, 1967), 65.

37. Thomas Hobbes, *Leviathan* (New York, 1964), 84–85; emphasis ours.

38. Mark Twain, *Roughing It* (New York, 1962), 118–20.

39. De Pauw, as quoted in H. S. Commager and E. Giordanetti, eds., *Was America a Mistake?: An Eighteenth-Century Controversy* (New York, 1967), 94–95.

40. Mártir, *Décadas,* 41–42 (Déc. 1., cap. 4).

41. Ibid., 226–27 (Déc. 3, cap. 8).

42. Diego de Landa, *Yucatán Before and After the Conquest* (New York, 1978), 24–25.

43. For an overview of the topic at hand, the "Black Legend," see R. Carbia, *Historia de la Leyenda Negra hispanoamericana* (Madrid, 1944); J. Juderías, *La Leyenda Negra* (Madrid, 1954); S. Arnoldsson, *La leyenda negra: Estudios sobre sus orígenes* (Stockholm, 1960); idem., *La conquista española de América según el juicio de la posteridad* (Madrid, 1960); W. S. Maltby, *The Black Legend in England: The Development of Anti-Spanish Sentiment, 1558–1660* (Durham N.C., 1971); C. Gibson, *The Black Legend: Anti-Spanish Attitudes in the Old World and the New* (New York, 1971); A. Caponnetto, *Hispanidad y Leyenda Negra: La Teología de Liberación y la Historia de América* (Buenos Aires, 1989); M. Molina Martínez, *La Leyenda Negra* (Madrid, 1991); see also E. Núñez, *España vista por viajeros hispanoamericanos* (Madrid, 1985). For broader contexts belonging to the immediate historical setting, see the standard survey by J. H. Elliott, *Imperial Spain, 1469–1716* (New York, 1966); and also a classic study by H. Kamen, *The Spanish Inquisition* (New York, 1975).

44. L. Hanke, *La lucha española por la justicia en la conquista de América* (Madrid, 1959), 16; for Las Casas in general, see also Hanke, *Bartolomé de Las Casas* (Bogotá, 1965), and also the "Black Legend" materials cited in note 43.

45. A. de Altolaguirre, *Don Pedro de Alvarado, conquistador del Reino de Nueva Granada* (Madrid, 1927), 9. For the citations following, dealing with Las Casas *in malo,* see R. Ricard, *La "conquête spirituelle" du Mexique: Essai sur l'apostolat et les méthodes des Ordres Mendiants an Nouvelle Espagne de 1523 à 1572* (Paris, 1933), 48; and, especially, R. Menéndez

Pidal, *La lengua de Cristóbal Colón, el estilo de Santa Teresa y otros estudios sobre el siglo XVI* (Madrid, 1958), 85–100 ("¿Codicia insaciable? ¿Ilustres hazañas?"); for more of the same, and at greater length, see also his *El Padre de Las Casas* (Madrid, 1963).

46. In this case, as pointed out in C. Bayle, *España en Indias* (Vitoria, 1934), 65. Since 1934, this diagnosis of the decimation of Native Americans has become a commonplace, and now much better documented: see the more recent studies cited in note 25 above.

47. For Actopán, see S. Sebastián et al., *Arte Iberoamericano*, in *Summa Artis* (Madrid, 1985), vol. XXVIII, 49–51.

48. Carbia, *Historia de la Leyenda Negra*, 84.

49. In this case, we are mostly quoting from a recent reprinting of the *Brevísima relación*, as included in a collection of Las Casas's polemical treatises dealing with Native American topics: J. Alcina Franch, ed., *Bartolomé de Las Casas: Obra indigenista* (Madrid, 1985); for this passage, see p. 68.

50. Ortiz's diatribe, besides as given in note 28 above, is also quoted by Bayle, *España en Indias,* 50–51.

51. Las Casas, *Brevísima relación de la destrucción de las Indias* (Madrid, 1986), 73.

52. Ibid.

53. Ibid., 77.

54. Ibid., 81.

55. Ibid., 85.

56. Ibid., 93.

57. Ibid.

58. Ibid., 94.

59. Ibid., 100.

60. Ibid., 102.

61. Ibid., 139.

62. Ibid., 105.

63. Ibid., 108.

64. Ibid., 133.

65. Ibid., 104.

66. Ibid., 140.

67. Ibid., 78.

68. B. de Las Casas, *Brevísima relación,* 102–3. For the later tradition of the "atrocity picture," in (North) America and in Europe, see J. F. Moffitt, "Francisco Goya y Paul Revere: Una matanza en Madrid y una matanza en Boston," in F. Calvo Serraller, ed., *Goya Nuevas Visiones: Homenaje a Don Enrique Lafuente Ferrari* (Museo del Prado, Madrid, 1987), 257–90.

69. M. Mexía Restrepo, *Discurso en la Academia Colombiana de Historia* (Caracas, 1930), as quoted by Bayle, *España en Indias,* 40. For a rare surviving account written by one of those Protestant "corsairs, pirates, and filibusters," which actually does support Restrepo's emotional response, see Jean Esquemeling, *The Buccaneers of America* (New York, 1967).

70. G. Benzoni, *Historia del Mondo Nuovo* (Roma, 1572), fol. 52; as reprinted in the recent, and well annotated, Spanish translation of this important work: *Girolamo Benzoni: Historia del Nuevo Mundo* (Madrid: Alianza Editorial, 1987), 144–45 (for similar mistreatment accorded blacks by the Spaniards, see pp. 161–62: "Los malos tratos dados

a los esclavos negros"). On Benzoni, see also J-P. Duviols, *L'Amérique espagnole vue et rêvée* (Paris, 1986), 177–82; Carbia, *Historia de la Leyenda Negra*, 62, 78; B. Keen, *La imagen azteca* (Mexico City, 1984), 52–53.

71. Sebastian Brant, *Das Narrenschiff*, H. A. Junghans, ed. (Stuttgart, 1980), 238–39; E. H. Zeydel, ed., *The Ship of Fools by Sebastian Brant* (New York, 1962), 222.

72. H. J. König, "La visión alemana del indio americano en los siglos XVI y XVII," in *Imagen del indio*, 127–56.

73. S. Sebastián, ed., *Alquimia y emblemática: La Fuga de Atalanta de Michael Maier* (Madrid, 1989)(introduction by J. F. Moffitt).

74. The flagship volume of De Bry's *Voyages* is readily available in an affordable Dover paperback edition: *Thomas Harriot, A Briefe and True Report of the New Found Land of Virginia (The Complete 1590 Theodore De Bry Edition)* (New York, 1972).

75. For contextual (and rather epistemological) readings of de Bry's *Voyages,* see B. Buchner, *Le sauvage aux seins pendants* (Paris, 1977), in English: *Icon and Conquest: A Structural Analysis of the Illustrations of De Bry's "Great Voyages"* (Chicago, 1981); M. Duchet, *L'Amérique de Théodore de Bry: Une collection de voyages protestant du XVIe siècle* (Paris, 1987).

76. P. Houlton, "The Persistence of the White-de Bry Image of the North American Indian," in *Imagen del indio*, 405–15.

77. Duviols, *L'Amérique espagnole*, 187–201. Besides Bucher (as in note 75), for a handy selection of Theodore de Bry's American print-series, see M. Alexander, ed., *Discovering the New World* (New York, 1976).

78. Anonymous Nahautl chronicler, as given in M. León-Portilla, ed., *The Broken Spears: The Aztec Account of the Conquest of Mexico* (Boston, 1966), 74–76.

79. "Annals of Tlatelolco," as in G. Brotherston, ed., *Image of the New World: The American Continent Portrayed in Native Texts* (London, 1979), 34–35. For various other Native American texts, also including a few accounts belonging to the "reverse view" of the Conquest, see various titles in the Primary Sources section of the Bibliography, especially M. León-Portilla, ed., *El reverso de la Conquista: Relaciones aztecas, mayas e incas* (Mexico City, 1964); N. Wachtel, ed., *The Vision of the Vanquished: The Spanish Conquest of Peru through Indian Eyes, 1530–1570* (London, 1977).

80. Jean Esquemeling, *Buccaneers of America*, 36–37.

81. For dozens of modern narratives of neo-colonialist racist massacres, in this instance as done by American troops and told with all the gruesome detail of Las Casas's accounts, see "Vietnam Veterans Against the War," *Winter Soldier Investigation: An Inquiry into American War Crimes* (Boston, 1972). New ones have since surfaced, due to yet other gratuitous internecine wars perpetrated by as many different "tribes," as in Iraq, Somalia, Bosnia, Rwanda, and so forth (unfortunately).

82. A. de Zorita, *Life and Labor in Ancient Mexico. The Brief and Summary Relation of the Lords of New Spain* (New Brunswick, N.J., 1963), 216–18.

83. R. Bambrough, ed., *The Philosophy of Aristotle* (New York, 1963), 385; for the feral motif of *homo homini lupus* during the sixteenth Century, see H. Haydn, *The Counter Renaissance* (New York, 1960), 405–24.

BIBLIOGRAPHY

Primary Sources

Acosta, José de. *Historia natural y moral de las Indias.* Mexico City, 1940.

Adler, E. N., ed. *Jewish Travellers in the Middle Ages: Nineteen Firsthand Accounts.* New York, 1987.

Alberti, Leon Battista. *L'architettura (De re aedificatoria).* Edited by G. Orlandi and P. Portoghesi. Milan, 1966.

———. *On Painting.* Edited by J. R. Spencer. London, 1966.

Alcina Franch, J., ed. *Floresta literaria de la América indígena: Antología de los pueblos indígenas de América.* Madrid, 1957.

Alexander, M., ed. *Discovering the New World, Based on the Works of Theodore de Bry.* New York, 1976.

Alfonso X. *Antología de Alfonso X el Sabio.*

Edited by A. G. Solalinde. Madrid, 1941.

Alvarez, M. C., ed. *Textos coloniales del Libro de Chilam Balam de Chumayel y textos glíficos del Códice de Dresde.* Mexico City, 1974.

Arber, E., ed. *The First Three English Books on America (A.D. ?1511–1555), Being Chiefly Translations, Compilations, &c., by Richard Eden . . . With Extracts, &c., from Works of Other Spanish, Italian, and German Writers of the Time.* Birmingham (England), 1885.

Arguedas, J. M., ed. *Poesía quechua.* Buenos Aires, 1966.

Ariosto, Ludovico. *Orlando Furioso (The Frenzy of Orlando).* Edited by B. Reynolds. Harmondsworth, 1973.

Aristotle. *The Philosophy of Aristotle.*
Edited by R. Bambrough. New
York, 1963.
———. *Aristotle's Poetics: Translation and
Analysis.* Edited by K. A. Telford.
Chicago, 1965.
Arrian. *The Campaigns of Alexander.*
Edited by A. de Sélincourt.
Harmondsworth, 1971.
Astrov, M., ed. *American Indian Prose and
Poetry.* New York, 1962.
Augustine of Hippo, Saint. *The City of
God.* Edited by V. J. Bourke. Garden
City, 1958.
———. *La Ciudad de Dios.* Biblioteca de
Autores Españoles. Madrid, 1965.
———. *Concerning The City of God
Against the Pagans.* Edited by
H. Bettenson. Harmondsworth,
1984.
Bacon, Francis. *New Atlantis. See* White,
1955.
Benedeit, Archbishop. *El viaje de San
Brandán.* Madrid, 1983.
Benjamin of Tudela. *See* Adler, 1987;
Komroff, 1989.
Benzoni, Girolamo. *Historia del Nuevo
Mundo.* Madrid, 1989.
Bergon, F., and Z. Papanikolas, eds.
*Looking Far West: The Search for the
American West in History, Myth, and
Literature.* New York, 1978.
Berlín, H., ed. *Historia Tolteca-Chichimeca:
Anales de Cuauhtinchan.* Mexico City,
1949.
———, ed. *Unos anales históricos de la
nación mexicana (1528).* Mexico City,
1948.
Bernáldez, Andrés. *Memorias del reinado de
los Reyes Católicos.* Madrid, 1962.
Bible: *The Holy Bible . . . Commonly
Known as the Authorized (King James)
Version.* Nashville, 1970. *The Holy
Bible: Revised Standard Version . . .
with the Apocrypha/ Deuterocanonical*

Books. New York, 1973. *Biblia Sacra
juxta Vulgatam Clementinam.* Madrid,
1977.
Biedermann, H., ed. *Altmexikos Heilige
Bücher.* Graz, 1971.
Bierhorst, J., ed. *Four Masterworks of
American Indian Literature: Quetzal-
coatl; The Ritual of Condolence; Cuceb;
The Night Chant.* New York, 1974.
———, ed. *The Red Swan: Myths and
Tales of the American Indians.* New
York, 1976.
Blake, J. W., ed. *Europeans in West Africa,
1450–1560.* Lichtenstein, 1975.
Boccaccio, Giovanni. *Genealogiae.* Venice,
1494; facs. ed. New York, 1976.
Boethius. *The Consolation of Philosophy.*
Edited by I. Edman. New York,
1943.
Brant, Sebastian. *Das Narrenschiff.* Edited
by J. A. Junghans. Stuttgart, 1980.
———. *The Ship of Fools by Sebastian
Brant.* Edited by E. H. Zeydel. New
York, 1962.
Brendan, Saint. *See* Gardiner, 1989.
Brinton, D. G., ed. *The Maya Chronicles.*
Philadelphia, 1882.
———, ed. *The Rig Veda Americanus:
Sacred Songs of the Ancient Mexicans.*
Philadelphia, 1890.
Brotherston, G., ed. *Image of the New
World: The American Continent
Portrayed in Native Texts.* London,
1979.
Bry, Theodore de. *See* Alexander, 1976;
Harriot, 1972.
Burland, C., ed. *Magic Books from Mexico.*
Harmondsworth, 1953.
Cabeza de Vaca, Alvar Núñez. *Naufragios
y Comentarios con dos cartas.* Madrid,
1957.
———. *Adventures in the Unknown Interior
of America,* Edited by C. Covey. New
York, 1961.
Cadogán, L., ed. *Ayvu Rapyta: Textos*

míticos de los Mbya-Guaraní del Güaira. São Paulo, 1959.

Caesar, Julius. *The Conquest of Gaul.* Edited by S. A. Handford. Harmondsworth, 1958.

Camões (Camones), Luis Vaz de. *The Lusiads.* Edited by W. C. Atkinson. Harmondsworth, 1952.

Campanella, Tommaso. *City of the Sun. See* White, 1955.

Cárdenas, Juan de. *Problemas y Secretos maravillosos de las Indias.* Madrid, 1988.

Castañeda, Pedro de. *The Journey of Coronado.* Edited by G. P. Winship. New York, 1990.

Cervantes de Salazar, Francisco. *México en 1554 y el túmulo imperial.* Edited by E. O'Gorman. Mexico City, 1963.

Cervantes Saavedra, Miguel de. *El ingenioso hidalgo Don Quijote de la Mancha.* Madrid, 1960.

———. *The Adventures of Don Quixote.* Edited by J. M. Cohen. Harmondsworth, 1963.

Cesariano, Cesare di Lorenzo. *Di Lucio Vitruuio Pollione de Architectura Libri Dece traducti de latino in Vulgare affigurati . . .* Como, 1521; facs. ed. New York, 1968.

Chilam Balam. See Alvarez, 1974; Roys, 1933.

Cicero. *The Speeches: Pro Sestio and In Vatinium.* Edited by R. Gardner. London, 1966.

Cieza de León, Pedro. *La Crónica del Perú.* Madrid, 1984.

Cobo, Bernabé. *Historia del Nuevo Mundo.* Madrid, 1956.

Colón, Hernando [Ferdinand Columbus]. *Vida del Almirante don Cristóbal Colón.* Buenos Aires, 1947.

———. *The Life of Admiral Christopher Columbus by His Son Ferdinand.* Edited by B. Keen. New Brunswick, N.J., 1959.

Columbus, Christopher. "Relaciones, cartas y otros documentos concernientes a los cuatro viajes que hizo el Almirante Don Cristóbal Colón para el descubrimiento de las Indias occidentales." In *Colección,* edited by M. Fernández de Navarrete. Madrid, 1824; rpt. Madrid, 1954 (the first publication ever of Columbiana; also see Fernández de Navarrete below).

———. *Select Letters of Christopher Columbus, with Other Original Documents, Relating to His Four Voyages to the New World.* Edited by R. H. Major. London, 1847; facs. rpt. New York, 1961.

———. *Raccolta di documenti e studi pubblicati dalla Regia Commissione Colombiana per il cuarto centenario della scoperta dell'America.* Edited by C. de Lollis. 14 vols. Rome, 1892–94 (also including, after vols. I–III, many relevant materials not actually written by Columbus).

———. *Journals and Other Documents on the Life and Voyages of Christopher Columbus.* Edited by S. E. Morison. New York, 1963.

———. *Cristóbal Colón: Textos y documentos completos: Relaciones de viajes, cartas y memoriales.* Edited by C. Varela. Madrid, 1982.

———. *Cristóbal Colón: Diario, Relaciones de viajes.* Edited by Bartolomé de Las Casas. Madrid, 1985.

———. *The Four Voyages of Columbus: A History in Eight Documents, Including Five by Christopher Columbus, in the Original Spanish, with English Translations.* Edited by L. C. Jane. New York, 1988.

————. *The Journal of Christopher Colum-bus.* Edited by L. C. Jane. New York, 1989.

————. *The "Libro de las profecías" of Christopher Columbus: An "En Face" Edition.* Edited by D. C. West and A. Kling. Gainesville, 1991.

Commager, H. S., ed. *America in Perspec-tive: The United States Through Foreign Eyes.* New York, 1947.

Commager, H. S., and Giordanetti, E., eds. *Was America A Mistake?: An Eighteenth-Century Controversy.* New York, 1967.

Conti, Natale. *Mythologiae, sive explicatio-num fabularum. Libri decem.* Venice, 1567; facs. ed. New York, 1976.

Cortés, Hernán. *Five Letters, 1519–1526.* Edited by J. B. Morris. London, 1928.

————. *Cartas de la conquista de México.* Madrid, 1985.

————. *Hernán Cortés: Letters from Mexico.* Edited by A. Pagden. London, 1986.

Cosmas Indicopleustes. *The Christian Topography of Cosmas.* Edited by J. W. McCrindle. London, 1897.

D'Ailly, Pierre. *Ymago Mundi de Pierre D'Ailly, Cardinal de Cambrai et Chancelier de l'Université de Paris (1350–1420), Texte latine et tra-duction française des quatre traités cosmographiques de D'Ailly et des notes marginales de Christophe Colomb. Etude sur les sources de l'auteur.* Edited by E. Buron. Paris, 1930.

Dante Alighieri. *La Divina Commedia II: Purgatorio,* Milan, 1902.

————. *Dante: The Purgatorio.* Edited by J. Ciardi. New York, 1961.

Dawson, C., ed. *The Mongol Mission: Narratives and Letters of the Franciscan Missionaries in Mongolia and China in the Thirteenth and Fourteenth Centuries.* London, 1955.

De l'Orme, Philibert. *Le Premier Tome de l'Architecture.* Paris, 1567.

Díaz del Castillo, Bernal. *Historia verdadera de la conquista de la Nueva España.* Madrid, 1985.

————. *The Conquest of New Spain.* Edited by J. M. Cohen. Harmonds-worth, 1963.

Dickens, Charles. *The Life and Ad-ventures of Martin Chuzzlewit.* Harmondsworth, 1986.

————. *American Notes for General Circulation.* Harmondsworth, 1989.

Donne, John. *The Complete English Poems.* Edited by C. A. Patrides. London, 1985.

Drimmer, F., ed. *Captured by the Indians: Fifteen Firsthand Accounts, 1750–1870.* New York, 1985.

Durán, Diego. *Historia de las Indias de Nueva España y Islas de la Tierra Firme.* Mexico City, 1967.

Eden, Richard. *The First Three English Books on America, A.D. 1511–1555. See* Arber 1885.

Espinosa, Alonso de. *The Guanches of Tenerife: The Holy Image of Our Lady of Candelaria and the Spanish Conquest and Settlement.* Edited by C. Markham. London, 1907.

Esquemeling, Jean. *The Buccaneers of America.* New York, 1967.

Expositio Totius Mundi et Gentium. Edited by J. Rongé. Paris, 1966.

Fernández de Navarrete, M., ed. *Colección de los Viages y Descubrimientos que hicieron por Mar los Españoles desde fines del siglo XV.* 5 vols. Madrid, 1825, 1829, 1837; rpt. Biblioteca de Autores Españoles, 3 vols. (BAE, nos. 75–77). Madrid, 1954, 1964.

Filarete, il. *Il Trattato.* Edited by L. Grassi and A. M. Finoli. Milan, 1972.

————. *Filarete's Treatise on Architecture, Being the Treatise by Antonio di Piero Averlino, Known as Filarete.* Edited by

J. R. Spencer. New Haven, Conn., 1965.

Forbes, J. D., ed. *The Indian in America's Past.* Englewood Cliffs, 1964.

Garcilaso de la Vega, "el Inca." *Comentarios reales: El origen de los Incas.* Barcelona, 1968.

———. *The Incas. The Royal Commentaries of the Inca Garcilaso de la Vega.* Edited by A. Gheerbrant. New York, 1971.

Gardiner, E., ed. *Visions of Heaven & Hell Before Dante.* New York, 1989.

Garibay, K. A. M., ed. *Poesía indígena.* Mexico City, 1940.

———, ed. *Veinte himnos sacros de los Nahuas.* Mexico City, 1958.

———, ed. *Poesía náhuatl.* Mexico City, 1965–68.

Giorgio Martini, Francesco di. *Trattati di architettura, ingegneria e arte militare.* Edited by G. Maltese. Milan, 1967.

Gómara, Francisco López de. *Historia general de las Indias.* Barcelona, 1966.

Guaman Poma de Ayala, Felipe. *Nueva Crónica y buen gobierno.* facs. ed. Paris, 1936.

———. *Felipe Guamán Poma de Ayala: Nueva crónica y buen gobierno.* Edited by L. Bustios Gálvez. La Paz, 1944.

Hakluyt, Richard. *Voyages and Discoveries: The Principal Navigations, Voyages, Traffiques and Discoveries of the English Nation.* Edited by J. Beeching. Harmondsworth, 1972.

Handlin, O., ed. *This Was America, As Recorded by European Travelers to the Western Shore in the Eighteenth, Nineteenth, and Twentieth Centuries.* New York, 1964.

Harriot, Thomas. *A Briefe and True Report of the New Found Land of Virginia: The Complete 1590 Theodore de Bry Edition.* New York, 1972.

Herodotus. *The Histories.* Edited by A. de Sélincourt. Harmondsworth, 1965.

Herrera, Antonio de. *Historia general de los hechos de los castellanos en las islas y tierra firme del mar océano.* Madrid, 1936.

Hesiod. *The Homeric Hymns and Homerica.* Edited by H. G. Evelyn-White. London, 1964.

Hobbes, Thomas. *Leviathan.* New York, 1964.

Homer. *The Odyssey.* Edited by W. H. D. Rowse. New York, 1960.

———. *The Odyssey.* Edited by G. H. Palmer. New York, 1971.

Horace. *The Complete Odes and Epodes with the Centennial Hymn.* Edited by W. G. Shepherd. Harmondsworth, 1983.

Hulton, P., and D. B. Quinn, eds. *The American Drawings of John White, 1577–1590, with Drawings of European and Oriental Subjects* (exh. cat.). London, 1964.

Humboldt, Alexander Freiherr von. *Cristóbal Colón y el descubrimiento de América.* Edited by L. Navarro y Calvo. Buenos Aires, 1946.

Isidore Hispalensis. *San Isidoro de Sevilla: Etimologías.* Edited by L. Cortés y Góngora. Madrid, 1951.

Joinville, Jean de. *Chronicles of the Crusades.* Edited by M. R. B. Shaw. Harmondsworth, 1967.

Keen, B., ed. *Readings in Latin-American Civilization, 1492 to the Present.* Boston, 1955.

Kingsbury, S. M., ed. *The Records of the Virginia Company of London.* Washington D.C., 1906–35.

Kirkconnell, W., ed. *The Celestial Cycle: The Theme of "Paradise Lost" in World Literature, with Translations of the Major Analogues.* London, 1953.

Knorozov, Y. V., ed. *Selected Chapters from the Writing of the Maya Indians.* Cambridge, Mass., 1967.

Komroff, M., ed. *The Contemporaries of Marco Polo, Consisting of the Travel Records to the Eastern Parts of the World, of William of Rubruck [1253–1255]; "The Journey" of John of Pian de Carpini [1245–1247]; "The Journal" of Friar Odoric [1318–1330] & "The Oriental Travels" of Rabbi Benjamin of Tudela [1160–1173]*. New York, 1989.

Koran: *The Glorious Koran*. Edited by M. M. Pickthall. London, 1956. *El Corán*. Edited by J. Cortés. Madrid, 1980.

Lambert, J-C., ed. *Les Poésies mexicaines: Anthologie des origines à nos jours*. Paris, 1961.

Landa, Diego de. *Yucatán Before and After the Conquest*. Edited by W. Gates. New York, 1978.

Las Casas, Bartolomé de. *Historia de las Indias*. Biblioteca de Autores Españoles. Madrid, 1927.

———. *Historia de las Indias*. Mexico City, 1951.

———. *History of the Indies*. Edited by A. Collard. New York, 1971.

———. *Bartolomé de Las Casas: Obra indigenista*. Edited by A. Franch. Madrid, 1985.

———. *Brevísima relación de la destrucción de las Indias*. Madrid, 1986.

Lattimore, O., ed. *Silk, Spices, and Empire: Asia Seen Through the Eyes of its Discoverers*. New York, 1971.

León Pinelo, Antonio de. *El paraíso en el nuevo mundo*. rpt. Lima, 1943.

León-Portilla, M., ed. *Visión de los vencidos: Relaciones indígenas de la Conquista*. Mexico City, 1959

———. *The Broken Spears: The Aztec Account of the Conquest of Mexico*. Boston, 1966.

———, ed. *El reverso de la Conquista: Relaciones aztecas, mayas e incas*, Mexico City, 1964.

———, ed. *Trece poetas del mundo azteca*. Mexico City, 1967.

Léry, Jean de. *History of a Voyage to the Land of Brazil, Otherwise Called America*. Edited by J. Whatley. Berkeley, 1990.

Livy, Titus. *Livy with an English Translation*. Edited by E. I. Sage. London, 1957.

———. *The Early History of Rome: Books I–IV of The History of Rome from its Foundations*. Edited by A. de Sélincourt. Harmondsworth, 1960.

———. *The War with Hannibal: Books XXI–XXX of The History of Rome from its Foundations*. Edited by A. de Sélincourt. Harmondsworth, 1972.

———. *Rome and the Mediterranean: Books XXXI–XLV of The History of Rome from its Foundations*. Edited by H. Bettenson. Harmondsworth, 1976.

Lollis, C. de, ed. *Raccolta, etc. See* Columbus.

Lorant, S., ed. *The New World: The First Pictures of America*. New York, 1965.

Lorenzo de'Medici. *Opere*. Edited by A. Simioni. Bari, 1939.

Lucretius. *On the Nature of the Universe*. Edited by R. E. Latham. Harmondsworth, 1970.

Magnusson, M., ed. *The Vinland Sagas: The Norse Discovery of America (Graenlendinga Saga and Eirik's Saga)*. Harmondsworth, 1965.

Maier, Michael. *Atalanta Fugiens. See* Sebastián, 1989.

Mandeville, Sir John. *The Travels of Sir John Mandeville: Facsimile of Pynson's Edition of 1446*. Edited by M. Seymour, Exeter (England), 1980.

———. *The Travels of Sir John Mandeville*. Edited by C. W. R. D. Moseley. Harmondsworth, 1983.

———. *Juan de Mandeville: Libro de las maravillas del mundo.* Madrid, 1984.

Martyr of Angleria, Peter. *The Decades of the Newe World or West India . . .* Edited by R. Eden. London, 1555 (as reprinted in Arber, 1885).

———. *De Orbe Novo.* Edited by F. MacNutt. New York, 1912.

———. *Pedro Mártir de Anglería: Décadas del Nuevo Mundo.* Edited by J. Torres Asensio. Madrid, 1989.

———. *Pedro Mártir de Anglería: Cartas sobre el Nuevo Mundo.* Edited by J. Bauzano. Madrid, 1990.

Mela, Pomponius. *La España del siglo I de nuestra era según P. Mela y C. Plinio.* Edited by A. García y Bellido. Madrid, 1945.

Mendieta, Jerónimo de. *Historia eclesiástica indiana.* Mexico City, 1870.

Migne, J-P., ed. *Patrologia Latina, cursus completa.* 221 vols. Paris, 1844–82.

Milton, John. *Paradise Lost; Samson Agonistes; Lycidas.* New York, 1961.

· Montaigne, Michel de. *The Selected Essays of Montaigne.* Edited by J. Florio. New York, 1959.

———. *Michel de Montaigne: Essays.* Edited by J. M. Cohen. Harmondsworth, 1958.

Montequîn, F-A. de., ed. *Maps and Plans of Cities and Towns in Colonial New Spain, the Floridas, and Louisiana: Selected Documents in the Archivo General de Indias of Seville.* Ann Arbor, 1974.

———. *Cities of the Hispanic World: Documentation for the Study of Urban Planning in Spain and Her Colonies.* Monticello, Va., 1981.

More, Sir Thomas. *Utopia.* Edited by P. Tanner. Harmondsworth, 1965.

Motolinía, Toribio de Benavente o. *Historia de los Indios de la Nueva España.* Madrid, 1988.

Navarrete. *See* Fernández de Navarrete.

Nordenskjöld, A. E., ed. *Facsimile-Atlas to the Early History of Cartography.* New York, 1973.

Núñez, E., ed. *España vista por viajeros hispanoamericanos.* Madrid, 1985.

Odorico da Pordenone. *Journal. See* Komroff, 1989.

Omont, H., ed. *Livre des Merveilles: Réproduction des 265 Miniatures du Manuscrit Français 2810 de la Bibliothèque Nationale.* Paris, 1907.

Ovid. *The Metamorphoses of Ovid.* Edited by M. M. Innes. Harmondsworth, 1961.

Oviedo y Valdés, Gonzalo Fernández de. *Historia general y natural de las Indias, islas y Tierra-Firme del Mar Océano.* Seville, 1851–55; rpt. Madrid, 1959.

———. *Natural History of the West Indies.* Chapel Hill, 1959.

Pané, Fray Ramón. *Relación acerca de las antigüedades de los Indios.* Edited by J. J. Arrom. Mexico City, 1947.

Péret, B., ed. *Anthologie des mythes, légendes et contes populaires d'Amérique.* Paris, 1960.

Philoponus, Honorius. *Nova typis transacta navigatio novi orbis Indiae Occidentalis.* Linz, 1621.

Philostratus the Elder. *Imagines.* Edited by A. Fairbanks. London, 1969.

Piano de Carpini, John of, *The Journal. See* Komroff, 1989.

Pigafetta, Antonio. *Magellan's Voyage Around the World.* Edited by J. A. Robertson. Cleveland, 1902.

———. *Primer viaje alrededor del mundo.* Madrid, 1985.

Pindar. *The Odes.* Edited by J. Sandys. London, 1968.

Plato. *Timaeus.* Edited by F. M. Cornford. Indianapolis, Ind., 1959.

———. *Timaeus, Critias, Cleitophon,*

Menexenus, Epistles. Edited by R. G. Bury. London, 1961.

Pliny the Elder, Caius. *La España del siglo I de nuestra era según P. Mela y C. Plinio.* Edited by A. García y Bellido. Madrid, 1945.

———. *Natural History in Ten Volumes.* Edited by H. Rackham. London, 1968.

Plutarch. *Lives of the Noble Greeks.* Edited by E. Fuller New York, 1959.

———. *Makers of Rome: Nine Lives by Plutarch.* Edited by I. Scott-Kilvert. Harmondsworth, 1965.

Polo, Marco. *The Travels of Marco Polo.* Edited by R. E. Latham. Harmondsworth, 1959.

Popol Vuh. *See* Recinos, 1951.

Ptolemy, Claudius. *Geography.* Edited by E. L. Stevens. New York, 1932; facs. rpt. New York, 1991.

Purchas, Samuel, ed. *Hakluytus Posthumus, or Purchas his Pilgrimes.* 20 vols. Glasgow, 1905–7.

Quinn, D. B., ed. *New American World: A Documentary History of North America to 1612.* New York, 1979.

Recinos, A., ed. *Crónicas indígenas de Guatemala.* Guatemala City, 1957.

———, ed. *Popol Vuh: The Sacred Book of the Ancient Quiché Maya.* London, 1951.

Rifkin, S., ed. *The Savage Years.* New York, 1967.

Ripa, Cesare. *Iconología, overo Descrittione d'Imagini delle Virtú, Vitii, Affetti, Passioni humane, Corpi celesti, Mondo e sue parti.* Padua, 1611; facs. ed. New York, 1976.

———. *Iconología.* Padua, 1611; facs. ed. Madrid, 1987.

Rocha Pinto, J. *A viagem: Memória e espaço. A literatura portuguesa de viagems: Os primitivos relatos de viagem ao Indico, 1497–1550.* Lisbon, 1989.

Ross, J. B., and M. M. McLaughlin, eds. *The Renaissance Reader.* New York, 1960.

Roth, L. M., ed. *America Builds: Source Documents in American Architecture and Planning.* New York, 1983.

Roys, R. I., ed. *The Book of Chilam Balam of Chumayel.* Washington D.C., 1933.

Rubruck, William of, *The Journal. See* Komroff, 1989.

Ruiz de Alarcón, Hernando. *Tratado de las supersticiones de los naturales de esta Nueva España.* Mexico City, 1953.

Sahagún, Bernadino de. *Historia general de las cosas de Nueva España.* Mexico City, 1979.

———. *A History of Ancient Mexico by Fray Bernadino de Sahagún: The Religion and Ceremonies of the Aztec Indians.* Edited by F. R. Bandelier. Glorieta, N.M., 1976.

Santarem, Vicomte M. F. de Barros e Sousa de. *Atlas composé de mappemondes, de portulans et de cartes hydrographiques dépuis le VIe jusqu'au XVIIe siècle.* Amsterdam, 1985.

Schedel, Hartmann. *Liber Cronicarum. Das Buch der Chroniken und Geschichten,* Nuremberg, 1493; facs. ed. New York, 1966.

———. *Liber Chronicarum cum figuris et imaginibus ab initio mundi,* Nuremberg, 1493; facs. ed. Cologne, 1976.

Schmidel, Ulrich. *Relatos de la conquista del Río de la Plata y Paraguay, 1534–1554.* Madrid, 1986.

Sebastián López, S., ed., *Alquimia y emblemática: La Fuga de Atalanta de Michael Maier.* Madrid, 1989.

Shakespeare, William. *The Complete Works.* Edited by H. Craig. Glenview (Illinois), 1973.

Sidney, Sir Philip. *The Complete Works.*

Edited by A. Feuillerat. Cambridge (England), 1912.

———. *The Countess of Pembroke's Arcadia.* Edited by M. Evans. Harmondsworth, 1987.

Sigüenza y Góngora, Carlos de. *Triumfo Parthénico.* rpt. Mexico City, 1960.

Staden, Hans. *Verdadera historia y descripción de un país de salvajes desnudos, feroces y caníbales.* Barcelona, 1983.

Strabo. *España y los españoles hace dos mil años, según la "Geografía" de Strabón.* Edited by A. García y Bellido. Madrid, 1945.

Suárez de Peralta, Juan. *Tratado del descubrimiento de las Yndias y su conquista (transcripción del manuscrito autógrafo de 1589).* Madrid, 1990.

Tacitus. *The Annals of Imperial Rome.* Edited by M. Grant. Harmondsworth, 1964.

———. *The Agricola and the Germania.* Edited by H. Mattingly. Harmondsworth, 1970.

Tudela, Benjamin of. *Travels. See* Adler, 1987; Komroff, 1989.

Twain, Mark. *Roughing It.* New York, 1962.

Vespucci, Amerigo. *The Letters of Amerigo Vespucci and Other Documents Illustrative of His Career.* Edited by C. R. Markham. London, 1894.

———. *Vespucci Reprints, Texts, and Studies.* Edited by G. T. Northrup. Princeton, N.J., 1916.

———. *Américo Vespucio: Cartas.* Madrid, 1983.

———. *El Nuevo Mundo: Viajes y documentos completos.* Madrid, 1985.

Villehardouin, Geoffroy de. *Chronicles of the Crusades.* Edited by M. R. B. Shaw. Harmondsworth, 1967.

Virgil. *Virgil's Works.* Edited by W. C. McDermott. New York, 1950.

Vitruvius. *The Ten Books on Architecture.* Edited by M. H. Morgan. New York, 1960.

———. *Vitruvius on Architecture.* Edited by F. Granger. London, 1962.

Vogel, V. J., ed. *This Country Was Ours: A Documentary History of the American Indian.* New York, 1974.

Wachtel, N., ed. *The Vision of the Vanquished: The Spanish Conquest of Peru through Indian Eyes, 1530–1570.* London, 1977.

Washburn, W. E., ed. *The Indian and the White Man.* Garden City, 1964.

White, F. R., ed. *Famous Utopias of the Renaissance.* New York, 1955.

White, John. *See* Harriot, 1972; Hulton, 1964; Lorant, 1965.

Winter Soldier Investigation: An Inquiry into American War Crimes by the Vietnam Veterans Against the War. Boston, 1972.

Zárate, Agustín de. *Historia del descubrimiento y conquista de la provincia del Perú.* Madrid, 1947.

———. *The Discovery and Conquest of Peru.* Edited by J. M. Cohen. Harmondsworth, 1968.

Zorita, Alonso de. *Life and Labor in Ancient Mexico. The Brief and Summary Relation of the Lords of New Spain.* Edited by B. Keen. New Brunswick, N.J., 1963.

Secondary Sources

Adams, P. C. "The Discovery of America and European Renaissance Literature." *Comparative Literature Studies* XIII (1976): 100–15.

———. *Travel and Travel Liars, 1660–1880.* New York, 1980.

Adorno, R. "El sujeto colonial y la construcción de la alteridad." *Revista de*

Crítica Literaria Latinoamericana XIV, no. 28 (1988): 55–68.

Aerts, W. J., ed. *Alexander the Great in the Middle Ages.* Nijmegen, 1978.

Alden, J., and D. C. Landis, eds. *A Chronological Guide to Works Printed in Europe Relating to the Americas, 1493–1776.* 2 vols. New York, 1980–82.

Alegría, R. E. *Las primeras representaciones gráficas del indio americano, 1493–1523.* Barcelona, 1978.

Alexandre, M. "Entre ciel et terre: Les premiers débats sur le site du Paradis (Gen. 2, 8–15 et ses réceptions)." In *Peuples et pays mythiques,* edited by F. Jouan, Paris, 1988, pp. 187–224.

Allard, G-H., ed. *Aspects de la marginalité au Moyen Age.* Montréal, 1975.

Allen, D. C. *Mysteriously Meant: The Rediscovery of Pagan Symbolism and Allegorical Interpretation in the Renaissance.* Baltimore, 1970.

Altolaguirre, A. de. *Don Pedro de Alvarado, conquistador del Reino de Nueva Granada.* Madrid, 1927.

America: Bruid van de zoon. 500 jaar Latijns-Amerika en de Lage Landen (exh. cat.). Antwerp, 1992.

L'Amérique vue par l'Europe (exh. cat.). Paris, 1976.

Anastos, M. V. "Pletho, Strabo, and Columbus." *AIPHOS* XII (1952): 1–18.

Antei, G. "Iconología americana: La alegoría de América en el Cinquecento florentino." *Cuadernos de Arte Colonial* V (1989): 5–33.

Arciniegas, G. *Amérigo Vespuccio y el Nuevo Mundo.* Madrid, 1990.

Arens, W. *The Man-Eating Myth.* Oxford, 1979.

Arentzen, J-G. *Imago Mundi Cartographica: Studien zur Bildlichkeit mittelalter-licher Welt- und Oekumenekarten unter besonderer Berücksichtigung des Zusammenwirkens von Text und Bild.* Munich, 1984.

Armstrong, E. *Ronsard and the Age of Gold.* Cambridge (England), 1968.

Arnoldsson, S. *La leyenda negra: Estudios sobre sus orígenes.* Göteborg, 1960.

———. *La conquista española de América según el juicio de la posteridad: Vestigios de la leyenda negra.* Madrid, 1960.

Atkinson, W. C. *A History of Spain and Portugal.* Harmondsworth, 1961.

Azcárate, J. M. de. "El tema iconográfico del salvaje." *Archivo Español de Arte* XXI (1948): 81–99.

Babcock, W. H. *Legendary Islands of the Atlantic: A Study in Medieval Geography.* Plainview, N.Y., 1975.

Bagrow, L., and R. A. Skelton. *History of Cartography.* London, 1964.

Bakeless, J. B. *America as Seen by the First Explorers: The Eyes of Discovery.* New York, 1961.

Baldry, H. C. "Hesiod's Five Ages." *Journal of the History of Ideas* XVI, no. 4 (1956): 553–54.

Ballesteros Gaibrois, A. *Figuras Imperiales: Alfonso VII, el Emperador—Colón—Fernando el Católico—Carlos V—Felipe II.* Buenos Aires, 1947.

———. *Génesis del descubrimiento.* Barcelona, 1947.

———. *Descubrimiento y fundación de Potosí.* Zaragoza, 1955.

Baltrusaîtis, J. *Le moyen age fantastique: Antiquités et éxotismes dans l'art gothique.* Paris, 1981.

———. *Imaginäre Realitäten: Fiktion und Illusion als produktive Kraft.* Cologne, 1984.

Baransky-Job, L. "The Problem and Meaning of Giovanni di Paolo's *Expulsion from Paradise.*" *Marsyas* VII (1959): 1–6.

Barghahn, B. von, ed. *Temples of Gold, Crowns of Silver: Reflections of Majesty in the Viceregal Americas.* Washington D.C., 1991.

Baring-Gould, S. *Curious Myths of the Middle Ages.* London, 1869.

Bataille, G. M., ed. *The Pretend Indians: Images of Native Americans in the Movies.* Ames, Iowa, 1980

Bataillon, M. *Etudes sur Bartolomé de Las Casas.* Paris, 1965.

Baudet, H. *Paradise on Earth: Some Thoughts on European Images of Non-European Man.* New Haven, Conn., 1965.

Baudot, G. *Utopía e Historia en México.* Madrid, 1983.

Bayle, C. *España en Indias.* Vitoria, 1934.

Bazin, G. *Paradeisos: The Art of the Garden.* London, 1990.

Beazley, C. R. *The Dawn of Modern Geography: A History of Exploration and Geographical Science.* London, 1897–1906.

Benito Ruano, E. *San Borodón, octava isla canaria.* Valladolid, 1978.

Berkhofer, R. F. *The White Man's Indian: Images of the American Indian from Columbus to the Present.* New York, 1979.

Bernheimer, R. *Wild Men in the Middle Ages: A Study in Art, Sentiment, and Demonology.* New York, 1970.

Bevan, W. L., and H. W. Phillott. *Medieval Geography: An Essay on the Illustration of the Hereford Mappa Mundi.* London, 1873.

Blanckhagen, P. H. von. "Narration in Hellenistic and Roman Art." *American Journal of Archaeology* LXI (1957): 78–83.

Boas, G. *Essays on Primitivism and Related Ideas in the Middle Ages.* New York, 1978.

Boas, G., and A. O. Lovejoy. *Primitivism and Related Ideas in Antiquity.* New York, 1973.

Boland, C. M. *They All Discovered America.* New York, 1961.

Bonet Correra, A. *El urbanismo in España e Hispanoamérica.* Madrid, 1991.

Boorsch, S., ed. *Images of the New World.* New York, 1975.

Boorstin, D. J. *The Image, or What Happened to the American Dream.* Harmondsworth, 1963.

———. *The Discoverers.* New York, 1983.

Börsch-Supan, E. *Garten-, Landschafts- und Paradiesmotive im Innenraum: Eine ikonographische Untersuchung.* Berlin, 1967.

Bowie, T., ed. *East-West in Art: Patterns of Cultural and Aesthetic Relationships.* Bloomington, Ind. 1966.

Bozeman, T. D. *To Live Ancient Lives: The Primitivist Dimension in Puritanism.* Chapel Hill, N.C., 1988.

Brandon, W. *The American Heritage Book of Indians.* New York, 1961.

———. *New Worlds for Old: Reports from the New World and Their Effect on the Development of Social Thought in Europe, 1500–1800.* Athens, Ohio, 1986

Braudel, F. *The Mediterranean and the Mediterranean World in the Age of Philip II.* London, 1975.

Braunfels, W. *Abendländische Stadtbaukunst.* Cologne, 1976.

Brenner, A. *Idols Behind Altars: The Story of the Mexican Spirit.* Boston, 1970.

Brigham, K. *Christopher Columbus: His Life and Discovery in Light of His Prophecies.* Barcelona, 1990.

Brown, L. A. *The Story of Maps.* New York, 1979.

Brummack, J. *Die Darstellung des Orient in den deutschen Alexandergeschichten des Mittelalters.* Berlin, 1966.

Brunhouse, R. L. *In Search of the Maya: The First Archaeologists.* New York, 1974.

Brunner, H. *Die poetische Insel: Inseln*

und Inselvorstellungen in der deutschen Literatur. Stuttgart, 1967.

Bryant, T. A., ed. *The New Compact Bible Dictionary.* New York, 1976.

Buarte de Holanda, S. *Visão do Paraíso: Os motivos edénicos no descobrimento e colonização do Brasil.* Rio de Janeiro, 1959.

Bucher, B. *La sauvage aux seins pendents.* Paris, 1977.

————. *Icon and Conquest: A Structural Analysis of the Illustrations of de Bry's Great Voyages.* Chicago, 1981.

Bucher, F. "Medieval Landscape Painting: An Introduction." In *Medieval and Renaissance Studies: Proceedings of the Southeastern Institute of Medieval and Renaissance Studies,* edited by J. M. Headley, 119–69. Chapel Hill, N.C., 1968.

Bunbury, E. H. *A History of Ancient Geography Among the Greeks and Romans From the Earliest Ages Till the Fall of the Roman Empire.* New York, 1959.

Burke, J. *The Day the Universe Changed.* Boston, 1986.

Burman, E. *The World Before Columbus, 1100–1492.* London, 1989.

Bury, J. B. *The Idea of Progress: An Inquiry into Its Origin and Growth.* New York, 1955.

Cafritz, R. C., ed. *Places of Delight: The Pastoral Landscape.* Washington D.C., 1989.

Campbell, M. B. *The Witness and the Other World: Exotic European Travel Writing, 400–1600.* Ithaca, N.Y., 1988.

Capel, H. *La física sagrada.* Barcelona, 1985.

Caponnetto, A. *Hispanidad y Leyenda Negra: La Teología de Liberación y la Historia de América.* Buenos Aires, 1989.

Carbía, R. D. *La nueva historia del descu-*

brimiento de América. Buenos Aires, 1936.

————. *Historia de la Leyenda Negra hispanoamericana.* Madrid, 1944.

Carpenter, R. *Beyond the Pillars of Hercules: The Classical World Seen Through the Eyes of Its Discoveries.* London, 1973.

Cary, M., and E. H. Warmington. *The Ancient Explorers.* Harmondsworth, 1963.

The Catholic Encyclopedia. New York, 1913.

Céard, J. *La Nature et les prodiges: L'insolite au XVIe siècle en France.* Geneva, 1977.

Ceram, C. W. *The First Americans: A Story of North American Archaeology.* New York, 1971.

Chaunu, P. *L'Amérique et les Amériques.* Paris, 1964.

————. *L'Expansion européenne du XIIIe au XVe siècles.* Paris, 1969.

————. *Conquête et exploitation des nouveaux mondes, XVIe siécle.* Paris, 1969.

Chiapelli, F., ed. *First Images of America: The Impact of the New World on the Old.* Berkeley, 1976.

Chinard, G. *L'Exotisme américaine dans la littérature française au XVIe siècle, d'après Rabélais, Ronsard, Montaigne.* Paris, 1911.

————. *L'Amérique et le rêve éxotique dans la littérature française au XVIIe et au XVIIIe siècles.* Paris, 1934.

Chueca Goitia, F. *Breve Historia del Urbanismo.* Madrid, 1968.

————. *Invariantes Castizos de la Arquitectura Española e Hispanoamericana.* Madrid, 1981.

Cirot, G. *Les histoires générales d'Espagne entre Alphonse X et Philippe II, 1284–1556.* Paris, 1904.

Clark, K. *The Nude: A Study in Ideal Form.* Garden City, 1956.

Cocchiara, G. *Il paese di Cuccagna ed altri studi di folklore.* Turin, 1956.

―――. *L'eterno selvaggio: Presenza e influsso del mondo primitivo nella cultura moderna.* Milan, 1961.

Cohn, N. *The Pursuit of the Millennium: Revolutionary Millennarians and Mystical Anarchists of the Middle Ages.* London, 1978.

Coleman, T. *Passage to America: A History of Emigrants from Great Britain and Ireland to America in the Mid-Nineteenth Century.* Harmondsworth, 1974.

Coli, E. *Il Paradiso Terrestre Dantesco.* Florence, 1897.

Colin, S. *Das Bild des Indianers im 16. Jahrhundert.* Idstein, 1988.

Collier, J. *Indians of the Americas.* New York, 1947.

Collis, M. *Cortés and Montezuma.* New York, 1978.

Conant, K. "The After-Life of Vitruvius in the Middle Ages." *Journal of the Society of Architectural Historians* XXXVII (1968): 33–38.

Cordy-Collins, A., ed. *Pre-Columbian Art History: Selected Readings.* Palo Alto, Calif., 1977.

Costa, G. *La leggenda dei secoli d'oro nella letteratura italiana.* Bari, 1972.

Cro, S. *Realidad y utopía en el descubrimiento y conquista de la América Hispana (1492–1682).* Madrid, 1983.

Crone, G. R. *The World Map by Richard of Haldingham in Hereford Cathedral.* London, 1954.

Crosby, A. W. *The Columbian Exchange: Biological and Cultural Consequences of 1492.* Greenwood, Conn., 1973.

―――. *Ecological Imperialism: The Biological Expansion of Europe, 900–1900.* Cambridge (England), 1993.

Crowe, J. A. *Spain: The Root and the Flower. An Interpretation of Spain and the Spanish People.* Berkeley, 1985.

Cruden, A. *Cruden's Useful Concordance of the Holy Scriptures, Comprising Most of the References Which are Really Needed.* Old Tappan, N.J., 1970.

Curtius, E. R. *European Literature and the Latin Middle Ages.* New York, 1963.

Cuttler, C. D. "Errata in Netherlandish Art: Jan Mostaert's 'New World' Landscape." *Simiolus* XIX (1989): 191–97.

Danielou, J. "Terre et Paradis chez les Pères de l'Eglise." *Eranos-Jahrbuch* XXIII (1954): 433–72.

Davidson, J. W., and M. H. Lytle. *After the Fact: The Art of Historical Detection.* New York, 1982.

Davies, N. *Voyagers to the New World.* Albuquerque, N.M., 1986.

Deak, G. G. *Picturing America, 1497–1899.* Princeton, N.J., 1988.

Defaux, G. "Un Cannibale en haut de chausses: Montaigne, la différence et la logique de l'identité." *Modern Language Notes* XCI (1982): 919–57.

Delumeau, Jean. *History of Paradise: The Garden of Eden in Myth and Tradition.* New York, 1995.

D'Este, M. *In the Canaries with a Camera.* London, 1909.

Deuel, L. *Testaments of Time: The Search for Lost Manuscripts and Records.* Baltimore, 1970.

―――, ed. *Conquistadors Without Swords: Archaeologists in the Americas.* New York, 1974.

Dickason, O. P. *The Myth of the Savage and the Beginnings of French Colonialism in the Americas.* Edmonton, 1984.

Dixon, L. S. "Giovanni da Paolo's Cosmology." *Art Bulletin* LXVII (1985): 604–13.

Dobschütz, E. von. "Wo suchen die Menschen das Paradies?" *Mitteilungen der Schlessischen Gesellschaft für*

Volkskunde XIII/XIV (1911/12): 246–55.

Doggett, R., ed. *New World of Wonders: European Images of the Americas, 1492–1700.* Washington D.C., 1992.

Donnelly, I. *Atlantis: The Antediluvian World.* Blauvelt, N.Y., 1971.

Drinnon, R. *Facing West: The Metaphysics of Indian-Hating and Empire-Building.* New York, 1990.

Duchet, M. *L'Amérique de Théodore de Bry. Une collection de voyages protestantes du XVIe siècle.* Paris, 1987.

Dudley, E., and M. E. Novak, eds. *The Wild Man Within: An Image in Western Thought from the Renaissance to Romanticism.* Pittsburgh, Penn., 1972.

Duncan, J. E. *Milton's Earthly Paradise: A Historical Study of Man.* Minneapolis, Minn., 1972.

Durán, M. A. *Fundación de ciudades en el Perú durante el siglo XVI.* Sevilla, 1987.

Durazzo, P. *Il planisfero di Giovanni Leardo.* Mantua, 1885.

Dussel, Enrique. *The Invention of the Americas: Eclipse of "The Other" and the Myth of Modernity.* New York, 1995.

Duviols, J-P. *L'Amérique espagnole vue et rêvée: Les livres de voyages, de Christophe Colombe à Bougainville.* Paris, 1985.

Edgerton, S. Y. "Florentine Interest in Ptolemaic Cartography as Background for Renaissance Painting, Architecture, and the Discovery of America," *Journal of the Society of Architectural Historians.* XXXIII (1974): 275–92.

———. *The Renaissance Rediscovery of Linear Perspective.* New York, 1975.

Edwardes, C. *Rides and Studies in the Canary Islands.* London, 1888.

Egbert, D. D. *Socialism and American Art in the Light of European Utopianism, Marxism and Anarchism.* Princeton, N.J., 1967.

Egger, G., ed. *Theatrum Orbis Terrarum: Die Erfassung des Weltbildes zur Zeit der Renaissance und des Barocks* (exh. cat.). Vienna, 1970.

Egry, A. de. *O Apocalipse do Lorvão e a sua relação com as ilustrações medievais do Apocalipse.* Lisbon, 1972.

Eliade, M. *Mitos, sueños y misterios.* Buenos Aires, 1961.

———. *Myths, Rites, Symbols: A Mircea Eliade Reader.* Edited by C. Beane and W. G. Doty. New York, 1975.

Elliott, J. H. *Imperial Spain, 1469–1716.* New York, 1966.

———. *The Old World and the New, 1492–1650.* Cambridge (England), 1970; rev. ed., 1992.

———. *El Viejo Mundo y el Nuevo, 1492–1650.* Madrid, 1972.

———. *Spain and its World, 1500–1700.* New Haven, Conn., 1989.

Esche, S. *Adam und Eva.* Düsseldorf, 1957.

Esteve Barba, F. *Historiografía indiana.* Madrid, 1984.

Evans, J. M. *Paradise Lost and the Genesis Tradition.* New York, 1968.

Exotische Welten-Europäische Phantasien (exh. cat.). Stuttgart, 1987.

Fagan, B. M. *Clash of Cultures.* New York, 1984.

Fairchild, H. N. *The Noble Savage: A Study in Romantic Naturalism.* New York, 1928.

Farb, P. *Man's Rise to Civilization, as Shown by the Indians of North America, from Primeval Times to the Coming of the Industrial State.* New York, 1969.

———. *Humankind.* New York, 1980.

Feest, C. F. "The Virginia Indian in Pictures, 1612–1624." *Smithsonian*

Journal of History II, no. 1 (1967):
1–20.

Fernández Armesto, F. *Before Columbus:
Exploration and Colonization From
the Mediterranean to the Atlantic,
1229–1492,* Philadelphia, 1988.

Fernández-Flórez, D. *The Spanish Heritage
in the United States.* Madrid, 1965.

Feuter, E. *Geschichte der neueren Historiographie.* Munich, 1930.

Fick, B. W. *El libro de viajes en la España
medieval.* Santiago de Chile, 1976.

Finley, M. I. *The World of Odysseus.*
Cleveland, 1962.

Fiske, A. "Paradisus Homo Amicus."
Speculum XL (1965): 436–59.

Fleming, I. E. M. "The American Image
as Indian Princess." *Winterthur
Portfolio* II (1965): 65–81.

———. "From Indian Princess to Greek
Goddess: The American Image,
1783–1815." *Winterthur Portfolio* III
(1967): 37–66.

Franco, J. *The Modern Culture of Latin
America: Society and the Artist.*
Harmondsworth, 1970.

Franco de Melo, A. A. *O indio brasileiro e a
revoluçao francesa: As origins brasileiras
da theoria da bondade natural.* Rio de
Janeiro, 1937.

Frankl, P. *The Gothic: Literary Sources and
Interpretations through Eight Centuries.*
Princeton, N.J.: 1960.

———. "Die Begriffe des mexikanischen
Kaisertüms und der Weltmonarchie
in den 'Cartas de Relación' des
Hernán Cortés." *Saeculum* XIII
(1962): 1–34.

———. *El "Antijovio" de Gonzalo Jiménez
de Quesada y las concepciones de realidad
y verdad en la época de la Contrarreforma
y del Manierismo.* Madrid, 1963.

Friede, J., and B. Keen, eds. *Bartolomé de
Las Casas: Towards an Understanding of*

the Man and His World. De Kalb, Ill.,
1971.

Friedman, J. B. *The Monstrous Races
in Medieval Art and Thought.*
Cambridge, Mass., 1981.

Frye, N. *The Return of Eden.* Toronto,
1965.

Gadol, J. *Leon Battista Alberti: Universal
Man of the Early Renaissance.* Chicago,
1969.

Gagnon, F. "Le Thème médiéval de
l'homme sauvage dans les pre-
mières représentations des Indiens
d'Amérique." In *Aspects de la marginalité au Moyen Age,* edited by G-H.
Allard, Montréal, 1975, pp. 83–103.

Galinsky, H. "Naturae Cursus: Der Weg
einer antiken kosmologischen
Metapher von der Alten in die
Neue Welt: Ein Beitrag zu einer
historischen Metaphorik Welt-
literatur." *Arcadia: Zeitschrift für
vergleichende Literaturwissenschaft* I
(1966): 277–311; II (1967): 11–78,
139–72.

Gandía, E. de. *Historia crítica de los mitos
y leyendas de la conquista americana.*
Madrid, 1929.

García y Bellido, A. *Veinticinco Estampas de
la España Antigua.* Madrid, 1967.

Gatz, B. *Weltalter, goldene Zeit und sinnverwandte Vorstellungen.* Hildesheim,
1967.

Gaus, J. "Die Urhütte. Über ein Modell in
der Baukunst und ein Motiv in der
bildenden Kunst." *Wallraf-Richartz
Jahrbuch* XXIII (1971): 7–70.

Gerbi, A. *The Dispute of the New World:
The History of a Polemic, 1750–1900.*
Pittsburgh, 1973.

———. *Nature in the New World, from
Christopher Columbus to Fernández de
Oviedo.* Pittsburgh, 1985.

German, G. "Höhle und Hütte." *Jahrbuch*

des Bernischen Historischen Museums
LXIII/LXIX (1983/84): 121–30.

Germán Romero, M. *Juan de Castellanos:
Un examen de su vida y obra.* Bogotá,
1964.

Gewecke, F. *Wie die neue Welt in die alte
kam.* Munich, 1992.

Giamatti, A. B. *The Earthly Paradise and
the Renaissance Epic.* Princeton, N.J.,
1966.

Gibson, C. *The Aztecs Under Spanish Rule:
A History of the Indians of the Valley of
Mexico, 1519–1810.* Palo Alto, Calif.,
1964.

————. *Spain in America.* New York,
1966.

————. *The Black Legend: The Anti-
Spanish Attitudes in the Old World and
in the New.* New York, 1971.

Gil, J. *Mitos y utopías del descubrimiento:
Colón y su tiempo.* Madrid, 1989.

Gilmore, M. P. *The World of Humanism,
1453–1517.* New York, 1962.

Giraldo Jaramillo, G. "Humboldt y el descubrimiento estético de América."
El Farol (Caracas), no. 181 (1959):
10–19.

Gisbert, T. "Los Incas y los Reyes Magos."
Traza y Baza VII (1973): 39–43.

Glacken, C. J. *Traces on the Rhodian Shore:
Nature and Culture in Western Thought
from Ancient Times to the End of the
Eighteenth Century.* Berkeley, 1967.

Gliozzi, G. *La scoperta dei selvaggi: Antropologia e colonialismo, da Columbo a
Diderot.* Milan, 1971.

————. *Adamo e il nuovo mondo.* Florence,
1977.

Gold und Macht: Spanien in der Neuen Welt
(exh. cat.), Vienna, 1986.

Goldstein, T. *The Dawn of Modern Science.*
Boston, 1980.

Gombrich, E. H. *Art and Illusion: A
Study in the Psychology of Pictorial
Representation.* Princeton, N.J., 1960.

————. *Norm and Form: Studies in the Art
of the Renaissance.* London, 1966.

————. *Reflections on the History of Art:
Views and Reviews.* Berkeley, 1987.

Gómez Canedo, L. "¿Hombres o bestias?"
Estudios de Historia Novohispana I
(1966): 29–51.

Gonnard, R. *La légende du bon sauvage:
Contribution à l'étude des origines du
Socialisme.* Paris, 1946.

Graf, A. *Miti, Leggende e Superstizioni del
Medio Evo.* Turin, 1892; facs. ed.
Hildesheim, 1985.

Graves, R. *The Greek Myths.* New York,
1959.

Greenblatt, S. *Marvelous Possessions: The
Wonder of the New World.* Chicago,
1991.

————, ed. *New World Encounters.*
Berkeley, 1993.

Greenleaf, R. E., and M. C. Meyer, eds.
*Research in Mexican History: Topics,
Methodology, Sources, and a Practical
Guide to Field Research.* Lincoln,
Neb., 1973.

Griffiths, J. G. "Archaeology and Hesiod's
Five Ages." *Journal of the History of
Ideas* XVII, no. 1 (1956): 108–19.

————. "Did Hesiod Invent the Golden
Age?" *Journal of the History of
Ideas* XIX, no. 1 (1958): 91–93.

Grimm, R. R. *Paradisus coelestis, Paradisus
terrestris.* Munich, 1977.

Guldan, E. *Eva und Maria.* Graz, 1966.

Hagen, V. von. *The Aztec: Man and Tribe.*
New York, 1961.

Hale, J. R. *Renaissance Exploration.* New
York, 1968.

Hall, J. *Dictionary of Subjects & Symbols in
Art.* New York, 1974.

Hamblin, D. J. "Has the Garden of
Eden Been Located at Last?"
Smithsonian XVIII, no. 2 (1987):
127–35.

Hanke, L. *The Spanish Struggle for Justice in*

the Conquest of America. Philadelphia, 1949; rpt. Boston, 1965.

———. *La lucha española por la justicia en la conquista de América*. Madrid, 1959.

———. *Aristotle and the American Indian: A Study in Race Prejudice in the Modern World*. London, 1959.

———. *Bartolomé de Las Casas*. Bogotá, 1965.

———. *All Mankind is One: A Study of the Disputation Between Bartolomé de Las Casas and Juan Ginés de Sepúlveda in 1550 on the Intellectual and Religious Capacity of the American Indians*. De Kalb, Ill., 1974.

Harley, J. B. *Maps and the Columbian Encounter*. Milwaukee, 1990.

Harris, M. *Cannibals and Kings: The Origins of Cultures*. New York, 1978.

Harrisse, H., ed. *Bibliotheca Americana Venustissima: A Description of Works Relating to America, 1492–1551*. New York, 1866.

———. *Biblioteca Americana Venustissima*. Madrid, 1960.

Hartog, F. *Le Miroir d'Hérodote: Essai sur la représentation de l'Autre*. Paris, 1980.

Harvey, P. D. A. *The History of Topographical Maps: Symbols, Pictures and Surveys*. London, 1980.

Haydn, H. *The Counter Renaissance*. New York, 1960.

Heikamp, D. *Mexico and the Medici*. Florence, 1972.

Heilige Experimente: Indianer und Jesuiten in Südamerika (exh. cat.). Vienna, 1989.

Heisig, K. "Woher stammt die Vorstellung vom Paradiesapfel?" *Zeitschrift für neutestamentliche Wissenschaft* XLIV (1952/53): 111–18.

Heitz, C. "Vitruve et l'architecture du Haut Moyen Age." *Settimana* XXII (1975): 725–57.

Helleiner, K. "Prester John's Letter: A Medieval Utopia." *The Phoenix* XIII, no.2 (1959): 47–57.

Hellkerstedt, K. J. *Gardens of Earthly Delight: Sixteenth and Seventeenth-Century Netherlandish Gardens*. New York, 1986.

Henige, D. *In Search of Columbus: The Sources for the First Voyage*. Tucson, Az., 1991.

Heninger, S. K. *Sidney and Spencer: The Poet as Maker*. University Park, Penn., 1989.

Henning, R. *Wo Lag das Paradies: Rätselfragen der Kulturgeschichte und Geographie*. Berlin, 1950.

Henríquez Ureña, P. *A Concise History of Latin American Culture*. New York, 1966.

Hermann, P. *Conquest by Man*. New York, 1954.

———. *The Great Age of Discovery*. New York, 1958.

Hodge, F. W., ed. *Handbook of the American Indians North of Mexico*. Washington D.C., 1907.

Hodgen, M. T. *Early Anthropology in the Sixteenth and Seventeenth Centuries*. Philadelphia, Penn., 1964.

Höffner, J. *Christentum und Menschenwürde: Das Anliegen der spanischen Kolonialethik im Goldenen Zeitalter*. Trier, 1947.

Holloway, M. *Heavens on Earth: Utopian Communities in America, 1680–1880*. New York, 1966.

Holly, M. A. *Panofsky and the Foundations of Art History*. Ithaca, N.Y., 1984.

Honour, H., *The European Vision of America* (exh. cat.). Cleveland, 1975

———. *The New Golden Land: European Images of America, from the Discovery to the Present Time*. New York, 1976.

Horgan, P. *Conquistadors in North American History*. New York, 1963.

Howard, D. R. *Writers and Pilgrims: Medieval Pilgrimage Narratives and Their Posterity.* Berkeley, 1980.

Huddleston, L. E. *Origins of the American Indians: European Concepts, 1492–1729.* Austin, Texas, 1967.

Hughes, R. *Heaven and Hell in Western Art.* London, 1968.

Huizinga, J. *Men and Ideas: History, the Middle Ages, the Renaissance.* New York, 1959.

Hulme, P. "Columbus and the Cannibals: A Study of the Reports of Anthropophagy in the Journal of Christopher Columbus." *Ibero-Amerikanisches Archiv* IV (1978): 115–39.

———. *Colonial Encounters: Europe and the Native Caribbean, 1492–1797.* London, 1986.

Husband, T. *The Wild Man: Medieval Myth and Symbolism.* New York, 1980.

Imagen del indio en la Europa moderna. (no editor named). Seville, 1990.

Ingstad, H. *Westward to Vinland: The Discovery of Pre-Columbian Norse House-Sites in North America.* New York, 1972.

Janson, H. W. *Apes and Ape Lore in the Middle Ages and the Renaissance.* London, 1952.

Jara, R., and N. Spadaccini, eds., *1492–1992: Re/Discovering Colonial Writing.* Minneapolis, 1989.

Jennings, F. *The Invasion of America: Indians, Colonialism, and the Cant of Conquest.* New York, 1976.

Jennings, G. *Aztec.* New York, 1980.

———. *Azteca.* Barcelona, 1986.

Jones, H. M. *O Strange New World.* New York, 1964.

Jones, W. R. "The Image of the Barbarian in Medieval Europe." *Comparative Studies in Society and History,* XIII (1971): 376–407.

Joris-Zavala, H. "L'allégorie de l'Amérique." In *Mémoires d'une Amérique,* 1–34. La Rochelle: Musée du Nouveau Monde, 1980.

Jos, E. "Impugnaciones a la *Historia del Almirante* escrita por su hijo." *Revista de las Indias* III (1942): 189–221.

———. *El plan y la génesis del Descubrimiento.* Valladolid, 1980.

Jourdain, C. de. *L'Influence d'Aristote et de ses interprétations sur la découverte du Nouveau Monde.* Paris, 1888.

Juderías, J. *La Leyenda Negra.* Madrid, 1954.

Kadir, D. *Columbus and the Ends of the Earth: Europe's Prophetic Rhetoric as Conquering Ideology.* Berkeley, 1992.

Kaemmerling, E., ed. *Ikonographie und Ikonologie: Theorien—Entwicklung—Probleme.* Cologne, 1979.

Kalstone, D. *Sidney's Poetry: Contexts and Interpretations.* New York, 1970.

Kamen, H. *The Spanish Inquisition.* New York, 1975.

Kappler, C. *Monstruos, demonios y maravillas al fin de la Edad Media.* Madrid, 1986.

Katzenellenbogen, A. *Allegories of the Virtues and Vices in Medieval Art.* New York, 1964.

Kaufmann, U. M. *Paradise in the Age of Milton.* Victoria, B.C., 1978.

Kellner, H. *Language and Historical Representation: Getting the Story Crooked.* Madison, Wis., 1989.

Keen, B. *La imagen azteca.* Mexico City, 1984.

———. *The Aztec Image in Western Thought.* New Brunswick, N.J., 1985.

Kerrigan, W., and Braden, G. *The Idea of the Renaissance.* Baltimore, 1991.

Killermann, S. "Die ersten Nachrichten und Bilder der Kokospalme und vom Drachenbaum." *Naturwissenschaftliche Wochenschrift* XIX (1920): 305–10.

Kimble, G. H. T. *The Catalan World Map of the R. Biblioteca Estense at Modena.* London, 1934.

———. *Geography in the Middle Ages.* London, 1938.

Kirkpatrick, F. A. *The Spanish Conquistadors.* New York, 1971.

Kirschbaum, E. et al. *Lexikon der Christlichen Ikonographie.* Freiburg-im-Breslau, 1968–72.

Kirschner, J. *Die Darstellung des ersten Menschenpaares in der bildenden Kunst.* Stuttgart, 1903.

Klein, H. S. *Slavery in the Americas: A Comparative Study of Virginia and Cuba.* New York, 1971.

Knipping, B. *De Iconographie van de Contra-Reformatie in de Nederlanden.* Hilversum, 1939–40.

Koch, H. *Vom Nachleben des Vitruv.* Baden-Baden, 1951.

Koch, R. A. "Martin Schongauer's Dragon Tree." *Print Review* V (1976): 114–19.

Kohl, K-H., ed. *Mythen der Neuen Welt: Zur Entdeckungs-geschichte Lateinamerikas* (exh. cat.). Berlin, 1982.

———. *Entzauberter Blick: Das Bild von Guten Wilden.* Frankfurt, 1986.

Krinsky, C. H. "Seventy-Eight Vitruvian Manuscripts." *Journal of the Warburg and Courtault Institutes* XXX (1967): 36–70.

Krumrine, M. L., ed. *Art and the Native American: Perceptions, Realities and Influences.* University Park, Penn., 1995 (in press).

Kubler, G. *Mexican Architecture of the Sixteenth Century.* New Haven, Conn., 1948.

———. *Esthetic Recognition of Ancient Amerindian Art.* New Haven, Conn., 1990.

Lach, D. F. *India in the Eyes of Europe: The Sixteenth Century.* Chicago, 1968.

———. *Southeast Asia in the Eyes of Europe.* Chicago, 1968.

Ladner, G. B. *The Idea of Reform, Its Impact on Christian Thought and Action in the Age of the Fathers.* London, 1967.

Langlois, C. V. *La Connaissance de la Nature et du Monde au Moyen-Age d'après quelques écrits français à l'usage des laïcs.* Paris, 1927.

Laporace, T. G., and R. Almagia. *Il mappamondo di Fra Mauro.* Venice, 1956.

Larsen, E. "Once More Jan Mostaert's West-Indian Landscape." In *Mélanges d'archéologie et de l'histoire de l'art offerts au Professeur Lavelleye,* 127–37. Louvain, 1970.

Lascelles, M. M. "Alexander and the Earthly Paradise in Medieval English Writings." *Medium Aevum* V (1936): 31–47, 79–104, 173–88.

Lauber, A. W. *Indian Slavery in Colonial Times Within the Present Limits of the United States.* New York, 1969.

Laurencich-Minelli, L. "Oggetti americani studiati da Ulisse Aldrovandi." *Archivio per l'Antropologia e la Etnologica* CXIII (1983): 187–206.

Lavado, P. J. "En torno a la figura del salvaje y sus implicaciones iconográficas." *Actas del V. Congreso Español de Historia del Arte.* 231–37. Barcelona, 1984.

Le Corbeiller, C. "Miss America and Her Sisters: Personifications of the Four Parts of the World." *Metropolitan Museum of Art Bulletin* (April 1961): 208–23.

Lee, R. W. *Ut Pictura Poesis: The Humanistic Theory of Painting.* New York, 1967.

Lehmann-Hartleben, K. "The *Imagines* of the Elder Philostratus." *Art Bulletin* XXIII (1941): 16–44.

Leonard, I. A. *Don Carlos de Sigüenza y Góngora: A Mexican Savant of the Seventeenth Century.* Berkeley, 1929.

———. *Books of the Brave, Being an Account of Books and Men in the Spanish Conquest and Settlement of the Sixteenth-Century New World.* rev. ed., Berkeley, 1992.

———. *Baroque Times in Old Mexico: Seventeenth-Century Persons, Places, and Practises.* Ann Arbor, Mich., 1966.

Lestienne, P. *Saint Malo ou Maclou: Sa vie et son culte.* St. Malo, 1954.

Lestringant, F. "Le Cannibalisme des 'Canibales'." *Bulletin de la Société des amis de Montaigne* IX/X (1982): 27–40; XI/XII (1982): 19–38.

———. "Le nom des 'cannibales' de Christophe Colomb à Michel de Montaigne." *Bulletin de la Société des amis de Montaigne* XVII/XVIII (1984): 51–74.

———. *Le Huguenot et le sauvage: L'Amérique et la controverse coloniale en France au temps des Guerres de Religion.* Paris, 1990.

Letts, M. *Sir John Mandeville: The Man and His Book.* London, 1949.

Levenson, J. A., ed. *Circa 1492: Art in the Age of Exploration.* Washington DC, 1991.

Levin, D. *History as Romantic Art: Bancroft, Prescott, Motley, and Parkman.* New York, 1963.

Levin, H. *The Myth of the Golden Age in the Renaissance.* Bloomington, Ind., 1969.

Levinas, E. *L'Humanisme de l'autre homme.* Montpellier, 1972.

Lévi-Strauss, C. *Tristes tropiques.* Paris, 1962.

Ley, W. *Another Look at Atlantis.* New York, 1969.

Ley, W., and L. Sprague de Camp. *De la*

Atlántida a El Dorado. Barcelona, 1960.

———. *Lands Beyond.* New York, 1993.

Lipsker-Zarden, E. *Der Mythos vom goldenen Zeitalter in den Schäferdictungen Italiens, Spaniens und Frankreichs zur Zeit der Renaissance.* Berlin, 1933.

Litvinoff, B. *1492: The Decline of Medievalism and the Rise of the Modern Age.* New York, 1992.

Livermore, H. *A History of Spain.* New York, 1960.

Lotts, L. "Die wilden Leute in der deutschen Graphik des ausgehenden Mittelalters." *Philobiblon* VIII (1964): 260–72.

Lotz, W. *Studies in Italian Renaissance Architecture.* Cambridge, Mass., 1981.

Lovejoy, A. O. *Essays in the History of Ideas.* New York, 1960.

———. *The Great Chain of Being: A Study of the History of an Idea.* New York, 1960.

Luce, J. V. *The End of Atlantis: New Light on an Old Legend.* London, 1975.

Luttervelt, R. van. "Jan Mostaert's West-indiesch Landschap." *Nederlandsch Kunsthistorisch Jaarboek* X (1949): 105–17.

Marle, R. van. *Iconographie de l'Art profane au moyen âge et à la Renaissance.* The Hague, 1931.

McClung, W. A. *The Architecture of Paradise: Survivals of Eden and Jerusalem.* Berkeley, 1983.

McDannell, C., and B. Lang. *Heaven: A History.* New York, 1990.

McEvedy, C. *The Penguin Atlas of Medieval History.* Harmondsworth, 1961.

McNeill, W. H. *The Rise of the West: A History of the Human Community.* Chicago, 1963.

———. *Plagues and Peoples.* New York, 1976.

Madariaga, S. de. *Christopher Columbus;*

Being the Life of the Very Magnificent Lord Don Cristóbal Colón. New York, 1940.

Magnaghi, A. *Amerigo Vespucci: Studio critico, con speciale risguardo ed una nuova valutazione delle fonti.* Rome, 1926.

Mâle, E. *L'art religieux du XII siècle en France.* Paris, 1966.

————. *The Gothic Image: Religious Art in France of the Thirteenth-Century.* New York, 1958.

————. *L'Art religieux de la fin du XVIe siècle, du XVIIe siècle et du XVIIIe siècle: Etude sur l'iconographie après le Concile de Trente.* Paris, 1951.

Maltby, W. S. *The Black Legend in England: The Development of Anti-Spanish Sentiment, 1558–1660.* Durham, N.C., 1971.

Mannix, D. P. *Black Cargoes: A History of the Atlantic Slave Trade, 1518–1865.* New York, 1962.

Manuel, F. E. *Utopian Thought in the Western World.* Cambridge, Mass., 1979.

Manuel, F. E., and P. Fritzie. *Sketch for a Natural History of Paradise: Myth, Symbol and Culture.* New York, 1971.

Manzano Manzano, J. *Colón y su secreto: El predescubrimiento.* Madrid, 1982.

Maravall, S. A. "La utopía político-religiosa de los Franciscanos en Nueva España." *Estudios Americanos* I (1949): 199–27.

Martí, A. *Islas Canarias.* Madrid, 1969.

Mason, J. A. *The Ancient Civilizations of Peru.* Harmondsworth, 1961.

Massingham, H. J. *The Golden Age: The Story of Human Nature.* London, 1927.

Mateo Gómez, I. "Consideraciones iconográficas sobre el drago, la palmera y el manzano del 'Jardín de las Delicias' del Bosco." *Traza y Baza* I (1972): 9–18.

Meinig, D. W. *The Shaping of America: A Geographical Perspective on 500 Years of History.* Vol. 1, *Atlantic America, 1492–1800.* New Haven, Conn., 1986.

Menéndez Pidal, R. *La lengua de Cristóbal Colón, el estilo de Santa Teresa y otros estudios sobre el siglo XVI.* Madrid, 1958.

————. *El Padre de Las Casas.* Madrid, 1963.

Mercer, J. *Canary Islands: Fuerteventura.* Harrisburg, 1973.

Michel, E. "Un tableau colonial de Jan Mostaert." *Revue Belge d'Archéologie et de l'Historie de l'Art* I (1931): 133–41.

Milanich, J. T. and S. Milbrath, eds. *First Encounters: Spanish Explorations in the Caribbean and the United States, 1492–1570.* Gainesville, Fla., 1989.

Milhou, A. *Colón y su mentalidad mesiánica en el ambiente franciscanista español.* Valladolid, 1983.

Miller, K. *Mappae Mundi. IV: Die Herefordkarte.* Stuttgart, 1896.

Mintz, S. *Sweetness and Power: The Place of Sugar in Modern History.* New York, 1986.

Moffitt, J. F. "Francisco Goya y Paul Revere: Una matanza en Madrid y una matanza en Boston." In *Goya Nuevas Visiones: Homenaje a Don Enrique Lafuente Ferrari,* edited by F. Calvo Serraller, 257–90. Museo del Prado, Madrid, 1987.

————. *Occultism in Avant-Garde Art: The Case of Joseph Beuys.* Ann Arbor, 1988.

————. "Archetypal Micro-Architecture: Prologemena to the *Custodias Procesionales.*" *Konsthistorisk Tidskrift* XII (1989): 47–62.

————. "'Hut-and-Tortoise': An 'Ecological' Topos from Vitruvius in George Wither's *Collection of Emblemes.*" *Ars Longa: Cuadernos de Arte* I (1990): 35–42.

———. "Philostratus and the Canaries." *Gerion* VIII (1990): 241–61.

———. "Filostrato, sus *Imágines* y la imagen de las Islas Canarias en la Antigüedad." Vol. II. In *Homenaje al Profesor Dr. Telesforo Bravo,* 437–60. Universidad de la Laguna, 1990.

———. "Leonardo's *Sala delle Asse* and the Primordial Origins of Architecture," *Arte Lombarda* 92/93 (1990): 76–90.

———. "An Airborne Rescuer from the North in El Paso: 'Ruggiero' or 'Perseus'? 'Hippogriff' or 'Horse'?" *Journal of the Rocky Mountain Medieval and Renaissance Association* IX (1990): 79–99.

———. "Vitruvius in a Carolingian Eden: The Genesis Cycle from the *Moûtier-Grandval Bible.*" *Source* XII, no. 1 (1992): 7–12.

———. "Medieval *Mappaemundi* and Ptolemy's *Chorographia.*" *Gesta* XXXII, no. 1 (1993): 59–68.

———. "'*Een West-Indien Lantschap met Vreemt Ghebouw*': Jan Mostaert on the Architectural Primitivism Characterizing a 'Golden Age' Reborn in the New World." In *Art and the Native American: Perceptions, Realities and Influences,* edited by M. L. Krumrine. University Park, Penn., 1995 (in press).

Moir, A. L. *The World Map in Hereford Cathedral.* Hereford, 1977.

Molina Martínez, M. *La Leyenda Negra.* Madrid, 1991.

Moorehead, A. *The Fatal Impact: An Account of the Invasion of the South Pacific, 1767–1840.* New York, 1967.

Morales Padrón, F. *Historia del descubrimiento y conquista de América.* Madrid, 1990.

Morison, S. E. *Admiral of the Ocean Sea: A Life of Christopher Columbus.* New York, 1962.

———. *The European Discovery of America: The Northern Voyages, A. D. 500–1600.* New York, 1971.

———. *The European Discovery of America: The Southern Voyages, 1492–1616.* New York, 1974.

Moseley, C. W. R. D. "Behaim's 'Globe' and Mandeville's 'Travels'." *Imago Mundi* XXXIII (1981): 89–91.

Moynihan, E. B. *Paradise as a Garden in Persia and Mughal India.* New York, 1979.

Mund-Dophie, M. "L'extrême-Occident de l'Antiquité classique et la découverte du Nouveau Monde: Une manipulation de textes à des fins idéologiques." *Nouvelle Revue du Seizième Siècle* VIII (1990): 27–49.

Murphy, J. J. *Rhetoric in the Middle Ages: A History of Rhetorical Theory from Saint Augustine to the Renaissance.* Berkeley, 1974.

———, ed. *Medieval Eloquence: Studies in the Theory and Practice of Medieval Rhetoric.* Berkeley, 1978.

Nabakov, P., and R. Easton. *Native American Architecture.* New York, 1988.

Naipaul, V. S. *The Loss of El Dorado: A History.* New York, 1984.

Nakam, G. *Les "Essais" de Montaigne: Miroir et procès de leur temps.* Paris, 1984.

Neuber, W. *Fremde Welt im europäische Horizont: Zur Topik der deutschen Amerika-Reiseberichte der frühen Neuzeit.* Berlin, 1991.

Die Neue Welt: Österreich und die Erforschung Amerikas (exh. cat.). Vienna, 1992.

Neumeyer, A. "The Indian Contribution to Architectural Decoration in Spanish Colonial America." *Art Bulletin* XXX, no. 2 (1948): 104–21.

Newton, A. P., ed. *Travel and Travellers of the Middle Ages.* New York, 1926.

Nilsson, M. P. *Homer and Mycenae.* London, 1933.

Nisbet, R. *History of the Idea of Progress.* New York, 1980.

Nordenskjöld, A. E. *Periplus: An Essay on the Early History of Charts and Sailing Directions.* Stockholm, 1897.

Nordhoff, C. *The Communistic Societies of the United States.* New York, 1875.

Nunn, G. E. *The Geographical Conceptions of Columbus: A Critical Consideration of Four Problems.* New York, 1924.

Nuttal, Z. "Royal Ordinances Concerning the Laying Out of New Towns." *Hispanic American Historical Review* V (1922): 249–59.

O'Gorman, E. "Sobre la naturaleza bestial del indio americano." *Filosofía y Letras* I (1941): 141–58, 305–15.

———. *La invención de América: Investigación acerca de la estructura histórica del Nuevo Mundo y del sentido de su devenir.* Mexico City, 1958.

———. *The Invention of America: An Inquiry into the Historical Nature of the New World and the Meaning of Its History.* Bloomington, Ind., 1961.

———. *Cuatro Historiadores de Indias, Siglo XVI: Pedro Mártir de Anglería, Gonzalo Fernández de Oviedo y Valdés, Fray Bartolomé de Las Casas, Joseph de Acosta.* Mexico City, 1972.

Olaechea Labayen, J. B., *El descubrimiento persistente de América: Dialéctica racial y convivencia humana como paradigma.* Granada, 1989.

Olschki, L. *Storia letteraria delle scoperte geographiche: Studi e ricerche.* Florence, 1937.

———. "What Columbus Saw on Landing in the West Indies." *Proceedings of the American Philosophical Society* LXXXIV (1941): 633–59.

———. "Ponce de León's Fountain of Youth: History of a Geographic Myth." *Hispanic American Historical Review* XXI (1941): 361–85.

———. *Marco Polo's Asia: An Introduction to His "Description of the World".* Berkeley, 1960.

Ong, W. J. *Orality and Literacy: The Technologizing of the Word.* London, 1982.

Ordax, S. Andrés. "El Palacio Moctezuma en Cáceres." *Memorias de la Real Academia de Extremadura* I (1983): 83–85.

———. "Los frescos de las salas romana y mejicana del Palacio de Moctezuma de Cáceres." *Norba* V (1984): 97–115.

Oster, P. *The Mexicans: A Personal Portrait of a People.* New York, 1990.

Pagden, A. *The Fall of Natural Man: The American Indian and the Origins of Comparative Ethnology.* Cambridge (England), 1982.

———. *Spanish Imperialism and the Political Imagination: Studies in European and Spanish-American Social and Political Theory, 1513–1830.* Yale UP, 1990.

———. *European Encounters With the New World, From Renaissance to Romanticism.* New Haven, Conn., 1992.

Palm, E. W. "La Aportación de las Ordenes Mendicantes al Urbanismo en el Virreinato de la Nueva España." In *Verhandlungen des XXXVIII.* Vol. 4, Internationalen Amerikanisten Kongresses, 131–40. Stuttgart, 1968.

———. "La representación de la Ciudad Precolombina en el Siglo XVI: Realidad americana y concepto ideal." *Academia: Boletín de la Real Academia de Bellas Artes de San Fernando* XLIX (1979): 123–38.

———. "Amerika oder die eingeholte Zeit: Zum Lob des Vespucci von Johannes Stradanus." In *Gedenkschrift Gerdt Kütscher,* Vol. 2, 11–23. Berlin, 1984.

———. *Los Monumentos Arquitectónicos de la Española.* Santo Domingo, 1984.

———. *Heimkehr ins Exil: Studien zu Literatur und Kunst.* Cologne, 1992.

Panofsky, E. *Meaning in the Visual Arts: Papers In and On Art History,* Garden City, N.Y. 1955.

———. *Life and Art of Albrecht Dürer.* Princeton, 1955.

———. *Studies in Iconology: Humanistic Themes in the Art of the Renaissance.* New York, 1962.

———. *Renaissance and Renascences in Western Art.* New York, 1969.

———. *Early Netherlandish Painting.* New York, 1971.

———. *La prospettiva come "forma simbolica" e altri scritti.* Edited by G. D. Neri. Milan, 1979.

———. *Vida y arte de Alberto Durero.* Madrid, 1982.

Parker, J. *Discovery: Developing Views of the Earth, from Ancient Times to the Voyages of Captain Cook.* New York, 1972.

Parry, E. *The Image of the Indian and the Black Man in American Art, 1590–1900.* New York, 1974.

Parry, G. *Seventeenth-Century Poetry: The Social Context.* London, 1985.

Parry, J. H. *The Spanish Theory of Empire in the Sixteenth Century.* Cambridge (England), 1940.

———. *The Establishment of the European Hegemony, 1415–1715: Trade and Exploration in the Age of the Renaissance.* New York, 1961.

———. *The Age of Reconnaissance: Discovery, Exploration and Settlement, 1450–1650.* Berkeley, 1981.

Patch, H. R. *The Other World According to Descriptions in Medieval Literature.* Cambridge, Mass., 1950.

Paz, O. *Sor Juana Inés de la Cruz, o Las Trampas de la Fe.* Mexico City, 1985.

Pearce, R. H. "Primitivist Ideas in the *Faerie Queene.*" *Journal of English and German Philology* XLIV (1945): 139–51.

———. *The Savages of America: A Study of the Indian and the Ideas of Civilization.* Baltimore, Md., 1953.

———. *Savagism and Civilization: A Study of the Indian and the American Mind.* Baltimore, Md., 1965.

Pearsall, D., and E. Salter, *Landscapes and Seasons of the Medieval World.* New York, 1967.

Pendle, G. *A History of Latin America.* Harmondsworth, 1965.

Penrose, B. *Travel and Discovery in the Renaissance, 1460–1620.* New York, 1975.

Pérez de Tudela y Bueso, J. *Mirabilis in Altis: Estudio crítico sobre el origen y significado del proyecto descubridor de Cristóbal Colón.* Madrid, 1983.

Peters, E. *Quellen und Charakter der Paradiesvorstellungen in der deutschen Dichtung vom 9.–12. Jahrhunderts.* Breslau, 1915.

Peterson, J. F. *The Paradise Garden Murals of Malinalco: Utopia and Empire in Sixteenth-Century Mexico.* Austin, Tex., 1993.

Pfister, F. "Das Nachleben der Überlieferung von Alexander und den Brahmanen." *Hermes* LXXVI (1941): 143–69.

Phelan, J. L. *The Millennial Kingdom of the Franciscans in the New World: A*

Study in the Writings of Gerónimo de Mendieta, 1525–1604. Berkeley, 1956.

———. *El reino milenario de los franciscanos en el Nuevo Mundo.* México, 1962.

Phillips, W. D. and C. R. *The Worlds of Christopher Columbus.* Cambridge (England), 1992.

Pickering, C. *Chronological History of Plants.* Boston, 1879.

Pigler, A. *Barockthemen: Eine Auswahl von Verzeichnissen zur Iconographie des 17. und 18. Jahrhunderts.* Budapest, 1956.

Pizarro Gómez, F. J. "La iconografía del Nuevo Mundo y su repercusión en las artes españolas y portuguesas." In *Actas del V. Simposio Hispano-Portugués de Historia el Arte,* 16–38. Valladolid, 1990.

Pochat, G. *Der Exotismus während des Mittelalters und der Renaissance: Voraussetzungen, Entwicklung und Wandel eines bildnerischen Vokabulars.* Stockholm, 1970.

Poeschel, S. *Studien zur Ikonographie der Erdteile in der Kunst des 16.–18. Jahrhunderts* Munich, 1985.

Pohl, F. J. *Amerigo Vespucci, Pilot Major.* New York, 1945.

Pope-Hennessy, J. *Giovanni di Paolo.* London, 1937.

Polleross, F., ed. *Federschmuck und Kaiser-krone: Das barocke Amerikabild in den habsburgischen Ländern.* Vienna, 1992.

Porter, H. C. *The Inconstant Savage: England and the North American Indian, 1500–1660.* London, 1979.

Prescott, W. H. *The Conquest of Peru.* New York, 1961.

———. *The Conquest of Mexico.* New York, 1964.

Prest, J. *The Garden of Eden: The Botanic Garden and the Re-Creation of Paradise.* London, 1981.

Prieto, C. *La minería en el Nuevo Mundo.* Madrid, 1969.

Provost, F., ed. *Columbus: An Annotated Guide to the Study of His Life and Writings, 1750–1988.* Detroit, 1990.

Ramírez Domínguez, J. A. *Cinco Lecciones sobre Arquitectura y Utopia.* Málaga, 1981.

———. *Edificios y Sueños (Ensayos sobre Architectura y Utopia).* Málaga, 1983.

———. *Construcciones ilusorias: Arquitec-turas descritas, arquitecturas pintadas.* Madrid, 1983.

Rammage, N. H. *Roman Art: Romulus to Constantine.* Englewood Cliffs, N.J., 1991.

Ramos, D. *El mito del Dorado: Su génesis y proceso.* Caracas, 1973.

Ramsey, R. H. *No Longer on the Map: Discovering Places that Never Were.* New York, 1973.

Reallexikon zur deutschen Kunstgeschichte. Stuttgart, 1948–.

Réau, L. *Iconographie de l'art chrétien.* Paris, 1958.

Reed, E. E. "The Ignoble Savage." *Modern Language Review* LIX (1964): 53–64.

Reinhard, W., ed. *Humanismus und Neue Welt.* Weinheim, 1987.

Ricard, R. *La "conquête spirituelle" du Mexique: Essai sur l'apostolat et les méthodes missionaires des Ordres Mendiants en Nouvelle Espagne de 1523 à 1572.* Paris, 1933.

Riding, A. *Distant Neighbors: A Portrait of the Mexicans.* New York, 1986.

Rienits, R. *The Voyages of Columbus.* London, 1970.

Ringbom, L. I. *Graltempel und Paradies: Beziehungen zwischen Iran und Europa im Mittelalter.* Stockholm, 1951.

———. *Paradisus Terrestris: Myt, Bild och Verlighet.* Helsinki, 1958.

Rodríguez Monegal, E. *Noticias secretas de América.* Barcelona, 1984.

Rogers, F. M. *The Quest for Eastern Chris-*

tians: Travels and Rumor in the Age of Discovery. Minneapolis, 1962.

Rolf, H. R. "An Experimental Epidemic of Reiter's Syndrome." *Journal of the American Medical Association* CXCVIII (1966): 693–98.

Romeo, R. *Le scoperte americane nella consienza italiana del Cinquecento.* Milan, 1954.

Romeu Palazuelos, E. *Las Islas Canarias.* Madrid, 1981.

Rosenau, H. *La ciudad ideal: Su evolución arquitectónica en Europa.* Madrid, 1983.

Rosien, W. *Die Ebstorfer Weltkarte.* Hannover, 1952.

Ross, D. J. A. *Alexander Historiatus.* London, 1963.

Roth, L. M. *A Concise History of American Architecture.* New York, 1979.

Rowland, B. *The Classical Tradition in Western Art.* Cambridge, Mass., 1963.

Ruano, E. B. *La leyenda de San Borondón, octava isla canaria.* Valladolid, 1978.

Rücker, E. *Die Schedelsche Weltchronik: das grösste Buchunternehmen der Dürer-Zeit; mit ein Katalog der Städteansichten.* Munich, 1973.

Rule, J. C., ed. *The Character of Philip II: The Problem of Moral Judgments in History.* Boston, 1963.

Ryan, M. T. "Assimilating New Worlds in the 16th and 17th Centuries." *Comparative Studies in Society and History* XXIII (1981): 519–38.

Ryan, S. A. *Christopher Columbus in Poetry, History and Art.* Chicago, 1917.

Rykwert, J. *On Adam's House in Paradise. The Idea of the Primitive Hut in Architectural History.* Cambridge, Mass., 1981.

Sale, C. *The Conquest of Paradise: Christopher Columbus and the Columbian Legacy.* New York, 1990.

Sanders, R. *Lost Tribes and Promised Lands: The Origins of American Racism.* New York, 1992.

Sanford, C. L. *Quest for Paradise: Europe and the American Moral Imagination.* Urbana, Ill., 1961.

Santiago Páez, E. "Algunas esculturas napolitanas del siglo XVIII en España." *Archivo Español de Arte* XL (1967): 125–36.

Sanz, C. *El gran secreto de la Carta de Colón.* Madrid, 1959.

———. *El nombre América: Libros y mapas que lo impusieron.* Madrid, 1959.

———. *Mapas antiguos del mundo (siglos XV-XVI).* Madrid, 1962.

Sanz Hermida, Mª., and A. M. Armand. "La alegoría en geografía: Estudio iconológico de los frontispicios de los Atlas holandeses de los siglos XVI y XVII." *Actas del Congreso del CEA,* 115–26. Cáceres, 1990.

Sariola, S. *Power and Resistance: The Colonial Heritage in Latin America.* Ithaca, N.Y., 1972.

Sauer, C. O. *Sixteenth-Century North America: The Land and the Peoples as Seen by the Europeans.* Berkeley, 1971.

Saxl, F. *Lectures.* London, 1957.

Scheicher, E. *Die Kunst- und Wunderkammern der Habsburger.* Vienna, 1979.

Schenk, H. "Martin Schongauers Drachenbaum." *Naturwissenschaftliche Wochenschrift* XIX (1920): 775–80.

Schiller, G. *Iconography of Christian Art.* London, 1971–72.

Schlosser, J. *La letteratura artistica: Manuale delle fonti della storia dell'arte moderna.* Florence, 1967.

———. *Die Kunst- und Wunderkammern der Spätrenaissance.* Braunschweig, 1978.

———. *Las cámaras artísticas y maravillosas*

del renacimiento tardío: Una contribución a la historia del coleccionismo. Madrid, 1988.

Schuller, B. "The Oldest Known Illustration of South American Indians." *Museum of the American Indian-Heyde Foundation Indian Notes* VII (1930): 484–97.

Schulten, A. *Tartessos.* Madrid, 1972.

Schulz, J. "Jacopo de' Barbari's View of Venice: Map-Making, City Views, and Moralized Geography Before the Year 1500." *Art Bulletin* LX (1978): 425–74.

Schweitzer, M. W., ed. *Espagne: Guides Hachettes.* Paris, 1961.

Scully, V. *American Architecture and Urbanism.* New York, 1969.

Sebastián López, S. *Album de arte colonial.* Tunja, 1963.

———. "La significación salomónica del templo de Huejotzingo." *Traza y Baza* III (1973): 25–31.

———. *Arte y Humanismo.* Madrid, 1978.

———. *Arte Iberoamericano.* Vol. 28, *Summa Artis.* Madrid, 1985.

———. *Contrarreforma y barroco: Lecturas iconográficas e iconológicas.* Madrid, 1989.

———. "El empleo y actualización de los modelos europeos en México y América Latina." In *Simpatías y diferencias: Relaciones del arte mexicano con el de América Latina,* 113–25. Mexico City, 1988.

———. *Iconografía medieval.* San Sebastián, 1988.

———. "Lo maravilloso y lo monstruoso en el grabado valenciano del Protorrenacimiento." *I Coloquio de Arte Valenciano,* 5–18. Valencia, 1989.

———. *El Barroco Iberoamericano: Mensaje iconográfico.* Madrid, 1990.

———. *Iconografía del indio americano.* Madrid, 1992.

Seymour, M. *Mandeville's Travels.* New York, 1967.

Seznec, J. *The Survival of the Pagan Gods: The Mythological Tradition and its Place in Renaissance Humanism and Art.* New York, 1961.

Shepard, P., *Man in the Landscape,* New York, 1967.

Silverberg, R. *The Realm of Prester John.* New York, 1972.

Simon, U. *Heaven in the Christian Tradition.* New York, 1958.

Simpson, L. B. *Many Mexicos.* Berkeley, 1961.

Skelton, R. A. *Explorers' Maps: Chapters in the Cartographic Record of Geographical Discovery.* London, 1958.

Slessarev, V. *Prester John: The Letter and the Myth.* Minneapolis, 1959.

Smith, B. *European Vision and the South Pacific, 1768-1850: A Study in the History of Art and Ideas.* New York, 1960.

Smith, H. N. *Virgin Land: The American West as Symbol and Myth.* Cambridge, Mass. 1970.

Snowden, F. M. *Blacks in Antiquity.* Cambridge, Mass., 1970.

Snyder, J. "Jan van Eyck and Adam's Apple." *Art Bulletin* LVIII (1976): 511–15.

———. "Jan Mostaert's West Indies Landscape." In Chiapelli, ed., *First Images of America,* 495–502.

———. *Northern Renaissance Art: Painting, Sculpture, the Graphic Arts, from 1350-1575.* New York, 1985.

Sommer-Mathis, A., and C. F. Laferl. *Das Bild Amerikas im barocken spanischen Fest.* Kassel, 1992.

Soustelle, J. *The Daily Life of the Aztecs.* New York, 1962.

Speck, G. *Myths and New World Explorations.* Edmonds Wash., 1979.

Sprague de Camp, L. *Citadels of Mystery:*

Ancient Ruins and Archaeology. New York, 1973.

———. *Lost Continents: The Atlantis Theme.* New York, 1975.

Stampp, K. M. *The Peculiar Institution: Slavery in the Ante-Bellum South.* New York, 1956.

Stanislawski, D. "The Origin and Spread of the Grid-Pattern Town." *The Geographical Review* XXXVI (1946): 105–20.

———. "Early Spanish Town Planning in the New World." *The Geographical Review* XXXVII (1947): 95–105.

Starnes, D. T., and W. W. Talbert. *Classical Myth and Legend in Renaissance Dictionaries.* Chapel Hill, N.C., 1955.

Steadman, J. M. *Nature into Myth: Medieval and Renaissance Moral Symbols.* Pittsburgh, Penn., 1979.

Stevens, W. M. "The Figure of the Earth in Isidore's '*De Natura Rerum*'." *Isis* LXXI (1980): 268–77.

Stewart, J., ed. *Handbook of the South American Indians.* New York, 1963.

Stewart, G. R. *Ordeal By Hunger: The Story of the Donner Party.* New York, 1971.

Stocchi, M. P. "Il '*De Canaria*' boccaccesco e un *Locus deperditus* nel '*De Insulis*' di Domenico Silvestri." *Rinascimento* X (1959): 143–56.

Strong, R., *Arte y Poder: Fiestas del Renacimiento, 1450–1650.* Madrid, 1988.

Struever, N. *The Language of History in the Renaissance.* Princeton, N.J., 1989.

Sturtevant, W. C. "The First Images of America." In Chiapelli, ed., *First Images of America,* 417–54.

Summers, D. *Michelangelo and the Language of Art.* Princeton, N.J., 1981.

Sumption, J. *Pilgrimage: An Image of Medieval Religion.* London, 1975.

The Sun King: Louis XIV and the New World (exh. cat.). New Orleans, 1984.

Swan, B. F. "The Ruysch Map of the

World (1507–1508)." *Papers of the Bibliographical Society of America* XLV (1951): 219–36.

Sweet, L. I. "Christopher Columbus and the Millenial Vision of the New World." *Catholic Historical Review* LXXII (1986): 369–82.

Tabor, J. D. *Things Unutterable: Paul's Ascent to Paradise.* University Press of America, 1986.

Tannahill, R. *Flesh and Blood: A History of the Cannibal Complex.* New York, 1988.

———. *Food in History.* New York, 1989.

Taviani, P. E. *Christopher Columbus: The Grand Design.* London, 1985.

Taylor, J. C. *America as Art.* New York, 1976.

El teatro descubre América: Fiestas y teatro en la Casa de Austria (1500–1700) (exh. cat.). Madrid, 1992.

Tervarent, G. de. *Attributs et symboles dans l'art profane, 1450–1600.* Geneva, 1958.

Tierney, P. *The Highest Altar: Unveiling the Mystery of Human Sacrifice.* New York, 1989.

Thacker, C. *The History of Gardens.* Berkeley, 1970.

Thomas, C. W. *Adventures and Observations of the West Coast of Africa, and its Islands.* New York, 1860.

Todorov, T. *La conquête de l'Amérique: La Question de l'Autre.* Paris, 1982.

———. *The Conquest of America: The Question of the Other.* New York, 1992.

Tooley, R. V. *Maps and Map-Makers.* New York, 1990.

Tovar, A. *Lo medieval en la Conquista y otros ensayos americanos.* Madrid, 1970.

Truettner, W. H., ed. *The West as America: Reinterpreting Images of the Frontier* (exh. cat.). Washington: Smithsonian, 1991.

Tuffrau, P. *Le merveilleux voyage de Saint*

Brandan à la recherche du Paradis. Paris, 1925.

Turner, A. R. *The Vision of Landscape in Renaissance Italy.* Princeton, N.J., 1974.

Tuveson, E. L. *Millennium and Utopia: A Study in the Background of the Idea of Progress.* New York, 1964.

Tyler, R. *Visions of America: Pioneer Artists in a New Land.* New York, 1983.

Uhden, R. "Zur Herkunft und Systematik der mittelalterlichen Weltkarten." *Geographische Zeitschrift* XXXVII (1931): 321–40.

———. "Die antiken Grundlagen der mittelalterlichen Seekarten." *Imago Mundi* I (1935): 1–29.

Vaillant, G. C. *Aztecs of Mexico: Origin, Rise, and Fall of the Aztec Nations.* Harmondsworth, 1965.

Veit, W. *Studien zur Geschichte des Topos der Goldenen Zeit von der Antike bis zum 18. Jahrhunderts.* Cologne, 1961.

Verger, P. *Fiestas y danzas en el Cuzco y en los Andes.* Buenos Aires, 1945.

Verlinden, C. *L'Esclavage dans l'Europe médiévale.* Bruges, 1955.

Vian, F. *La guerre des Géants. Le mythe avant l'époque hellénistique.* París, 1952.

Vicens Vives, J. *Approaches to the History of Spain.* Berkeley, 1972.

Vignaud, H. *Toscanelli and Columbus: The Letter and Chart of Toscanelli.* London, 1902.

———. *Études critiques sur la vie de Colomb avant ses découvertes.* Paris, 1905.

———. *Histoire critique sur la grande entreprise de Christophe Colombe.* Paris, 1911.

———. *Le vrai Christophe Colomb et la légende.* Paris, 1921.

Vigneras, L. A. *La búsqueda del Paraíso y las legendarias islas del Atlántico.* Valladolid, 1976.

Viola, H. J., and C. Margolis, eds.

Seeds of Change: A Quincentennial Commemoration. Washington, 1991.

Vuippens, I. Ayer de. "Où plaça-t-on le Paradis Terrestre?" *Etudes Franciscaines* XXXVI (1924): 117–40, 371–98, 561–89; XXXVII (1925): 21–44, 113–45.

Wagner, H. R. "Peter Martyr and His Works." *Proceedings of the American Antiquarian Society* LVI (1946): 239–88.

Warren, F. B. *Vasco de Quiroga and His Pueblo-Hospitals of Santa Fé.* Washington D.C., 1963.

Washburn, W. E. "The Meaning of 'Discovery' in the Fifteenth and Sixteenth Centuries." *American Historical Review* LXVIII (1963): 1–21.

Watts, P. M. "Prophecy and Discovery: On the Spiritual Origins of Christopher Columbus's 'Enterprise of the Indies'." *American Historical Review* XC (1985): 73–102.

Wauchope, R. *Lost Tribes and Sunken Continents: Myth and Method in the Study of American Indians.* Chicago, 1962.

———, ed. *Handbook of the Middle American Indians.* Austin, Tex., 1964–75.

Weckmann, L. "The Middle Ages in the Conquest of America." *Speculum* XXVI (1951): 130–41.

Weinberg, B. "Montaigne's Readings for 'Des Cannibales'." In *Renaissance and Other Studies in Honor of William Leon Wiley,* 264–79. Chapel Hill, 1968.

Weismann, G. *They All Laughed at Columbus: Tales of Medicine and the Art of Discovery.* New York, 1987.

Weiss, E. "Ein neues Bild Jan Mostaerts." *Zeitschrift für Bildende Kunst* XX (1909/10): 215–17.

West, D. C. "Christopher Columbus, Lost Biblical Sites, and the Last Crusade."

Catholic Historical Review LXXVIII (1992): 518–41.

Westrem, S. D., ed. *Discovering New Worlds: Essays on Medieval Exploration and Imagination.* New York, 1991.

White, F. R., ed. *Famous Utopias of the Renaissance.* New York, 1955.

White, H. *The Content of the Form: Narrative Discourse and Historical Representation.* Baltimore, 1987.

White, J. *Birth and Rebirth of Pictorial Space.* Cambridge, Mass., 1987.

Wilford, J. N. *The Mapmakers.* New York, 1973.

Williams, G. H. *Wilderness and Paradise in Christian Thought.* New York, 1962.

Williams, S. *Fantastic Archaeology: The Wide Side of North American Prehistory.* Philadelphia, Penn., 1991.

Wilson, A. *The Making of the Nüremberg Chronicle.* Amsterdam, 1976.

Wirth, P. "Bemerkungen zum Nachleben Vitruvs im 9. und 10 Jahrhunderts und zu dem Schlettstäder Vitruv-Codex." *Kunstchronik* XX (1967): 281–91.

Wittkower, R. "Marvels of the East." *Journal of the Warburg and Courtauld Institutes* V (1942): 159–97.

———. *Architectural Principles in the Age of Humanism.* New York, 1965.

———. "Marco Polo and the Pictorial Tradition of the Marvels of the East." *Oriente Poliano* (Rome) (1957): 32–46.

———. *Gothic vs. Classic: Architectural Projects in Seventeenth-Century Italy.* New York, 1974.

———. *Allegory and the Migration of Symbols.* London, 1977.

Woodward, D. "Reality, Symbolism, Time and Space in Medieval World Maps." *Annals of the Association of American Geographers* LXXV (1985): 510–21.

———. "Medieval *Mappaemundi.*" In *The History of Cartography.* Vol. 1,

Cartography in Prehistoric, Ancient, and Medieval Europe and the Mediterranean. Edited by J. B. Harley and D. Woodward, 286–370. Chicago, 1987.

———, ed. *Art and Cartography: Six Historical Essays.* Chicago, 1987.

Wright, J. K. *The Leardo Map of the World, 1452 or 1453, in the Collection of the American Geographical Society.* New York, 1928.

———. *The Geographical Lore of the Time of the Crusades: A Study in the History of Medieval Science and Tradition in Western Europe.* New York, 1925; rpt. Dover, 1965.

———. *Human Nature and Geography: Fourteen Essays, 1925–1965.* Cambridge (U.K.), 1966.

Wright, L. B., ed. *West and by North: North America Seen Through the Eyes of Its Seafaring Discoverers.* New York, 1971.

Wyndham, H. A. *The Atlantic and Slavery.* New York, 1935.

Zacher, C. *Curiosity and Pilgrimage: The Literature of Discovery in Fourteenth-Century England.* Baltimore, 1976.

Zamora, M. *Reading Columbus.* Berkeley, 1993.

Zavala, S. *La "Utopía" de Tomás Moro en Nueva España y otros estudios.* Mexico City, 1937.

———. *Sir Thomas More in New Spain.* London, 1955.

———. *Las instituciones jurídicas en la Conquista de América.* Mexico City, 1971.

Zechlin, E., "Columbus als Ausdruck der mittelalterlich-neuzeitlichen Epochenscheide." *Studi Colombiani* II (1951): 101–11.

Zerubavel, E. *Terra Cognita: The Mental Discovery of America.* New Brunswick, N.J., 1992.

INDEX